M000213565

ROYAL PORTRAITS IN HOLLYWOOD

ROYAL PORTRAITS IN HOLLYWOOD

Filming the Lives of Queens

Elizabeth A. Ford
and
Deborah C. Mitchell

THE UNIVERSITY PRESS OF KENTUCKY

ROCKINGHAM COUNTY PUBLIC LIBRARY
OUTREACH   EDEN
MADISON   REIDSVILLE
MAYODAN   STONEVILLE

791.43
F

Copyright © 2009 by The University Press of Kentucky

Scholarly publisher for the Commonwealth,
serving Bellarmine University, Berea College, Centre
College of Kentucky, Eastern Kentucky University,
The Filson Historical Society, Georgetown College,
Kentucky Historical Society, Kentucky State University,
Morehead State University, Murray State University,
Northern Kentucky University, Transylvania University,
University of Kentucky, University of Louisville,
and Western Kentucky University.
All rights reserved.

Editorial and Sales Offices: The University Press of Kentucky
663 South Limestone Street, Lexington, Kentucky 40508–4008
www.kentuckypress.com

13 12 11 10 09   5 4 3 2 1

Library of Congress Cataloging-in-Publication Data

Ford, Elizabeth, 1946–
    Royal portraits in Hollywood : filming the lives of queens / Elizabeth
A. Ford and Deborah C. Mitchell.
        p.   cm.
    Includes bibliographical references and index.
    ISBN 978-0-8131-2543-5 (hardcover : alk. paper)
    1. Queens in motion pictures. 2. Biographical films—United
States—History and criticism. I. Mitchell, Deborah C., 1951–
II. Title.
PN1995.9.Q35F67 2009
791.43'65262—dc22
                                2009008873

This book is printed on acid-free recycled paper meeting
the requirements of the American National Standard
for Permanence in Paper for Printed Library Materials.

Manufactured in the United States of America.

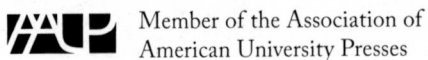

Member of the Association of
American University Presses

For Jean McClure Kelty and Carolyn G. Heilbrun—
two uncommon women

Contents

Acknowledgments

The sum of any manuscript is more than its authors. Ours is no different. We owe a debt of gratitude to all the biographers, historians, scholars, filmmakers, and actors who have enriched our project with their research and talent.

We would like to thank several people in particular. Mary Jo Dunne did some important fact-checking for us. Julie Tvaruzek's artistry provided us with beautiful images to accompany several presentations based on this work. Perc Kelty gave us access to Jean McClure Kelty's extensive library; using Jean's books and reading her marginal notes gave our work added meaning.

To Lou Giannetti, always a guiding spirit, we thank you for listening and for validating our efforts. To Joseph Brown, our copyeditor, we thank you for your careful and thoughtful reading. Your suggestions improved our text.

Of course, we appreciate our families' capacity to understand and live through the process, especially the bunker mentality that characterizes the wrapping-up phase. And, finally, to the excellent students we have taught and learned from—thank you for keeping us alive as teachers and scholars.

Introduction

Duty first, self second; that's how I was brought up. That's all I've ever known.
—Queen Elizabeth II to Tony Blair in *The Queen*

When Helen Mirren, authentically coiffed and costumed as Elizabeth II, turns to the camera in *The Queen* (Stephen Frears, 2006), she presents a perfect amalgam of royal personae, a queen playing a queen. Mirren is unarguably one of the most revered stars in the English-language cinema, and Elizabeth II is the *queen*, still so awe inducing that Jack Straw, a "former socialist" and the current lord chancellor, backed out of her royal presence at the 2007 opening of Parliament as meekly as a sixteenth-century courtier might have done (Lyall, "Ever Backward"). Elizabeth II wasn't Mirren's only royal role in 2006. She also played Elizabeth I in the critically acclaimed HBO miniseries *Elizabeth I*. This unprecedented double-queen sweep netted Mirren an Oscar, an Emmy, a Golden Globe, and a BAFTA award for her dead-on portrayals. Mirren's tour de force portraits of two larger-than-life female British monarchs may have been unprecedented, but the early twenty-first century's preoccupation with queens' lives on film is not. Queens are in vogue, sometimes literally.

The September 2006 cover of *Vogue*, for example, features a living, breathing Marie Antoinette, headlined as the "Teen Queen Who Rocked Versailles," dressed in rose pink satin, coiffed à la mode. Of course, it's not the real Marie Antoinette so serenely gazing out from her pink-damasked chamber but Kirsten Dunst, who starred as the French queen in Sofia Coppola's *Marie Antoinette* (2006). The catalyst for *Vogue*'s interest—the controversial, rock-enhanced biopic—is just one of the more recent high-profile cinematic rebirths of an enigmatic queen. *Elizabeth: The Golden Age* (2007), a feature-length biopic covering Elizabeth I's relationship with Sir

Walter Raleigh, allowed Cate Blanchett to reprise her 1998 role as the iconic Tudor queen, while 2008 releases included Justin Chadwick's *The Other Boleyn Girl*, starring Scarlett Johansson and Natalie Portman. As this book went to press, a new *Mary, Queen of Scots*, directed by Phillip Noyce and also featuring Johansson, was in production, and *The Young Victoria*, directed by Jean-Marc Vallée and starring Emily Blunt, Miranda Richardson, and Jim Broadbent, was in postproduction. Multiple media sources report that Catherine Zeta-Jones and Hugh Jackman are in talks concerning an epic, 3-D musical version of Cleopatra's life, to be directed by Steven Soderbergh.

Questions about what has triggered the recent wave of interest in female sovereigns headline news stories and give entertainment anchors monarch manna to munch on. Reviewers like Manohla Dargis wonder whether there's "something in the air, say the stench and decline of empire" ("However Heavy"). We would respond to Dargis by insisting that it's not a "stench" driving these film choices but the scent of change. Led by audience interest in character actresses like Blanchett and Mirren, the film industry may be gradually undergoing a seismic shift, awakening to the possibility that not only leading men gain depth and sophistication with maturity. Revived interest in the queens also reflects altered political reality. High-profile elections around the world have demonstrated that *equal* might, at long last, mean "equality," as glass ceilings shatter and women vie for high-ranking posts. Even before the 2006 U.S. midterm elections, which dramatically increased the number of women in Congress and made Nancy Pelosi the first female speaker of the House, the *New York Times* recognized the "three-continent long-jump for women in politics" (qtd. in Powers 268). The leap can end in a rough landing or even prove fatal. Benazir Bhutto, Ségolène Royal, Angela Merkel, Michelle Bachelet, Ellen Johnson-Sirleaf, and Hillary Rodham Clinton represent a long line of women willing to risk everything for a chance to lead. Their precursors stretch back to another group of powerful women, the famous queens of the past, most of whom had little choice but to rule.

The urge to adapt these royal lives for the screen is hardly something new. Biopics about queens have always punctuated a genre that, as George Custen points out, has traditionally been focused on men; the lives of men "account for 65 percent of all biographies, more than twice the number of female biopics." Custen also notes that *royalty* is one of the few categories in which biographical films about women outnumber those about men, giving them "a particular weight, for they are instances in which the male domination of the power structure is disrupted by female eminence" (103). Silent film initiated the royal biopic; early viewers could see Sarah Bernhardt's four-reeler *Queen Elizabeth* (Henri Desfontaines and Louis Mercanton, 1912) or Theda Bara's *Cleopatra* (J. Gordon Edwards, 1917). The 1930s added the dimension of sound, which gave biographical film what it needed, the combined power of action and language.

The lives of queens dominated the output of female biopics in the 1930s, as this list of eight titles shows: *Queen Christina* (1933), *Cleopatra* (1934), *The Scarlet Empress* (1934), *Catherine the Great* (1934), *Mary of Scotland* (1936), *Victoria the Great* (1937), *Marie Antoinette* (1938), and *The Private Lives of Elizabeth and Essex* (1939). In a single decade, the 1930s presented an essential set of female royal lives that film biographers would revisit. These eight 1930s royal biopics are the touchstones of our study. Instead of organizing the chapters according to the historical chronology of the queens' births, we follow film history, devoting a chapter to each queen, "screening" the films in the order in which they were released, from *Queen Christina* in chapter 1 to *The Private Lives of Elizabeth and Essex* in chapter 7. In each chapter, we follow a discussion of the 1930s film with analyses of subsequent English-language film versions of that queen's life. Royal biopics resonate with the rhythms of the decades, but only the 1990s and the early years of the twenty-first century repeat the high concentration visible in the 1930s.

Dargis's question (Why now?) might well be applied to the 1930s touchstone films. Why then? What cultural catalyst sparked the early spate of queen biopics? The answer lies in Hollywood's starmaking machinery. Recent awards acknowledged Helen Mirren's membership in an elite group of luminaries like Judi Dench, Vanessa Redgrave, and Meryl Streep, all celebrated as queens of their craft, but Hollywood's fixation with its own queens is also nothing new. Americans love democracy, but we adore the glamour of monarchy wherever we find it. Having invested in European stars like Greta Garbo and Marlene Dietrich, Hollywood sought lucrative projects for them. What could be better than casting them as famous European queens while fashioning them into queens of the cinema? Royal biopics follow the arc of popularity and the "turning away from the foreign and the exotic, and toward more everyday issues associated with the U.S. milieu" (Landy 167). But why limit the crowning of queens to European stars? By the 1930s, every major studio had one department whose sole purpose was to manufacture stars and another to sell them as Hollywood royalty. Early fan magazines are rife with references to stars as queens. One photo caption from a 1930 *Photoplay* refers to "Queen Garbo shaking hands with the first American actor who helped her" (Griffith, ed., 213). In another *Photoplay* article, Leonard Hall writes of Garbo: "There is only one queen, aloof and majestic on a lonely mountain top, who can do no wrong" (4).

By casting its studio queens as real royals, Hollywood assured its own system of succession with an eternal stream of worshipping subjects and built a tight homology between reality and fantasy, between the private and the public. The public clamored for details of their favorites' private lives. Working in the dream factory for most stars meant walking in the glare of a high-voltage spotlight. As films quickly moved from novelty to entertainment mainstay, a double view of stars just as quickly became the norm, especially for women, and not much has changed since then. Just as our current fashion magazine covers declare stars unreachably lovely while the national tabloids front their woes and their cellulite, so early issues of Hollywood trades like *Photoplay* ran glamour shots of "goddesses" alternating with less flattering pieces with titles like "Pictures They Wish They'd Never Posed For." Hollywood in the 1930s, as in all successive years, declared, coronated, and often deposed its queens.

The public happily joined the feasts of veneration, participating just as happily in orgies of venality. Public attitudes toward the monarchy, especially toward princesses and queens, provide a historical corollary for such bipolar swings. Perhaps only Grace Kelly, who reigned on-screen and in Monaco, wore an untarnished crown. Her children, however, have drawn just the kind of damning scrutiny she avoided. The ecstatic adoration and rabid gossip-mongering that followed Princess Diana in life and death are the most recent manifestations of the phenomenon that placed her "at the crossroads of royalty and celebrity" (James). When Diana died, Elton John didn't have to write a new song for her. He simply rewrote the lyrics for "Candle in the Wind," his elegy for Marilyn Monroe, underscoring the link between two kinds of royal icons. Perhaps because it acknowledged that link, "Goodbye, English Rose" seemed the most apt tribute at Diana's funeral. The 1930s focus on royal women launches an excellent metaphor for the love/hate relationship between the public and female Hollywood stars. We examine the tension between private and public selves experienced by queens and by the actors chosen to portray them.

The wish to see the private woman behind the crowned head and robed body put literary and film biographers on similar paths. Many of the first literary biographies of women were also the lives of queens, proof of their enduring, cross-genre fascination. And, while the lives of women raised to rule may seem incredibly distanced from those of all other women, biographers agree that they are at once exceptional and quite ordinary. Though these queens' decisions shaped history, their lives followed the rhythms of most women's lives. They could rarely escape pressures of appearance, marriage, childbirth, and motherhood. These lives, which commoners regarded as privileged, were, like all lives, lived in response to circumstance. Both literary and film biographies attest to the difficulty of wresting precious, private life away from mandated paths.

Given our current national penchant for biographical films, an examination of these earlier incarnations helps illuminate the ongoing challenge of visualizing real lives. Roland Barthes once called a biography "the novel that dare not speak its name" (qtd. in Heilbrun 28), and so too the biographical film risks the pitfall of becoming only a narrative that the writer or director yearns to believe. When the casting makes viewers catch their breath, when the cultural surround signals its solidity, when the screenplay and direction ring with insight, a biopic becomes the evocation of a life we long to understand, albeit a dramatized one. We're not suggesting that there can be a "true" version of a life. Biographies, autobiographies, and histories resound with selective memory, and sometimes art, not fact, provokes the best insight.

Like an artist's portrait, the biopic becomes an interpretation of the real person, and that interpretation can be so close the portrait almost breathes, like Leonardo's *Mona Lisa.* Or it can be a likeness that captures the spirit of the living being, as the *Rainbow Portrait,* attributed to Issac Oliver, does of Elizabeth I. Then again, the interpretation might be as loose as Picasso's *Portrait of Uhde.* All these are choices fraught with challenges for filmmakers and audiences alike. We compare literary and film texts to pose questions about selection, sequence, and emphasis. As Linda Seger says: "A life defies cinematic neatness" (49). What slice of the life do film biographers choose to tell? Which events are treated, which deleted? Does the film chronology mirror or depart from the life's time line? Are fictional scenes added? If so, how do these affect the overall view of the subject? We do not intend to coronate films that slavishly follow their sources, but we are interested in recognizing the spin of creative license. How far is too far from established truth? What responsibility does an auteur have to the life held up for viewers' pleasure?

For more direction in reading the film texts, we turn to Carolyn Heilbrun's classic feminist work *Writing a Woman's Life,* which begins with this assertion: "There are four ways to write a woman's life; the woman herself may tell it, in what she chooses to call an autobiography; she may tell it in what she chooses to call fiction; a biographer, woman or man, may write the woman's life in what is called a biography; or the woman may write her own life in advance of living it, unconsciously, and without recognizing or naming the process" (12). In our study of the fifth way of writing a woman's life, biographical film, we consider concerns Heilbrun voices about literary accounts of women's lives. She notes that objectivity, that illusive goal, hardly seems possible when biographers routinely delete anger and "unwomanly ambition" (17–18), erase female childhoods, "mock" or undervalue female friendships (100), and rarely depict any but the most conventional male/female relationships (92). Perhaps, as Heilbrun suggests, the most important condition needed for all the others to coalesce is the willingness to examine the whole person.

In the 1930s, to watch the life of a queen was to see, acted out, the difficulty of attaining, or even articulating, an independent goal, a problem that had to be meaningful to women of the time, who were living, for the most part, according to a prescribed format or struggling mightily to break the mold. As current remakes show, these lives matter to men and women today, who still coexist in a world where "one of the unknowns is how to live together as partners" (Gordon). Female leaders have started to imagine what kind of global reality they might create. Michelle Bachelet, the president of Chile, "believes that women (if they dare) can develop a non-male style of leadership" that could be "firm . . . caring, nurturing" (Powers 270). Texts about the difficult lives of queens allow us to look back as we walk ahead toward new possibilities.

Our study begins with two film views of the most atypical of queens,

Christina of Sweden, who found her crown too heavy. Unwilling to pay the price it exacted, she abdicated, looked for, and found an environment that would give her freedom and comfort—Rome. Once settled there, she continued to wield power, often selfishly and rashly, although she had neither title nor throne.

Chapter One

ᥱ

Queen Christina of Sweden

It is impossible for me to marry. I am absolutely certain about it. . . . I have
prayed God fervently that my inclination might change, but I simply cannot
marry.
—Queen Christina

O nly two biopics of Queen Christina exist: Rouben Mamoulian's 1933
Queen Christina and Anthony Harvey's 1974 *The Abdication,* and,
though vastly different interpretations, as the forty-one years between
them might suggest, both capture the spirit of an unconventional life.
Christina was born in 1626 under the shadow of her mentally unstable
mother, Maria Eleonora of Brandenburg, and her legendary father, the
Vasa king Gustav Adolph, also known as Gustav the Great and the Lion
of the North for his political and military acumen. Disappointed in a female heir, King Gustav nevertheless insisted on educating his daughter in
the manner befitting any prince. When he died in the Battle of Lützen in
1632 during the Thirty Years War, Christina was six—and the new queen
of Sweden.

According to Faith Compton Mackenzie's 1931 biography, *Sibyl of the
North,* Christina, for the most part, served her country well for twenty
years. She certainly had her faults, but she was hardworking, attending
every session of Parliament, fighting for peace, putting an end to Catholic
persecution, and insisting on religious tolerance in her country even though
she, herself, cared little for her father's Protestant religion, which insisted
that she marry and breed for the good of Sweden. A great reader, Christina's dream was to bring art and culture to her remote and icy realm, and, to
that extent, she tried to cultivate her own intellectual image. Intelligent,
yes. Brilliant, maybe. But she was not the genius she purported to be. She

Queen Christina of Sweden. (Courtesy Erich Lessing/Art Resource, New York.)

seems destined always to have missed the mark of her revered father. She found no strong role model in her mother, who doted on her great husband but hated his country. Maria neglected her daughter until King Gustav died, at which point she clung to Christina, forcing the child to sleep with her, the king's heart suspended above them in a box (Mackenzie 22). Her mother's hysterical wailings bred a lifelong contempt of her own sex, and possibly sex in general, in Christina. As Veronica Buckley points out: "She took her model of all women from her mother, and declared that, of all human defects, to be a woman was the worst" (55). Consequently, during her lifetime, Christina often dressed in men's clothing and surrounded herself with male attendants, like Aage, her valet and confidant, in *Queen Christina* or Birgito the dwarf in *The Abdication*.

Finally, at twenty-seven, sick of duty and responsibility, and refusing, as she put it, to be bartered in marriage or become a breeder for some man "the way a peasant uses his fields" (Buckley 197), Christina abdicated the throne, turned the reins of power over to her cousin Charles, converted to Catholicism, and moved to Rome. Seduced by the beauty and warmth of Italy, she befriended popes and artists the likes of Bernini, and lived as though she still wore the crown, demanding all the rights and privileges of a monarch. The Vatican, finding her conversion a real feather in its miter, tried to accommodate her, but it's hard to be queen when you have no country, no government, no subjects, and no money. Christina always exceeded the modest income she received from Sweden; she spent lavishly and borrowed heavily.

The former queen also shocked and outraged Europe with her scandalous and crude behavior. Almost immediately on moving to Italy, she linked herself romantically with Cardinal Decio Azzolino. Tongues wagged around the globe. Whether they consummated their relationship or not, he remained the one steadfast, loyal, and positive influence in her life for thirty years, dying only two months after she did. Intrigue after intrigue, Christina lived large on the European landscape. Once she tried to proclaim herself queen of Naples. People rolled their eyes and shook their heads: "Oh, that's just Christina." But one scandal, in particular, proved the final undoing of her reputation. She had always favored young, handsome sycophants and scoundrels who abused her trust and cheated her, as she herself often used and abused those who had her best interests at heart. One rogue, in particular, Marchese Gian-Rinaldo Monaldeschi, tried to frame fellow scoundrel Francesco Santinelli to make him look bad in the eyes of the queen, who had heretofore chosen to ignore their cheating and scheming. When Monaldeschi's plan backfired, Christina had him executed. The brutal details of his death, recorded by Prior Père Le Bel of Fontainebleau's monastery, appalled and sickened not only France, where the events unfolded, but all Europe. To make matters worse, Christina showed no remorse. It was within her rights as a monarch to administer punishment to her subjects, she felt, and she was answerable to no one but God (Buckley 234). Christina never recovered from the scandal. The royal, the great, the rich, and the famous, previously tolerant of her eccentric behavior because of who and what she was, turned their backs on her and closed their doors to her—except for Azzolino, who tried to establish some sense of order in her life in Italy.

Such a life no one had thought to bring to the screen until a Swedish import named Greta Gustaffson inspired the possibility of an adaptation, an adaptation that compelled every major studio to hitch its own reigning queen to a real-life royal and launch a series of "queen" films that stretches into the present day. By the time the Mackenzie biography of Christina came out in 1931, Greta Garbo was a name to be conjured with and a woman as hard to ignore as the Queen of the North—inspiring awe, wielding enormous power, and garnering serious box-office dollars. She had, by all accounts, long been disenchanted and unhappy with her movie roles and ready to abandon Hollywood when MGM's lure of a new contract pulled her back. She was offered her own production company, an unheard-of salary for the time, director and costar approval, and a green light on the Queen Christina project. Several of Garbo's biographers mention her keen interest in the Swedish queen, and Barry Paris carefully lays out the genesis of the film. He points to Inga Gaate, Marie Dressler, and Mercedes de Acosta as people who suggested the role to Garbo, but it was Garbo's close friend Salka Viertel who ultimately drafted the script that the star then read as she was returning to Hollywood from Sweden on a freighter "dressed as a strapping young boy" (qtd. in Paris 288).

Biographies and photos of Garbo make clear her identification with Christina. Both longed to flee their gilded cage, both liked dressing in men's clothing, and, by some accounts, both leaned toward bisexuality. Any similarities between the Queen of Cinema and the queen of Sweden end here, however. As late as 1962, S. N. "Sam" Behrman, the playwright who had been called in to do the rewrites on *Queen Christina*, remembered that Garbo considered herself "closer personally to the character of Christina than any other," but, as Behrman came to know Garbo, he disagreed with her comparison: "No one could have been less like the actual Queen Christina than Garbo." Behrman praised Garbo, calling her portrayal of the Swedish queen "beautiful" and "modest" (qtd. in Vieira 190).

The real Christina was anything but modest. As Veronica Buckley writes: "Christina was to be trained to only two conventionally feminine habits, modesty and virtue, though in the former, at least, she was to fail spectacularly" (49). Headstrong, arrogant, and boastful, she bears little resemblance to the beautiful, contemplative, reclusive Garbo or the noble film persona.

Historical and biographical accounts would suggest that the queen relished life in the limelight, making a spectacle of herself wherever she went, while Garbo lived even her public life in private. The actress refused to play Hollywood's publicity game, which added to her mystique but frustrated press and paparazzi. One disappointed journalist wrote at the height of Garbo's fame: "She has failed as a private life star" (Shirley 133). So MGM actually hired a Garbo look-alike, Geraldine De Vorak, to stand in for Garbo at public affairs. In a *Photoplay* article, Lois Shirley wrote of De Vorak: "She is Greta Garbo's private life" (133). Did Christina ever feel that tension between her public duty and her private desires? Of course. The tug was so strong that she abdicated, throwing off heavy crown, royal robe, and the responsibilities that came with them, but not without great angst and personal cost.

Physical descriptions of Christina too defy any similarities with the tall, stunning star who inspired the director Rouben Mamoulian to recall: "No matter how you lit Garbo the result was beautiful" (qtd. in Vieira 182). Descriptions of Christina abound in her biographies since those who saw her noticed her physical eccentricities first. Buckley writes: "Despite her small stature and fairly delicate build, the young queen's movements and gestures were far from feminine. She walked like a man, sat like a man, and could eat and swear like the roughest soldier. Her voice was deep and gruff, and her temper warm—her servants were no strangers to blows or bruises" (63). Etchings and paintings of her in later life show a squat, unkempt, sexually ambiguous figure in men's jackets and shoes. Garbo, who never saw herself as glamorous and retired in her prime to eschew makeup and designer clothes for a more natural look and masculine attire, might have found Christina's casual, often careless attitude toward her appearance amusing, but it's doubtful she would have approved the public antics, coarse behavior, and false bravado that often made Christina the object of public ridicule.

Mamoulian's film airbrushes away Christina's behavioral and physical warts, the rough edges smoothed and polished by the mere casting of Greta Garbo, whose surname in Italian means "grace." The name fits the actress perfectly, like one of those Adrian gowns she often wore in her MGM films. Several versions of how Greta Gustaffson acquired the name Garbo turn up in the biographies, but one in particular suggests that the director Mauritz Stiller (credited with discovering the teenaged actress) "knew the Italian musical term *con garbo,* 'with grace,'" and liked the way it sounded with Greta (Paris 50). Luigi Barzini, in his excellent national portrait *The Italians,* writes that *garbo* is an essential part of the Italian character: "[It] keeps everything within the boundaries of credibility and taste" (76). The word beautifully describes the actress's performance as Christina: she makes the Swedish queen, so lacking in grace herself, palatable, always within "the boundaries of credibility and taste" (Barzini 76).

Queen Christina (1933)

Christina's father, Gustav the Great, makes a brief appearance in the exposition of *Queen Christina,* but his giant specter and legacy remain in every frame of the film—from the wall-sized portrait of him that hangs above the queen's desk to his daughter's mannerisms and clothing. Two soldiers find Gustav dying on the battlefield of Lützen and ask, "Who are you?" He replies: "I *was* the king of Sweden." Mamoulian dissolves to a shot of the crown and scepter and the coronation of Gustav's daughter, the feisty young Christina striding confidently through a gauntlet of officious-looking men in black robes. She approaches her throne. How high it seems. Chancellor Axel Oxenstierna (Lewis Stone) tries to help her up. No thanks. She can do it herself. The scene becomes a metaphor for her life, which, ultimately, she will live on her own terms, regardless of how her father lived his. The child's address to Parliament is taken almost verbatim from Christina's actual speech.

Twenty years pass before we see Christina again. Looking every inch the cavalier in her wide-brimmed hat, long velvet jacket, breeches, and knee-high boots—a costume ready-made for a kinetic queen—she rides at breakneck speed across the snowy landscape, companion Aage (C. Aubrey Smith) and dogs trailing behind. Into the courtyard they ride. We see her only from behind as she dismounts and takes the palace stairs two at a time, her Great Danes struggling to keep up. Through vast hallways she clips, her freedom of movement diminishing with every fateful footstep toward duty and decisions. Only when she turns a profile to the camera and removes her hat do we realize that the "king" is a beautiful woman, as the casting of Garbo ensures.

But this is no lovely figurehead; this is a working, worried queen. Trapped behind her huge desk, dwarfed by the portrait of her father filling the wall behind her, and hemmed in by Chancellor Oxenstierna on one side and Lord Treasurer Magnus De la Gardie (Ian Keith) on the other, Christina reads, signs, and comments on the documents they keep handing her. Sweden's victorious war machine needs more funds. "How many men have we lost?" she asks. Ten thousand, Oxenstierna tells her. "A few more victories like this, and we'll have to hire foreigners to fight our battles," she quips. The war is too expensive. What about her people? Oxenstierna informs the queen that her people clamor for war, they clamor for her marriage to Prince Charles (Reginald Owen), and they clamor for a Swedish heir. "In short, Chancellor, they clamor," Christina says, sidestepping what has now become a familiar refrain as she prepares to meet with Parliament.

The mise-en-scène in this film so neatly captures her sense of entrapment that, while the script says that Christina abdicates for the sake of love, the mise-en-scène tells another story, the real story: she's worn the crown for a long time, and she's tired of it all. Sitting before Parliament and the people, she weighs all opinions before she speaks. A series of close-ups captures the fanatic zeal of her triumphant cousin Charles, the archbishop (David Torrence), and the body politic as they shout on about war and "crushing the enemy" while the peasants just feel powerless. It is a tired, angry queen who finally speaks: "Peace. There must be an end. . . . We have been fighting since I was in the cradle and many years before. . . . There are other things to live for than wars." Christina wants art and literature, security and happiness, not death, for her people. But she must fight through the din of male voices to have her final say: "I want peace, and peace I will have."

This press for peace echoes the views of an earlier monarch, Elizabeth I, who hated the waste and uncertainty of war. In this and other respects, Christina must have found a kindred spirit in the Virgin Queen so close to her in time. Both felt the weight of ruling men in a man's world and the oppressive harangue of marrying and producing an heir when they weren't inclined in that direction. Both highly educated, they carved out a lifelong path of study and needed intellectual stimulation as others needed air. Both toed a more tolerant line with regard to religious practices than the extremists around them. They ultimately made vastly different decisions about their lives, but the connections are hard to ignore. Buckley's research reveals that Christina read William Camden's biography of the English queen "as part of her training in statecraft": "The Protestant queen Elizabeth was widely known and admired in Sweden, and during Christina's girlhood, memories of her were still fresh in many minds." Christina appreciated "the English queen's wide culture, her strength of mind, and, not least, her mastery of statecraft" that had made England one of the greatest powers in Europe. Buckley states that, while Christina railed against women rulers in general, she never included Elizabeth I in her rants (55). How much of an influence was Elizabeth in Christina's life? Did Elizabeth's choices hold some sway over Christina's own choice to fend off the pressure to marry? It's possible that, in comparing herself to Elizabeth, not to mention her own father, Christina found herself wanting and unequal to the rigors of ruling and decided to step down. This speculation, however, feels much too facile, the decision to abdicate most likely being founded on a complex combination of the political, the religious, and the sexual.

At the beginning of the film, Christina's decisions, actions, and gestures can only be coded male. She assumes the male role in statecraft and love, while her manservant, Aage, takes on the "lady-in-waiting" duties. He wakes the queen early each morning even though she's usually already awake and reading in bed (an accurate reflection of Christina's real-life habits). He fusses about his mistress, combing her cropped tresses and fitting her boots over her trousers while she splashes some snow on her face. The queen's masculine habits don't seem to bother the ambitious Magnus De la Gardie either. He's got power and romance on his mind, but, when he enters the queen's chambers, his dialogue and attitude reflect a stereotypical female position. He kisses Christina, complaining that it's been too long since he's seen her. She quips that she's just seen him yesterday. Magnus pouts a little, but she has no time to "soothe" him, she says. But, Magnus insists, he is her destiny. Christina sighs that she longs to escape her destiny. Their witty, role-reversal banter sets up Christina's real interest: the beautiful Ebba Sparre (Elizabeth Young), who enters and wants to go for a sleigh ride. Christina placates her with a kiss on the lips and a promise to go away for two or three days in the country after her business with Parliament wraps up, but, when she overhears Ebba complaining to her own lover that Christina is demanding, interested only in her own concerns, she jealously and angrily tells her that she needn't fear her domination any longer. Is it any wonder that she wants to escape with Aage? "To hunt, Your Majesty?" he asks. "At least not to be hunted," Christina responds.

Thus, the opening sequence of *Queen Christina* sets up truthfully the major conflicts of the queen's life. Exhausted from fighting through the cacophony of male voices, the burdens of state, the worries of war, Magnus De la Gardie's insatiable ambitions for more power and more of her time, Oxenstierna's one-note song about marrying her cousin Charles Gustavus and producing an heir, and her own strong feelings for the beautiful Ebba Sparre, Christina longs "to forget the world." Private conversations with her chancellor render her more feminine desires. Why can't she remake the world? Artists do it. Scientists do it. Sweden's real queen promoted education, inviting scholars from all over Europe to her court. In the film, Christina tells the French ambassador that Descartes is coming, but, of course, we never see him arrive. Her reported disappointment in the philosopher's physical appearance and his subsequent death from pneumonia because she wouldn't let him return to the warmer climate of his native France are conveniently left out of this romanticized version. Rather than lead her people to destruction, Garbo's Christina wants to guide them "beyond themselves, to grace and freedom." Oxenstierna is not an idealist. For him, it's about duty. "You are your father's daughter," he reminds her, as if she needs reminding. "Must we live for the dead?" she asks. Yes, to live for the great dead, she must smile for the masses and marry Charles. She doesn't want to do either. "You can't die an old maid," he cautions. "I have no intention to, Chancellor. I shall die a bachelor," Christina winks.

There's almost a contemporary feel to the film, just as there is to this woman who defied convention and insisted on life on her own terms. Molly Haskell suggests that the film feels modern because it was made before the Production Code "went into full force" and, before 1934, "women were entitled to initiate sexual encounters, to pursue men, even to embody certain 'male' characteristics without being stigmatized as 'unfeminine' or 'predatory'" (91). But two scenes in particular are daring even for pre-Code Hollywood. The scene in which Christina greets Ebba with a kiss on the lips suggests what some believe to be their lesbian relationship. Irving Thalberg, second in command at MGM, found that aspect of Christina "interesting" and told Salka Viertel she could keep it in the film if she handled the scene with taste (Vieira 176). Walter Wanger, the film's producer, and Rouben Mamoulian, the director, also fought the censors over the second, "bedroom" scene and won the right to keep it in the film as well.

Pounded by the pressures of duty, Christina rides out with Aage when they happen on the carriage of the Spanish envoy, stuck in the snow. Don Antonio de la Prada, envoy extraordinary from the king of Spain (played by John Gilbert, Garbo's former lover, who she insisted play the role), is cold and cranky. He's on his way to see the queen, and he comes bearing King Philip's portrait and proposal of marriage. Christina finds it amusing that he doesn't recognize her. Why would he? She's dressed like a man. For the first time in the film, Christina laughs out loud and directs the carriage out of the rut. The inn is not far, she tells him.

Don Antonio tosses her a coin with her own image on it for her troubles. Visually, we see Christina start to ride away and then change her course, racing toward the inn and her destiny. Antonio and Christina find themselves locked in conversation with each other for the evening as they discuss their countries, their climates, their people, and their notions of love. The Spanish ambassador argues: "Great love, perfect love, has to be nurtured." Christina doesn't believe in perfect love. It's an illusion. The punctuation mark to their conversation comes when they are called on to settle an argument. How many lovers has the queen had this year? Six, one patron says. Nine, says another. A brawl ensues. Christina settles it with a gunshot and a declaration: the queen has had twelve lovers this year. "Long live the queen!" the customers shout. The joke will come back to haunt her.

Christina and Antonio end up in the same bedroom, the landlord unwittingly launching their romance. He has rented the last room to Christina, but, since "the young nobleman" and Antonio have hit it off so well, why not share the room? Antonio can't understand why Christina is so reluctant to undress until she takes off her jacket. John Gilbert, who never quite succeeded in converting his fame and fortune to the talkies, does a classic silent screen double take here as he joyfully cries: "Of course, I felt it. Life is so gloriously improbable." Still unaware of just who she is, Antonio spends several blissful days—and nights—snowbound with Christina at the inn. They never leave their room. His servant brings them chocolates. They lie before the fire, sensually eating grapes from his hacienda in Spain. They talk. They love. At one point, Christina walks, almost in a dreamlike state, around the room, touching everything. Is this love? Is this an illusion? She wants to feel solidity. Seductively, she lies on the bed, caressing her lover's pillow. The scene plays out in total silence. William Daniels's lighting and Mamoulian's close-ups of Garbo's extraordinary face carry the moment. "What are you doing?" Antonio eventually asks. "I've been memorizing this room," she replies. "In the future, I will live a great deal in this room."

The transition between this scene and the next lies in Antonio's next question: "Why did you come dressed as a man?" Christina explains that, in her home, she is "very constrained." She likes to get away from it all, "to be free." Her response erases any doubts we might have of the queen's heterosexuality. What, these breeches? Just a disguise, nothing more. Mamoulian visualizes the result of Christina's affair with Antonio. He cuts to the palace, where Christina is preparing to meet the Spanish ambassador as her real self, the queen. For the first time, she wears an elaborate gown, and women attend her while Aage glowers from a distance. Her clothing indeed marks a turning point in her behavior. Her meeting with the French ambassador elicited no such sartorial shift. Her goal has become "to be just a woman in a man's arms," as the costume change suggests. The transformation stuns Antonio. In public, before the court, he recovers from his shock and carries out his command. In private, he is angry. After all, he is her "unlucky" thirteenth lover. Christina, wearing another off-the-shoulder, sexy velvet frock, wants to soothe this lover. "I fell in love with you, Antonio. Forgive me for being a queen," she cajoles.

Christina uses a different tactic to calm her subjects, who have been whipped up into an anti-Spanish frenzy by the jealous Magnus. Protesting the queen's possible marriage with a foreigner, they storm the palace. "Let them in," she commands her guards. "I am not afraid of my subjects." Like Elizabeth I, Christina always knew how to keep the goodwill of her people. They never forgot her after she vacated the throne. It didn't seem to matter

Queen Christina. Are there enough crowns in this shot? Perhaps they're meant as reminders of what Christina is giving up in the film's abdication scene. Casting the beautiful, regal Greta Garbo in this early biopic ensures a romantic vision of the unattractive seventeenth-century Swedish queen who found the crown too heavy to bear. (Courtesy Jerry Ohlinger's Movie Material Store.)

whether she converted to Catholicism, stirred up intrigue and scandal all over Europe, or made herself ridiculous wherever she went. She was still Gustav the Great's daughter. Her infrequent visits to Sweden after her abdication, mainly to secure her annuities, were met with dread from the powers that be, but the people poured into the streets, cheering the last of the Vasas. In Mamoulian's film, when they storm the palace, she alone faces them, calming them with her mere presence and her words: "My father died for Sweden, and I live for her. Now, my good people, go home to your work, and leave me to mine."

Christina is, however, smart enough to realize that her people will never accept a foreigner on the throne. Like so many of the powerful women represented on film, she can't have it all. This queen must choose between crown and country or love. (It seems that only Victoria got both, but not without a great deal of compromise with Albert.) Aside from polishing the Swedish queen's rough edges, *Queen Christina*'s insistence on a romanticized motivation for abdication and an improbable ending pervert reality. No less than seven screenwriters worked on the screenplay at various times, and most felt that the real reason Christina abdicated wasn't dramatic enough. Therefore, with the exception of the short exposition introducing us to the main characters and conflicts, the film picks up her life, as so many of these royal biopics do, when she meets "the man," Don Antonio in this case, thus foregrounding a romantic reason for giving up her throne.

Garbo anguished over this important change imposed on Christina's life, and she feared what the real Swedes would think of the film: "I often wake up and think with horror about the film coming to Sweden. . . . They'll think I don't know any better. Just imagine Christina abdicating for the sake of a little Spaniard. I managed to believe for ages that it would look as though she did it because she was weary of it all and from a boundless desire to be free" (qtd. in Vieira 190). This, of course, is exactly why the real Christina abdicated. But Garbo needn't have worried. As one of her own biographers writes: "Swedish moviegoers accepted her portrayal of Christina wholeheartedly. They knew full well that the real queen was ugly and fickle and were happy to have Garbo rewrite history" (Vieira 190).

In the film, we see a high-angle long shot of Christina in her nightgown, walking to her throne room in the middle of the night. Wrestling with thoughts of abdication, she sits bathed in candlelight, head down, shoulders hunched with the weight of her decision. Oxenstierna enters, and she tells him: "I have grown up in a great man's shadow. A symbol. . . . I'm tired of being a symbol. I long to be a human being. . . . After all, Chancellor, one's life is all one has." Oxenstierna can deliver no sympathy, only another credo for a queen: "Greatness demands all." He disappears as a slow, pull-out long shot frames Christina's solitary figure sitting head in hands on her throne, the high-contrast lighting heightening her sense of isolation.

Mamoulian chooses to keep faith with Christina's abdication scene, incorporating her simple white dress, Oxenstierna's refusal to remove her crown, and the peasant who rushes up to her with tears running down his face, saying: "Keep your crown on your head . . . and we will help you the best we can to bear your burden" (qtd. in Buckley 157). Some of the dialogue is taken from contemporary sources. Relinquishing the emblems of power, Christina walks toward the camera as her subjects clutch at her gown, envisioning a life with Antonio that is not to be. He has challenged Magnus to a duel and lost, and now lies mortally wounded on the ship that was to carry them to Spain. He dies in her arms, the overhead shot signaling that their fate has played out. Christina looks up, tears streaming down her face, and, in the still of the moment, covers his face. The real Don Antonio Pimentel de Prado was a general sent to "assess Sweden's military strength, and to determine whether the queen had any plans to marry" (Buckley 146). Christina, on the other hand, thought that he came with information from the king of Spain about her secret plans to convert to Catholicism. Buckley reveals that their private meetings "led many people to believe that the two were lovers" (147). It seems unlikely, but no one can say for sure whether they were or weren't. We do know that Don Antonio helped arrange accommodations for Christina when she left Sweden, visited her in Rome, and eventually left Italy to serve in Flanders when she began to replace her Spanish friends with French ones (199). He never dueled Magnus, nor did he die in Christina's arms. He simply faded out of the picture, an anticlimactic end to the romantic hinge he plays in the film.

The last shot of Queen Christina is perhaps one of the most famous in film history. Christina stands alone at the bow of the ship, Aage behind her. As she looks off to the horizon and toward Spain, Mamoulian slowly zooms in to an extreme close-up of her face. Garbo wanted to know what she should be thinking in the final shot. What expression should she convey? Mamoulian told her: "Nothing. Absolutely nothing. You must make your mind and your heart a complete blank. Make your face into a mask" (Vieira 185). The director later explained that, in this way, every viewer could "write in his own emotions" (read: write his own ending) instead of being disappointed in a predetermined film viewpoint (189). Grief, hope, determination—any emotion might apply to Garbo's face and, thus, dictate Christina's fate. As Roland Barthes writes in *Mythologies:* "Garbo still belongs to that moment in cinema when capturing the human face still plunged audiences into the deepest ecstasy, when one literally lost oneself in a human image as one would in a philter, when the face represented a kind of absolute state of the flesh, which could be neither reached nor renounced" ("The Face of Garbo" 56). By the end of *Queen Christina*, artist and subject entwine, creating an ambiguity that sends us reeling into "the deepest ecstasy." Garbo's portrait flatters, revealing a woman with the purest of intentions who tried to rule in a world of men and who finally cast off her men's clothing and crown for love.

Who was Christina? Was she the intellectual who read into the wee hours of morning, combing the globe for rare books, and building one of the finest libraries in the world? Was she the peacemaker who tried to steer her country away from the devastating costs of war? Was she the beleaguered, tired, frustrated queen who threw away her power in a desperate bid for personal freedom? Was she the fool, surrounded by a ragtag band of rogues and cheats? Was she the woman in love, as her letters to Azzolino indicate, with a man already bound and married to the church of Rome? Was she so open-minded with regard to sexual persuasion and religious tolerance that she was light years ahead of her time? Would her political antics and bawdy behavior cause even a blip on the rich and famous radar today? "Nobody really knows the truth about her," Liv Ullmann told Howard Kissel in 1974 (qtd. in Long 54), even after reading biographies and bits of her own life that Christina sketched. So we read and we watch with Carolyn Heilbrun's caution always in mind: "Biographers of women have had not only to choose one interpretation over another but, far more difficult, actually to reinvent the lives their subjects led, discovering from what evidence they could find the processes and decisions, the choices and unique pain, that lay beyond the life stories of these women" (31). Christina was a fascinating paradox, a fact that we never quite get from watching Mamoulian's film. While Anthony Harvey's 1974 portrait of the Swedish queen tracks closer to this shifting persona, his decision to adapt only the weeks following Christina's abdication and her arrival in Rome leave us intrigued but exasperated at unfulfilled potential. Most of Christina's adventures and exploits unfold in the second chapter of her life, in Italy, but, as of this date, we have yet to see them enacted on-screen.

The Abdication (1974)

Forty-one years after Garbo introduced Queen Christina to an American public, the Norwegian actress Liv Ullmann, the star of six Ingmar Bergman films, landed the role she still considers "a human being's dream part" (qtd. in Long 59). Ullmann, who read Christina's "torment" as a universal human condition, told John Crittenden: "I've never done any part that I felt so much for.... I feel like her problems are what in different ways most women and maybe men have in common. In our world today we don't find our place, so we stretch out and people don't want us and then we don't want people. And you have to put this into a costume picture, into Queen Christina. She's a modern woman, yet a woman of all times" (qtd. in Long 59). She later told David Sterritt of the *Christian Science Monitor*: "Queen Christina's problems have never been mine. But her human condition— being afraid in a situation, lonely—that has to be mine. And everybody's" (qtd. in Long 80).

Thus, while Mamoulian and Garbo present an airbrushed, romanticized portrait of Christina, Ullmann and Anthony Harvey (who also directed *The Lion in Winter* [1968]) attempt an unvarnished portrait in *The Abdication*, based on Ruth Wolff's play and subsequent screenplay. There's a sensitivity about this adaptation that seems to be missing from the Mamoulian version and so many other royal biopics, a real attempt to understand the private woman under all the public bluster by digging deep into Christina's childhood, adolescence, and young adulthood. Wolff, one of the only two female writers in the long string of queen biopics we explore in this book, read both widely and deeply about the Swedish queen, distilling her life into one critical decision that reveals character.

At times, it feels like we're privy to a lengthy therapy session, and, in many ways, we are. Christina arrives in Rome about a year after her abdication, but, before she can meet the pope and be received by him into the church, she is detained by Cardinal Decio Azzolino (Peter Finch), who has been appointed her confessor. It seems that the church has received some rather racy reports of Christina's exploits during her trek to the Holy See, and Azzolino must separate fact from fiction. Will Christina's behavior prove an embarrassment to the church? Is she worthy to enter the Catholic faith? We find out through her sessions with the cardinal, which are intercut with flashbacks from key events in her past. Harvey seamlessly transitions between past and present, bits of dialogue or gestures in the present dissolving into pieces of Christina's memory.

The result is a tantalizing look into the psyche of a woman, an anointed queen, trapped since the age of six in a gilded cage of duty and responsibility. Pressed relentlessly to wield power and think like a man but to marry and breed an heir (preferably a male one) like a woman—having little to no parental guidance or support and few companions or friends to confide in—Christina never attained sexual equilibrium or emotional stability. Some of her biographers suggest that she used God as an escape clause. In this film adaptation, she explodes in frustration at her chancellor, proclaiming: "I am dedicating my maidenhead to God." She tells Azzolino: "It was the only thing I could say to stop them pestering me." Christina had never been particularly religious, but she astutely saw that, whereas Catholics viewed virginity as a divine state, Protestants did not. She would be a Catholic.

In reality, His Holiness Pope Alexander VII (Fabio Chigi) met Christina immediately on her arrival, welcoming her to Rome and the Vatican, showering gifts, including a carriage designed by Bernini, on his most recent and prestigious convert. But, within the psychoanalytic bent of the 1970s, in which both play and film were written, the confessional/therapy session narrative structure works as a handy plot device, peeling back layer after layer of Christina's complex persona and giving modern female audiences a woman they can relate to, one with problems—in some cases just like theirs. Must a woman always wield power like a man? Are there no other models? What should she do with newfound opportunities? What if she doesn't want to be a wife and mother? What if she chooses the life of the mind? What if she doesn't fit the prevailing societal/male vision of beauty and womanhood? What if her relationships and sexuality are unconventional? How will she reconcile her needs and desires with society's demands on her? What better case study of the universality of these private versus public issues than the life of Christina, queen of Sweden, a woman who literally gave away a kingdom because she couldn't comply with the standards imposed on her?

In many respects, *The Abdication* is also indicative of the 1970s departure from Hollywood's classic genres, conventions, themes, and sensibilities. In the 1930s, the era of the Great Depression, America still viewed European royalty through a romantic lens, a view reflected in Garbo's screen version of Queen Christina. Royals and celebrities alike seemed as far removed from ordinary mortals as the planet Venus. But, by the 1970s, such illusions had largely disappeared. And, when the film focus returned to Christina, it turned out that, underneath all that propriety and ice, the Scandinavian countries were, after all, just hot springs of sexual freedom, a primer for free love. This makes the Norwegian Liv Ullmann an interesting casting choice for a modern Christina since she has that look of smoldering sexuality underneath that cool, blonde exterior. Several scenes throughout the film have her writhing in bed, under ornate, stirring ceilings of cherubs and half-clothed angels of God.

Given Vietnam, Watergate, corporate scandals, rising inflation, and escalating violence in general, the 1970s world was a darker place—and Hollywood films mirrored the headlines and all the doubt and fear they generated. As Louis Giannetti and Scott Eyman point out in *Flashback*, filmmakers captured the ambiguities of the age on-screen: "The new filmmakers tended to prefer loose, episodic structures. Their movies were more personal, more like European movies. The endings of these films are often unpredictable and inconclusive, not neatly resolved to give a sense of closure to the dramatic materials. Life goes on, even after the final fade-out. . . . Filmmakers tended to be more interested in exploring the complexities of character rather than the intricacies of plot" (399). The tormented Christina made for an interesting character study, and, though far removed from us in time, her story brought into sharp relief the problems of contemporary women who didn't fit the classic mold of wife and mother, who wanted more and were willing to ride the centerline of the women's movement to see where it would take them. Once their cage doors opened, however, they weren't quite sure which direction to take or what they were flying toward.

After her abdication, Christina found herself in just such a predicament. Relieved of her royal responsibilities, the only thing she had known, and filled with a mixture of fear and uncertainty, elation and excitement, she traded her robes and carriages for riding breeches and a sword, turned her face toward the sun, circled the cage, and fled via a circuitous route to Rome, the pope, and the church. Surely the 1970s woman would understand her paradoxical persona of bravado and self-doubt, desire and revulsion. The idea of experiencing the world, with all its uncertainties and ambiguities, both fascinated and frightened her. Wolff, it would seem, grounds her play and screenplay firmly in the sensibilities of her own time.

Comparisons between Mamoulian's 1933 *Queen Christina* and Harvey's 1974 *The Abdication*, between Garbo's version and Ullmann's, seem inevitable, but Ullmann's take dismisses any significant connections: "In the Garbo movie, Queen Christina was beautiful, everything about her was beautiful. She abdicated over a man she loved who was killed in a duel. The real Christina was nothing like that. She was not beautiful. She was ugly, appallingly so. She did not care for men. She had no companions. . . . *The Abdication* tries to show you a woman undergoing a trauma, but when it's over you still don't know all the answers about her. It's a completely different picture" (qtd. in Long 54). The "lonely, tormented creature who abdicated because she couldn't bear men, because she couldn't bear the thought of having children" (Long 80–81), is a far cry from Garbo's romantic romp in the snow with John Gilbert, though, to be fair, Garbo too tries to impart Christina's sense of conflict. And, although there's nothing appalling about Liv Ullmann's looks, she manages to capture the inner struggles of a woman who cannot resolve her duties as a woman and her disgust with them. Educated as a prince—taught to ride, hunt, and rule like a man—she rejects her femaleness. Her mother, Maria Eleonora (Kathleen Byron), appears in this film adaptation only in Christina's dreamlike state: an unhappy, severe, mentally unstable woman who keeps the heart of her dead husband in a box by her bed and pulls the head off Christina's doll. We assume that we're meant to read this as representative of the mother-daughter relationship since Christina calls herself "the doll queen." No warmth here. Christina's relationship with her mother was certainly a troubled one, and the film reflects the truth of it. She confesses to Azzolino: "Thank God I have no daughter. I couldn't bear anyone to feel about me as I felt about my mother." The primary influences in the child-queen's life were Chancellor Oxenstierna (Cyril Cusack) and her male tutors. At one point, she tells Azzolino: "They tutored me night and day on Aristotle and Plato. They taught me mathematics and geometry until I could do them in

The Abdication. Liv Ullmann's Christina comes closer to the mark, though her own beauty, like Garbo's, invests the real queen with a stateliness she never had. Note how heavy that crown looks. She will soon remove it and run from her cold, dark, oppressive palace into the sunlight and Rome, where most of the film plays out. (Courtesy Jerry Ohlinger's Movie Material Store.)

my sleep. They made sure I knew Latin, French, Spanish, Greek, economics, poetry, diplomacy—but what they were *really* raising me for was for *breeding!*" It's a dilemma that Christina cannot easily resolve. She's been repeatedly asked to "put a man at the center of [her] life and to allow to occur only what honors his prime position" (Heilbrun 20–21). The result, as Heilbrun points out, is to make "one's own desires and quests . . . always secondary" (21). She had no narrative, or life quest, of her own.

Wolff focuses her treatment of Christina on the particular problems of women navigating power in a man's world and rigid male/female role expectations. "Shall I rule with a hand of iron or a heart of love?" she wonders. Worn out and worn down from her inability to answer that question, Christina eventually comes to the conclusion that she is unfit for her occupation:

> Sometimes I've prayed to turn into a man. And then for a moment I feel strong and able. I stride through events and move them. I am Power. I am Strength. And then I fade. . . . My will seems to wither, like decaying flowers. I cry out to be loved and loving, but if it were to happen, I'd be all the more confused. . . . Look at me! I am a grotesque! A freak! Look at my man-woman brain, my man-woman heart, my man-woman body! Look at me! Two sexes! Both at once and neither! I'm being torn apart! I must give up the crown. (Wolff 104–5)

Later she cries: "God, let me be not a queen or not a woman!" (105).

The bifurcated image of obedient "doll queen" and rude, rebellious prince in both play and film points up Christina's gender confusion. Christina has arrived in Rome under cover of night one week earlier than expected, with only her dwarf, Birgito (Michael Dunn), for a companion. Looking disheveled and dirty in her male breeches and shirt (a sight not so jarring by standards of the 1970s), she demands to see the pope at once. Decio Azzolino comes instead to greet her, and in her he finds a brilliant enigma with a randy reputation who matches him wit for wit. Would she like to rest and freshen up? "No. I'm never tired. I always look like this. Rest does not improve me," she declares. Ullmann and Finch, both fine character actors, are in perfect sync here as they banter back and forth. "Why did it take you a year to make the journey from Stockholm to Rome?" Azzolino asks Christina. "The roads were muddy," she quips. He holds up a copy of *The Pleasures and Depravities of Christina, Queen of Swe-*

den and exclaims: "Your escapades are single-handedly keeping a continent of gossips alive!"

> AZZOLINO: In this you are the harlot of the Northern Hemisphere.
> CHRISTINA: How picturesque.
> AZZOLINO: In this you are a man in disguise.
> CHRISTINA: Unlikely, but possible.
> AZZOLINO: Why did you give up the crown?
> CHRISTINA: It was too heavy.
> AZZOLINO: Why did you never marry?
> CHRISTINA: I'm allergic to gold rings.
> AZZOLINO: Why did you become a Catholic?
> CHRISTINA: To come to a better climate.

Christina's defenses are up. It seems that, in the year following her abdication, she was enjoying herself for the first time in her life, and her actions, recorded along the way by priests and bishops, reached Rome and the pope. Are the rumors true? If Christina chooses not to confess, she will not be accepted into the faith. Azzolino holds the trump card. A Protestant Queen who has given up her religion and her crown for Catholicism has nowhere to go. She must tell her story. After some resistance, she consents to Azzolino's examination and his demand for seriousness and obedience. "Seriousness and obedience.... Have I come all this way once again to become the doll queen?" she asks. As she begins to tell her confessor that she was "the best-behaved child you could ever wish to know," Harvey cuts to a blonde, blue-eyed doll/child, obviously female, acquiescing to Axel Oxenstierna's every command. But Azzolino reminds Christina that she grew up as a boy. Harvey cuts to the same child, now precocious, dressed as a boy. "Which of these creatures are you?" he asks. "None of them! Both of them! Neither!" Christina cries.

Further evidence of her gender confusion in the film lies in Christina's sexual attraction to both Ebba Sparre (Ania Marson), a beautiful lady-in-waiting, and Magnus De la Gardie (James Faulkner), the son of the high marshal. Throughout the film, Harvey repeatedly cuts back to Christina's complex relationships with her two favorites. Many of their scenes are shot in mist or darkness, signifying Christina's lack of clarity with regard to her own sexual feelings. For example, when Christina notices Ebba and Magnus falling in love with each other, it's through fog in the forest or in shadow. The young Christina (played by Suzanne Huddart) reacts by cutting off her hair, donning men's attire, and professing her love for Ebba. When Azzolino calls it "unnatural" love, Christina responds: "I loved that woman more than I ever loved another. Love is so rare. Should we deny it when we find it?" In truth, Christina did love Ebba, or "Belle," as she called her. Veronica Buckley posits: "She had probably never been a lover of women in the fullest sense, lacking the courage, or the self-knowledge, to engage in sexual relationships with women who were not themselves overtly lesbian, or even, perhaps, with those who were. As with men, it seems, so with women: Christina preferred the unconcluded game" (210). After leaving Stockholm, Christina never saw Ebba again, though she later wrote: "I am yours as much as ever I was, no matter where I may be in the world" (qtd. in Buckley 187). In the film, Ebba marries Magnus, but, in life, she actually married Magnus's brother, Count Jacob De la Gardie.

Christina's affections in the film also extend to Magnus, and, at one point, she declares to Oxenstierna that she will marry him, but Magnus wants Ebba. Reeling from her loss, yet curious as to what the act of sex is all about, she begs Ebba to let her "watch" as she makes love with Magnus. "I want to know what it's like," she pleads. Ebba reluctantly consents. Camera angles shift from straight to oblique, suggesting a world out of kilter as we see a young Christina, hidden in the shadows of their bedroom, a single tear tracking down her cheek as they climax. Magnus offers to show Christina how it's done (considerate of him), but, when she refuses him, he roughly tells her: "No one will ever love you. You don't know how to love." In the meantime, Oxenstierna presses Christina to marry her cousin Charles Gustavus (Richard Cornish), here portrayed as a shy, stammering, besotted, ineffectual young man. "Have you noticed that all our friends are married?" he asks Christina. "Doesn't it make you want anything?" She quickly replies: "It makes me want to widen my circle of friends." Clearly, Charles is no match for Christina, as Azzolino tells her. "Who in God's name would be a match for me?" she asks, looking knowingly at Azzolino.

Christina has come to Rome to forget the trauma of having to choose between her throne and marriage. She's had a meltdown, and, after years of repressing her desires and anger, she hurls documents across the room and casts herself to the ground in despair. She realizes that a crown does not come with a guarantee of control over one's private or public life. One critical scene in both the play and the film crystallizes this moment. In the present, Christina is talking with Azzolino on a Vatican balcony about being forced to marry Charles. A dissolve to the past finds her on her balcony at Tre Kronor Palace in Sweden talking with Oxenstierna: "I am queen of Sweden. By reason of my exalted rank and privilege, I am allowed anything I want. I am allowed to marry a man I do not love. I am allowed, by night, to submit to God-knows-what idiotic fumblings and horrors and, by day, to rule the fumbler and the entire world." Kings have more fun. They pursue, and women take the consequences. They go off to battle, and women await news of their sons. "Find me a man who will bear my children!" As she tells Oxenstierna, "I swear that I will never give myself to a man . . . ," she turns and now faces Azzolino to finish the sentence: ". . . unless it be to you." Harvey holds them in silhouette against a brilliant sunset and fades to black.

By this time in the film, it's obvious that these two people are kindred spirits. Whether consummated or not, their love affair/friendship was real and lasted thirty years. They met when Azzolino was a young cardinal, a member of the "flying squadron," Vatican intelligentsia who frequented Christina's Palazzo Farnese and, later, her Palazzo Riario to discuss subjects as diverse as politics and poetry. Sparks flew between Christina and the cardinal, but Azzolino assured the pope that all was innocent when rumors and placards suggested otherwise. Their relationship survived the gossip as well as Christina's political intrigues and wild spending. He helped put her financial house in order and provided emotional stability when he could.

In Harvey's film, we see a middle-aged Azzolino with his own ambitions and checkered past. He's "known" a woman but has rededicated himself to God and aims for the papal seat itself. He's been maneuvered into the position of confessor to one of the church's most prized converts, Christina, by another cardinal and his cadre, who wish to see Azzolino discredited. Neither the church nor those within its walls are above a little underhanded business (another illusion destroyed). If Azzolino finds Christina unworthy, he will be criticized for turning away a useful, living advertisement for Catholicism. If he recommends her to the pope and she fails to live up to her faith, he will be reprimanded for not doing a better job. If he falls for Christina . . . well, even better. One less rival for the miter.

The binary movement of the film mirrors Azzolino and Christina's growing attraction and parallels Christina's awakening. The film moves from Stockholm to Rome, from Oxenstierna to Azzolino, from past to present, from cold to hot, from frigid to inflamed, from darkness to light, from indoors to outdoors, from stone walls to lush fountains, from men's breeches to women's décolletage, from mist to clarity, from concealment to disclosure, from self-doubt to self-awareness.

The film opens in darkness; only pinpoints of candle flames illuminate Christina's abdication scene. When the ceremony is over, she runs through the vast, dark corridors of Tre Kronor toward the light and the open door. Outside, she casts off her robe, twirls around, and stretches her arms wide toward the sun. This opening scene establishes the movement of the film: Christina's journey toward freedom and enlightenment. Her abdication is the catalyst for the transformation of her life from a conventional one to a nontraditional, eccentric one. And, as Heilbrun argues: "The woman who writes herself a life beyond convention, or the woman whose biographer perceives her as living beyond conventional expectations, has usually early recognized in herself a special gift without name or definition. Its most characteristic indication is the dissatisfaction it causes her to feel with appropriate gender assignments" (96). This dissatisfaction causes Christina to ask at one point: "Is marriage the most natural or unnatural state?" The idea of *reinventing*, or *renegotiating*, marriage and relationships probably never occurred to Christina, but her actions and sensibilities indicate that that's exactly what she tried to do. She reached for love outside gender and social norms, building a life on her own terms.

Christina's scenes with Azzolino suggest her growth arc. She first meets him in darkness. The Vatican is asleep. It's late. She's arrived early. They begin their discussions in closed rooms; stone walls and shadows fill the background. As their relationship progresses, we see them sitting outdoors, in the sunlight, around beautiful fountains. In one scene, Christina arrives for her session in an eye-popping, low-cut gown. "What are you doing?" a smitten Azzolino asks. "Courting you," Christina replies. Finally free to choose her own lover, she opts for the unconventional, an ordained priest and cardinal, a strong contender for the papal seat.

Azzolino, in his turn, does not want to lose himself but feels himself giving in to his own desire for Christina, whom he calls a "strange, tormented creature, [a] confused, courageous, brilliant creature." When Vatican gossip prompts a colleague to warn Azzolino about his relationship with the queen, he cries: "Is there no possible connection between a man and a woman besides that! God save me from the common mind!" A beat later, he whispers to himself: "God save me from myself." Resistance is futile. He confesses to Christina: "My fault is . . . I do love. What is worse, I do not think it is a sin. I do not even think it a weakness. I do love. I do want. I do desire." His desire crosses the line of Catholic doctrine. They would be damned. "You and I will be living private lives," he says. "I don't want to look at you across public spaces," she responds. But one passionate kiss later, a dying pope, like a rival lover, determines their fate. The pope will embrace Christina as his newest convert, and Azzolino must renew his commitment to the church.

At the end of the film, we see Christina, now in a simple peasant-looking dress of black and white, walking against a sea of red (cardinals gathering for the conclave) to Azzolino, who turns toward her with a look of longing and pain, saying: "God's kingdom . . . must be served." Christina replies: "Are we not the world's strangest couple? Saying no to each other— and that's the greatest gift we each can give." In Wolff's play, he says "I love you" before the final curtain, but their locked gaze visualizes their angst in the film. Moving beyond the ambiguity of the film frame and the prosce-nium arch, Christina and Azzolino renegotiated their relationship into a thirty-year affair of the heart and mind that worked for them. In the next chapter, we meet another queen who walked an unconventional path, ac-cepting her royal marriage, and using that position to take the crown. In this way, she carved out a life quest for herself that served her public and private needs.

Chapter Two

⤙❧

Catherine the Great

At the bottom of my soul I had something, I know not what, that never for
a single moment let me doubt that sooner or later I would succeed in becoming the sovereign Empress of Russia in my own right.
—Catherine II of Russia, *Memoirs* (1745)

The 1930s introduced the first in a quartet of Disney fairy-tale adaptations: *Snow White* (David Hand, 1937), *Cinderella* (Clyde Geronimi et
al., 1950), *Sleeping Beauty* (Clyde Geronimi, 1959), and *Beauty and the Beast*
(Gary Trousdale and Kirk Wise, 1991). In these enduringly popular films,
becoming a princess is the panacea. The complex lives of real queens provide antidotes to stories that equate a happy ending with a crown, some
gorgeous gowns, and an adoring prince. Christina, born to rule and placed
on the throne as a child, couldn't put aside her royal burden quickly enough
when she became an adult, attempting to keep the privileges of high birth
while discarding the constrictions of a life lived according to a prescribed
pattern. In contrast, Catherine the Great, whose progress toward the throne
began with her marriage, reached for her crown. She seized the rule of
Russia from her husband and adopted his country as her own. The words
of Catherine that serve as this chapter's epigraph, an apologia for the act
that made her empress, reveal her willingness to follow her impulses, even
when they led to a coup d'état.

Catherine had "no claim whatsoever" to the throne, as Isabel de Madariaga reminds us in her biography (1). She seized it nevertheless, and for
thirty-four years she tried with all her will to do what she thought best for
Russia. Like Christina's, Catherine the Great's vivid story cries out to be
told visually. In 1744, fourteen-year-old Princess Sophia of Anhalt-Zerbst,
a minor German province, traveled to Russia to meet Grand Duke Peter,
who was Empress Elizabeth's nephew and the heir to the throne. Renamed

Catherine the Great. (Courtesy Bildarchiv Preussischer Kulturbesitz/Art Resource, New York.)

Catherine, Sophia married the erratic, unattractive Peter in an elaborate Orthodox ceremony. Was Peter the father of the son she bore in 1754? Questions about Paul's legitimacy and Catherine's affairs initiated continuing gossip. Before her death, Elizabeth came to doubt Peter's ability to rule, but she still passed the crown to him. She could have chosen differently. Peter the Great had altered the process of succession, allowing a czar or czarina to ignore blood ties in the selection of a successor. Peter III's stumbling three-month reign engendered noble and military support for Catherine's 1762 takeover. Peter's death, suspicious at best, darkened Catherine's rise to power (Erickson, *Great Catherine*, 226).

Talk about Catherine's string of male companions punctuated the long reign of this "working ruler," who was, by all biographical accounts, committed and diligent, if vain and self-promoting (de Madariaga 24). Early scholars criticized Catherine II—who admired Enlightenment ideas but believed in absolutism—for not tackling the plight of the serfs and for accomplishing far less than she attempted. Most twentieth-century historians credit her with helping to set "the intellectual tone of modern Russia" (Wren 215). She discouraged torture, improved education, and was "the first ruler of Russia to conceive of drawing up legislation setting out the corporate rights of the nobles and the townspeople, and the civil rights of the free population of the country." She also "established . . . courts to which the state peasants had access" (de Madariaga 217). Inspired by the French philosophes, Catherine labored to lift her huge country.

Biographers concentrate on the years of Catherine's reign. Filmmakers, however, demonstrate little interest in her efforts to rule. More than half a century separates two full-length biographical films, Josef von Sternberg's *The Scarlet Empress* (1934) and Paul Czinner's *Catherine the Great* (1934), from two made-for-television specials, Michael Anderson's *Young Catherine* (1991), and Marvin J. Chomsky's *Catherine the Great* (1995). Like the Disney princess films, these versions of Catherine II's life fixate on the getting of the crown. They provide bipolar views of the young princess who became the mature empress, hammering Catherine into flat representations of good or bad, saint or sinner.

Catherine the Great (1934)

The contemporary reviewer Mordaunt Hall liked *Catherine the Great*, the film that "succeeded *Queen Christina* on the Astor screen." Hall remarked on its treatment of history, which he saw as a combination of "facts" and "an efficient actress" (Hall, "'Catherine the Great,'" 48). Paul Czinner's version of the Russian empress's life deploys the occasional fact, as in a scene that reflects one of the real empress's policies. Catherine (Elisabeth Bergner) has the intelligence and insight to advise Empress Elizabeth (Flora Robson) during a famine-induced peasant uprising, saying that she would send "flour and corn" first and "hang the governors" next, instead of punishing the starving peasants. Generally, however, *Catherine the Great* eschews facts, preferring to massage the unwieldy blob of history into a more accommodating shape. This drawing-room tragedy burnishes its main characters into noble types and reduces Catherine's life to an epigram: power cannot trump love.

To make this version viable, Peter must be rendered lovable, a difficult assignment made simpler by investing him with Douglas Fairbanks Jr.'s glamour. The choice to showcase Peter's state of mind in the first scene identifies the thrust of a movie that doesn't quite fit its title. Shaped as an elegy for Peter's dark figure, it subordinates Catherine's rise to his fall. No establishing shots convey the vastness of Russia; most of the action plays out on interior sets designed by A. Hallam and Vincent Korda, beginning with the grand duke's lair, his hunting lodge. Russian in a stereotypical way, the lodge, with its flickering firelight, handsome officers, exotic women, surplus of alcohol, and strains of a balalaika, frames Peter in his environment of choice; the Prussia-loving Peter hated Russia, but the frame helps the film's romanticizing agenda. Hall observed: "Mr. Fairbanks does good work in this role, but he hardly gives the impression that Peter is mentally unbalanced." Fairbanks could probably have created a convincing madman—as the equally hunky Brad Pitt did when he played the insane Jeffrey Goines in *Twelve Monkeys* (Terry Gilliam, 1995)—but a certified lunatic wouldn't have fit Czinner's vision. Empress Elizabeth describes her nephew as "unstable, moody, dangerous and bad," while Peter thinks of himself as "cruel, suspicious, disloyal, and vain." Fairbanks's glamour leavens the heavy chain of negatives, and the screenplay selects characteristics that feed his Byronesque pose.

The true beauty in the film, Peter wears a court plaster and eye makeup to fit the mood of the eighteenth-century Russian court, which favored all things French. Slender, and dressed in black, the sexiest Hamlet imaginable, his grumbling at the lodge introduces his idée fixe: "What am I, a child to be fetched and married . . . by a parcel of women?" Czinner's film parlays the real Catherine's first, short-lived impression that the grand duke might be tolerable into this dramatic figure. De Madariaga calls Peter "not stupid," just "lacking in common sense" (3), but other biographers treat him less generously, detailing his cruelty and immaturity. Peter, whom Wren characterizes as "mentally defective, brutal and vulgar," idealized Prussia and disliked Russia (199). He lived an insulated, limited life, preferring the company of his roughest servants. He drank too much and wasn't squeamish about torturing animals. A creature of impulse, he once bored a hole through the wall of the empress's chamber so that he could spy on her private moments (Alexander 36). Time and intimacy reversed Catherine's initial impression of her husband. In her journal, she gives a blunt assessment of Peter. "I needed a husband endowed with common sense," she says, "and this man didn't have any" (Alexander 36). By the time he lurched drunkenly into their bridal chamber and passed out, she knew that their marriage, unconsummated for years, would be a disaster.

"I loathe the idea of marriage," Peter tells Grigory Orlov (Griffith Jones) in the opening scene. The real Peter did not. At first, he saw Catherine as someone who "shared many of the same problems" experienced by young royals (Alexander 26). Their orchestrated engagement followed protocols of diplomacy and nobility, a ballet choreographed by Empress Elizabeth. To bring the couple together in a way that dramatizes Peter's resistance, the screenplay by Lajos Biro, Arthur Wimperis, Melchior Lengyel, and Marjorie Deans uses a shopworn plot device reminiscent of an operetta. Catherine and her mother have arrived at Elizabeth's court, but Peter refuses to meet them, storming out of his aunt's presence. Catherine too runs away from her mother, hurt by the grand duke's rejection. Of course they bump into each other. This scene takes place in a liminal space, the vaulted palace rotunda, an elaborately tiled, arched, and pillared zone that separates the doings of the court from life in the outer world. Czinner returns the action to the same space when Elizabeth dies and, again, when Peter exits the palace. Catherine and Peter meet-cute there, and she asks for "the way out." She confesses her disappointment at not seeing Peter. "Do you know him?" she asks. She charms Peter by insisting that she has "dreamed about" the grand duke and planned to marry him since she was a child and that she doesn't "care about ruling Russia."

Catherine the Great. Although the dainty Elisabeth Bergner and the handsome Douglas Fairbanks Jr. look like a picture-perfect pair, they hold this pose for a few moments only; they rarely touch in this film, which treats their disastrous marriage as if it were a romantic tragedy. (Courtesy Jerry Ohlinger's Movie Material Store.)

This fictionalized meeting showcases Elisabeth Bergner's girlishness. She fumbles with her ribbons and lowers her head in shy disappointment. Bergner was one of the stream of European imports who sought wider success on Western film screens; *Catherine the Great* and *The Scarlet Empress* mark the tapering of the European rush. Not that such imports ceased. Sophia Loren, Catherine Deneuve, Juliette Binoche, and Penélope Cruz have continued the tradition, but our increasingly accessible planet circumscribes magnetism born of difference. In the 1930s, however, Bergner, like Garbo and Dietrich, emitted the pull of a culturally and geographically distant Europe. Bergner never achieved the elevated status of a recognized queen of cinema, but she was no stranger to larger-than-life roles ("Bergner, Elizabeth," 101). In the theater, Bergner had played Juliet, Queen Christina, and Camille, and, like Dietrich in *The Scarlet Empress,* she had a complex relationship with her director, Czinner being her husband (101). Although Marlene Dietrich called Bergner "[my] idol" (Frewin 33), Bergner must have felt overshadowed by Dietrich's quick rise and enormous popularity. Her desire to stake out some cinematic territory of her own rings in this loaded comment about Dietrich, whom she thought "just a little too beautiful." Such beauty, she suggests, might be an impediment. "If I were as beautiful as Dietrich," Bergner remarked, "I shouldn't know what to do with my talent" (Frewin 37).

Catherine the Great worried that she was not beautiful enough, although portraits document her regal carriage and striking, animated face. One of her lovers, Stanisław Poniatowski, describes her "complexion of dazzling whiteness" and her "large expressive blooming blue eyes, eye lashes that were dark and very long," and "a mouth that seemed to invite kisses" (qtd. in Waliszewski 1:132). Garbo brought glamour to Queen Christina, who had very little. The petite Bergner had no physical resemblance to the real empress, whom Poniatowski called "big," but her persona fits the interpretation in *Catherine the Great.* Bergner's Catherine bemoans her size, knowing that she lacks the dignity of height. Empress Elizabeth affectionately dubs her "Little Catherine," a nickname that signals her continued girlishness. The real Catherine was a thirty-three-year-old woman when she took the throne. *Catherine the Great* elides time, and Catherine, whose age is unclear, remains substantially innocent.

Like all the film versions of Catherine's life, Czinner's ticks off public, state events—Catherine's selection, the marriage ceremony, the death of the empress, Peter's ascension, Catherine's coup—while keeping the camera on Catherine and Peter's marriage. The private (but rarely personal) focus, however, promotes a single concept: Catherine loves Peter and only Peter. Peter begins to distrust his wife even before their marriage takes place when a counselor suggests that she faked their meeting and that she recognized and manipulated him. As emperor, he orders her off to "the kitchen" or into "the nursery," but those commands do not alter her feelings. His initial disparagement provokes her clearest statement of undying love. During their marriage ceremony, the camera focuses on the paraphernalia of orthodoxy: statues of saints, icons, bearded patriarchs. It's clear that Catherine takes her vows seriously, but Peter's offhanded rendition of "Till death us do part" makes his smarmy mistress, Elizabeth Vorontsova, giggle. He spends the wedding night with Vorontsova (Diana Napier), not Catherine. Wearing a rosebud-decorated nightgown, a tiny figure alone in a big bed, a teary Catherine explains to Elizabeth that it's easy to love good men but that "the others," the bad ones, "need our love."

To keep her love pure (to avoid dealing with any messy love affairs), the screenplay concocts an elaborate conceit. Hoping to pique Peter's jealousy, Catherine dons a uniform and adopts a regiment, trying to fake adultery. Her ruse works; Peter drags her to his apartment for an explanation. When Catherine admits to "seventeen lovers" (a complete lie), he is impressed, and he regales her with his exploits. "I'm beginning to like you," he declares. Their chat morphs into a romantic dinner, served by Peter's French manservant, Lecoco (Gerald DuMaurier), who exists solely to demonstrate that the grand duke has a softer side. Finally, Catherine admits her deception. "You idiot," she says, confessing that she loves him only. The fade to black at their bedside stands for the conception of Catherine's son Paul, who never appears in the film.

This reinterpretation of fact sidesteps the inconvenient reality of Catherine's lovers, historical figures who don't fit Czinner's vision. The screenplay recasts details, even Catherine's donning of regimentals, to serve its fiction. The real Empress Elizabeth and Catherine II did, occasionally, don men's clothing. The empress would call for a turnabout ball at which the men dressed as women and vice versa. Some vanity was involved in this decision because Elizabeth knew she looked well in her elaborate male attire. Catherine too found the garb flattering. Most important, during her takeover, Catherine changed from a black dress into the colors of the Preobrazhensky Regiment, which supported her (Erickson, *Great Catherine*, 220). This military image of Catherine crossed European borders via, for example, engravings of her in uniform that circulated in prerevolutionary France, eventually becoming part of the Russian ruler's "political iconography" (Weber 83). A "seven [foot] square" copy of a portrait by Vigilius Ericksen featuring Catherine on horseback in her regimentals still hangs in the Peterhof (Alexander between 178 and 179).

In *Catherine the Great,* the uniform is just part of the lie about her "seventeen lovers," and Bergner looks sprightly, not sexy, in the costume, a little soldier on a big campaign to woo her husband. Flora Robson—a featured player in many royal biopics—portrays Empress Elizabeth as flirtatious, rapacious, capricious, and obsessed with looking young, but, generally, she's protective of and motherly toward Catherine. She seeks her input on national affairs, and she supports her attempt to capture Peter's love, counseling: "Every beast of a man begins to want you when he thinks you belong to some other beast of a man." The real Elizabeth, a pragmatist, understood that Peter would not, perhaps could not, produce an heir. She did not deign to notice that a handsome young courtier, Sergei Saltykov, was wooing the grand duchess. After two miscarriages (events not acknowledged in any Catherine biopic), Catherine conceived, and Peter was purported to be the father of her son Paul. Many in the court believed otherwise, but, as de Madariaga points out, no one can be completely sure (1). Elizabeth's feelings for Catherine fluctuated. When she had Elizabeth's favor, Catherine encouraged the empress's growing dissatisfaction with Peter's behavior, hoping to gain the throne. Since *Catherine the Great* emphasizes Catherine's faithfulness and deletes her ambition, she refuses Elizabeth's deathbed offer of Russia, even after the empress calls Peter a "lunatic" and says that Catherine "should rule." Catherine, who looks imperial in a sparkling hair ornament and matching necklace, still insists that Peter is "good and wise," although he has begun courting supporters, plotting revenge, and planning his coronation before his aunt dies.

To make the denouement—Catherine's accession—palatable, Peter must become a little more, but not completely, crazy and unlovable. Czinner indicates the chilling effects of Czar Peter's spontaneous commands via a montage of cruel proclamations that punish innocents for fun. Catherine tries to mediate these and to interpret Peter's orders to the military, translating his ramblings into respect for the common soldier. Refusing the possibility that he is mad and that she might take power, Catherine insists: "I don't want to be anything but [Peter's] wife."

A climactic state dinner from the pages of history catalyzes Catherine's action; biopics bend the event to suit different needs. At the dinner, which took place six months after Elizabeth's death and two weeks before Catherine's coup, Peter humiliated his wife in front of five hundred guests. He ordered a toast to the royal family and, when Catherine would not stand, sent a servant to instruct her to do so. Catherine explained that she would not stand because that would be like honoring herself. Peter screamed "Doura, doura" (idiot, idiot), and Catherine "burst into tears." Quickly, she calmed herself and regained her poise (Haslip 112–13). A gauntlet finally having been thrown down, the dinner made public the chasm between them.

Catherine the Great shapes the dinner to make the narrative of Catherine's continuing love for Peter possible. Catherine's costumes, by John Armstrong and Vincent Korda, add to her royal aura. In her dressing room, she relaxes in an ermine wrap. When summoned to the dining room, she dons an elaborate gown similar to one of Elizabeth's that emphasizes her own natural nobility and links her to the dead empress. Although she's clearly made miserable by Peter's foul behavior, Catherine directs her anger at Elizabeth Vorontsova, who sits in the position of honor, beside him. "A woman can sit at the foot of a table and still be the head of it," Catherine comments, while "another can sit at the head of a table and be the last of all women." Peter orders the serving man to take the order of St. Catherine from his wife, and—bang—the scene ends abruptly, with a fade to black. Peter doesn't berate Catherine, and Catherine doesn't cry or give him the glance of "cold, unadulterated hatred" remembered by some guests (Haslip 113). In the next scene, Orlov, who has changed sides, begs Catherine to take command and pledges her his love. The absence of the explosive confrontation between Catherine and Peter matters more than the glimmering of a new romance because it enables the last, lamest conceit that keeps *Catherine the Great* on its narrow path.

After the high of the dinner party, the film falls to its conclusion, a moment that elevates Peter and diminishes Catherine. A long shot of onion-like domes and spires that says *Moscow* to Western viewers, close-ups of running, booted feet, and the stirring sound of bells tolling and trumpets calling stand for the coup. Catherine wears a black redingote and a skirt, not trousers, for this scene in which she promises her people to be a "good mother" and to lead Russia to history and peace. She greets her ministers with the affection a niece might show a favorite uncle. Crosscuts to Peter being escorted into a carriage parallel Catherine's assumption of control. In the short-lived czar's last moments, *Catherine the Great* brings his elegy to an amazing conclusion: Byron mutates into Sydney Carton. Calm and self-possessed, Peter assures his guards that he is "very tired" and "very glad to go on this journey." He politely asks for death, exhorting Feodor, the guard who accompanies him, to help him "reach the end of the journey" quickly. As Peter hears mounting cheers for the new empress, he smiles, his eyes glisten, and he says: "Well done, Little Catherine; well done." Listen, you can almost hear the famous lines that end Dickens's *A Tale of Two Cities:* "It is a far, far better thing that I do, than I have ever done; it is a far, far better rest that I go to, than I have ever known." Was Peter's cruelty a strategy to force Catherine into carrying his burden? In her grand salon, Catherine sinks to the floor, overwhelmed by the crowd's reception, reveling in their love for her. Peter's death turns her joy into despair.

Carolyn Heilbrun warns: "There will be narratives of female lives only when women no longer live their lives isolated in the houses and stories of men" (47). Although at the end of Czinner's film Catherine rules "all Russia," it's clear that the men who surround and, literally, tower over her still have control. Even the now-dead Peter encouraged the violation of her first command: "not to touch a hair of his head." Peter's murder taints her victory, as it did the real Catherine's, but Bergner's Catherine implies a damaging, long-term effect. The film ends as it began, with the spotlight on Peter. "That poor unhappy man," Catherine mourns. "He always used to call me Little Catherine." Like an echo, his words, *Little Catherine,* reaffirm her diminutive position: smaller than, weaker than, less than a man.

The Scarlet Empress (1934)

As Marcia Landy notes, *The Scarlet Empress* begins with the echo of a fairy tale: "About two centuries ago, in a corner of the Kingdom of Prussia, lived a little princess . . . chosen by destiny to become the greatest Monarch of her time." The once-upon-a-time opening doesn't lead to a happy ending. Instead, the little princess becomes what the blurb describes: "the ill-famed

Messalina of the North." Characters in a later royal biopic beg to be told the juicy part of her story. In W. S. Van Dyke's *Marie Antoinette* (1938), a group of French noblewomen cluster around a dashing young count whom, they believe, is Russian. Marie Antoinette raises her glass and toasts Catherine the Great, calling her "your naughty empress." The others pester the count for "intimate details" of Catherine's life and for any "personal experience" of her that he can share. This fiction reflects a reality. The crowned heads of Europe solicited news and gossip of each other and seemed to get it quickly, even in their technologically challenged age. It's amusing that these bejeweled, effete members of the doomed French aristocracy, including Marie Antoinette, see Catherine—not themselves—as the supreme signifier of decadence. The tyranny of rumor linked the French and Russian queens. Like Marie Antoinette's, Catherine's image comes to our time dragging its baggage of slander.

The Scarlet Empress, directed by Josef von Sternberg and starring Marlene Dietrich, poses as truth, crediting a secret "diary of Catherine II arranged by Manuel Komroff" as its source. Von Sternberg dropped his first title for the film, *Her Regiment of Lovers,* fearing censorship, but he didn't drop the plan to highlight the queen's sexuality. Although he knew that Czinner had chosen the same subject and was filming in England, Sternberg went ahead with his project, believing that he and Dietrich could create something better. It would be difficult to declare one of these biopics the winner, but it's simple to notice their differences as most critics do, declaring them "180 degrees removed from" each other (Landy 172). Artistically and ideologically, they are opposites. Czinner's picture, an accessible historical romance, takes place on interior sets designed to look the way audiences expect palaces to look, and dialogue carries the romanticized story. Czinner imagines a system that still has the grace to crank out a few beneficent monarchs. "I intend [the film] to be not necessarily an authentic work," von Sternberg said about *The Scarlet Empress* (Frewin 76). Giannetti and Eyman note that *The Scarlet Empress* uses "more titles for purposes of exposition and story clarity than most silent films" (78). That's because image, not dialogue, dominates this compulsively composed music video of Catherine's life from her childhood to the year she took power, and von Sternberg must throw the audience narrative transitions—like life preservers—to keep them from drowning. His film depicts a nest of vipers capable only of becoming more foul.

Casting, too, dictates a difference between the films. Marlene Dietrich, von Sternberg's protégée, is the visual node around which the others— Empress Elizabeth (Louise Dresser), Count Alexei (John Lodge), and Peter III (Sam Jaffe)—coalesce. By the release date of *The Scarlet Empress*, von Sternberg's *The Blue Angel* (1930) had made Dietrich so widely famous that her name alone could draw crowds. To publicize his *Dishonored* (1931), airplanes painted with one word, *Dietrich*, flew low over New York (Frewin 55). For years after the great wave of her film popularity had crested, Dietrich's presence could generate excitement, luring fans eager to see Hollywood royalty. In our blue-collar hometown of Youngstown, Ohio, her appearance to spur the sale of war bonds filled the central square. Dietrich couldn't control the publicity or the creation of the persona that brought her such fame. Giannetti and Eyman comment that both "Dietrich and von Sternberg were amused by the Trilby-Svengali publicity put out by Paramount" (138). Dietrich's amusement wore thin; even before she filmed *The Scarlet Empress*, she threatened (as did Garbo) to escape to Germany, where she would return to the stage. Public rapacity for information about Dietrich's marriage and her relationship with her married director fed the flip side of veneration. Her fans thirsted to know whether she was a "love Pirate" (Bach 148).

The situation more than amused von Sternberg, who perpetuated the gossip swirling around him and his stunning star during their seven-picture collaboration, and who insisted that "no press stories" could be released by Paramount without his approval (Frewin 55). On-screen and off, the view of Dietrich had a single filter. The 1930s film critic C. H. Rand acknowledges this: "I see [Dietrich] through the eyes of Josef von Sternberg. . . . Marlene is a myth, a symbol, an idea" (qtd. in Frewin 60). Von Sternberg's myth, symbol, and idea of Dietrich, whose name he superimposes over a crown in the title sequence of *The Scarlet Empress*, pervades his films and the publicity he crafted. She is "the classic temptress" (Frewin 43), a preoccupation that dominates *The Scarlet Empress*. Von Sternberg alters Catherine's life to fit the persona he created for Dietrich; certainly, his view should differ dramatically from Czinner's take on Bergner's Catherine, that faithful wife and reluctant ruler. Regardless of their differences, these two films share similar indelible cultural imprints. For all its artistic trappings, and for all its vaunted emphasis on sexuality, *The Scarlet Empress* swings between creation and convention as it shapes Catherine's life.

Catherine the Great skips Catherine's life before Peter; it begins on the day she meets the prince. We don't care for this convention of female biopics, used more often and more recently than you might imagine. (Christine Jeffs's *Sylvia* [2003], e.g., begins its dark take on American poet Sylvia Plath's life on the day she meets her love and her nemesis, Ted Hughes.) Although it deletes her childhood, *Catherine the Great* strains to show Catherine's essential childishness, a perpetual state. Sternberg promises to follow the development of an innocent into a virago in *The Scarlet Empress*, but he argues that virago genes are hardwired, merging historical detail from Catherine's childhood with a glimmering of her precocious psyche.

By modern standards, the little princess's life was less than idyllic. Bright and sensitive Sophia, like all girls in her class, could have only one purpose, to improve her family's position by marrying well. Always studious, Sophia could read French by four (Erickson, *Great Catherine*, 2), but such accelerated learning dictated a brief childhood. At seven, "all her toys and dolls were taken away" to promote her intellectual growth (9). Her liveliness was punished with "slaps and blows" (5), while a fall left her with a curved spine that she wore a brace to correct (6–7). In *The Scarlet Empress*, Sophia's mother (Olive Tell) banishes her daughter's toys, declares that she will marry a king, and watches the doctor prescribe "a harness" for her. In a cross-generational blending of actress and subject, Dietrich's daughter, Maria Seiber (credited as Maria Riva), is cast as the young Sophia, who claims that she would rather be a "toe-dancer" or a "hang-man" than marry. A schoolmaster who entertains Sophia by reading about Russia's notorious czars triggers a stream of images, a glimpse into the child's imagination. Besides pillaging Cossacks and murderous nobles, erotic scenes of nubile women enduring bondage and torture—horrors that might have been set loose by the mention of wearing a harness—center her vision. A nearly nude woman emerges from an iron maiden; another turns on a wheel; several others roast at the stake. If these are the fruit of the child's imaginings, what else might lurk inside her?

The scary montage dissolves from the spectacle of a young man, bound and swinging as the human clapper of a bell, to the marriageable Sophia, now played by Dietrich, in a flower-bedecked swing. The sweetness of the swing scene doesn't erase the dissonant clang of the opening with its notion that one does not become but is born a scarlet empress with a "penchant for cruelty even as a child" (Landy 176). Reviewers who complained that Dietrich couldn't portray innocence may not have recognized that the transformation in *The Scarlet Empress* parallels the motion of a makeover plot, in which a beautiful star masquerades as a plain woman until her loveliness reemerges. The satisfaction of watching that process comes, not from a surprise, but from the predictability of the outcome. During the course of the film, the star sheds the signifiers of ugliness (heavy brows, glasses, bulky torso) and regains the face and body familiar to fans.

The fascination of seeing Dietrich masquerade as an innocent, innocence being a state as antithetical to her as frumpiness, reaches its peak in the layered wedding scene. Empress Elizabeth presides over the union, smiling from a box above the crowded floor of Our Lady of Kazan. Scores of bearded monks, hundreds of lit candles, clouds of incense, fill the cathedral floor below her, and pierced screens surround the knave, increasing the atmosphere of claustrophobia. Catherine radiates light, even in this shadowy, orthodox melange. Her white mesh veil transforms her face into a matte-finish portrait, separating her from other, coarser humans. Multiple close-ups in the film, especially in this scene, "graft the folklore of stardom onto the folklore of royalty" (Landy 173). The camera lingers long enough to merge Dietrich's beauty and Catherine's dawning understanding. Part of the pleasure of watching these famous extreme close-ups comes from anticipating the restoration of the ironic, heavy-lidded Dietrich, who had made a career out of playing prostitutes and near prostitutes. The perpetually innocent Catherine of *Catherine the Great* and the perpetually evil Catherine of *The Scarlet Empress* occupy end points on the same essentialist spectrum.

As the young Catherine learns in *Catherine the Great,* once you enter, there is no real "way out" of Peterhof Palace. Von Sternberg's innovative set underscores that point, providing the perfect contrast to the flowery Prussian bower where Sophia played with her friends. Eighteenth-century Russian royals adopted French fashion and culture. *Catherine the Great* mimics that reality, but Hans Dreier's expressionistic Peterhof is no Versailles. Groups of five or six labor to open the massive doors, distorted icons fill the wall space, and freestanding gargoyles (sculpted by Peter Ballbusch) intrude on the action. The gargoyles, sometimes larger than life, even draw attention away from Empress Elizabeth when she sits on a gigantic throne decorated with the Russian emblem—a double-headed eagle. To be absorbed into the concentric circles of court life might have felt like entering this lurid interior, an experience that art can transmit better than accuracy. The Peterhof waits for its proper queen, a woman who doesn't mind the excesses pressing in on her.

Travis Banton adapts Catherine's wardrobe to her environment. Veils, fur, and feathers abound, but two costumes, like bookends, play with the idea that the scarlet empress lies right beneath the surface of the innocent. Before Catherine takes a lover, she runs into her dressing room clad only in her undergarments. From the waist down, she's encased in a hoop skirt, a cage of black wire. This kitschy iron maiden offers a full view of Dietrich's famous legs in tight-fitting pantaloons, predecessors of footless leggings. Over this, she settles a froufrou of a gown. After many conquests, Catherine appears in an outerwear version of this getup, a strapless, backless, transparent black sheath under a transparent black hoop skirt trimmed with black marabou.

Where's the Disney Prince wearing tights and ermine? *Catherine the Great* and *The Scarlet Empress* rearrange the real Catherine's marriage and love affairs into safer patterns, but neither promises a Prince Charming. *Catherine the Great* dismisses the empress's lovers as a figment of her imagination. Her son Paul, who exists only in a reference to the nursery, results from a single night in Peter's bed. She's the perfect Victorian wife, a doll who exudes no sexual knowledge even after producing an heir. *The Scarlet Empress* trumpets Catherine's sexual conquests but denies her any affection, making her act out the fate of the archetypal bad girl. Sure, she can get sex, but how about love? Von Sternberg never intends Sam Jaffe's grand duke to kindle any emotion but repulsion. By the time Peter stands next to Catherine, grinning witlessly through their wedding, von Sternberg has made his mental state clear. No nuances shade this characterization. When *The Scarlet Empress* received bad reviews, von Sternberg complained that the critics had missed the humor in the film, but many found Jaffe, who fiendishly drills that hole through the empress's wall, funny. Threatening music heralds his first appearance, and, if his frazzled wig, frowsy fur cape, and blank stare aren't enough, his toy soldiers and his glee at going to "witness an execution" stamp him as unequivocally nutty. To prevent any misunderstanding, a title declaring him a "royal half-wit" underscores the visual message. The screenplay doesn't shade Peter's attitude toward Catherine. "I hate my wife," Jaffe's Peter tells his aunt. "I don't want her."

Catherine wants Alexei, a fictional character who escorts the princess from her home to Moscow. He is the first Russian man she sees, and she falls for his sultry looks, tangled locks, and stolen kisses. John Davis Lodge, gorgeous even in a towering fur hat like those worn by the palace guards in *The Wizard of Oz*, gives *The Scarlet Empress* its Douglas Fairbanks Jr. Dressed in black, like Peter at the start of *Catherine the Great,* Alexei lacks the potency of Fairbanks's misunderstood isolate, but he's the only character who could be considered a foil for Catherine. The innocent princess falls for him while she's wearing a hair ribbon, like Snow White. When she dons a hat for her trip to Russia, the hat bears a similar bow at the crown, an insistent, and very funny, marker of virginity. Catherine wakes up to Alexei's first kiss with self-remonstrances. "I deserve punishment," she tells him.

Titles decry Catherine's status as a brood mare, but props and action play with the equestrian metaphor that links sex and horsemanship. All this horseplay—who will whip or be whipped; who will ride or be ridden—emits a nasty squeak of the "scandalous pornographic tales" about Catherine that include bestiality, the "product of male imaginations" (Alexander viii). At an inn on the way to Russia, Alexei tells Sophia's mother that he can find her a room in the stables if she doesn't like her accommodations; then he hands Sophia his whip so that she can punish him for desiring her. When next they meet, she and her ladies gallop through the palace halls the week after her marriage. The titles claim that Catherine's exuberance, her "joyous existence," is the result of "the carefree spirit of youth," but all the running in the following sequence of scenes reeks of sexual frustration. Well on her way back to being Dietrich, Catherine wears a riding habit, darker makeup, and a growing cynicism. While Alexei petitions her for an audience, she flexes her whip and smartly raps the bannister, but they do meet, alone, to act out the only romantic scene in *The Scarlet Empress.*

Literally in the hay, the two would-be lovers hover face-to-face in the stable. Catherine whispers breathily and swings between desire and action on a convenient loop of rope. She falls on her back and places a straw between her lips like a cigarette. Alexei removes it. They repeat the straw sequence, von Sternberg's idea of hot foreplay, *five times* (and again later in the film). Finally, Catherine falls into an eyes-closed kiss with Alexei, her left hand displaying her wedding ring. A whinnying horse brings Catherine, a filly, to her senses, away she gallops, and that's it for romance. Catherine ends things with Alexei (the only man she feels affection for) when she learns that he has been Elizabeth's lover. She humiliates him by forcing him to watch another handsome guardsman slip through a secret door into her chamber. Catherine fulfills her brood mare duties by random assignation, stumbling on her first lover in the garden of the Peterhof, a raw recruit who thinks she is a "kitten." None of her other lovers (a whole regiment?) make that mistake. In *The Scarlet Empress,* Paul appears as a bundle of blankets, and a black mesh veil indicates Catherine's postpartum state. The coarse crosshatching abstracts Dietrich's features into a composition of sharp angles and shadowy hollows like a fuzzy, but recognizable, still of the star.

As she describes a scene that von Sternberg created for *The Scarlet Empress,* Marcia Landy argues that whether the content is "historically documentable" is "irrelevant"; the power of the biopic to critique genres and norms matters more than accuracy (182). It's culturally relevant, however, to consider the historically documentable content that biopics leave as lacunae. Each of the two 1934 versions wraps Catherine's marriage and sexuality in a package recognizable to viewers: the faithful wife and the insatiable wanton, opposite stereotypes, but both less risky than presenting Catherine's stark sexual dilemma to the Hayes office or to audiences. She needed a pregnancy. Her husband rebuffed her. Courtiers wooed her. Her advisers looked askance. The cold pragmatism of Empress Elizabeth—hinted at in *The Scarlet Empress*—fits no convenient genre schema. Neither do Catherine's miscarriages, her subsequent pregnancies, or her search for emotional and political support.

Neither film attempts a reading of Catherine's complex approach to power. Biographers describe her dedication and her ambition; she sought to prepare herself for the throne by learning Russian, reading political theory, and forming alliances with military—especially the Orlov brothers—and political figures, and she coldly monitored Empress Elizabeth's decline. *Catherine the Great* refuses any such notion, keeping relations between Catherine and Elizabeth cordial and the coup the outcome of necessity. *The Scarlet Empress* acknowledges Orlov's presence and codes Catherine's ambition red, casting her accession as an emblem of a rotten system that replaces one murderous wretch with another. Although titles promise to reveal Catherine's "youthful ideals" giving way to her "ambitious pursuit of power," neither phrase fits the visual agenda. Even in her faux innocence, Catherine never looks beyond the Peterhof. She and Elizabeth, sexual ri-

The Scarlet Empress. Heralded by patriarchs, and held aloft by Cossacks, Catherine is carried toward the throne of all the Russias in this stirring scene from *The Scarlet Empress,* but Josef von Sternberg's patriotic closing doesn't reflect the focus of the film: Dietrich/Catherine's sexuality. (Courtesy Jerry Ohlinger's Movie Material Store.)

vals, have no conversations about the throne, and, when a priest offers Catherine backing from his "political machine," she voices no interest in "petty conspiracy." As does *Catherine the Great, The Scarlet Empress* uses a montage of proclamations to stand for Peter's cruelty, and crosscuts show Catherine's response: a game of blindman's bluff with her friends. Her ambitions, represented by a smirking review of a regiment rife with upright officers and her selection of Orlov (Calvin Gordon), have little to do with governance.

The historic banquet in *The Scarlet Empress* seals Catherine's viciousness, although von Sternberg floats the weak suggestion that she might not be irredeemably selfish. Alms for the poor, solicited by a priest, paint Catherine, Orlov, and Alexei as more generous than Elizabeth Vorontsova, who pitches a bit of bread into the salver, and Peter, who slaps the priest. "There are no poor in Russia," Peter insists. Although Catherine shucks off an armful of bracelets (but not her pearls), her ironic smile while she knots her napkin, a noose for Peter, steals the scene. After she leaves the hall, Peter stabs an apple as he orders her death, but this Eve has the jump on him. Orlov strangles Peter behind an orthodox cross in nothing flat, and his death causes no blip on the Russian radar screen. Catherine needs no prompting to assume her uniform with its tight-fitting white trousers. Von Sternberg goes for stirring patriotism—punctuated by shots of Dietrich in those tight pants—with the coup that culminates in a noisy, horseback rush up the staircase where she flirted with Alexei. Dvorak's *New World* Symphony may sound like a bright future, but the face that centers the religious and patriotic swirl is the Old World face of Dietrich, dark lips smiling, eyes glinting with avarice.

Young Catherine (1991)

Why did the same year produce two Catherine the Great biopics? The ethos surrounding the Czinner versus von Sternberg attempts probably helped. The world depression spurred audiences to schadenfreude, making the old truism that money (even heaps of it) can't buy you love or happiness a crowd-pleaser. The specter of Stalin and enforced collectivism too must have made fairy-tale/horror-story depictions of the Russian aristocracy a draw. A half century later, in the shadow of an unraveling Soviet Union, a look at the life of Catherine the Great combines nostalgia for the past with a democratizing homily from the present. Set amid the splendor of czarist Russia, it trumpets the righteous dedication of a ruler who wasn't produced by blood succession.

The fantastic sweep of a gilded reception room, rich, polished parquet floors, tapestry-covered love seats with scrolled embellishments, elaborately paneled walls, incredible paintings and objets d'art—the actual trappings of empire—give this made-for-television special the clout born of filming on location. *Young Catherine,* a lavish Turner Home Entertainment spectacle shot in Russia and directed by Michael Anderson, selects the same slice of the empress's life as the two 1934 biopics. This leisurely look at Catherine's youth includes political intrigue and portraits of the figures around the throne as it marches to its incessant drumbeat. *Young Catherine* molds Catherine the Great into a figure more palatable to late-twentieth-century viewers; she's closer to Bergner's reluctant ruler than to Dietrich's temptress, but she's updated with a healthy dose of self-determination. Even during her carriage ride toward Russia, Princess Sophia (Julia Ormond), who neither looks nor acts like a teen (Ormond was twenty-five), reveals that she has been thinking protofeminist thoughts about the lives of royal women. She gently chastises her mother for calling ruling "man's work." Russia, she comments, "is ruled by a woman. England has been. So has Sweden."

One of the great strengths of *Young Catherine* is its portrait of the female ruler who represents the old, bad, monarchical way. Vanessa Redgrave's energetic performance as Empress Elizabeth convinces from the moment the character appears, graciously welcoming Catherine as one of the contenders for her nephew's hand. Redgrave—a DBE (dame commander of the British Empire) who has also played Guinevere and Mary, Queen of Scots—makes it clear just how someone so quixotic could be completely beguiling. Elizabeth's charisma emanates from her childlike joy, and Redgrave knows how to exaggerate this central characteristic to make it the root of Elizabeth's rigidity and destructiveness.

When the empress discovers that Princess Sophia's mother, Johanna (Marthe Keller), has been corresponding secretly with Frederick, the emperor of Prussia, she flies into a towering rage, confronting Johanna with an intercepted letter, and screaming that she will "never, never, never" forgive her. "I have thrown people into dungeons, in chains, for life, for less," she thunders, an assertion of a willingness to exact physical punishment that sounds, and is, true. According to Waliszewski, "two thousand tongues, two thousand pairs of ears" were once cut off at her request (1:58–59). Elizabeth sends the kneeling supplicant off to pack for an immediate departure. Then, with startling speed, she becomes all sunshine. Looking angelic and lovely in her bright yellow frock, she fans herself until calm and cool. Turning to Sophia, the witness of her terrifying wrath, she bestows her own mother's name, Ekaterina, on the shaken, teary-eyed girl with the gaiety of someone conferring a special birthday treat, apparently oblivious that her chastising of the mother might have upset the daughter. Her behavior here provides a context for later actions.

After petting and spoiling Catherine when she becomes pregnant, Elizabeth virtually steals the newborn Paul from her. Beautifully gowned and coiffed, Elizabeth leaves Catherine to sweat on the birthing couch (an accurate portrayal). Since Catherine has produced an heir, she's extraneous until her next lying-in. Neither protestations nor tears move Elizabeth into sharing the child with his mother. Redgrave's performance conjures up the reality of absolute power, a drug as addictive and destructive as heroin. Elizabeth's assumption that she can do as she wishes to anyone at any time offers a possible outcome for Catherine's future; she could become as certain of her dominance as her predecessor is of hers.

What little *Young Catherine* shows of Catherine's childhood steers her character away from such an outcome. Her loving father insists on her education and sends her off to Russia with duty foremost in her mind. Catherine's mother, a calculating player, disappears from the court and, apparently, from her daughter's heart because she is an expedient manipulator. Another strength of this version is that it attempts, as the incident with Johanna demonstrates, a more complete picture of competing forces inside and outside the Russian court. An empress "with no enemies," Elizabeth declares, "is no empress." From outside, King Frederick of Prussia (Maximilian Schell), not a friend, works to consolidate his power. He enlists a willing Johanna and anticipates no trouble from Catherine and Peter, "two obedient children." From inside the court, Elizabeth's adviser, Vorontsov (Franco Nero), and his wife (Anna Kanakis) mount a plot to poison Catherine so that they can put their niece in the princess's place.

Young Catherine even addresses Elizabeth's attempts to control what went on in Catherine and Peter's marriage bed. After she discovers the lack of procreative activity, the empress puts the young couple in lockdown under the surveillance of the fertile, fecund Choglokovs, husband and wife, as role models and spies (a form of internal surveillance she really did institute). Even in her own apartments, Catherine must bear the constant irritation of the empress's agenda. Prior film Catherines got no chance to vent or to confide. Both, encircled by ladies-in-waiting, have no conversation with anyone but the other main characters. Ormond's Catherine has a friend and confidante in Princess Deshkova (Laurie Holden), who listens to her woes and applauds her triumphs. Deshkova's presence provides a rationale for personal conversations, an important addition to the screenplay since they enable Catherine to voice her determination to persevere after Peter is changed by smallpox because she has "come hundreds of miles . . . embraced a new faith . . . and learned a new language." Near the time of her coup, Catherine states her fervor for Russia, "a country worth dying for," to Deshkova. Another of Catherine's confidants and supporters, not a member of the Russian court, adds depth to her portrait. No other biopic of 'Catherine's life foregrounds Lord Hanbury-Williams, Catherine's real-life friend and mentor.

In this version, the English ambassador (Christopher Plummer), who sees all the qualities mandatory for a great ruler in the young princess, encourages her to begin considering what might happen after Elizabeth's death. In life, Catherine discussed her position at court with the ambassador, corresponded with him, and considered him an audience for her memoirs (*Memoirs* x). "He had great wit and knowledge," Catherine wrote, "and we had a conversation as pleasant as it was merry" (146). The garden scenes between them are visual metaphors for Catherine's blooming. High-angle shots and close-ups show the friends traversing the geometric garden paths as they discuss court affairs. With the garden as background, Hanbury-Williams helps Catherine weigh the political benefits and deficits of taking a lover. Their film relationship gave Chris Bryant, the screenwriter, a chance to add exposition; when Peter develops smallpox just before their wedding, Catherine is ignored and excluded. Hanbury-Williams explains the mood and culture of the court. The courtiers are practicing expediency. If Peter recovers, Catherine will, of course, become a central figure, and everyone will want to count her as a friend. If Peter should die, Catherine will be valueless to them and will end up "the tiniest footnote to history." When courtiers cluster around Catherine as she next enters the reception room, she, and the audience, understands that the grand duke has recovered.

Hanbury-Williams's presence adds outside/inside context. Like King Frederick's, it illustrates the investment that other countries had in monitoring progress in Russia, a factor missing from the enclosed worlds of *Catherine the Great* and *The Scarlet Empress*. More significantly, he provides another rationale for Catherine's coup, suggesting to her that diplomats like him already realize Peter's inability to rule, even "a line." When he leaves, he charges her with taking Russia "out of the Dark Ages." Her discussions with him allow Catherine to test ideas about her public self, but they don't make it clear that she was developing an "independent policy" beyond his manipulation, as she did in life (Haslip 85). She demonstrates her independence when she refuses to bow to Frederick's pressure. "I am grand duchess now," she tells his emissary.

Young Catherine makes Catherine's relationship with Peter a testament to her growing understanding. She's no eternally faithful wife, although she tries to like her husband, whom she sees, initially, as "very nice" but childish. Reece Dinsdale's grand duke neither leers like Sam Jaffe nor smolders like Douglas Fairbanks, but he's obviously unstable and incapable of mature action. Peter's childishness—he wants to play hide and seek—keeps viewers off guard. At first his antics amuse; then they alarm. Increasingly, we see, as Catherine does, that Peter's instability portends a catastrophe for Russia. Dinsdale's mix of innocence, weakness, malice, and dissipation, which he practices with the slutty Lizzie Vorontsova (Katharine Schlesinger), corresponds with accounts of his "childlike" behavior (Erickson, *Great Catherine,* 40). There's a horror-film ethos in the shadowed scene in which Peter, disfigured by smallpox, reveals his bald head and face covered with oozing sores.

Young Catherine acts out the rumor that the grand duke suffered from a slight physical impediment to sex (Haslip 48). To repair his infirmity, a group of guards get him too drunk to realize he's undergoing the surgery he's been avoiding—the slitting of a tight foreskin. The operation must take place so that the pregnant Catherine can make her husband sleep with her at least once to give her child the appearance of legitimacy. (In this version, Catherine's clearly pregnant before the surgery.) To inflame Peter's desire, Catherine dresses in the uniform of the imperial guard and "drills" with Peter's soldiers (something Peter forced the real Catherine to do). This fictional guess at how they might have come together adds a little black humor to an otherwise deadly serious venture. An excited Peter "disciplines" Catherine by spanking her with his sword, behavior that leads to lust. Perhaps only Julia Ormond could have kept Catherine looking squeaky clean in these circumstances. Ormond goes for repugnance masked by sprightly determination, a stance that is in accordance with Catherine's father's teachings about duty and that allows *Young Catherine* to follow its rhythm of rightness.

Ormond is up to the task of creating an appealing and serious character. Trained as a stage actress, her on-screen success escalated after she played this role, obviously shaded to fit her persona. Unlike Vanessa Redgrave, who was born into stage royalty, Ormond, who didn't inherit such a name or position, was being marketed as an upscale ingenue. *Legends of the Fall* (Edward Zwick, 1994), her first starring role in a major motion picture, placed her opposite the sizzling newcomer Brad Pitt. In *First Knight* (Jerry Zucker, 1995), she played Queen Guinevere to the sizzling old-timers Sean Connery as King Arthur and Richard Gere as Lancelot. Roger Ebert upped the ante for *First Knight* when he compared it to *Casablanca* (Michael Curtiz, 1942), with its difficult choice between passion and allegiance. He makes a similar comparison between Ormond, with her "apple cheeks . . . full lips . . . wide-set, grave eyes," and Ingrid Bergman (rev. of *First Knight*).

When Ormond played the title role in *Sabrina* (Sydney Pollack, 1995), a remake of Billy Wilder's 1954 classic, Edward Guthman continued Ebert's "who does she look like" game, asserting that her "cool patrician looks and . . . gorgeous voice" remind him more of Grace Kelly than Audrey Hepburn. These weren't the only critics who lauded Ormond's person more than her acting. Janet Maslin, hardly an easy sell, dropped the comparisons but gave Ormond credit for "considerable glamor" and "crispness" in *Smilla's Sense of Snow* (Bille August, 1997), an adaptation of Peter Høeg's best-selling novel. Ormond's progress toward queen status stopped when she stopped—press stories say—to take some time off. *Young Catherine* carries the flavor of the up-market slot that she was expected to fill.

Catherine is often shown with a book in her hand, a habit confirmed in her memoirs. "The most boring book," Catherine says, seems a "delicious amusement" in contrast to Peter (*Memoirs* 105). *Catherine the Great* doesn't worry about Catherine's intellect. *The Scarlet Empress* gives a glimpse of Catherine reading but fixes its lens on her seductions. *Young Catherine* depends on its portrayal of a more intellectual heroine to give credence to a critical stage in Catherine's personal development, an event ignored by both 1934 biopics. In 1759, after a lonely winter of solitary reading and thinking, Catherine felt that she had to make a change. Heilbrun asks us to look for such a "life crisis," especially in the "lives of women who died before the middle of the twentieth century" (47). Many women, Heilbrun explains, escaped from conventional society by taking a lover, an act defined as a "sexual sin," or by initiating some other social act that put them beyond the pale. Christina did this by abdicating. Catherine, hardly living a "conventional" life, tried for a reversal of her position. She petitioned the empress for release, claiming that she wanted to return to Germany because she served no purpose at the Russian court.

In her memoirs, Catherine describes the letter she wrote demanding

Young Catherine. As if offering her full support, Empress Elizabeth stands behind Catherine, regarding her with affection. The film traces Elizabeth's vacillating feelings for the grand duchess, swings from approval to disparagement that demonstrate the empress's mercurial temperament more than Catherine's worth. (Courtesy Jerry Ohlinger's Movie Material Store.)

an audience. She characterizes herself as "alone and abandoned" and declares that she is "hated by the Grand Duke and not at all loved by the Empress" (*Memoirs* 197). It was certainly true that her husband disliked her and that the empress had refused to let her visit her two children. (Catherine had borne a daughter by a second lover.) While the meeting with Elizabeth did not win her freedom, it did help her regain the empress's attention, which may have been her real aim, and it stood as a personal turning point. After the experience, she writes: "In whatever situation it should please Providence to place me, I should never find myself without those resources that intelligence and talent give to each according to his natural abilities" (199).

Young Catherine uses high-contrast lighting and the dynamics of space and position to mark Catherine's rise and Elizabeth's decline. Elizabeth sits, her power waning, her hair loose and disheveled. Catherine stands, young and regal, carefully coiffed and dressed in deep blue velvet, a paradigm of someone ready to rule. Tightly framed close-ups underscore the tension between the decadent, dying ruler and the ascendant empress. Later, on her deathbed, Elizabeth whispers her last, unfinished thought to Catherine. "I wish . . . ," she says, leaving the suggestion that she might have anointed Catherine her heir at the end. Catherine's inner certitude also dominates *Young Catherine*'s version of the banquet scene. In this rendition, which deletes Catherine's nervousness, her calm strength stands against Peter's trembling hysteria. The carefully established framework for Catherine's coup makes her takeover a foregone conclusion. By the time she mounts her white stallion and dons her regimentals, Catherine exudes the authority of a Minerva come down to earth to claim her rightful territory.

Ormond's casting helps make Catherine an empathetic character, and the screenplay nicely interjects Catherine's personal growth into its treatment of court politics. The justification for her acts, however, depends substantially on spin that highlights the princess's conversion and sanitizes her sexuality. It's true that abandoning her Lutheran upbringing posed a dilemma for Catherine, who knew that her father opposed the move, and true as well that she received intellectual guidance from a charismatic Orthodox priest. Ultimately, however, as Carolly Erickson explains, it was convert or go home, and Sophia made the choice to become the Russian Orthodox Catherine as a sign of allegiance to "her new parent," the empress (*Great Catherine*, 54). *Young Catherine* credits no biographical source, but it seems to be channeling Erickson's pages, especially in the conversion scene, a visual depiction of Erickson's description: Catherine kneels in the "womblike darkness of the Palace chapel," intoning "the confession of faith" that she has "painstakingly memorized, parrot fashion" (52). Erickson notes that the real Catherine wore a "crimson gown," but Ormond's Catherine is dressed in creamy white. The difference in dress signals a split in interpretation. Erickson treats Catherine's acceptance of the Orthodox faith as a pragmatic step toward becoming Peter's wife, while the film overdramatizes the journey toward conversion, spending half an hour of the two-and-a-half-hour run time on the change. Repeated shots of a kneeling Catherine, wearing a hooded, monk-like robe, surrounded by icons, make religion a central component of the narrative and of her nature. The choice to exalt her Orthodox religiosity panders to the pro–family values, ultrapatriotic segment of the viewing audience. Catherine's carefully shaped love life promotes the belief that someone so patently pious and in love with Russia would never do anything immoral; such a queen should, and does, find a Disneyesque prince.

A saccharine musical theme underscores the romance. Every time Catherine falls into the arms of Gregory Orlov (Mark Frankel), a schmaltzy crescendo repeats. *Young Catherine* borrows from *The Scarlet Empress* the notion that Catherine fell for the handsome, dark-haired guard (reprise John Lodge) who conveyed her to Russia. Orlov offers Catherine his sword and his life after the trip, and he hovers in her vicinity, a watchful guardian. He's the one who fetches Empress Elizabeth from a retreat at a convent when the princess is being poisoned, and it's he who orders the guards to salute Catherine on her wedding day. In *Young Catherine,* the empress designates Orlov as the approved stud, but Catherine already loves him. The affair scoots outside the parameters of romance when Catherine discusses the outcomes of such a merger with Hanbury-Williams, but this scene exists to provide more validation. She knows, she tells the affirming ambassador, just who she will choose for the job. So do we.

Catherine's pregnancy happens overnight—as soon as the night contains Orlov, another sign that their coming together is right. The glamorous Frankel and Ormond look perfect together, almost like brother and sister; on a stolen weekend, their costumes, by Larisa Konnikova, match. He wears tight red pants, she a red skirt, and they both sport full, white blouses, kitschy peasant garb that links them to Mother Russia, not to the decadent monarchy. It's Orlov who sires Catherine's son, he who enlists the guard to protect her, he who supports and plots toward her takeover. When Orlov is arrested by Vorontsov (a fiction), Catherine adds saving his life to her mission of saving Russia. *Young Catherine* does not show Orlov murdering Peter, but Catherine's confessor (John Schrapnel) insists that he must die to keep her safe, absolving Orlov even before he acts. This endless love feels good, but, historically, things were hardly so simple. Sergei Saltykov, Catherine's courtly lover, did exist, and Catherine, duped into thinking he adored her, learned his affection was part of a larger plan. *Young Catherine* sidelines the blunt hurt that results from such a stab to the heart. Saltykov or Peter, not Orlov, fathered Catherine's first child. After Catherine produced an heir, Saltykov looked elsewhere for passion, and

Catherine selected her next lover, not Orlov, but Stanisław Poniatowski, the secretary to Hanbury-Williams and father of her second child, Anna Petrovna. Orlov came third, and he gave Catherine military support during her coup as well as another son, Gregory Bobrinski.

It's true that Catherine formed a long-term attachment with Orlov, that their affair lasted twelve years, and that she admired his certainty, his "primitive strength" (Haslip 101). It's also true that many biopics judiciously merge characters in aid of creating a tighter, more focused story. *Young Catherine*, however, implies a purpose for this romantic fantasy that has little to do with the consolidation of too many minor characters. Filmed during the first Bush presidency, *Young Catherine*, which also purges Empress Elizabeth of lovers, leaves the impression that saintly, nearly monogamous Catherine, Orlov, and little Paul, who clearly resembles his parents, will become the permanent royal family. As Catherine lifts the sparkling crown and holds it above her head, she looks straight at the camera, as if accepting her audience's approval.

Catherine the Great (1995)

Potemkin, the man who seemed most intellectually and physically capable of giving Catherine comfort and peace, followed Orlov, and others followed Potemkin, but that part of the empress's life—the part in which she ruled Russia and pursued a satisfying private relationship—isn't covered in *Young Catherine*. *Catherine the Great*, an A&E made-for-television movie, starring Catherine Zeta-Jones, Jeanne Moreau, and Omar Sharif, attempts a larger slice of Catherine's life, moving beyond her 1762 coup d'état to end in the 1770s. Because it considers this greater span, it could showcase her development into a worthy empress and a mature woman. Sometimes, it takes that option, for example, when it depicts Catherine's growing intellectual strength and political savvy and when it touches on her relationship with Potemkin, the man the real empress regarded as a soul mate. But these random flashes of enlightenment simply don't add up to a satisfying whole. Instead of trying to create an evocative portrait of a complex woman, Marvin J. Chomsky, who directed *Gunsmoke* and some episodes of *Star Trek* early in his career, crafts an exploitative response to Catherine Zeta-Jones's beautiful body. John Goldsmith and Frank Tudisco's screenplay aids him in his preoccupation; it makes sense that these writers do not ac-

knowledge a source because they rampage through Catherine's life, stitch-
ing together a fabric that's part bodice ripper, part political thriller. The
result is a bit like *The Scarlet Empress* on steroids, with less artsy presump-
tion and more bare flesh.

The speed with which *Catherine the Great* rockets through the princess's life signals its focus. A first-person voice-over by Catherine glosses
the opening shot of Peter (Hannes Jaenicke) and the young Catherine
(Catherine Zeta-Jones) at the altar, clarifying the date, 1745, and describing the circumstances of the royal marriage: "We were both pawns in a
political game." Then, in less than two minutes, we're yanked ahead seven
years (the accurate length of time) to the day on which Empress Elizabeth
(Jeanne Moreau) learns that the marriage has not been consummated. This
version doesn't bother with Catherine's childhood or her parents. There's
no Emperor Frederick and only a few words to gloss Catherine's selection
as Peter's wife. *Young Catherine* dwells on her religious conversion, but, in
this film, it's a fait accompli and never mentioned. Instead, *Catherine the
Great* fast-forwards to Empress Elizabeth's very physical interview with
Sergei Saltykov (Craig McLachlan). While she questions the strapping
young man, whom she characterizes as "a stag in rut," the empress care-
lessly flicks his jacket aside with her fan, the better to gauge the size of his
private parts. He'll do as Catherine's first lover, she decides.

As you can see, this first chunk of Catherine's life, which should feature
Don Henley's "The End of the Innocence" as background music, gets to her
deflowering as fast as it can. And there's no fade to black à la Bergner and
Fairbanks to leave the circumstances of that event a mystery. Saltykov and
Catherine, trapped in a hunting lodge by a thunderstorm, get an opportunity they can't ignore. This situation is not too far from the truth implied
by Catherine's journals, which recount a private "hour and a half" conversation during a hunt that, Catherine says, "pleased me rather well" (*Memoirs* 110). From that kernel, however, this production explodes into corn.
While the other biopics privilege Catherine's private life, *Catherine the
Great* bypasses private on its sprint to prurient, placing viewers right between the sheets. Through a convenient peephole, one of the empress's
advisers watches the couple as they couple, underscoring the voyeuristic
feel of the clichéd seduction scene, with its flickering firelight, white fur
rug, and intertwined nude limbs. The camera caresses Saltykov's massive
pectorals, bulging biceps, and corded neck, which look a lot more like the

results of a twentieth-century obsession with the Nautilus than the physique of an eighteenth-century Russian nobleman, while Jones's body, especially her perfect back, gets plenty of exposure.

The first nude interlude foreshadows more to come. Shortly after Catherine's tryst with Saltykov, Kovia—the Lady Bruce (Agnès Soral)—discusses the love affair with Catherine, who lounges in her royal bath, nipples barely covered by the water. It's intriguing to see how selectively the writers of these biopics choose supporting characters from Catherine's entourage (a considerable group). Bergner's Catherine depended on Elizabeth and, later, on Orlov. Dietrich's Catherine had no friends at all, underscoring von Sternberg's view of her as a solitary predator. *Young Catherine*, with its more wholesome, monogamous slant, chooses an aging British diplomat and a sedate lady-in-waiting, and this version features a companion better suited to a sensual agenda. Kovia's character is based on the real Lady Bruce, Praskovia Rumyantsev; *Catherine the Great* capitalizes on the gossip about this sycophantic follower whom, many believed, copied Catherine's every whim so slavishly that she even dallied with one of Orlov's brothers while the empress had an affair with Orlov (Erickson, *Great Catherine*, 330–31). In *Catherine the Great*, Catherine uses Kovia as a procuress, first, to fetch Orlov and, later, to convince Potemkin (whom she seems to know intimately) to return to her mistress. When Kovia brings Orlov to her, another nearly nude romp ensues. Catherine greets Orlov in sexy dishabille, her bare legs extended invitingly. The enterprising Orlov cuts the laces of her loose gown with a handy pocket knife, and, voilà, there's another opportunity to feature Zeta-Jones's back.

Costuming amps up the already high degree of titillation decreed by eighteenth-century fashion. The designer, Barbara Baum, revels in the period mandate that a woman's breasts be compressed, elevated, and exposed by giving Zeta-Jones the most daring décolleté in the cast. Her barely contained breasts dominate scenes so often that they could be billed as supporting players. One piece of dialogue seems to refer to them, creating a bit of unintentional humor in an almost humorless script. In the first flush of romance, Catherine and Potemkin stand in the moonlight. Catherine's breasts, again, feature prominently in this half shot, and, although Potemkin is speaking about the stars, he looks right at Catherine's heaving bosom as he says that they seem "close, as if one only had to reach out and touch them, . . . but . . . they're too high, beyond reach."

A child actor, who had become a seasoned professional by the age of twenty-six, when she played Catherine, the Welsh Zeta-Jones isn't bad at telegraphing the empress's shrewd intelligence, when she gets a chance. As a rising star, Zeta-Jones didn't rate the royal treatment that Ormond received, with all those comparisons to Audrey Hepburn and Ingrid Bergman, but she looked like money in the bank to Hollywood. Shortly after *Catherine the Great* aired, her movie career took off; she got good reviews and lots of audience exposure for her work with Antonio Banderas and Anthony Hopkins in *The Mask of Zorro* (Martin Campbell, 1998), with Sean Connery in *Entrapment* (John Amiel, 1999), and with her husband-to-be, Michael Douglas, in *Traffic* (Steven Soderbergh, 2000). These high-profile roles, while not particularly patrician, lifted Zeta-Jones into a royal circle of revenue-producing actresses and made her "the highest paid British woman in Hollywood" for several years (Woodcock 27). Critical acclaim followed with a Best Supporting Actress Oscar for her stunning dancing and singing in the musical *Chicago* (Rob Marshall, 2002).

Before Zeta-Jones became such an international celebrity, however, her turn as the rumor-burdened empress provided a taste of unwelcome public attention. While they filmed *Catherine the Great,* Zeta-Jones and Paul McGann, *Catherine the Great*'s Potemkin, became friends; Zeta-Jones got to know McGann's wife and child as well. Shortly after the production wrapped, she met McGann to share some cast photos. Paparazzi following Zeta-Jones snapped the two casually kissing hello, and several British tabloids carried the photo with stories claiming that McGann and Zeta-Jones were having an affair. Angry denials only fueled the gossip machine, and paparazzi began to hound Catherine, McGann, and his wife. The public devoured the story, apparently intrigued by the possibility that Zeta-Jones might be a home wrecker for whom McGann would abandon his wife and small child. Eventually, McGann and his wife had to move to another town to escape the persistent buzz. Zeta-Jones says that this incident helped her develop a shell; distance also helps her cope with the rigors of celebrity. She and Douglas have escaped the public eye by living on Bermuda, outside the media bubble.

When *Catherine the Great* shifts its gaze from Zeta-Jones's form to Catherine's character, it comes alive. Catherine quotes the French philosophes, she mentions her reading, and she acknowledges her plans for Russia. "I wanted a revolution," she says, in a voice-over, while she is crowned ruler of all the Russias. After taking over, she discovers that she can handle her two advisers, Bestuzhev and Vorontsov. These astute politicians begin as enemies, and Catherine learns to play them against each other. Eventually, the two form an uneasy alliance, frightened by Catherine's egalitarian sentiments. This subplot suggests that Catherine's loyalties, finally, lie with Vorontsov, but it never reaches a resolution.

Sketchy at best, scenes featuring the members of the royal family skimp on the talents of an impressive supporting cast. A production that boasts cameos by legends like Jeanne Moreau, Omar Sharif, and Mel Ferrer should have an attendant luster. A lengthier version of *Catherine the Great* released in Germany as a miniseries may have increased Ferrer's visibility, but, in the American cut, he's barely there. Sharif and Moreau fare a little better, shining as aging lovers in their few good scenes. Sharif plays Razumovsky, Elizabeth's "Emperor of the Night," whom she secretly married in real life. *Young Catherine* acknowledges the importance of the tension between Elizabeth and Catherine. Moreau, eternally alluring, creates an earthy, tough, cynical Elizabeth, but there's not much chance to examine her attitude toward Catherine. Except for a scene in which she brutally removes the newborn Paul from Catherine's arms and a truncated version of the important interview between the two women, they rarely interact.

Hannes Jaenicke has even less impact as Peter. Jaenicke's Peter plays the violin and loiters with his servants as the real Peter did, but that's about the extent of his activity, making him the blandest Peter of the lot. Only his one-time bedding of Catherine—a nasty business—illuminates his brutality. Minimal attempts to suggest his ineptitude and to clarify his ongoing threat to Catherine aren't enough to contextualize his murder. A trite visual metaphor accompanies Peter's extinction. First, in a series of crosscuts between the exiled emperor and the new empress, Peter peacefully plays his violin while a squad of army officers rides toward him through the moonlight. In Moscow, Catherine reads by candlelight. Back at Oranienbaum, the officers dismount and run to the palace. In Moscow, Catherine begins to snuff out the candles. The violin music halts abruptly as Orlov and his crew strangle Peter. Finally, Catherine extinguishes the last candle, and the flame—Peter's life—goes out. As a prelude to Peter's murder, Catherine's silly dialogue undercuts the seriousness of her triumph. "My Dear," she says to Kovia as the coup begins, "I am about to seize the throne of Russia. What on earth shall I wear?" In *Catherine the Great*, she chooses a black dress and a military jacket. This costume—a key historical detail—receives less attention than Catherine's more revealing ensembles.

Catherine the Great gives little thought to Empress Elizabeth or Peter, but it spends more than a third of its time on Catherine's romance with Potemkin, and this makes sense. A full-length film or a miniseries could devote itself to this slice of Catherine's life alone, without running out of material. *Catherine the Great* stakes out important biographical ground when it lingers on Catherine and Potemkin, but glitches skew its presentation. The least important of these, a weird casting choice, creates visual confusion. Three brothers from one family, Mark, Paul, and Stephen McGann, have roles in *Catherine the Great*. All three have a strong familial resemblance, but Mark and Paul McGann, who play Orlov and Potemkin, look distractingly alike. Consequently, Catherine's lovers, Orlov and Potemkin, also look alike, making it difficult to read the transition between them. The first time we watched the film, we had to rewind and look again to make sure it wasn't the same man answering to a different name. Costuming reinforces the confusion since both men are clad in officers' coats much of the time. Does the casting of these attractive men have any basis in reality? While some describe Orlov as dashing, many observers note that Potemkin was an "uncouth," heavy, "ungainly" man, with an "uncovered" blind left eye (Erickson, *Great Catherine*, 303), making it difficult to imagine that he looked anything like either handsome McGann.

Besides the clone/lover problem, there's the aging factor (or lack of it). When Catherine and Potemkin became lovers in 1774, Catherine was a mature woman of forty-five, disillusioned with her son, constantly entangled in Russia's problems. She was still physically attractive, if grayer and stouter, and she longed for a friend, lover, intellectual equal, and political ally, a combination she had never found in one man (Erickson, *Great Catherine*, 301). Voice-overs and superimposed dates alert viewers to passing time in *Catherine the Great*, but, after a battle scene labeled 1757, these markers disappear. Catherine Zeta-Jones's appearance does nothing to help establish the time frame because, apparently, she remains twenty-six throughout. While this film covers a larger slice of Catherine's life, it denies her the dignity of looking as if she has lived it. Even portraits painted in the 1760s, after Catherine had become empress, show her mature, womanly countenance. According to *Catherine the Great*, the empress's face

(centuries before Botox) remained a mask of youth, unmarked by experience. Finally, in the last scene, when Potemkin leaves Catherine alone, two
shiny, silver streaks dramatically highlight her lush, dark hair. How much
time has gone by? Only Catherine's vague remarks about Potemkin winning "the Crimea" for her indicate that part of her reign has passed and
there's more to come.

Catherine the Great labors to make viewers see that Catherine and
Potemkin's relationship was more than an affair. Catherine speaks Latin to
Potemkin; together they quote classic poetry. They share the pangs brought
on by ruling. "You've found that to command was to be alone," Catherine
says to a war-weary Potemkin. Weirdly, in this ultrafleshy production, Potemkin seems more aesthete than epicurean, and, in their most intimate
scenes, these passionate lovers look chaste. In bed, they talk to each other,
nightgowns buttoned up to their chins, instead of making love, as if sexual
pleasure and intellectual companionship can't coexist. Some believe that
the real Catherine married Potemkin secretly, citing possible dates, locations, and references to each other as "husband" and "wife" in their correspondence (Erickson, *Great Catherine,* 307). Whether or not theirs was a
marriage in fact, Catherine and Potemkin felt committed to each other.
They sparred over political and government issues; they shared a grand vision of Russia—literally—touring it together; they fed each other's delight
in things sensual. Potemkin, who had "burst in upon the court like a hot
wind off the faraway . . . desert," helped the driven, work-obsessed Catherine relax (303). They sometimes met in the steam baths, where they dressed
in comfortable caftans, lounged on divans, and ate delicacies. They must
have had what Heilbrun calls a "revolutionary marriage," which transcends
the passions of youth, and in which "both partners have work at the center
of their lives and must find a delicate balance that can support both together and each individually" (81).

As far as it goes, *Catherine the Great* tries to show something like this,
but the film takes a giant misstep when it insists on framing Emilian
Pugachev (John Rhys-Davies), a real and insistent figure in the history of
Catherine's reign, as the catalyst for their breakup. In an era of no DNA or
photographs, when many could be persuaded an imposter was the real
thing, this rebellious Cossack posed as the "true" czar, Emperor Peter. The
empress, according to this Cossack Peter, had not succeeded in killing him.
The violent "backward-looking" uprising he caused ended with equally

violent government reprisals. Ultimately, his own men turned him in to save themselves, and he was executed in 1774 (de Madariaga 60).

Although the film's chronology is close—Pugachev's rebellion played itself out during the period when Catherine and Potemkin came together—the film misrepresents the role that Catherine took in Pugachev's execution. In the film, Potemkin appeals to Catherine to pardon Pugachev. She refuses, and Pugachev is beheaded at her command. Potemkin declares that the killing stroke of that blade also signals the death of their relationship. In contrast, the real Catherine intervened mercifully, intending to save the culprit from excruciating pain. As a traitor who had led the underclass against the nobility, his fate was sealed; Pugachev would be put to death. His sentence, to be drawn and quartered, guaranteed him prolonged agony. The victim of this gruesome punishment was first hanged long enough to lose consciousness but not to die. Next, he was revived so that he could watch his own disemboweling. Finally, while the victim was often still alive, his limbs were severed and tossed to the four quarters of the earth. (Even violence addict Mel Gibson lets William Wallace escape into a vision as this punishment is enacted in *Braveheart* [1995].) Catherine's Enlightenment-inspired vision for Russia included a wish to diminish the use of draconian punishments, like this one, and she ordered that Pugachev be beheaded before his body was mutilated. Beheading sounds horrific to modern ears, but, in the eighteenth century, it was considered a quick, painless death. Catherine had to issue this command secretly to avoid outcry from the nobility (de Madariaga 63).

Catherine the Great uses its fiction about Pugachev's execution to bring a neat resolution to a relationship that, in reality, was messy and entangling. In the film's final scene, Potemkin storms in, full of rage and accusations. By condoning the execution, Catherine has intentionally thwarted him, he claims: "You deny me this, you won't see my face in court." He complains too that Catherine "won't tolerate an equal." Catherine answers that both of them are probably "damned," and Potemkin stamps out. In a handy voice-over, Catherine explains, vaguely, that Potemkin continued to do military service for her, but the visual reality of their clean break has a greater impact. The real Catherine maintained her friendship with Potemkin until his death in 1791 (de Madariaga 218). When their physical relationship cooled, their political alliance continued. In 1776, Catherine even gave Potemkin a title, "His Serene Highness," to the dismay of many who hated his influence on her. When Potemkin still figured in her private life, helping her meet younger men, rumors that he was little better than a procurer abounded (Erickson, *Great Catherine*, 331).

Catherine's refusal to pardon Pugachev in this film underscores another suggestion made by the final words in the screenplay. Anyone who could deny a lover such a favor, anyone who could order a man to be beheaded on the spot, must be cold and hard, certainly unwomanly. After Potemkin leaves, Catherine turns to mount the throne, alone. The voice-over now explains that she knows the French call her *Catherine le Grand*, and she stresses the male pronoun, *le*. "I think I earned the title," she says.

The double-headed eagle, an emblem rampant in each film, stood for imperial Russia's domination of the East and the West. It could also be a symbol for these polarizing biopics. Each film wars over Catherine's body; each champions a single head as a true portrait. Choosing the earliest part of Catherine's life facilitates such a simplistic reduction, for these films end where Catherine's career as a ruler began, dragging the idea that getting the crown is *all* right into the twenty-first century.

Chapter Three

౿

Cleopatra

I am Isis. . . . I broke down the governments of tyrants. . . . I made an end to murders. I compelled women to take the love of men. I made the Right stronger than gold and silver. I ordained that the True should be thought good. I devised marriage contracts. . . . I am queen of rivers and winds and sea.
—Isis's creed

Cleopatra VII had become a familiar cinematic subject by 1934, a boom year for royal biopics. *Catherine the Great* opened in February, *The Scarlet Empress* in September, and, in October, Paramount presented its lavish *Cleopatra*, starring Claudette Colbert, Warren William, and Henry Wilcoxon, and directed by that king of spectacle, Cecil B. DeMille. From our vantage point at the start of the film-saturated twenty-first century, the 1930s seem a distant, early decade in the development of the cinema, yet *Cleopatra* (1934) was the third American biopic of the Egyptian queen's life, preceded by two silent films: in 1912, Helen Gardner produced and starred in Charles L. Gaskill's *Cleopatra*, "one of the first 'full-length' American feature films" (Solomon 62); that film was followed five years later by J. Gordon Edwards's *Cleopatra* (1917), starring Theda Bara. Stills of Bara in full vamping regalia and the tagline "The Vampire Supreme" transmit the tone of the lost film.

The potent lure of Cleopatra's dangerous otherness has long teased modern imaginations, and the mystery of deep time escalates her fascination. Furthest from us of all the queens we discuss, Cleopatra was born in 69 or 70 B.C. and died in 30 B.C., and the key events in her life have inspired artists of all genres. The last Ptolemy to sit on the throne of Egypt and the first to learn Egyptian, Cleopatra grew up in Alexandria, educated by scholars, and surrounded by treachery. The teenaged Cleopatra VII watched

Cleopatra, by Michelangelo. (Courtesy Scala/Art Resource, New York.)

her older sister, Berenice, seize the throne from their father, Auletes (Ptolemy XII). Once he regained power (with Rome's help), Auletes put Berenice to death in public and named Cleopatra and her younger brother, Ptolemy XIII, as his heirs. Auletes's death sparked a sibling struggle for the throne that resulted in Ptolemy's triumph and Cleopatra's exile from Alexandria. Like her father, Cleopatra needed Rome's support to rule. She sought it, catalyzing her collaboration with Julius Caesar in a legendary meeting. Although Ptolemy XIII had forbidden her to return to Alexandria, the queen hid herself in a carpet and had it delivered to the emperor. Enchanted by her, Caesar restored Cleopatra's throne (with her brother as coruler) and began a love affair with the young queen. In 47 B.C., Cleopatra gave birth to a son, Caesarion, and Caesar acknowledged the queen's importance to him by inviting her to Rome.

After Caesar's dramatic murder in the Roman senate, Cleopatra returned to Egypt, where she ruled for three years while an uneasy triumvirate of Octavian (Caesar's nephew), Marc Antony, and Lepidus divided control of the Roman Empire. Feeling the pull of Roman power, Cleopatra again linked her public and private fates. Her meeting with Marc Antony on the royal barge also became legend. During their hedonistic years together, the two produced three children. Marc Antony's marriage to Octavian's sister complicated but did not end their alliance.

Antony's attempts to enlarge Egypt's holdings and to legitimize Caesarion and his own half-Ptolemaic children enraged Octavian. The triumvirate broke, and another Roman civil war erupted. In a desperate sea battle against Octavian at Actium, Marc Antony and Cleopatra suffered a crushing defeat. They returned to Egypt, where both chose suicide over subservience. Neither left life unobtrusively. Antony fell on his sword, surviving long enough to die in the arms of the queen. Cleopatra died by poison, cheating Octavian of a triumph over her. Legend says that the poison was delivered by an Egyptian cobra; Shakespeare called it an asp. Accompanied by her handmaidens, arrayed in her royal robes, and lying in state in her tomb, Cleopatra made an incredible exit, one that, like her incredible life, begs for visual interpretation.

Objects associated with the queen of Egypt—the carpet, the barge, the asp—have become as familiar as images in a fairy tale. A group of historical figures surrounds Cleopatra: Apollodorus, the Sicilian merchant who delivered her to Caesar; Iras and Charmion, her ladies-in-waiting; Arsinoe, Berenice, and the Ptolemies, her power-hungry siblings; Caesar and Antony, her lovers; Caesarion, her oldest son, and her other offspring; Octavian, her nemesis. They form a cast of characters as well known as those in a play, and many have *become* characters in famous plays by Shakespeare and Shaw. *Biopic* becomes an even more ambiguous term when applied to this queen, more persona than biographical subject, so we include analyses of these key dramatic versions of her life in our discussion.

All these givens cluster around Cleopatra, but she presents a perplexing puzzle. Portraits of Christina, Catherine, Mary, Victoria, Marie Antoinette, and Elizabeth I suggest their features, their bearing, their queenly garb. The collective testimony of these paintings and, in the case of Victoria, photographs and film offers generations to follow fairly consistent images of these queens. Although artists like Michelangelo and the Pre-Raphaelite Alma-Tadema have imagined her, only brief descriptions in ancient sources and likenesses on a few coins hint at Cleopatra's appearance. "Not one single surviving portrait-bust that can be confidently believed to represent her" remains (Grant 66). Was Cleopatra black? Francesca Royster finds the question important. She traces the queen's "afterlife," claiming that the "struggle by contesting racial camps for ownership" of Cleopatra's image speaks of her continuing cultural power (8).

The scant physical evidence seems almost generous when compared to first-person records of her thoughts and desires. There are none. All those "seeking to learn about Queen Cleopatra . . . , one of the most influential women in a world dominated largely by men, are hampered by the lack of any separate biography devoted to her" ("Summary of Ancient Sources"). Our understanding of the key events in her life, all views of Cleopatra, all biographical, fictional, and cinematic interpretations of her life, spring from just a few ancient sources produced by men, reflecting the biases of their places and times, and discussing her only to the extent that she is involved in the affairs of men. Caesar includes her as a player in *The Civil War*. She figures in Plutarch's *Lives*, first in Julius Caesar's and more prominently in Marc Antony's biography, and in Suetonius's *Lives* as well. Dio Cassius wrote about her Roman visit to Caesar in his *History of Rome*.

Lacking her words, we chose as this chapter's epigraph an excerpt from Isis's creed because Cleopatra identified with the goddess (Grant 119–20). From Shakespeare's words in *Antony and Cleopatra*, "Age cannot wither her, nor custom stale / Her infinite variety" (2.3.276–77), we craft a template for examining four full-length film views of the queen's life (*Cleopatra* [1934], *Caesar and Cleopatra* [1945], *Cleopatra* [1963], and *Antony and Cleopatra* [1972]) and three made-for-television productions (*Antony and Cleopatra* [1975], *Cleopatra* [1999], and *Rome* [2005–2007]). In all the chapters of this book, we pay close attention to the physical evocations of the queens we discuss, but, because history provides the least detail about her person, Cleopatra's presence deserves an ultrasensitive reading, depending, as it does, on the combined vision of writers, directors, designers, and actors. We flip Shakespeare's claim about Cleopatra into a question: Does "custom stale" the queen's image, or is she given new life, "infinite variety," on film?

Cleopatra (1934)

Even tales about the genesis of Cleopatra biopics have become the stuff of legend. In 1959, Walter Wanger (the producer of *Queen Christina*) and Spyros Skouras (the president of Twentieth Century–Fox) considered remaking *Cleopatra*. It should be simple, Skouras conjectured, to update the Theda Bara silent version. Wanger had something grander in mind. He wanted Elizabeth Taylor for the title role (Walker, *Elizabeth*, 214–15). The result of their talk was the bloated *Cleopatra* (1963), starring Taylor, Rex Harrison, and Richard Burton.

Accounts of that fateful conversation, now part of Hollywood lore, don't mention whether Paramount's 1934 biopic ever came up; Wanger knew of and had surely seen Cecil B. DeMille's *Cleopatra*, starring Claudette Colbert, with whom he had worked. In the best of all possible worlds, Skouras and Wanger would have put aside the Bara script long enough to watch and talk about DeMille's film (the first *Cleopatra* with sound). If they had, they might have noted that energy and humor drive the Colbert version, qualities that the Taylor/Burton production could have used more of. The frenetic trailer features DeMille gazing at costume sketches, mobs crowding the steps of the Roman senate, dancers cavorting on Cleopatra's barge, Cleopatra vamping, and Cleopatra and Antony sharing a big movie kiss. Never static or boring, the film attacks the generous slice of Cleopatra's life that most film versions cover, beginning when she meets Caesar, and ending with her death. The combination of the sweep through time, a larger-than-life subject, and DeMille's direction signals that the personal will be sacrificed to public spectacle. *Cleopatra* fractures history, flattens characters into stereotypes, and, often, dissolves into silliness. While most of its elements conspire to make this a clichéd version of Cleopatra's life, the film adds up to more than the sum of its parts. It exudes a reckless sexuality, and, most important, Claudette Colbert takes her part seriously, working hard to give this portrait of the queen's public life a private shadow.

Cleopatra opens with a title sequence that would make Edward Said twitch, a checklist of signifiers that scream of Orientalism: pyramids, palms, a chained priestess raising two incense burners, a profile of the Sphinx. These images conjure up a generic Hollywood Egypt where all that's missing is a mummy. No titles remind us that the pyramid builders were as far back in time from Cleopatra as she is from us or that the setting is Alexandria. Instead, the opening duns the audience, "Hey, here comes EGYPT," setting the tone for the whole. Roland Anderson and Hans Dreier, the art directors, and Waldemar Young and Vincent Lawrence, the screen-writers, elevate surface over substance, making good the trailer's promise of "luxury and lavishness," qualities the Depression-era audience probably yearned for more than historical accuracy.

Louis Giannetti and Scott Eyman point out that DeMille—neither a critical nor a political favorite of our time—could always tell a story (46), and *Cleopatra,* shot in southern California, follows a hard-driving story line that discards or alters inconvenient truths. There's little suggestion, for example, that Caesar (Warren William), recently embroiled in a civil war, entered another conflict in Alexandria. Instead of fighting for the city, Caesar dallies with Cleopatra, so not a book in the Alexandria library gets singed, as some did when Caesar's battles came right into the central city (Grant 71). In fact, no one mentions the library, the dual harbors, or the lighthouse, Alexandria's celebrated landmarks. They're also missing from the cinematographer Victor Milner's artful deep shots that let the eye roam from fabric-draped interiors, to outer walls, to distant horizons.

Young and Lawrence's screenplay, based on an adaptation of unspeci-fied "ancient sources" by Bartlett Cormack, reduces Cleopatra's family to a mention of her single, rival brother, who never appears. This Cleopatra-as-temptress story cleanses the queen of motherhood, erasing all her children. The writers add a dramatic and probably fictional scene of the queen enter-ing Rome behind Caesar's chariot. She's dressed in flowing metallic cloth and a cobra headdress, riding on a slave-borne palanquin. It's tempting to imagine an even more spectacular procession, and the 1963 *Cleopatra* out DeMilles DeMille by blowing this scene up exponentially. In DeMille's *Cleopatra*, the queen's entry into Rome encourages East/West polarization, opposing the smoldering Cleopatra to the dowdiness of the Roman matrons watching her. According to the biographer Michael Grant, Caesar staged such triumphs to showcase the spoils of war, including captured royals: think humiliation, not honor. Although Arsinoe, one of her ambitious sisters, marched into Rome in chains, Cleopatra, accompanied by her brother and her son, probably entered Rome quietly (Grant 86). As she is carried into the city, Cleopatra looks the part of a woman who decimates her two Roman lovers. In *Cleopatra,* neither man needs to be more than a stereotype because his function in this film is to fall.

Cleopatra fashions Caesar into a CEO motivated by ruthless ambition. He first appears buried in paperwork, having turned the Egyptian palace into his office. The contemporary reviewer Mordaunt Hall comments that this scene is "so modern" that "the mighty Caesar" might be expected to have a "typewriter" (rev. of *Cleopatra*). DeMille takes this shortcut—Caesar as executive—to speed the story, exploiting the anticorporate prejudices of his time. Casting helps, for Warren William often played an amoral businessman, a type Depression-era audiences loved to hate. Since the screenplay deletes the battle for Alexandria, William (who was forty) has little chance to demonstrate the fifty-two-year-old Caesar's ruggedness. Cornered, in the midst of heated fighting, the real Caesar, dressed in full battle armor, jumped into the Alexandria harbor and swam to safety, holding important documents above the water (Grant 73). This Caesar never lifts a weapon and lacks a soldier's survival instincts. Cleopatra, not Caesar, spots the toe of Pothinus's sandal under a curtain in her boudoir and runs the villain through with a pike. The camera often shoots Caesar from the side to showcase his hallmark hairdo, the combed-forward bang, "the little flag," as Roland Barthes puts it, that says "Ancient Rome" ("The Romans in Films," 26).

Only geographic foreplay gets Caesar out of his chair. He follows the "pretty little queen" when she dangles India, not just her slender form, before him. He doesn't caress or kiss her, and it takes a major suspension of disbelief to imagine that their walk up Cleopatra's staircase, hands linked, ends in anything but a merger. It makes sense that this stolid Caesar, obsessed with wealth and power, doesn't scent his own death.

If Caesar stands for greedy ambition, Marc Antony (Henry Wilcoxon) embodies lust. This brawny man's man appears at Calpurnia's party leading two Great Danes. Calpurnia's silly soiree—Rome via 1934 Hollywood—features bias-cut togas and conversation that sounds more like studio gossip than Roman banter. The illicit relationship between Caesar and Cleopatra gives the revelers plenty to discuss behind Calpurnia's back. "The wife is always the last one to know," one guest titters. Marc Antony, "an insatiable lover of women," liked to compare himself to Hercules (Grant 112–13). DeMille translates the historical figure into a caricature. His Marc Antony could have come directly from a restaurant in twenty-first-century Rome that caters to tourists. In that Disney-like environment, big plates of spaghetti circulate, and raffia-encased bottles dispense chianti. A praetorian guard, tackily resplendent in leather and polished metal, salutes guests and poses for photo ops.

When he enters Calpurnia's party, Antony wears a similar, stagy costume. The Roman babes, with their marcelled hair and penciled eyebrows, squeal as if he were Mick Jagger. Marc's *so vain,* striding through his female admirers with a jock strut. (Warren Wilcoxon's performance as Marc Antony pleased DeMille, who cast him as King Richard the Lion-Hearted in *The Crusades* [1935].) After Caesar's death, Marc Antony promises to bring Cleopatra "to Rome, in chains." He's no match for Cleopatra, who topples this big boy as easily as she could knock over a Hercules action figure. The promised wealth of the East, not sex, enticed Caesar, but fleshy pleasures suborn Marc Antony.

A Cleopatra biopic would seem incomplete without a re-creation of the queen's royal barge, one of those powerful images emblematic of her life. *Cleopatra* quickly rolls out and dispenses with the famous carpet-delivery device, but DeMille and his designers, Anderson and Dreier, love the barge, lingering on its possibilities. The description in Plutarch provides enough fuel to launch eternal voyages of fancy. He writes of a "barge with a poop of gold," "purple sails," and "oars of silver" where Cleopatra lounges "beneath a canopy of cloth of gold," fanned by "boys costumed as Cupids," and attended by a crew of "the most beautiful of her waiting women" (qtd. in Grant 115). DeMille's black-and-white film paints the barge as an erotic alternate reality, the site of some of the most lavish and sexually charged scenes in the film.

From the moment he steps on board, Antony enters a magical zone, a setting a little like Rapunzel's fairy-tale tower, a slim cylinder from without, a palace within. Exterior shots show a narrow barge with high sails, but the interior opens out into several stage-sized areas for spectacles, with Marc Antony's fall booked as the main act. The sequence of *Cleopatra*'s two seduction scenes has the fairy-tale feel of repetition: the male dominates, the queen offers herself, the male balks, the queen proffers an additional prize, the male is subdued, the queen triumphs. Wealth alone, an effective aphrodisiac for Caesar, won't do for Marc Antony, who believes that women should be "playthings." On board her vessel, Cleopatra tempts Antony with herself; then she ups the ante with visions of bondage and subservience. Fan-waving serving girls prostrate themselves before Antony as he traverses the deck leading to Cleopatra's high, plumed dias. The queen, in a position physically lower than Antony's, remains on her divan when he harshly orders her to come with him. She refuses, rising only to draw his attention to her tight, pearl-encrusted sheath. (Like Caesar, Antony needs nudging.) Cleopatra "confesses" her plan to seduce him.

"What do you care for this, for instance," she asks, clapping her hands to start the show. Antony's fate is to become a plaything, and, if he weren't so dull, he could see it in the first tableau. He gapes as male and female dancers—who walk sideways, like Egyptians in ancient murals—lead forward an unresisting bull chained with flowers and gentled by sweet caresses. All subsequent acts play to Antony's fantasy, presenting women as playthings. While Nubian slaves serve him food and plenty of wine, Cleopatra pretends drunkenness but keeps a clear eye on his testosterone and intoxication levels. Cool, and in control, she signals for the coup de grâce.

DeMille favors scenes with plenty of witnesses, but he denies Cleopatra's crew and theater audiences access to this private love scene, virtually crossing out the climax of all this foreplay. First, slaves form an *x* by raising two slanting poles hung with drapes to mask the divan where Antony and Cleopatra embrace. Next, more slaves cross two long, flowered streamers in another *x*-shape in front of the already crossed drapes. Could this be the very first X rating? Even though the couple's embrace is hidden, every element of the scene reads as sexual energy. Rudolph Kopp's theme, which has been repeating throughout the film, surges here, sounding a little like

Ravel's *Bolero*. The barge sails forward, "a muscular conductor pounds out a throbbing beat on the drum as the music climaxes" (Solomon 64), and the oarsmen thrust their oars through the water.

The Hollywood Production Code, written in 1930 and enforced beginning in 1934, forbids scenes that might "stimulate the lower emotions" (Giannetti and Eyman 162). Although it crosses out explicit sex, *Cleopatra* exists to stimulate "lower," meaning "libidinal," emotions. Sexual innuendo resonates throughout, but sexuality escapes its supporting role in the film to take on a life of its own. The opening pan reeks with the scent of the forbidden. A blurb explains that Egypt comes next on "ambitious" Caesar's list for world domination and that Cleopatra and her brother are fighting for its rule. These words hardly prepare the audience for the first visual—a peek into a disheveled bedchamber. The camera moves from the rumpled bed to a soldier lying facedown amid a jumble of objects: a wine decanter, a robe, a tray. The camera keeps moving to the right, where a live ibis stands between the prone soldier and another gagged and trussed black soldier who's suspended in front of a heavy satin drape, his muscled body forming the base of a triangle made by a knotted silken cord that binds his ankles to his wrists and then travels up to the ceiling. Only when the door opens and Charmion (Eleanor Phelps), Cleopatra's sexy lady-in-waiting, screams, "Oh, the queen! Where's the queen?" does it become clear that this is the queen's room, that these are dead guards, and that the queen has been abducted. Before the door opens, however, the audience could be getting a voyeuristic peep into the "aftermath of an orgy" (Royster 91). What kind of queen reigns here?

The Scarlet Empress (1934) turns Catherine into a sexual predator. Even that frenetic film, however, provides the queen of Russia with some biographical context. *Cleopatra* rejects the scant biography available. Without exposition about her family, with no comment on her childhood or education, with little reference to Isis, without her children, Cleopatra becomes a character motivated by survival alone. Claudette Colbert works around this narrow interpretation. According to DeMille, she strove to "do something different with Cleopatra" (qtd. in Quirk 68). Different than what DeMille doesn't say. "She stamped her own personality on the role. She emerged from it most vividly," he concludes (68).

Colbert, who died in 1996, said that she lacked any "deep, dark miseries to report" and would, therefore, never write an autobiography (Quirk

2). Trying to glimpse Colbert's "own personality" in Lawrence J. Quirk's biography—the most detailed of those available—proves almost as exasperating as trying to see the real Cleopatra through the available historical sources. Volume of information isn't the problem; Quirk offers an avalanche of material about Colbert, and he presents a plot summary for *every one* of her sixty-five films, most of them made as a contract player for Paramount. Quirk, whose uncle edited and published *Photoplay*, calls on his Hollywood contacts in this work. He interviewed Colbert and many of those who worked with her. With few exceptions, the remarks of these producers, directors, and actors emphasize her professionalism, spunk, niceness, and lack of vanity. But a weird current swirls beneath the surface of this laudatory ocean. Quirk's questions to all the men who knew or worked with Colbert invariably lead to the potency of her attraction. He's determined to prove that Colbert was sexually attractive to men, that this "dame" was "hot as hell" (45). He reports the "film lead" Edmund Lowe's assertion, "Believe you me, she was sexy" (45), and Mitchell Leisen's comment, "Claudette was man oriented, no doubt about that" (79). He even quotes male fans who wrote to *Photoplay*. "You just know she is one warm responsive woman," one gushes (70). Quirk mounts his fevered insistence that Colbert was heterosexual in response to rumors in the 1930s about her intense friendships with women and her two cool marriages; many current scholars include her on their lists of potentially lesbian stars (Mann 31).

Simply mentioning the debate around Colbert's sexuality would have been enough. But Quirk makes denial his cause célèbre, skewing the biography in the process. He should have paid more attention to his own acknowledgment that a person's work, not his or her sexual orientation, matters most. As he concludes his comments on the female director Dorothy Arzner, "known as a butch number," Quirk says: "Whatever her private life, she had a knack for early feminist-oriented films and was at her best handling dramas in which women tried to hold their own in a man's world" (34). Colbert, known to be "liberal and understanding about homosexuals and bisexuals" (78), would probably be less invested in certifying her hetero status than Quirk is. "If you live only for the opinions of others," Colbert told Quirk, "you'll never leave your imprint" (3).

Undeveloped threads in Quirk's text hint at a woman with good professional instincts and the courage to follow them. When *It Happened One Night* (Frank Capra, 1934) catapulted her into the top ten, Colbert leveraged her stature as one of Hollywood's queens into control over her working environment, announcing that she would not film after five o'clock. She also decided, literally, how the public would see her, encouraging directors and photographers to shoot her so that the left side of her face was featured. In one of the few critical comments included in Quirk's biography, Mary Astor quips: "The right side of [Colbert's] face was called the other side of the moon because nobody ever saw it" (110).

Quirk gives Colbert's explanation: a "tiny bump" on the right side of her nose (the result of a childhood accident) gave her a "bad" side (3). It's amazing to see how often Colbert got what she wanted. *Cleopatra* has few full-faced shots of the actress and almost no right-face–prominent views. That means nearly every shot featuring Colbert (at least three-quarters of the shots in the film) had to be composed around her left-to-the-camera positioning. But was that "tiny bump" the only issue? The few shots of Colbert's right profile reveal it to be sharper, with pronounced angles of nose and chin, while her left profile—her public face—is softer, more conventionally pretty, less distinctive. Keeping her left side to the camera also meant that Colbert occupied the position the human eye normally scans toward; the "intrinsic heaviness of the right" gives that side of the frame natural dominance (Giannetti, 11th ed., 70). An actress who could manage her projected image, effectively crossing out one side and offering up the other, was capable of projecting whatever self she wanted to reveal. Octavian calls Cleopatra an "Egyptian snake" (a subtle epithet) in his speech leading to the battle of Actium. It's not a giant leap from his invective to freezing Cleopatra into a symbol of female corruption who exists to attract, poison, and destroy men. Quirk's dogged insistence that Colbert was a man magnet reveals the limitation of a one-note approach to a life. The costumes in *Cleopatra* transmit a similar one-note interpretation of its subject as one "sexy dame."

Cleopatra's eclectic trailer draws attention to its queen-creating team of DeMille and Travis Banton with a shot of DeMille reviewing sketches for Colbert's costumes. Banton, a top designer in the 1930s, insisted that costumes had to help "tell a story" (Mann 45). Some of Cleopatra's attire evokes Egypt, like her jewels based on items from the tomb of King Tutankhamen. Colbert loved her bangs, so she probably liked the wig she wore as Cleopatra, a banged, shoulder-length bob reminiscent of figures in Egyptian tomb paintings. In several scenes, Cleopatra's hair more closely resembles the coin profiles of the queen, which show a Grecian style, a low bun with waves held back from her face by bands. Colbert's makeup for *Cleopatra* didn't raise critical hackles as did the "lipstick, rouge, and eye-makeup" she wore as a fashion-forward Puritan heroine in *Maid of Salem* (Frank Lloyd, 1937) (Quirk 93). Her plucked, arched brows and dark mouth may not be Ptolemaic, but evidence suggests that the real "Cleopatra's makeup was probably elaborate," involving "antimony . . . and lamp black" (Grant 67).

Many of Cleopatra's costumes have a lot less to do with the Alexandria of Cleopatra's time than they do with the streets of Paris and New York, where the "sophisticated and assured" grown-up clothes of the 1930s replaced the childish flapper silhouette of the 1920s (Lurie 71). All her evening gowns (this Cleopatra has no day wear) are made of luxurious fabrics cut to cling, as were the gowns of the time. By 1934, films were mirroring and inspiring fashion trends in a kind of leakage from screen to street. It pays to conflate character and actor, and the synthesis accelerates when the queens of Hollywood are desirable in culturally relevant ways.

Cleopatra's generally contemporary gowns tell DeMille's version of the story. Bands of lamé stand in for bodices, and strategically sprinkled spangles simultaneously cover and highlight erogenous zones. These body-conscious costumes boost Cleopatra/Colbert's seduction quotient, showcasing her figure, especially her beautiful legs. Velvet—a ridiculous choice for the Egyptian climate—makes perfect sense as a costume for Cleopatra if you want to initiate her characterization with body language. She first appears as a prisoner in a racing chariot, gagged, partially hooded, barefoot, and bound with the same thick cording used to truss the guard in her boudoir. She communicates her rage by struggling, drawing attention to her bondage. A crossed cord, artfully threaded under one breast and around her waist, gives the garment definition, while the velvet nap catches the light to emphasize each twist of her flexible body and to announce that she's wearing nothing underneath. Like Virginie Gautreau's strapless, black velvet evening gown in John Singer Sargent's most famous portrait, *Madame X,* Cleopatra's velvet shift plays on the combination of sumptuous fabric and naked flesh, an overture for her costumes to come.

As a sign that the queen's body is luscious and forbidden, Banton often uses an *x* motif, embellishing and canceling out Cleopatra's charms at the same time. An *x* marks her waist and supports her skirt, or seams meet to form ruched x-shapes. Trim that crosses and recrosses her body traces several x's in the costume the queen dons for her appearance before the Roman senate (a visit preempted by Caesar's murder). This elaborate, mermaid-style gown of transparent chiffon makes her dependent on others. Cleopatra needs seven maidens to help her arrange the train, and, when she learns of Caesar's death, she must be lowered into a chair, weakened as she is by her sorrow and immobilized by her clothing, a nice conjunction of narrative and fashion.

Colbert, listed in the 1930s as one "of the ten best-dressed women in the country" (Quirk 114), told Quirk that she regretted the time she had spent in fittings and, in general, "over clothes" (181), but her on-screen image illustrates why designers loved to dress her. Colbert wears her Cleopatra costumes effortlessly, at ease whether she is still or moving fluidly around the sets. Mordaunt Hall found Colbert "even more attractive than usual" in this persona. Given the nature of DeMille's *Cleopatra*—it's an epic first and a biopic second—and given the character prescribed by screenplay and costume design, Colbert could have phoned this one in. She could have worked the sexy getups and collected her salary. William and Wilcoxon seem to have internalized a get-that-paycheck ethic; neither tries to exit the stereotype zone. Colbert, however, strains against the stale temptress-only interpretation to thaw and give nuance to the queen's character.

DeMille commented that Colbert put "herself" into the part, but Jon Solomon attributes the queen's character, "as complex as the layered gauze wrapping around a mummy," to her words—Colbert was the first film Cleopatra who could talk. Solomon claims that this Cleopatra's character relies on her "charming, calculating, yet vulnerable chatter" (63). We think that Solomon overstates Colbert's vulnerability and the chatter and pays too little attention to her persona. The real Cleopatra's tumultuous life in the Alexandrian court must have given her maturity beyond her years. Scholars agree that "the fascination of the young queen herself," not only her physical beauty, attracted the worldly Caesar to her when it would have been politically easier to side with her brother (Grant 64). DeMille briefly nods to the gap in their ages (at least twenty-three years). Cleopatra, abandoned in the desert, childishly worries about her stomach. "I've had no breakfast; I'm hungry," she whines to Apollodorus. (The Sicilian rug merchant who delivered her to Caesar morphs into Cleopatra's counselor figure.) Her whining stops here, and she needs little help from Apollodorus to figure out her next move.

"How old is this Caesar?" she wants to know. But how old is Cleopatra? Although nearly twenty years pass in the course of the film, there's no attempt to clarify that time span or to age Colbert via makeup and hairstyle. DeMille's collapsing of time creates little space for maturation, and, throughout the film, Colbert plays Cleopatra as an adult who sees her life as darkly funny. Cleopatra's laugh, hearty, a little rueful, says that she knows being unrolled from a carpet is a ridiculous introduction, and her springy rise from that low position suggests strength as much as charm or sexuality. Colbert remembered being on target for this "difficult" scene, which was captured in one take (Quirk 68). Although she must state her case before the murderous Pothinus, her brother's supporter, Cleopatra neither begs, nor clings, nor cowers. When she moves, once, to put Caesar's chair between her and Pothinus, she turns the action into a gesture of intimacy, stooping to speak into his ear.

"If I leave you now, I'll be killed," Cleopatra tells Caesar, punctuating the line with wry offhandedness. Although Caesar calls her a "pretty little queen," everything in her posture and tone says *woman*, not *girl*. This queen is alert to Alexandria's (and Hollywood's?) realpolitik, where life and death (and stardom?) depend on a command. Cleopatra has life and death power over others, and Colbert invests the scenes that demonstrate this with black humor. Just before she cooly skewers Pothinus, she flips the javelin from her left hand to her right, an expert move that makes Caesar's eyes open wide. After she watches Pothinus die, she smirks as she asks Caesar: "And now am I worth talking to?" Francesca Royster says that Cleopatra becomes "the eye of the director" during the scenes on the barge, a position that distances her from the action and highlights the hierarchical nature of the film (88). The rush of spectacle gives the queen only a few scenes designed to show her contemplative side, and in these she does not function as a lens for DeMille. One moment comes before she meets Marc Antony. "No plan yet?" asks Apollodorus. For an answer, we get a close-up of the queen gazing away from her counselor, a study in concentration. She doesn't speak, but her expression transmits the weight of her situation.

In a silly scene featuring a bubbling cauldron and a mad-scientist high priest, Cleopatra considers poisoning Antony to gain Octavian's favor. She summons a condemned man and hands him a beaker of wine stirred with a poison-laced rose. As he drinks and falls dead, the camera stays on the queen's mask-like face. She turns to her priest. "Was there any pain?" she wonders. When the priest answers, "A little," she shakes her head impatiently, annoyed by the difficulty of finding an easy death for her lover and, perhaps, herself. The close-up gives the scene another dimension. If Cleopatra has to ask that question, whom was she watching? What was she thinking? As members of a generation trained to be aware of the camera's gaze *at* a female subject, we long to look into the queen's interior life.

Quirk notes that Colbert had to learn to tone down her stage-variety acting for the screen (14). In *Cleopatra*, she relies on more restrained gestures, so her exaggerated reactions pop out, campy and vampy. When Caesar visits Cleopatra before he leaves for the Roman senate (and his death), she poses, silhouetted against some foliage. Hyperdramatically, she throws back her head and extends her arms as she rushes to meet him. Similar exaggeration marks her decision not to poison Marc Antony. A long shot captures her lunge, which knocks a poisoned wine cup from his hand. From a full-body embrace, she slithers—against him—to her knees. As the camera moves in, her eyes roll back under her lids—a scary moment. "I've seen a god come to life," she quavers. While most of Colbert's performance has an edge, these scenes evoke silent film's naïveté, an effect that DeMille probably liked. The ending of his epic echoes that tone. To allow Octavian a grander entrance, the director rearranges Cleopatra's most private moment, her death. In *Cleopatra*, the queen dies alone on her throne, sitting upright, not in her tomb attended by her two ladies, an underscoring of the thrust toward public spectacle. When the camera goes wide, to show the front wall of the royal chamber, Octavian and a crowd of his men share the view of Cleopatra, posed like a mannequin.

Some contemporaries protested that her modern essence kept Colbert from being convincing in period roles. Colbert wanted to play Saint Joan, for example, but didn't get the part. We wonder whether, by *modernity*, those critics actually meant *self-confidence, humor,* and *irony,* timeless qualities that any star (or any queen) has to cultivate. Given the costumes and lines of a temptress, denied any portrayal of Cleopatra as a child, a daughter, a sister, a priestess, a lover of Egypt, an educated ruler, or a mother, Colbert still creates a queen who "emerge[s] . . . most vividly," a Cleopatra who made an attempt to exert some control over her life.

Cleopatra. Even as she sits on her throne arrayed for death, Claudette Colbert exudes the 1930s glamour that permeates her performance as the Egyptian queen in Cecil B. DeMille's spectacle. (Courtesy Jerry Ohlinger's Movie Material Store.)

Caesar and Cleopatra (1945)

George Bernard Shaw approaches Cleopatra's life as if it is an exercise in need of correction. He ends his play *Caesar and Cleopatra,* produced on the London stage in 1901, with the words: "Hail Caesar!" Even if the play didn't finish with that salute, Shaw's affection for Caesar would be abundantly clear; his name appears first in the title, and the volume and wit of his words grant him dominance. Gabriel Pascal, who directed Shaw's adaptation of his play, adds a visual ending after the salute: a close-up of Cleopatra, with "a gleam in her eye, saying 'Marc Antony' under her breath" and, finally, a shot of Caesar's ship sailing for Rome (*Collected Screenplays of Bernard Shaw* 469). DeMille's *Cleopatra* emphasizes the queen's powers of entrapment, but Shaw's *Caesar and Cleopatra,* starring Vivien Leigh and Claude Rains, marks Caesar's escape from Egypt. History provided Shaw with the conjunction of these two lives, but Shaw tweaked history into a pattern he adored, one in which an older, brilliant misogynist mentors a younger, uneducated, not appropriately grateful or especially worthy woman. Shaw relished this story so much that he told it again in *Pygmalion* (1912), his most famous play. For a taste of the linkage between *Caesar and Cleopatra* and *Pygmalion,* consider the way the two main characters meet in each.

It's late afternoon in London; the rain is falling. *Pygmalion's* inciting incident takes place in front of St. Paul's (not the major Wren cathedral, but the "minor" Inigo Jones church) in Covent Garden where the rainstorm brings together the two protagonists. The world-weary linguist Henry Higgins uses the location to "take down" notes on the execrable English he hears around him; he loudly laments the mutilation of his native tongue. One of the most dastardly mutilators, the flower girl Eliza Doolittle, hears Higgins claim that he could lift her out of poverty, could "pass [her] off as the Queen of Sheba," by teaching her to speak correctly (*Collected Screenplays of Bernard Shaw* 231). When Eliza takes him up on his boast, the plot is set in motion.

It's night in Egypt; the moon is shining. *Caesar and Cleopatra's* inciting incident takes place in the desert in front of the Sphinx (not the "major" Sphinx, but a minor, "dear little kitten of a sphinx") where the protagonists meet. The world-weary Julius Caesar apostrophizes the Sphinx as if it is his equal, declaring that he too is "part god" with "nothing of man" in him "at all" (*Collected Screenplays of Bernard Shaw* 407). The teenaged Cleopatra, a "silly little girl" who believes the Romans—especially Caesar—to be cannibals, overhears him. Cleopatra knows that someone must teach her how to be "the Queen of Sheba" (i.e., Egypt) so that she can confront Caesar. She begs this "old gentleman" (whom she doesn't recognize as Caesar) to help her. "I will be your slave," she promises (410). Caesar accepts, and the plot is set in motion.

Besides demonstrating an inherent similarity in the two plays, this brief comparison reveals Shaw's chutzpah; he's not timid about reinventing one of the most famous meetings in history. Where's the carpet? Where's Apollodorus? Shaw refuses to give the audience what it expects. But the scene at the Sphinx does more than thwart expectation. Shaw shifts the balance of surprise. In stage-managing her carpet-roll arrival, Cleopatra figured out how to amaze a man who had seen it all. It's true that Caesar (Claude Rains) *is* amazed to find a "divine child" at the Sphinx, but the climax comes when Cleopatra discovers that the "old gentleman" who has started to tutor her in queenly etiquette is the fearsome Caesar. Later in the play, Shaw introduces Apollodorus (Stewart Granger) when he repackages the Cleopatra-rolled-in-a-carpet scene, making it his instead of history's. Angry at being left behind during the battle for Alexandria, Cleopatra has herself hidden in a carpet and delivered by Apollodorus to the Alexandria lighthouse, where Egyptian forces surround Caesar. Caesar is surprised to see the queen emerge from the carpet, but the moment still belongs to him. To escape capture, Caesar dives into the harbor; the squealing queen makes a less than majestic descent—she's tossed in after him. Shaw rewrites history; it's not important documents that Caesar swims to safety but the queen of Egypt.

These pivotal scenes go to Caesar, and that's hardly surprising since Shaw revels in extolling Caesar's virtues. Shaw and Pascal anguished over Caesar's casting. The classical actor Forbes Robertson had performed the role on the stage; for the film version, Pascal wanted classicism with a touch of the modern. He settled on Claude Rains, who, he believed, possessed those qualities. Shaw declared himself to be "perfectly satisfied in the first split second" after meeting Rains (Deans 73). In *Meeting at the Sphinx*, which details the Shaw/Pascal production, Marjorie Deans praises Rains for his "dry subtlety and strength" (73). Although this Caesar works all night while Cleopatra dreams, he's no dull CEO. He has wit, humor, and humanity, a Caesar who might be worth wooing, but his dryness underscores another Shavian notion.

While posters promoting *Caesar and Cleopatra*'s American premier featured a nearly nude Cleopatra in Caesar's arms, Shaw found the idea of a love affair between the two disgusting. His screenplay imagines a teacher/student relationship instead. To justify this authorial sleight of hand, Shaw has to adopt a one-note view of Cleopatra. His note, of course, must differ from DeMille's. Instead of highlighting her seductive power, Shaw fixates on Cleopatra's limited capacity to change, portraying her as perpetually primitive, a recalcitrant lump of clay that can't be molded to satisfaction. All Caesar's striving, Shaw implies, can't lift Cleopatra from her inferior position as an amoral being barely worth her breath. The film's end–of–World War II release intensifies *Caesar and Cleopatra*'s agenda of female unworthiness and male superiority.

DeMille elbows history out of the way any time it threatens to slow his pace. In contrast, Shaw sometimes welcomes accuracy, even when it halts action. He's happiest with lengthy dialogue—not a surprise to anyone who has read the prefaces and afterwords to his plays. His screenplay labors to recount the politics of Caesar's arrival in Alexandria, to describe the delicate balance between Egyptian and Roman interests, and to summarize Caesar's virtual imprisonment in the royal quarters. Although Gabriel Pascal "tampered with" some of Shaw's exposition (*Collected Screenplays of Bernard Shaw* 138–39), the whys and hows of Caesar's arrival are essentially accurate. The sets for Arthur Rank's production (a big budget project) reflect similar attention to detail.

Foreshadowing the nexus of problems surrounding the disaster-prone 1963 *Cleopatra*, the Shaw/Pascal collaboration, which started filming six days before D-Day and took two years to complete, had more than its share of difficulties. The set designers, John Bryan and Oliver Messel (who also designed the costumes), had to work around wartime shortages and threats, changes in location from England's Denham Studios to Alexandria, Egypt, and bad weather everywhere (even unusual cold in Egypt) to produce the stunning backgrounds for Shaw's story.

For all this getting it right, however, Shaw excises history that doesn't fit his vision of Cleopatra. "I do not feel bound," he says in a note following the play, "to believe that Cleopatra was well educated" (*Collected Screenplays of Bernard Shaw* 119). Leigh's performance in her audition for the part shows how completely she understood Shaw. Nearly thirty at the start of filming, Vivien Leigh played an ingenue—exactly what Shaw sought—aiming for the part of Cleopatra as artfully as she had aimed for the chance to play Scarlett O'Hara: "As near as possible, and without speaking any of the lines of the play she assumed the role she wanted" (Walker, *Vivien,* 163). After her audition, the eighty-seven-year-old Shaw harbored the false impression that she was shy. "I can knock all that out of her," Shaw excitedly told Gabriel Pascal, anticipating for himself a tutor's role that paralleled Caesar's. Leigh was right to wager that "maidenly demureness" would help her become Cleopatra (Walker, *Vivien,* 163).

This Cleopatra is so raw that she resists a daily bath. Shaw wrote a new scene for the screenplay in which the queen's attendant, Ftatateeta (Flora Robson), leads a whining Cleopatra toward a luxurious palace pool. This moment could provide a glimpse into Cleopatra's private life, but Shaw doesn't use the scene to explore her psyche or to reveal her flesh; *Caesar and Cleopatra* rigidly adheres to the Production Code, skirting those lower emotions. The bath might be a metaphor for the way Shaw washes away Cleopatra's history. The real Cleopatra grew up in a wing of the royal enclosure and was probably familiar with the essentials of grooming. Michael Grant thinks that the political turmoil of her father's reign gave the young princess "an exceptionally sharp and grim political education" that formed her into someone "very different from the ignorant, kittenish" figure in Shaw's play (26). When Cleopatra met Caesar, she had been on the throne of Egypt for three years; she was neither a seasoned ruler nor a raw novice. As queen, she had standardized the weight and value of brass currency (Grant 38), and she may have been the first Ptolemy to take part in religious rites at Hermonthis honoring the god Amon (Grant 47). The young Cleopatra must have understood the difficulty of staying on the throne. Even during her short rule, she suffered natural and political disasters. A bad harvest and the belief that she placed Roman over Egyptian interests enabled her brother's power play (Grant 49).

The real Caesar backed up his decision to give Cleopatra the throne with two Roman legions, but the young queen too had something to offer. She welcomed Caesar onto her royal barge and took him on a progress down the Nile; he saw the Old Kingdom monuments and the vast deserts. Cleopatra opened the door to the Egypt beyond Alexandria (Grant 81). Most significantly, she gave birth to the child she named Caesarion, whose presence and contested parentage created an ongoing "burning political issue" (Grant 84). Shaw's film, which covers about six months, deletes the trip down the Nile and Cleopatra's pregnancy from its narrow slice of the queen's life.

Cleopatra's person in *Caesar and Cleopatra* conforms to Shaw's slant. How old is this Cleopatra? Most sources place the queen's age at twenty or twenty-one when Caesar arrived, but the date of her birth can't be pinned down more accurately than at "the end of 70 or the beginning of 69 B.C." (Grant 63). Shaw based his play on *The History of Rome* by Theodore Mommsen. In this late-nineteenth-century work, Mommsen acknowledges the affair between Caesar and Cleopatra, but he makes other points about their history more consistent with Shaw's vision, for example, his claim that Cleopatra was "about sixteen years" when Caesar arrived (Deans 15). Shaw repeats this mantra in the note about Cleopatra that follows the play: "Cleopatra was only sixteen when Caesar went to Egypt" (*Collected Screenplays of Bernard Shaw* 119). In his direction of Leigh, Pascal follows Shaw's lead.

At first, Leigh plays Cleopatra as a sprite even younger than sixteen. Slight, and far from matronly at thirty, Leigh carries this off by skipping and skimming through the sets. She speaks rapidly and in a high voice, her cadence and pitch suiting a child/princess who has not yet learned to give orders, even to her nurse/slave Ftatateeta. During the twenty-year span covered by DeMille's *Cleopatra,* the queen appears unmarked by time. Shaw's *Caesar and Cleopatra* covers the much shorter period of six months, but no artifice is spared to illustrate Cleopatra's external change from child to woman. The queen's walk becomes more majestic, her voice deepens, and the pace of her speaking slows. Paradoxically, the whole point of the elaborate surface change is to highlight what remains the same.

Oliver Messel's costuming underscores Cleopatra's fast-forward trajectory. Colbert, her head covered by a hood, her body crisscrossed by cord, appears first as a bound sex object. In contrast, Leigh's first costume, a simple belted shift of off-white crystal-pleated silk, stamps her as an innocent. Her crimped black hair loose down her back, her feet shod in flat sandals, her body clothed in gauzy fabric, this childlike Cleopatra can play, crouching, kneeling, running, and springing, as she does when she leads Caesar back to her palace. Once there, he issues a quick lesson in giving orders, and she responds with vicious glee by beating a cowering slave with a snake skin, reveling in the feral impulse barely beneath her innocent surface. But her freedom of motion disappears when Caesar urges her to assume her state robes. The change stiffens her into a statue. Her hair has been covered by an elaborate headdress, and, while Caesar watches, her ladies fasten a confining gold mantle over her shift. Cleopatra assumes the crossed-arm posture of a ruler (or an image on a royal sarcophagus) as she holds the crook and the flail. Finally, Caesar lifts a heavy crown into place. "Is it sweet or bitter to be queen?" he asks her. "Bitter," she answers. This "bitter" transformation turns the teen into a tomb-ready idol, but her surface sophistication falls apart when she realizes that the "old gentleman" who has helped her is the feared Caesar. She falls, squealing, into his lap, reduced to childish joy.

Cleopatra looks like a royal but acts like a child when she sneaks into the court hidden behind her servant. She pops out, runs to the throne, yanks her little brother off, and pushes him to the floor. "This is how she treats me, always," Ptolemy (Anthony Harvey) whines to Caesar. Costuming links the two sibling rivals. Both look feminine and effete, with elaborate eye makeup and pale, powdered faces, and both wear tightly fitted gowns of white crystal-pleated silk with gold-encrusted front panels, bejeweled collars, and headdresses of the sort audiences would expect to see in a film set in Egypt. Their similarity carries a powerful visual message, especially when the two sit side by side on the throne, mirroring each other's posture. Beneath the surface, brother and sister share a "total absence of moral sense" (Grant 27). Each is perfectly willing—in fact eager—to have the other beheaded. While most biographers acknowledge this, perhaps inbred, trait, few see it as Cleopatra's only component of character. Ptolemy disappears after this scene, having helped document the pervasive Ptolemaic savagery.

Two exotic costumes, very different from her girlish shift or throne-room garb, emphasize Cleopatra's body and her Orientalism. After her bath, her servant, Ftatateeta, helps her don a tight-fitting, low-cut blue and gold sari for her audience with Caesar. Even when Cleopatra wears this opulent outfit, which showcases her lovely figure, Caesar calls her "little kitten" and "poor child," but Shaw and Pascal signal the image change. From across the forecourt Cleopatra walks toward the camera (no more running) to strains of a sweet violin serenade, and Leigh plays Cleopatra-as-temptress for all she's worth. Pascal's close-ups catch her coy, coral-lipped smiles and her glances through mascara-coated lashes at Caesar. Although the action that follows this scene takes place during the same day, Leigh sheds the sari for a costume that could have walked off the set of another Messel project, *The Thief of Bagdad* (Ludwig Berger et al., 1940). This close-fitting brilliant blue-green gown, sashed in vivid orange and trimmed in gold, has an Arabian Nights flavor, and so does Cleopatra's fantastic coiffure: two upturned plaits, each tipped with gold. Wearing this fairy-tale splendor, the young queen makes her journey to the lighthouse rolled in a carpet.

As soon as her carpet unrolled, Claudette Colbert's Cleopatra sat up, then athletically sprang to a standing position, astounding her audience. In contrast, Leigh's Cleopatra lies passively while the men unfold her carpet and uncover her from a nest of silken shawls—a Scheherazade moment. As he plays with her bare arm, Caesar drops his kitten analogy. Now he calls her "a pretty little snake," a loaded bit of dialogue that identifies her nature. The big time jump in *Caesar and Cleopatra* comes after Caesar's jump into the harbor and the swim that saves both queen and general.

During the six-month period while he awaits Roman reinforcements, Caesar counsels Cleopatra, action that takes place off-camera. *Caesar and Cleopatra* offers no montage like the one in *Pygmalion* (Anthony Asquith and Leslie Howard, 1938) that shows Henry Higgins (Leslie Howard) laboring over Eliza Doolittle's (Wendy Hiller) vowels. Only Cleopatra's person and behavior testify to Caesar's influence. After six months, a regal Cleopatra, wearing subtler gold jewelry and a veiled headdress, reads in her seraglio-like royal enclosure. The deep eggplant color of her vaguely Roman gown separates her from her brightly clad women, as does her demeanor. Shaw's Cleopatra, who rarely exhibits a sense of humor, barely smiles while her ladies giggle, teasing her, and mocking Caesar. A graceful, sophisticated queen has displaced child and temptress, an evolution that Ftatateeta disapproves of. "You want to be what these Romans call a New Woman," she complains. The phrase *New Woman* must be a Shavian joke, for this glimpse of Cleopatra's private world only reinforces the continuing contrast between her surface and her interior.

Time spent listening to Caesar and observing his rule of courtesy has provided Cleopatra with a pleasing mask and the assurance that she can rule—alone—when he leaves, a goal she makes clear to her brother's adviser, Pothinus (Francis L. Sullivan). The impulse that drove the childish

Cleopatra to beat a slave still drives the suave queen. In six months, she has become articulate enough to voice her self-knowledge. "Oh, if I were not ashamed to let [Caesar] see that I am as cruel at heart as my father," she warns a disrespectful lady, "I would make you repent." She needn't try so hard to dissemble, however. Shaw's wise Caesar has never been taken in by the fledgling queen. "I haven't trusted you," he tells her.

Her performance as Scarlett O'Hara in *Gone with the Wind* (Victor Fleming, 1939) marked Vivien Leigh as a full-fledged queen of stage and screen and forever linked her to that character. With their combined glamour and talent, Leigh and Laurence Olivier, her husband, glittered enough to wow British and American audiences. Marjorie Deans acknowledges Leigh's star power, but she conflates Vivien Leigh, "remarkably small and slender," and the girlish Cleopatra as she appears so vividly in the first scenes of *Caesar and Cleopatra*. Deans dubs Leigh a "darling of destiny" and says that she "cannot imagine" that Leigh ever had to "struggle and agonize to make her way in life." Such an untroubled passage, Deans remarks, may account for Leigh's "personality which is notably clear and unshadowed, giving a brilliant, princesslike quality of assurance and poise" (65). It's hard to imagine that these words could be anything but obfuscation. Deans, an uncredited writer and script supervisor, was close enough to *Caesar and Cleopatra* to write a book about its production. In a chapter titled "Production Difficulties," she notes that Leigh was "taken ill" during filming (93), but her bland phrase hardly communicates the reality. If Leigh had been asked, "Is it sweet or bitter to play Cleopatra?" she probably would have answered, "Bitter." Later, in 1951, Leigh enjoyed playing Cleopatra to Laurence Olivier's Caesar and to his Marc Antony in limited back-to-back performances of Shaw's and Shakespeare's plays, but she had suffered so acutely during the filming of the movie role she had avidly sought that, as her biographer Alexander Walker points out, "she was to let six years go by before she could bear to see [*Caesar and Cleopatra*]" (*Vivien* 171). Six weeks into filming, Leigh discovered that she was pregnant, an event that she gaily announced in a letter to her first husband, Leigh Holman: "I'm to have a baby. Everyone is *very, very* cross" (qtd. in Vickers 156). Pascal rearranged the shooting schedule, moving Leigh's scenes up. But her condition didn't alter the intensity of her performance or quench Pascal's thirst for perfection. After this film, Arthur Rank banned Pascal from future projects. His micromanagement sent *Caesar and Cleopatra* over schedule and over budget, and his inability to prioritize exhausted the cast. Flora Robson recalls him "wast[ing] three days over an actor who had one line to say" (qtd. in *Collected Screenplays of Bernard Shaw* 137). Stewart Granger blamed Pascal for not using a double for Leigh in the scene in which Cleopatra leaps around the audience hall, wildly beating a slave with a snake skin. In a letter to his wife, Granger described Pascal's request that Leigh repeat the scene again and again. During one of the takes, Granger explains, "she slipped and fell heavily" (qtd. in Vickers 156).

Leigh miscarried two days later (Vickers 156–57). Her weakened physical state and a subsequent period of depression constitute the "illness" to which Deans refers, but this was hardly an isolated, dark episode in an otherwise sunny existence. Deans's description of Leigh's personality as "unshadowed" would have amazed those who knew her well and who recognized the physical and mental stresses shadowing her adult life. Recurring bouts of pulmonary tuberculosis, which killed her in 1967, weakened her, and she suffered manic-depressive swings. Her fellow cast members witnessed a breakdown that halted the filming of a key scene in *Caesar and Cleopatra* (Walker, *Vivien,* 170). As it records a story, a film captures a real moment in the lives of the actors; the final scenes in *Caesar and Cleopatra,* especially, trap Leigh's troubled state.

That fragility is obvious in a scene set on the palace rooftop. Leigh was greeny-white as Indian marble and extremely thin, and her pallor and brittleness, symptoms of her distress, shade Shaw's portrait of a calculating, vengeful queen. Right before the start of a banquet, Pothinus tells Caesar the queen's secret—she wants him to leave so that she can rule without her brother. Although Caesar sees this as "natural," Cleopatra rages at Pothinus for speaking, and she sends Ftatateeta to kill him. Pothinus's death cry disrupts the party, and his murder triggers Caesar's disgust. "Oh, ignoble," he calls Cleopatra. In contrast, noble Caesar ascends. His reinforcements arrive, and upbeat music accompanies his reentry into the cheery all-male world of hand-to-hand combat. As fortune shifts in Caesar's favor, life truly becomes bitter to Cleopatra.

Her banquet costume, the most goddess-like and the most regal ensemble of the lot, heightens the impression that Cleopatra is isolated. She wears a heavy pyramidal headdress of dull metallic pellets, a severe contrast to Leigh's white face, and a close-fitting cloth-of-gold gown that draws

Caesar and Cleopatra. Dressed in the costume that most suggests her iconic status, Cleopatra gives a cool gaze that hints at the calculating mind behind that beautiful surface. George Bernard Shaw's version of Cleopatra as a flawed, feral creature centers Pascal's adaptation of Shaw's *Caesar and Cleopatra.* (Courtesy Jerry Ohlinger's Movie Material Store.)

attention to Leigh's thinness. The whole ensemble announces Cleopatra's status as icon, and the gown's decoration foreshadows her fate. Its bodice, cut lower over the left breast, features a phoenix-like appliqué, a golden bird with a tail that sweeps down to embellish the skirt. The phoenix's small, serpent-shaped head curls up onto the paper-white flesh over Cleopatra's left breast, anticipating the bite of the asp. A brutal death ends this scene. After Caesar rushes to battle, Rufio confronts Cleopatra. "Your man bungled the job," he tells her, complaining about the noisy nature of Pothinus's murder. When he learns that Ftatateeta slew Pothinus with her bare hands, he quickly slits her throat before joining Caesar. Ftatateeta's assassin potential catches Rufio's attention, but her progress from serving woman, to murderer, to murder victim should prick the curiosity of Shaw's audience.

In DeMille's *Cleopatra,* Iras and Charmion (named in ancient sources as Cleopatra's ladies-in-waiting) remain at the queen's side, but they are little more than sexy blonde ciphers. Shaw demotes Iras (Renee Asherson) to an insignificant member of the court and erases Charmion. In their place he puts Ftatateeta, a fictional figure with "the mouth of a blood-hound and the jaws of a bulldog" and "a powerful and handsome body . . . apparently naked," a description that combines ugliness, aggression, and sexuality (*Collected Screenplays of Bernard Shaw* 130). Messel picks up on the ugliness. Flora Robson, an attractive woman, becomes a parody of an Egyptian in a coarse black wig, dark makeup, heavy jewelry, and strips of fabric that bare her arms and shoulders. When she stands next to Leigh's glamorous Cleopatra, she looks as if she wandered off a vaudeville stage that wasn't part of the Orpheum circuit. Francesca Royster points out that Robson is, essentially, in blackface and that her presence offers an opposition to Vivien Leigh's whiteness, a marker of their slave/master relationship. Leigh had acted out this scheme before as Scarlett O'Hara, the "nursling" of a black mammy (Hattie McDaniel) in *Gone with the Wind* (Royster 127–28). Shaw, who played with the idea of re-creating the alphabet, gives this character a name resonant with vowels, like baby talk. Caesar sometimes shouts "Teeta," a sound close to *teat,* an utterance that might have been considered sly bawdiness on a set that adhered to the Production Code. Attempts to say her name—"Tota," "Tota-teeta"—become a vaudeville-like shtick, turning the character, no matter how consequential her actions, into the living punch line of a running joke. Such mockery reaches a climax in the last scene of *Caesar and Cleopatra.*

Shaw and Pascal's film ends years before Cleopatra's death, but the conclusion sets the tone for the queen's future. The final scene marks Caesar's triumph and Cleopatra's failure. The real Caesar left Rufio, the son of a slave, in charge of the Roman forces in Egypt (Grant 80). Shaw escalates Caesar's act into a diminishment of Cleopatra's power. Standing in the glow of the sun and of the cheering Alexandrians, Caesar appoints Rufio "Roman Governor," a male-to-male transfer that sidesteps the queen. In fact, Caesar forgets Cleopatra, as if she is a detail too minor to recall. Only her appearance reminds him that he should bid her farewell. The bright sunlight washes over Caesar, but the queen emerges like a shadow from a shadow world as she comes toward him from the palace. Bernard Dukore feels that Pascal's shot of Cleopatra, anticipating Marc Antony, "eyes gleaming and her lips smiling," subverts Shaw's agenda of Caesar worship: "Pascal suggests victory for the sexy charmer, and minimizes the implication that she failed to get what she killed for" (*Collected Screenplays of Bernard Shaw* 140). But, if Cleopatra's person is a talisman, and if Caesar's last words to her matter, the last scene has a darker tint than Dukore's words imply.

Cleopatra, veiled, wears the darkest of her costumes. Her unembellished charcoal-colored gown, mourning for Ftatateeta, is also the least Eastern of them. In this gathered, strapless chiffon number, Leigh could be a socialite headed for a smart end-of-the-war party, although there's nothing festive about her expression. In fact, there's little that seems alive about Cleopatra. Against the charcoal veil, the queen's chalky face and bright red lips recall the tagline for Theda Bara's *Cleopatra:* "The Vampire Supreme." Shaw, who became a champion of women's rights, seems to have relished sucking the life out of the two female figures in *Caesar and Cleopatra.* In his hands, the queen of queens becomes a footnote to Caesar, a sterile, stunted thing, and, as if that diminishment could not provide satisfaction enough, Shaw crafts a mother figure to mock and destroy, dealing an after-death blow to Ftatateeta, a coda that underscores the theme of the whole.

Although the queen demands justice—she wants Caesar to punish Rufio for killing Ftatateeta—Caesar declares the murder "well done." He asks Cleopatra not to be angry about "that poor Totateeta," still not bothering to pronounce the name correctly, a final refusal to extend his signature boon—

courtesy—to Cleopatra's dead nurse. But there's a last indignity. Shaw has Cleopatra laugh at Caesar's mangling of the name, "in spite of herself," revealing her utter shallowness (*Collected Screenplays of Bernard Shaw* 457). Seen in this context, Cleopatra's anticipation of Marc Antony underscores her membership in a lesser sex, a group inured to sacrificing its own.

The only woman Shaw likes in *Caesar and Cleopatra* is a man. To the Sicilian merchant Apollodorus Shaw gives the love of music and art and the ability to spin pleasing dinner conversation. Oliver Messel dresses macho Stewart Granger (horribly miscast) with a zest that almost trumps Shaw's affection. Granger worried that Shaw meant the character to be gay, "which," he noted, "was not exactly my scene" (qtd. in Vickers 155), and he does look a little less than comfortable in his minitunics accessorized with capes and jewels. Shaw marries Apollodorus's artsy graciousness to athleticism and an appetite for combat. Apollodorus is the first to dive from the lighthouse, and he pledges his sword, his "right arm," and his "heart and life" when Caesar rushes into battle after the banquet scene. Men alone, it seems, offer infinite variety in *Caesar and Cleopatra.*

Shaw's Cleopatra subsides into perpetual childishness when set against the pageantry of the glorious male sex, with its warships, banners, and trumpets. The film opened in the testosterone-high climate at the end of World War II, so it's hard not to read Shaw's indictment of Cleopatra as a broader censure. Especially in the last scene, in which she looks like a fashionable woman of the 1940s, her tragic flaw seems less an inheritance from the Ptolemaic dynasty and more a condition of gender. In a short note following *Caesar and Cleopatra,* Shaw points out that such childishness "can be observed ... at the present day in many women of fifty" (*Collected Screenplays of Bernard Shaw* 119). It's a woman's tendency, he suggests, to fixate on the "round strong arms" of a potential lover while willfully ignoring history's great landscapes. With this disparaging portrait, Shaw could be asking the question Henry Higgins asks Colonel Pickering in *My Fair Lady:* "Why can't a woman [even Cleopatra] be more like me?"

Cleopatra (1963)

Shaw's slant permeates *Caesar and Cleopatra.* But doesn't every author/auteur refashion Cleopatra's (or any queen's) life as if it were a dress? The most extreme tailoring demands the lopping off of limbs to ensure a fit.

Consider *Serpent of the Nile* (William Castle, 1953), a low-budget horror with a title yanked from Shakespeare's *Antony and Cleopatra*. This farce forces Cleopatra (Rhonda Fleming) into a straitjacket. She's a snake, a warmongering nymphomaniac. Fleming, jammed into some tacky prom gowns, slithers and pouts her way through the dreadful screenplay. It's no surprise that the men "subdue the golden wench" in this repulsive patchwork.

The producer Walter Wanger had a more flattering garment in mind for Cleopatra in 1959, even before Spyros Skouras, the head of Twentieth Century–Fox, handed him the Theda Bara script "almost old enough to be made of parchment" (Wanger and Hyams 8). Wanger never considered updating that screenplay. For $15,000—a bargain—he had bought the rights to a romanticized biography, Carlo Maria Franzero's *The Life and Times of Cleopatra* (3). Impressed by her "youth, power, and emotion," he hoped to cast Elizabeth Taylor, whom he had admired in *A Place in the Sun* (George Stevens, 1951), as Cleopatra. "She came through to me," Wanger explains, "as the one young actress who could play [the queen]" (3). Taylor's request for an unprecedented million-dollar salary raised the bar for star salaries and jump-started the relatively inexpensive beginning into the costly saga *Cleopatra,* directed by Joseph Mankiewicz, starring Elizabeth Taylor, Rex Harrison, and Richard Burton, one of the most written-about films in American cinematic history.

Film critics in the 1960s, fueled by studio publicity and dunned by a drumbeat of gossip, could hardly have objectively watched or written about a film that was an international obsession for five years from preproduction in 1959 to release in 1963. Public fascination with and outrage about *le scandal,* the affair between Taylor and Burton, reached a fever pitch before the film ever hit the theaters. When it did, the four-hour *Cleopatra,* an anticlimax to its creation, received both praise and derision, capped by Judith Crist's career-defining slap-down: "The mountain of notoriety has produced a mouse" (qtd. in "Super Pan"). Nearly fifty years after the initial reviewers had their say, *Cleopatra,* still eclipsed by the chatter it generated, has morphed into an unwieldy chunk of American pop culture.

Do you want to know how many miles of film were shot? What Burton said to Taylor at their first on-set meeting? What sneaky tactics the paparazzi adopted to get photos of the couple? When Taylor's husband, the singer Eddie Fisher, left Rome? How much it cost to free a cat and her kittens from beneath Cleopatra's bedroom? Why some disobedient elephants were "fired"? For fascinating factoids ad infinitum, see Walter Wanger's on-the-spot journal, *My Life with Cleopatra* (1963), and Jack Brodsky and Nathan Weiss's tell-all, *The Cleopatra Papers* (1963). The siren song of such seductive material sounds in most analyses of the film. Of the eight pages that Jon Solomon devotes to *Cleopatra*, for example, he spends five on film lore and has to snap himself back to "the film—ah, yes, the film" (70). Even *Magill's Survey of Cinema*, hardly a flighty tabloid, wallows in trivia and expounds on what Joseph Mankiewicz *might* have meant, instead of discussing the existing movie (see Hopkins). The ephemera swirling in *Cleopatra's* wake, however, can't stale its images, especially those of the queen. The cover of Francesca Royster's *Becoming Cleopatra* features one of the most haunting, a close-up of Taylor in full "Egyptian" makeup, her heavily shadowed eye looking out above the title. Royster joins the chorus of those who explore the indelible overlap of star and subject; she claims that "the conflation of [Taylor's] image. . . . with the Cleopatra character" will "ghost" the part for every actress who follows (94). At the epicenter of this lavish production, a film reflective of its time, lives a schizophrenic ghost worth raising.

Where should such an icon dwell? John De Cuir's designs for *Cleopatra* netted him an Oscar nomination, if not a win, but some critics were less than awed by the film's over-the-top look. Charles Hopkins summarizes the complaints of those who found *Cleopatra's* "surprising vulgarity" more akin to Caesar's Palace (the Las Vegas version) than Ptolemaic Alexandria (470, 471). The liquidity of temporal/spatial location doesn't have to be a flaw. To us, De Cuir's interiors look futuristic, prescient. Cleopatra's apartments are spare but opulent, with expanses of open floor and cut-stone wall punctuated by hits of deep aqua and pale orange. The camera glides past fabulous objets d'art and critically placed pieces of minimalist furniture. The whole reads more like an anticipation of Dubai than faux Ptolemy. This is a Middle Eastern ethos that modern viewers recognize, a context that helps free the story from its ancient-Egypt-only niche.

Conventional wisdom says that Joseph Mankiewicz (who replaced Rouben Mamoulian as director) had to create that story nightly, like Scheherazade, writing the next day's screenplay after slogging through each day's killer shooting schedule; the writers Nigel Balchin, Nunnally Johnson, and Lawrence Durrell had labored over *Cleopatra*, and Ranald Mac-

Dougall and Sidney Buchman are credited. It's also received knowledge that editing rendered the final cut all but incoherent. Even someone with no knowledge of Cleopatra's dealings with Rome, however, should be able to follow the arc from the queen's meeting with Caesar to her death, the same sweep of time DeMille chose. At first, this isn't DeMille's simplistic "queen as seductress" version. Mankiewicz shoots for double vision, going wide and zooming in, as he tries to capture both the scope of history and the pull of character. Before it clicks into replay, *Cleopatra* makes a grand attempt.

The film begins, not with the queen, but on a flaking fresco of a battlefield that comes to life as a narrating voice sets the scene. This method, collapsing representation into "reality," marks the transitions of time and location. Standing before a sea of Roman red, smelling the stench of death following his triumph at Pharsalia, Caesar (Rex Harrison) contemplates pursuing Pompey to Egypt. The brilliance of hindsight allows us to note that this cautionary tale about the danger of stepping into the political affairs of a distant, Eastern country seems amazingly appropriate to a nation teetering on the brink of involvement in Vietnam. More recent global entanglements suggest that it couldn't hurt to reconsider a saga infused with the problems of empire, one in which a superpower, ever seeking world dominance and wealth, enters a distant country to force a change in leadership.

Although Mankiewicz first considered opening on Cleopatra in her own encampment, the existing context frames the queen's dealings with Rome as a series of causes and effects. What happens after the head of state is toppled, some irreplaceable artifacts are torched, and the mission seems to be accomplished? Hopkins claims that Mankiewicz's ideal Cleopatra, a "Platonic philosopher queen,"..."a bluestocking"with a world vision, never made it to the screen (470), but enough of that person appears to make viewers want more. The queen sketched in the first half of the film is a powerful force loosed by Roman actions. After the intermission (the film runs four hours), a broader brush takes over, abstracting Cleopatra into expressionistic smears. Any light shining on her private world goes out well before she enters the tomb.

But, at the start, the queen sparkles, quickly signaling her power. Franzero describes the rolled-in-a-carpet meeting as if it were something "in a fairy tale" (49), but Mankiewicz favors realism. At first, his screenplay echoes Shaw's in its praise of Caesar, played here by Rex Harrison, a great Shaw fan. The general guesses the carpet's passenger and plans to stage-manage her appearance by having the carpet unrolled upside down so that he can inspect the "backside." Cleopatra, physically off balance for a few seconds, doesn't acknowledge his loaded comment. Instead, she rises to face Caesar with no slinking or shrinking. More than Colbert's or Leigh's, Taylor's Cleopatra demonstrates her capability to become queen of Egypt.

The biographer Alexander Walker calls Taylor's Cleopatra "a kittenish coed of a queen seducing her professorial Caesar" (*Elizabeth* 266). We disagree. Taylor, twenty-eight when filming began, always looked more mature than her years. Only eleven when she was cast as Velvet Brown in *National Velvet* (Clarence Brown, 1944), Taylor, who could pass for fourteen, already promised adult beauty. In *Cleopatra*, she's youthful but never precious. A veteran of adult projects like *Suddenly, Last Summer* (Joseph L. Mankiewicz, 1959) and *Butterfield Eight* (Daniel Mann, 1960), Taylor was accustomed to playing experienced women. Every action helps her establish her far-from-kittenish character. Cleopatra's treatment of Apollodorus (Cesare Danova) speaks of a mature relationship with those who serve her; her stride to the table for a golden beaker of wine says she's at home; her admonition to employ a food taster proves that she knows the peril of overconfidence; her critique of Caesar's maps reveals her familiarity with strategy. Even the little golden dagger strapped to her waist stamps Cleopatra as savvy, a queen who thinks in contingencies. She proves that *she*, not Ptolemy, and not Rome, controls the palace. After leaving Caesar's quarters, she spies on him and his advisers from a secret passage. A close-up of her eyes (an important motif throughout the film) staring through round peepholes makes her, not the Romans, the gazer; the audience looks with her, not at her. While she listens, Caesar's aides review her knowledge of language, history, and philosophy and affirm that, "if she were not a woman," she would be "an intellectual."

In this version, that claim isn't such a stretch, but the queen's sexual history, not her intelligence, arouses the most intense Roman interest. Cleopatra has had many men, they believe, and she chooses her lovers "in the manner of a man." This assumption contradicts Grant, who believes that Cleopatra was "murderous and chaste," with two lovers only (84). The report of her appetite for men works to her advantage in *Cleopatra*. Caesar has taken the measure of her brother, Ptolemy (Richard O'Sullivan), and of Pothinus (Gregoire Aslan), his eunuch regent. Their garish makeup, pink and gold robes, elaborate jewelry, and fancy headdresses stamp them effete, unhealthy, enervated, certain to provoke a knee-jerk antigay response in a 1960s audience. In contrast, Cleopatra looks healthy and hetero. In her first costume, a tight-waisted scarlet tunic, she burns like a live coal.

Even if she isn't wearing anything, she exudes self-possession. When Caesar fails to obey her command to appear at once, Cleopatra retaliates by staging a "special" audience for him when he does come, receiving him while she is in the nude. Wearing tons of eye makeup, swathed in gauze, attended by her ladies, she gives the Romans what they expect—a tableau of Eastern indolence. A display of power, the queen's performance proves that, if Caesar cannot come when called, the queen of Egypt can't be expected to alter her agenda for his convenience, even if it only involves throwing on a robe. Caesar takes the point, reacting with wit and interest. Eddie Fisher (Taylor's husband at the film's start) suggested playing the scene "properly and artistically" in the nude, and he and Taylor reviewed the footage and stills after it was shot (Wanger and Hyams 116). Fisher earned a salary for producing Taylor on time and in costume, but he couldn't render her compliant. Taylor resented the industry attitude that her body was its commodity. It seems doubtful that she would have OK'd the nude audience scene, which isn't particularly flattering or sensual, if she felt it to be gratuitous jiggle. A later bathing scene shows Cleopatra considering a plan for meeting Antony. These two scenes, the only truly fleshy footage in the film, help establish that all Cleopatra's moments, even those that might be considered private, have public significance.

It's easy to see why Taylor liked the wardrobe that Irene Sharaff designed for *Cleopatra* enough to keep some of the gowns for her private use. She wore a Sharaff creation "inspired by the one she wore when she and Burton did their first scene together on the Cleopatra set" for her first marriage to Burton in 1964 (Walker, *Elizabeth*, 272). Sharaff knew how to invest Taylor, who was quite small, with stature. The Oscar-nominated costumes evoke a more sophisticated sexiness than Travis Banton's peekaboo numbers for Claudette Colbert. Sharaff rejects bare midriffs, transparent bodices, and nipple-highlighting glitter for rich fabrics in jewel tones of amethyst, canary, emerald, turquoise, and ruby that complement Taylor's pale oval face, lavender eyes, and dark hair. These vivid gowns are conservatively cut, with natural waists and long, slightly flaring skirts (a silhouette popular in the 1960s) to focus attention on Taylor's small waist and generous bust. High slits reveal infrequent flashes of leg. This Cleopatra's clothing frames but doesn't flaunt her lushness.

Taylor could have worn most of these gowns off the set. Like Colbert's and Leigh's, her costumes reflect style at the time of the film, and, more specifically, they aid the conflation between star and role. Cleopatra's style *is* Taylor's style. The most Egyptian thing about Cleopatra—her eye make-up with its painted lids, sparkling lashes, and eye-extending liner—became Taylor's trademark. Taylor applied the heavy makeup herself and kept a muted version as a signature look for years. Twice, Cleopatra displays her nude body, but never, ever, does she reveal completely nude eyes. The liner (never the shadow) disappears only when she is preparing for sleep or giving birth. Her "kohled eyes," like a cartouche, affirm that Cleopatra never stops being queen (Royster 95).

The adoption of some of Cleopatra's trapping in her real life illustrates Taylor's ambiguity about the role, and her "identification with Vivien Leigh," her Cleopatra predecessor, speaks of her self-awareness (Walker, *Elizabeth*, 280). Leigh was a rare kindred spirit, someone else inhabiting a body that evoked other personae than her own. While their performances as the queen of Egypt differ greatly, the actresses share many personal parallels. Leigh had married a "great" actor and lived with that comparison, a situation Taylor faced with Burton. Leigh knew the self-doubt that resulted from being admired and resented for her beauty. Taylor balanced on that peak from preadolescence to late middle age. The pressures of containing several selves exacerbated Leigh's mental and physical problems (Walker, *Elizabeth*, 290). Taylor's health deteriorated as the stress of her career escalated. When Leigh succumbed to tuberculosis, no one found press tributes that described her as "the eternal Scarlett O'Hara" odd (Vickers 326). As Taylor accepted her million-dollar fee, as she hid from paparazzi, as she walked among a cast selected to support her performance, as she strolled into an Egypt built for her in Rome, and as she lifted the crook and flail, she had to ponder the strangeness of becoming a queen.

Cleopatra wears full queen regalia when Caesar places the double crown of Upper and Lower Egypt on her head. This scene has had an impact beyond the film because it produced the most familiar still of Taylor as Cleopatra, an image (fronting the most recent DVD of the film) for which Fox paid dearly. Shaw's childish Cleopatra describes the assumption of the crown as "bitter," but to this more mature Cleopatra, who smiles at its weight, the crown seals the "sweet" merging of private and public selves. She kicks off her reign with forethought. She has brought Caesar a kneeling pillow, a bit of humor with an edge. To prospective empire builders, the pillow should represent a daunting truth: those whom you annex may see *you*, not themselves, as ancillary. Caesar kneels, smiling at Cleopatra's cleverness. Perhaps he shouldn't.

After their first embrace, Cleopatra tells Caesar, "I promise you, you won't like me this way," indicating that she won't be a passive lover. The fruit of their relationship, their son, sets Cleopatra in motion. Unlike the Colbert version, this film includes Caesarion, acknowledging his importance as a catalyst for Cleopatra's visit to Rome. A private moment at the end of her entry into the eternal city, the "most spectacular pageant sequence ever filmed," captures the impact of the trip (Solomon 73). De-Mille's vision of the arrival looks low-key in comparison to *Cleopatra*'s explosion of the event. For inspiration, Mankiewicz might have turned first to Franzero, who depicts the Romans as critics, lined up to see whether Cleopatra is a "courtesan" or a "sorceress" with an "evil influence" on men. "Above all," Franzero thinks, the Romans regarded her as "an alien," the Eastern opposite of Western virtue (69). In his page-and-a-half description, Franzero names some of the players in the drama: "black slaves," "eunuchs" dressed "like women," an "almost naked" contingent of Egyptian soldiers, and, finally, the queen, a beautiful woman with a "golden" complexion, sensuous lips, and nearly bare breasts (69–70). The controversial high point of the procession is Caesarion, who "bore an astonishing likeness to Caesar" (70).

The biggest of *Cleopatra*'s big scenes takes place in a supersized forum constructed for the film where the black slaves and soldiers appear but not much of the ethnocentrism Franzero describes as the pervasive attitude of the Roman crowd. Mankiewicz shows a throng transfixed by the (Roman) tuba players, puffs of colored smoke, nearly naked dancing girls, archers, a shower of gold, and a dove-filled pyramid. At the climax, ranks of slaves pull a huge porphyry statue of a lion-bodied pharaoh through Constantine's Arch. This unlikely steed bears the queen and her son (Loris Loddi), who perch on an elevated seat. The intimate moment in this very public scene comes after Cleopatra and Caesarion, both glittering with gold, dismount and stand slightly below their host. Caesar nods to them; they bow deeply to him. Then the camera moves in on the queen's face. Deliberately, Cleopatra winks.

Solomon reads the wink as a joke between Caesar and Cleopatra, a shared acknowledgment "that Rome has been conquered" by Egypt's (read: Cleopatra's) exotic grandeur (74). After that close-up of the queen's heavily made-up eye tipping the wink, however, the camera doesn't cut back to Caesar, so we don't know if he's chuckling. There's no wink in Franzero's text; it wouldn't be in sync with the mood of a crowd that jeers at Egyptian animal gods (70). The easier-to-please observers in the film explode into cheers, overwhelmed, while stiff Roman matrons (coiffed à la Pat Nixon) follow Calpurnia's lead and rise to their feet. The screenplay mandated cheers for Cleopatra, but Taylor worried about the tone of the welcome she might receive. After all, *L'Osservatore della Domenica,* a weekly paper published by the Vatican, had declared her an unfit mother (Taraborrelli 201). How would the mob of Italian extras treat a woman the pope had blasted? The "ancient Romans," thrilled to see such a big star, screamed, "Leez," not "Cleopatra," siding with Taylor and against the pope, so Cleopatra's wink also indicates Taylor's relief.

Marc Antony (Richard Burton) is on target when he conjures up Rome's founders. "Nothing like this has entered Rome since Romulus and Remus," he tells Caesar. The grand display, while not based on history, underscores Cleopatra's mythic purpose. She has brought her child/god, not to pay homage to Rome, but to claim it. In this context, Cleopatra's wink means something infinitely simple. It says, "So, here we are," giving the scene an anticolonial edge. Is the dominant power really in control? Once Cleopatra and her heir roll into Rome's inner sanctum, the possibility of rewind vanishes. Mankiewicz's procession, a metaphor for the political landscape, beautifully enacts the phrase *the elephant in the room.* The spectacle delights the eye, but the pharaoh in the forum activates concerns that cannot be ignored. Will this Oriental pair remain in Rome? Will Caesar divorce Calpurnia? Legitimize Caesarion? A few scenes only separate Cleopatra's wink from Caesar's blood-stained body.

The wink also acts as a pivot. The high of the procession precipitates, not just Caesar's, but Cleopatra's fall as the film reneges on its promise of a vital portrait of the queen. Such retrograde motion reminds twenty-first-century viewers, like us, of a significant text that appeared in 1963, Betty Friedan's *The Feminine Mystique.* During the transformative years of the early 1960s, the promise of feminism, as glittering an image as Cleopatra perched near the top of the patriarchal monument, beckoned tantalizingly from the near future. As the screenplay looks back at the alliance between Cleopatra and Caesar, it steps forward, daring a little more than a father/daughter interpretation, rejecting the Shavian notion that Cleopatra, doomed by inheritance and biology, must be Caesar's inferior. Caesar and Cleopatra's mutual dependency and corresponding traits, like humor, wariness, a reverence for Alexander the Great, a fondness for being right, and a soupçon of lust, help Taylor and Harrison (who got an Academy Award nomination for Best Actor in a leading role in 1964) strike sparks in their scenes together. But in the transition to Antony and Cleopatra's romance— a more conventional context—Mankiewicz's screenplay retreats to familiar territory. Marc Antony later tells Cleopatra that, as he stood in the forum, he saw her approaching figure as a golden "doll," an image that echoes DeMille's Marc Antony, who knew that women should be playthings.

In her coming together with Antony, the real queen must have sizzled. In *Cleopatra*, she's frozen into a familiar figure: the destroyer. The screenplay discards the complexity of history for a catchy tune, repeating the refrain of the misguided woman who refuses to be a plaything, who won't "have love as [her] master." Even the queen of queens must learn, albeit too late, that to be mastered by love is all. A companion piece to the procession into the forum, the arrival of Cleopatra's royal barge in Tarsus begins the transition from ruler to spoiler. Wanger calls the exterior shots of Cleopatra's barge "right out of Plutarch" (Wanger and Hyams 170). While the boat with its Tyrian purple sails and glamorous crew looks perfect, a deeply tanned, glitter-haired Taylor standing rigid and alone in a miniature pillared shrine seems far from the sensuous being Plutarch imagined "reclined beneath a gold-flecked canopy, dressed like Aphrodite" (qtd. in "Summary of Ancient Sources"). She's distant too from the camera, as if its adoring eye has pulled back and fallen out of love. The remove encourages the view that this Cleopatra, gold glinting at her neck, comes, not in love, but with a single purpose.

The plot device that opens the "Antony" section suggests a rich path, one that Mankiewicz does not follow. Cleopatra wears a lure, a bib of gold coins, each bearing Caesar's image. This bauble signals her understanding of Antony, a pretty basic fellow, who confesses that he becomes tongue-tied in her presence. With the necklace, she labels herself Caesar's treasure, banking on Antony's urge to pillage. Cleopatra maps the way, in case Antony can't quite figure it out. The single entertainment at the barge party (less fun to watch than DeMille's) features Bacchus, a stand-in for Antony, who fondles a plump double for the queen. She's coiffed in the queen's 1960s miniflip, she wears a barer version of the queen's white and gold ensemble, and, of course, she sports a similar necklace. Brought to the sticking point by this vision, a sodden Antony leaps into Bacchus's throne to manhandle the faux Cleopatra. Like a lightning bolt, the realization that he could embrace the real queen strikes him. He strides into her boudoir, rends her bed curtain, and shouts: "Want to say something NOW. NOW." This is an utterance that sounds more caveman than consul. Finally, Antony yanks off the necklace, confronting his Harold Bloomian/Sigmund Freudian anxiety of influence/Oedipal blend of neuroses.

Besides giving Antony a target for his frustration, the bib of gold recalls the significance of coins to Cleopatra's history. Grant believes that Cleopatra "stage-managed" the dramatic meeting on the royal barge to lift herself and Antony into the divine realm where both were gods (117). Coins testify to the earthly dimension of their union. Like miniature texts, they hold the only attributable images of Cleopatra, and their existence documents her connection to Rome and to Antony. After Antony left Octavia, he returned to Egypt and enlarged Cleopatra's kingdom, an act commemorated by a minting of coins. Roman currency rarely featured women, and, when it did, they were Roman, not "foreigners." The coins bearing Cleopatra's profile were incendiary, an "unprecedented spectacle," material proof of the status Antony accorded her (Grant 169).

Cleopatra could use the coins to trace the transition from Caesar's profile to the queen's, but it doesn't. The Cleopatra-brought-down-Antony mode requires no fresh motif. Franzero assumes that Cleopatra enmeshed Antony in a net of pleasure. "But why," he begs the question, "did Cleopatra bring Antony down to the level of sensual debauchery?" (160). DeMille, who doesn't care why, uses that assumption for a plot. Solomon worries that the Fox *Cleopatra* diminishes the fall by failing to demonstrate Marc Antony's greatness: "This cinematic Antony starts at the bottom and falls sideways" (710). And it's true that the dour Burton exchanges his armor for a lounge lizard's robe and his sword for a flagon of wine before Cleopatra ever sets sail for Tarsus. If audiences are denied crucial explication, they are fully briefed on Mankiewicz's ultimate preoccupation, placing blame on the queen. Antony states it unequivocally. "You happened to me," he tells Cleopatra, in explanation of his post-Cleopatran sloth and ineptitude.

The process of that happening should be fun to watch, but more heat radiates from the publicity still on the front of Wanger's book than from the film's live-action embraces. The shot features Taylor and Burton, profiles to the camera, a few inches apart, held in a dynamic tension, like the lovers on Keats's Grecian urn. Lacking any sense of precious, suspended time, each of the infrequent love scenes comes accompanied by Cleopatra's directives about how Antony should challenge Rome. Given these two actors, the luxury of two hours, and the wealth of source material bordering on "sensual debauchery," focusing on Cleopatra's nagging, even if her guilt is the single point, seems sadistic.

In his life of the queen, Franzero provides as much gossip about the historic pair as the tabloids spewed about Taylor and Burton, more than enough to energize several films. He gives detailed accounts of the jokes the couple played on each other, the extravagant wagers they made, the fabulous feasts they planned, the secret societies they formed, the slumming forays they took into Alexandria's reddest zones, the sexual embraces they enjoyed, almost publicly. Even a taste of such hedonism would have helped define the dangerous attraction between Antony and Cleopatra. After their coupling on the barge, however, *Cleopatra* expects its audience to accept a fait accompli. The pair's terse dialogue has less poetry than text messaging, and only a glimpse of the childish Antony (his caveman impulses purged) paddling about in Cleopatra's bathing pool, and the sight of his togas, like limp pajamas, hanging in her boudoir, establishes their intimacy.

Because nothing—not a meal together, not an exotic party, not a glimpse of their languor—illustrates their mutual entanglement, key scenes have little impact. Cleopatra venting her rage at Antony's marriage reads as silly despite Taylor's herculean efforts to make it electric. Like a victim of Tourette syndrome, she shakes, screams, and inflicts a *Psycho*-inspired stabbing on Antony's garments. Cuts to Greece show Antony dining with Octavia, a wife as docile as Cleopatra is driven. Wouldn't a zoom-in on one of Cleopatra and Antony's wilder nights help audiences negotiate this confusing terrain?

Taylor's Cleopatra rages about being perceived as a "harlot," but Mankiewicz aims way beyond the familiar epithets of *whore* or *unfit mother* (both charges leveled at Taylor). To include any trace of their heirs would complicate the simple story line of a man reduced to infancy by an un-natural woman. The children's absence flattens the twenty-second glimpse of the donations at Alexandria into an indecipherable vignette. Wasn't Antony eager to leave Caesar's shadow? Why does he legitimize Caesar's child? For the actual ceremony, which took place in 34 B.C., Antony and Cleopatra dressed like gods. Antony "donated" a goodly hunk of the world to Cleopatra and Caesarion and gave a share to his own children by the queen. He also took care to make his oldest son, the child of his first wife, "his Roman heir," an act that showed his hesitation to empower Cleopatra and her children only (Grant 171). But any hint that Antony could think for himself would challenge this one-note song.

Cleopatra's characterization in the second section denies viewers var-ied perspectives. A few times, in the first half, the camera follows the queen into her inner world, a space entered by Iras, Charmion, Apollodorus, Cae-sar, and a few others only. Mankiewicz never mines what could be a rich vein. He reduces Iras and Charmion to signifiers—à la DeMille. In its dreary plod to the mausoleum, *Cleopatra* falls back on its budget, a strategy apparent in a montage depicting the queen's rage over Antony's marriage. Cleopatra, dressed in a kaleidoscope of gowns and headdresses, forces Antony to "total surrender." Although critics complained about the grating quality of Taylor's voice (never her strength), it's difficult to imagine any-one delivering lines like "I hear [Octavia] sleeps fully clothed" in calm, round, full tones. Irene Sharaff, not Taylor, Burton, Antony, or Cleopatra, does a star turn in this time-collapsing sequence and in the entire second section, with its more than twenty opulent wigs and costumes. Our study has shown us that, generally, royal biopics would rather risk visual disso-nance than age their subjects, outing the cultural dictum that only young women are beautiful and, thus, worth watching. (As we have seen, Cathe-rine Zeta-Jones in *Catherine the Great* grows from blossoming adolescence to ripe middle age, a passage of time marked by a single artistically placed silvery streak in her cloud of dark hair.) Although twenty years pass, the smooth-skinned Cleopatra looks younger and more hip in the last half, her longer hair gathered into a ponytail that suggests ancient Greece and fore-shadows Haight-Ashbury. But the luster of her appearance and apparel can't mask the absence of an insightful screenplay. The queen's gorgeous cobalt gown and matching high crown, worn with a leopard-skin-lined and -hooded cream cloak, for example, don't give the battle of Actium the

Cleopatra. This glittering costume, which practically encases Elizabeth Taylor, could be a metaphor for the way the role has overshadowed her identity. Few who write about Joseph Mankiewicz's *Cleopatra* can resist fishing for parallels in the lives of the two queens. (Courtesy Jerry Ohlinger's Movie Material Store.)

nuance it lacks. "They told me you were dead," Cleopatra whines, as she tries to explain her departure to Antony, but the rainbow array of gowns she wears as she stalks him from beach to tomb, not meaningful dialogue or action, steals the show. The portrait of an unnatural woman requires nothing but a mannequin; when she is reduced to such a caricature, Cleopatra becomes her clothing.

A predictably colored costume underscores the predictable shift of power in Antony and Cleopatra's relationship. In her final attempt to rouse Antony from his post-Actium torpor, Cleopatra comes to him in a brown robe like a penitent's cloak. They exchange bracing slaps, but he delivers his with enough force to knock her to the ground. Her robe falls back to reveal a plain red dress underneath. On the floor, with her hair down, her Hester Prynnish gown uncovered, and the confession "How wrong I was" springing to her lips, the queen declares that she now welcomes love's mastery, literally reaching the low that the screenplay blunders toward. After she has been reduced—too late—to an apologetic scarlet woman, the queen, as fresh as a bride, chirps happily about Antony's lack of fear as she anticipates their suicide. For their posttomb honeymoon, Cleopatra chooses her garment with care, asking her ladies to dress her in the gold ensemble she wore to enter Rome, explaining that it should enable Antony to recognize her, a sign that she now embraces his view of her as a "little gold doll."

Taylor, who vomited after watching *Cleopatra* at its premier, never provided specific insight about how it felt to experience the queen's humbling. She was no stranger to roles in which women learned hard lessons, but Mankiewicz crafts Cleopatra's life into the archetypal enactment of feminine crime and punishment. Words not spoken color Walter Wanger's disingenuous comment that Taylor was "the only woman" he had known who had "the necessary youth, power and emotion" to play the queen (Wanger and Hyams 3). She was also the only woman he had known whose life would conjure up so many parallels to Cleopatra's. Wanger understood that Fox would purchase her subtext along with her presence. By the time she accepted the role of Cleopatra, a queen who had been labeled a serpent, a scarlet woman, and a fatal lover, Taylor herself had been labeled a child star, a starlet, a sexpot, a serial bride, a glamorous mother, a grieving widow, an Oscar winner, and a home wrecker. Even before the Taylor/Burton affair, Fox was willing to ante up, to stake the studio on a pair of queens. Taylor insists that *Cleopatra* "wasn't a flop" for her; she earned over $7 million (Walker 237), but the role marked her. It placed her in an earning bracket that seemed unthinkable before she reached for it, and it enclosed her and Richard Burton in a circle of notoriety so isolating that only hereditary royals had experienced it.

Like Vivien Leigh before her, Taylor can't escape narrative. Even the sympathetic biographer Alexander Walker encourages readers to see Taylor's life as a pat film plot, a search for lasting love. The media, still trying to trade on her story, uses passing time to give its rehashing operations an aura of retrospection. In 1994, fifty years after her first starring role (in *National Velvet*), the *Ladies' Home Journal* celebrated the anniversary by producing a special issue entitled *Elizabeth Taylor: Portrait of a Legend*, an exercise in praise and blame. While it declares Taylor "a true beauty and a real survivor" and includes stills from her films, this glossy rag touts the "shocking candor" of excerpts from Burton's diaries (including details of Taylor's behavior when sloshed) and "the dramas and traumas of her private life." Illustrating the powerful urge to see the existence of a film queen as a study in extremes, the editors take care to enumerate the marriages of "Elizabeth Taylor Hilton Wilding Todd Fisher Burton Burton Warner Fortenay" before they canonize her, praising her involvement in charities, especially her work to lessen the stigma of AIDS. More valuable than the content, the portrait of Taylor on the cover, her lids darkly shadowed, a little liner extending the corners of her eyes, reminds us that, no matter how diligently we try, we can't read the private truth in the public life.

Antony and Cleopatra (1972)

George Bernard Shaw called *Antony and Cleopatra* an elevation of "sexual infatuation" (qtd. in C. Marshall 300). You could read Shaw's *Caesar and Cleopatra* as a response to Shakespeare's play, an extended meditation on the triumph of Roman (male) rectitude over Oriental (feminine) amorality. *Antony and Cleopatra*, however, doesn't depict the pair's sexual escapades; Shakespeare places accounts of Antony and Cleopatra's hedonistic behavior in the mouths of others. Much more than a paean to pleasure or a dogged allocation of blame, *Antony and Cleopatra*, an unacknowledged source for DeMille, Shaw, and Mankiewicz, insists that the attraction in the lovers' tale lies in the tension between legend and life, or, as Cynthia Marshall says: "Shakespeare offers mythic invocation alongside a chastening skepticism" (299). Although *Antony and Cleopatra* is a play, not a bio-pic, any discussion of the queen in film must consider this important work, with its descriptions of Cleopatra that transcend page, stage, and screen. Lines from Shakespeare, not Shaw, engraved on a plaque in Eaton Square, serve as a tribute to Vivien Leigh: "Now boast thee, Death, in thy posses-sion lies / A lass unparalleled" (qtd. in Walker, *Vivien*, 304).

Shakespeare understood that a goddess alone couldn't constitute an "unparalleled" lass. To give Cleopatra's portrait depth and dimension, he juxtaposes myth and motion, a very modern move. The most compelling mythic description of Cleopatra comes via Enobarbus, Antony's right-hand man, who reconstructs the vision he saw sailing into Tarsus: "The barge she sat in like a burnished throne, burned on the water" (2.2.227–28). Those famous words, lit from Plutarch's fire, enthrall Enobarbus's listeners. They hang on his picture of Cleopatra: "In her pavilion—cloth of gold, of tissue— / O'erpicturing that Venus where we see / The fancy outwork Na-ture" (2.2.236–38). They also hang on his even more famous claim about her inexhaustible charm: "Age cannot wither her, nor custom stale / her infinite variety. Other women cloy / The appetites they feed / But she makes hungry where she most satisfies" (2.2.276–79). Mankiewicz and De-Mille bring Cleopatra's arrival on the royal barge to life, but in the play, where large-scale scenes happen offstage, Shakespeare entrusts the Tarsus moment to Enobarbus.

Against this construct of memory Shakespeare places the personal Cleopatra, who teases, pouts, worries, chastises, and cheats, challenging viewers to merge the woman and the legend. No director, so far, has achieved an adaptation of *Antony and Cleopatra* that sings like Franco Zeffirelli's 1968 or Baz Luhrmann's 1996 visionary adaptations of *Romeo and Juliet* or like Kenneth Branagh's triumphant 1993 *Much Ado about Nothing*. The two film versions we examine—one grisly, one good—show how completely the queen's afterimage depends on interpretation and performance.

Hildegarde Neil, who played Cleopatra to Charlton Heston's Antony in the film *Antony and Cleopatra* (1972), directed by Heston, had to con-tend with more than the usual difficulties of learning a Shakespearean part and tuning it for the screen. There had been, after all, a very visible Cleopa-tra whose image still dominated the media. Even though nine years had passed since the release of Fox's behemoth, the flavor of that rich fare hadn't faded enough to make space for a fresh vision. Neil also faced the daunting task of playing Cleopatra to an actor who had internalized Antony. Charlton Heston turned to *Antony and Cleopatra* for his directorial debut as one turns to an old friend. In his youth, he played Antony in an amateur film; in a 1947 Broadway revival, he played Proculeius to Katharine Cornell's Cleopatra; in 1970, he played Marc Antony in a film adaptation of *Julius Caesar* starring Jason Robards. Pushing fifty in 1972, Heston shopped the idea of the film around and found financial backers (including himself). As Antony, in a work he knew "as well as any other script [he] ever worked on," he hoped to recapture the high of his Academy Award–winning performance as Judah Ben-Hur (Heston 346).

Heston's crude two-hour-and-forty-minute take on *Antony and Cleopatra* wasn't another *Ben-Hur* (William Wyler, 1959) or another *Cleopatra;* the film never made it to wide release. Bad reviews followed its London premier and its discouraging Washington, DC, opening in September 1973. *Antony and Cleopatra's* uneven pace and questionable editing, plus Heston's predilection for keeping the camera on himself, validate the critical thumbs-down. In the first ten minutes of the film, Antony, not Cleopatra, gets nearly naked in one eye-popping scene. As he changes his tunic, Heston strips down to the equivalent of a jock strap, revealing more than we expected (or wanted) to see of his body. That moment adds to the overwhelming impression that Heston would gladly have shortened the title to *Antony*, an abbreviation he uses consistently in his journals.

Heston's screenplay repositions Enobarbus's description of Cleopatra, significantly altering its impact. Shakespeare introduces the passage after Antony has promised to wed Octavia, Caesar's sister. Antony exits with the other members of the triumvirate, but Enobarbus remains with Octavian's inner circle. His words, delivered to these insiders, gloss Antony's promise.

Antony may not understand the depth of his involvement with Cleopatra, but his right-hand man, a keen observer, believes he does. The passage raises various apparitions for Enobarbus's auditors. Agrippa remembers the queen he has met; Maecenas imagines a goddess. Theatergoers must cast themselves back to the queen they have just seen while Enobarbus's words color their next view of her.

The most important purpose of the passage, however, is to convince Enobarbus's audience that Antony's return to Egypt is a foregone conclusion, his longing unquenchable. The queen? Unforgettable. Heston alters that crucial message. In the film, Antony's marriage to the chilly Octavia

(Carmen Sevilla) has already taken place. He strolls in the garden, where he overhears Enobarbus (Eric Porter) describing Cleopatra's arrival. Antony's off to Egypt. Although the next, stirring scene of his galley in full sail over a rippling sea gives the film some needed speed, the change in position alters the audience for and the point of the speech. Heston aims Enobarbus's words at Antony, making them his motive, as if Antony needs a spur to spark his passion, as if his memory of the queen is fading, as if Enobarbus's description, not the queen, arouses him.

Heston's queen, Hildegarde Neil, isn't convincing as Cleopatra. Of course, no one knows exactly what the real Cleopatra looked like, but the cool, pretty Neil, with her cloud of dark hair, deep blue eyes, sharp cheekbones, slender body, and nasal, cultured accent, looks and sounds less believably Mediterranean than Taylor, and she can't quite summon the fire that Cleopatra needs. Heston recognized Neil's dissonance but chose her anyway. He had considered and rejected Sophia Loren (not a native speaker of English), Glenda Jackson (not up to the part), and Irene Pappas (who "might be difficult to handle") (Heston 354). Neil's problems are compounded by the writer/actor/director tag team Heston throws at her.

Shakespeare begins his development of the living queen in act 1, scene 1. With consummate skill, Cleopatra presses Antony to measure his love for her while she mockingly urges him to hear a messenger just arrived from Rome. She insists that the call comes from Fulvia, his wife, or from Octavian, the "scarce-bearded" Caesar (1.1.24), both of whom, she intimates, can make Antony dance to their tunes. Heston cuts all (yes, *all*) Cleopatra's opening lines except for the first two about the bounds of love. While a romantic theme by Augusto Alguero swells, the queen lies, limp and mute, listening to Antony's declaration: "Let Rome in Tiber melt . . . / Here is my space." Shakespeare's Cleopatra teases Antony into those words. This Cleopatra moons over him. Antony's hairy chest peeking through a slit-to-the-waist embroidered robe, not the queen's wit, draws attention in this first scene. After he crops her words, Heston literally covers Neil in a full-body embrace.

Discarded lines and limited action keep Cleopatra a shadowy figure. Heston even manipulates Antony's death scene to diminish Cleopatra's importance. After her death, her enemy, Caesar Octavian, encourages her legend, drawing attention to her cold beauty: "She looks like sleep, / As she would catch another Antony / in her strong toil of grace" (5.2.415–18), but before her apotheosis comes a relentlessly human moment trapped by history. Cleopatra, grieving, imprisoned in her own mausoleum, was reunited with dying Antony, who had "to be hoisted through a window in the . . . upper story." Cleopatra and her women, "with the utmost difficulty," brought him in (Grant 223). Shakespeare follows history. In the play, Antony is brought to the monument, but Cleopatra cannot open the ground-level door, she says, because she is safe and prefers to die than risk capture. The queen acts as the catalyst for Antony's entry into the tomb, calling out: "Help, Charmion, Help, Iras, help! / Help, friends below! Let's draw him thither" (4.15.15–16).

Heston restages the scene. His Antony, macho to the finish, lurches to the tomb alone and beats on the door for entry. When Cleopatra appears above him, she speaks the lines about her own safety, but not those about "draw[ing] him thither." Antony grabs Cleopatra's dangling scarf as if it were a rope and begins hauling himself up. Only then does Cleopatra call for her ladies to help; the alternatives would be for her to topple from the tomb or be strangled by her lover's grip. Would she have refused him entry if he hadn't forced the issue? Antony steals the initiative, and his ninja climb leaves the audience pondering Cleopatra's loyalty. Neil's over-the-top performance complicates the already confusing mix. As if goosed into anguish, she screams and weeps, a different Cleopatra than the one who drifts through much of the film.

Antony and Cleopatra (1975)

Light bathes the television adaptation of Trevor Nunn's *Antony and Cleopatra* (1975), illuminating an Antony (Richard Johnson) and Cleopatra (Janet Suzman) worthy of Shakespeare's lines. The weakest thing about this performance is its minimalist look (to call the props a set would be a stretch). After a disturbing title sequence in which live actors teeter, trying to hold poses as figures in Old Kingdom murals, the designer Michael Bailey scatters a few rugs, drapes some veils, hands out alabaster goblets, and calls it Egypt. In the theater, where modern audiences have been trained to accept multipurpose cubes as stand-ins for beheading blocks and dining tables, such stylish signification would be more than fine, but, by 1975, television viewers were hardly strangers to movieworthy sophistication. *Masterpiece Theater,* for example, had already mounted the stunning, fully staged miniseries *Elizabeth R* starring Glenda Jackson. Perhaps the on-steroids hugeness of past epics should make the lean profile of this *Antony and Cleopatra* refreshing, but, to us, it just feels skimpy and tight. To mask the absence of anything interesting in the background, the camera must stay in motion or keep in close.

Another video version of *Antony and Cleopatra* (1983), part of a series aimed at teachers, unrolls on an even barer stage, a reproduction of the Globe Theater. Lynn Redgrave and Timothy Dalton star; they, and all the cast, enunciate so carefully that Shakespeare's poetry sounds like fodder for a learn-Elizabethan-English-while-you-drive CD. Perhaps to compensate for their monotonous delivery, the players adopt an unmodulated liveliness. Skip this almost parodic disaster for the Suzman and Johnson version, where it's clear, five minutes into the first act, that the cast, skillfully directed by Jon Scoffield, won't let the lack of ambience distract them from tone, shading, and pace.

It seems almost unfair to compare Hildegarde Neil's performance to Janet Suzman's. Suzman doesn't have to endure solipsistic editing or a shot-seeking costar (Johnson's powerful, not selfish), but the difference between them is greater than the sum of those problems. Suzman is just plain terrific; a nomination for a BAFTA award recognized her excellence. She too is light eyed, pale, slender, and in her early thirties (the same age as Neil). She too has a cultured accent, but the slight hook of her nose, the lift of her chin, the narrowing of her eyes, the calculated turn of her head, all suggest that Cleopatra's profile on those coins may have been an attempt to capture a woman a little like this. Suzman's Cleopatra also trades on the currency of the 1970s; her down-to-there straight bob marries the period look of the queen and the ethos of a flower chick. Her beauty comes from animation, and every inch of her is alive. In the first scene, her body moves with command, her gestures reinforce each nuance of her words. Heston and Neil only appeared in the opening scene, but a full retinue surrounds this Antony and Cleopatra, and the queen plays to that audience. When she explains that Caesar may want Antony to "take in that kingdom, and enfranchise that," she *becomes* Caesar, standing with her legs apart, pointing out, stiff armed, the direction of Antony's assignment.

Costuming defines Suzman's Cleopatra. Not come-hither (like Colbert's), or Oriental (like Leigh's), or overwhelming (like Taylor's), or nondescript (like Neil's), Suzman's body-conscious gowns underscore her flexibility. In color, texture, and concept, her first costume resembles Antony's; both wear gold-trimmed white pleated tunics and white robes. There the similarity ends. Cleopatra's small, firm breasts strain against her V-necked, sleeveless bodice. The fitted waist focuses attention on her supple middle, and the sash, belted twice around her waist, dips to mark her erogenous zone with a knot. Suzman's not buxom; her body is taut as a bowstring, strong and vital.

Suzman's strength intensifies Cleopatra's precarious position as she perches on the ledge of her mausoleum watching for Antony. No ambiguity clouds this Cleopatra's eagerness to bring her lover into her tomb. As soon as she sees his attendants carrying him, she leans out, stretching her arm toward him, her fingers hyperextended. Antony and Cleopatra give their last thoughts to each other, lip to lip, in a charmed circle that has its own atmosphere, like a pas de deux. Suzman earns her bloodcurdling shriek at Antony's death by building a character who's "no more but e'en a woman" (4.15.86) but no less than an eternally fascinating queen.

In Cleopatra's death scene, the designer Ann Curtis loses her deft touch. The queen's striped robe, cut in the shape of a mummy case, is meant to function as art, a heavy-handed attempt to confront audiences with the queen, packaged for the tomb, and ready for mythmakers. The cartoonish costume disrupts the tragic mode. Minor flaws, however, shouldn't keep viewers from seeking out this performance. The two most recent views of Cleopatra's life, another pair of opposites, do not sate our hunger to see a great actress play the queen in a great film, but they do predict future possibilities.

Cleopatra (1999) and Rome (2005–2007)

How do you translate a historic icon into a postmodern idiom? Although this question could be asked about all the queens we examine, the one furthest from us in time, the pre-Christian Cleopatra, should be the most difficult to update. No twenty-first-century feature film has tried, but two made-for-television productions prove the limitations of the conditional tense. Cleopatra and Rome agree that updating the queen's life is no big deal. These splashy sagas start from a common language, but their versions of the queen's life, like two distinct dialects, are light years apart in interpretation and execution.

Some grand exterior shots grant Hallmark Entertainment's *Cleopatra*, starring Leonor Varela, Timothy Dalton, Billy Zane, and Rupert Graves, an initial richness belied by its stupefying blandness. A stale exercise in surfaces, *Cleopatra* follows the DeMille path, but it assembles its bits and pieces without energy or humor. The two-hour-and-forty-minute special claims to be based on Margaret George's *The Memoirs of Cleopatra* (1997). George, who rides the upper edge of the history/romance genre, specializes in researched fictions about historic figures. Her pleasant, made-up memoir humanizes Cleopatra, imagining her fears, friends, and obsessions. But *based on* is always a relative term. The writers Stephen Harrigan and Anton Diether use a claw-machine approach to adaptation, randomly snagging and jettisoning bits of George's sprawling novel. They pluck up a few of Cleopatra's friends, like Olympos (Art Malik), and plop them into the action, where they flounder like fish, but—maddeningly—they don't try for George's best one hundred pages, a sketch of Cleopatra's childhood. Instead of going where no film has gone before, *Cleopatra* covers the mandatory chunk of Cleopatra's life from Caesar to the tomb. Ignoring George's attempts to be coherent, the adaptors go for pastiche, pushing *Cleopatra* straight into the palpitating heart of the romance genre.

Anyone who has seen the Catherine Zeta-Jones version of *Catherine the Great* (1995) understands that there's nothing new about launching a fresh face in a royal soap opera. Varela, at least, gets to leave her international mark on a role generally played by actresses who could pass for Nordic and who hail from America or England (Suzman comes from pre-reconciliation South Africa). Half Chilean, half French, the multilingual Varela, with her brown eyes, honeyed skin, and dark curls, broadens the casting pool. Her performance in *Sleep Dealer* (Alex Rivera, 2008) says that she's capable of more than she gives as the queen of queens. Franc Roddam, who directed a good television version of *Moby Dick* in 1998, settles for synecdoche in *Cleopatra*. Caesar swaggers; Marc Antony lifts his eyebrows; Octavian smirks; Cleopatra pouts. Varela's flat delivery can't lift the flatter dialogue, but this isn't *Moby Dick,* and flesh, not profundity, matters most in a bodice ripper.

Cleopatra and *Rome* agree that an update has to include more sex. A modern audience expects more flesh than Colbert and William's linked hands and more frequency than Taylor and Burton's minimal caresses. *Cleopatra* goes for jiggle, not sensuality. Carlo Franzero mentions Cleopatra's "tunic of a transparent tissue," a garment that makes the queen's "perfect breasts appear bare" (70). George, a swimmer in the same limited source pool, describes a gown "as transparent as early morning" (126). The designer Enrico Sabattini runs with that image. The combination of Varela's lush, entirely visible body and young Cleopatra's lack of sexual experience ups the titillation factor, a romance novel staple that Harrigan and Diether embrace. George imagines that Cleopatra's last night as a virgin was a learning experience. In the memoir, the princess interviews a prostitute before setting out to bed Caesar. The screenplay introduces Cleopatra in that scene. Varela listens behind a curtain while the prostitute rips away her veil of ignorance with valuable precoital tips like, "Men like to be touched." Cleopatra's second deflowering by Marc Antony (more violent and more graphic) demonstrates that the queen no longer needs instruction. Always satisfied with surface, *Cleopatra* assumes that Varela's body and the sex scenes adequately cover the area of sexual attraction.

Violence too escalates in both television versions of the queen's life. *Cleopatra* uses Arsinoe (Cassandra Voyagis), Cleopatra's ambitious sister, to introduce a smidgen of mean girls dialogue and a pinch of sadism. George sticks to history in her treatment of Arsinoe, whom Caesar marched into Rome in chains. Going against tradition, Caesar spared her life, an "act of mercy" that Cleopatra may not have appreciated (Grant 86). There's little mercy for Arsinoe in *Cleopatra*. Cleopatra orders her sister's assassination, then listens, nipples erect, while a guard strangles her. The screenplay's increased violence nudges *Cleopatra* closer to Varela's genre of choice. "One of my biggest dreams is to be in action movies," Varela told an interviewer in 2001. She got her wish in *Blade II* (Guillermo del Toro, 2002), a vampire vehicle starring Wesley Snipes, but her slow-motion carpet roll has the aura of the martial arts epic, and there's a quick glimpse of the queen in her chambers (more Radisson Courtyard than Ptolemaic palace) practicing an exercise regimen that looks suspiciously like tai chi.

Cleopatra capitalizes on Varela's training in "juggling, acrobatics, gymnastics and dancing" (Loos) to morph George's introspective queen into an action figure, trading up from Claudette Colbert's murderous jab at Pothinus. In another slow-motion sequence during Caesar's battle for Alexandria, the queen, robes floating around her, grabs a pike and impales an attacker, arcing his skewered body over her head. It wouldn't make sense for such a warrior to sit out the Battle of Actium, so *Cleopatra* adds a scene in which the queen, with teeth bared and sword aloft, rallies her troops to repel boarders and finishes off an enemy soldier with a neat thrust. These additions could be seen as profeminist if they weren't so blatantly focused on selling Varela's body and adding gore. *Cleopatra* happily abandons its literary source for a lower road, producing an easy, sleazy video-game update that reshuffles the givens.

Rome doesn't do that. The twenty-two-episode HBO/BBC series is obviously not a biopic, and Cleopatra is not its single focus. We include it because *Rome* proves that a modern look at Cleopatra can be more than a reheated ragout. This Cleopatra (Lyndsey Marshal), introduced in a first-season episode entitled *Caesarion,* captivatingly combines charm, self-preservation, and deceit. In a shot reminiscent of DeMille's in-the-boudoir opening, the camera travels up a chain to a foot, then to an ankle, then to an opium pipe. Finally, it rests on the sated, closed face of the presumptive ruler of Egypt, held captive by Ptolemy's faction. Marshal's little-boy haircut (and her opium high) could easily make the transition from Egypt to Tribeca. She's wearing a plain, stained linen shift and no makeup. This antivamp's sensuality has little to do with transparent robes, although she wears several. Marshal's Cleopatra understands sex and calculates the uses that pleasure might serve. She knows how to touch men. Once freed of her chains, she doesn't hesitate to raise a probing foot to investigate a Roman guard's state of arousal or, comically, to clap her thighs open in preparation for love. She orders one of the Roman guards who deliver her from her captors to "enter her" so that she can multiply her chances of pregnancy before she meets Caesar. That she will have sex with Caesar is, as far as she is concerned, a no-brainer. "I will have him or die," she informs Charmion (Catherine Hunt). William J. McDonald, the writer, and Stephen Shill, the director, don't bother with titillation. Cleopatra's women watch and applaud the acrobatic sex between their skilled mistress and Pullo, the Roman guard.

Aware of the historical sources for Cleopatra's life, and conscious of the film tradition they follow, *Rome*'s creators aim for the person, not the myth. They know that their view of Cleopatra's pragmatic sexuality breaks new film ground, as does their retelling of the carpet story. The two Roman guards (the characters who connect the episodes) deliver the queen to Caesar (Ciaran Hinds) in a linen gear bag (a possible translation of Plutarch). When the bag is unfastened, Cleopatra, sweating and dusty, sits up and brushes the sand from her arms. But don't imagine that the magic is missing from this meeting. When Cleopatra turns to Caesar, she straightens her shoulders, lifts her chin, and gracefully holds out her hand. As he helps her up, Caesar doesn't have to say that he finds her ravishing. Their eyes lock; their fates do too.

Filled with violence as graphic as the sex, *Rome* employs gore as exposition. Every severed head and pool of blood carries information about culture or character. In this spirit, Cleopatra and Mark Antony (James Purefoy) demonstrate the Ptolemaic attitude toward slaves. The besotted lovers play at indoor archery with real arrows and a stag (a slave in a deerskin) as their trembling target. Court followers applaud their shots, including the last fatal hit, while Roman messengers stare in disbelief. Could this kohl-eyed, skirted dissolute be Lord Antony? This episode *No God Can Stop a Hungry Man*, like Conrad's *Heart of Darkness*, beautifully illustrates going native. A later episode, *About Your Father*, with its court full of entangled bodies, a melange that could have been inspired by Hieronymus Bosch, frames Antony's and Cleopatra's death in sex and violence. Although we don't like *Rome*'s parodic take on the queen's suicide—she worries about bloating and discoloration—we admire its commitment, stated by the director, John Maybury, to "finding a new way in."

Rome's revisionist view throws its predecessors into sharp relief, clarifying their approaches. Invoking signifiers satisfied DeMille, while Shaw launched a corrective, pigeonholing the queen as an example of bad DNA and unfortunate biology. Mankiewicz, lapsing into a DeMillean portrait, couldn't combine the woman and the vistas. Films based on *Antony and Cleopatra* don't always transmit Shakespeare's modern vision of the complex being behind the icon. Margaret George's attempt at the first person gets lost in a lazy translation. Although *Rome* scraps the conventional collection of bits and goes for the person, infinite possibilities and a list of unattempted topics remain. Cleopatra's pre-Caesar years stay in the shadows. Her relationships with her women, the true insiders in her world, have yet to be imagined. The downhill slide that propelled Antony and Cleopatra to mutual destruction awaits a narrator. The world presses in on a postmodern audience ready to rethink, not retry, Cleopatra. Twenty-first-century Western viewers finally know the names and locations of Middle Eastern countries and struggle for any key to their complex histories. We are watching and listening, hoping to glimpse Cleopatra and to hear her voice, so long silent.

Chapter Four

Mary Stuart, Queen of Scotland

This realm being divided in factions as it is, cannot be contained in order, unless our authority be assisted and forthset by the fortification of a man who must take upon his person in the execution of justice.
—Mary, Queen of Scots

Carolyn Heilbrun has written: "Women who acquire power are more likely to be criticized for it than are the men who have always had it" (16). Witness the flurry of attention aimed at Katie Couric when she made the move from cohost of NBC's *Today Show* to solo anchorwoman of the *CBS Evening News.* Hair too severe, delivery too serious, delivery too light, stories too frivolous, and on and on the critics wagged. Was Katie happy? Was Katie sorry she made the move? Was she making too much money? Could she handle the CBS power seat occupied by giants like Walter Cronkite and Dan Rather? Wouldn't she be better off with a male coanchor? Brian Williams's shift from MSNBC to the anchor chair vacated by Tom Brokaw, on the other hand, caused little fanfare, nary a ripple in the broadcasting waters. And no one made any comments about the color of his hair and how he parted it or insisted that he work with a female coanchor.

With royal women, the criticism gets kicked up a notch. In the case of our queens (with the possible exception of Marie Antoinette, who had little, if any, real power), the prevailing wisdom wrestled with one central question: How could a mere woman wield all that power wisely or alone? A queen in particular defied the laws of God and man. To be a monarch was "a rare and unnatural phenomenon which could only be regularized by speedy union with a prince who would rule over her in private and guide her in her public, God-given role as queen" (Dunn 5). Every action, every decision, exposed a queen to criticism and challenge, while few people

Mary Stuart, Queen of Scotland. (Courtesy Bildarchiv Preussischer Kulturbesitz/
Art Resource, New York.)

dared question Henry VIII and lived to tell about it. Elizabeth I, Henry's daughter, foregrounded the problem when she explained to Parliament why she wouldn't execute Mary of Scotland even though the safety of her kingdom and her person depended on it: "We Princes . . . are set on stages in the sight and view of all the world duly observed. The eyes of many behold our actions; a spot is soon spied in our garments; a blemish quickly noted in our doings. It behooveth us therefore to be careful that our proceedings be just and honourable" (Pryor 89). This is probably one of the reasons Elizabeth had such a tough time making decisions, but not much has changed in four hundred years. Today's royals, like celebrities, live in glass castles, their every move watched, stalked, and reported to a hungry public by an emboldened press that refuses to recognize the moat. Tabloids now catalog the spots of princes, while art sways our perceptions of them by magnifying, minimizing, even erasing their blemishes. In the past hundred years, even screen images of royalty, women in particular, crackle with the dramatized conflicts and pitfalls of power and love, of public versus private selves.

John Ford's *Mary of Scotland* (1936) and Charles Jarrott's *Mary, Queen of Scots* (1971) focus on this issue of women and power. Both films privilege the private over the public, the woman over the monarch. *Mary of Scotland*, based on the 1933 Pulitzer Prize–winning historical play by Maxwell Anderson, sets up "the life-and-death struggle for supremacy" between Mary Stuart (Katharine Hepburn) and Elizabeth Tudor (Florence Eldridge) from its opening title card. Two heads on one coin, Mary's private face wins the toss here, while Elizabeth's public image recedes to the dark side of the hand. Since both Marian biopics centralize this dynamic between the queens, it seems appropriate to discuss a bit of Elizabeth's background also in this chapter. As Jane Dunn carefully, painstakingly lays out in her biography, *Elizabeth and Mary: Cousins, Rivals, Queens*, these two women, who shared the same royal bloodline and experienced firsthand what it was like to navigate power in a man's world, were shaped by vastly different forces.

Mary had every advantage. The great-granddaughter of Henry VII, she was declared queen of Scotland only days after her birth and her father's death; sent to the French court of Henry II when she was six; married to François, the dauphin of France, at sixteen; crowned queen of

France at seventeen; and widowed at eighteen. She returned to Scotland shortly thereafter, but her romantic and impetuous nature, her French sensibilities, her Catholic background, and her lack of any governing experience doomed her to failure. Though she possessed a certain charm and a fun-loving spirit that drew people to her, she had been petted, coddled, and raised with a sense of her own self-importance from the cradle and grew into a willful, moody, politically naive woman detached from her subjects (French or Scottish), lacking in discipline and self-control, and constantly involved in plots to usurp Elizabeth. Given this type of personality, as Rosalind Miles (*I, Elizabeth*) has pointed out, "at every single point of her life, she made the wrong decision" (interview with Rosalind Miles). Dunn explains that Mary's decisions always sprang from "impetuous feeling": "This was to make her attractive as a woman, compelling as a romantic heroine and impressive in command when things went her way. But it made her tragically fallible as a queen" (15). Right up until the ax fell, she refused to accept any culpability for her actions.

Tragic flaws aside, however, Mary never stood a chance of ruling over the Protestant Scottish clansmen with their shifting loyalties and quarrelsome spirit. Instead, this only child of James V and Mary of Guise became a lightning rod for every ambitious noble who aimed high. She was raised up and brought down by men and her own uncontrollable desires for them. She put men at the center of her life and her personal feelings over the welfare of her subjects. She lived her narrative through men.

Elizabeth was born to rule men and die a virgin. England was her husband, her people her children, as she was fond of pointing out to her councilors, nobles, ambassadors, foreign princes, and anyone else who badgered her to marry and produce an heir. Crowned queen of England at twenty-five, she quickly demonstrated her divine right to public power and her sovereignty over men. "I will have but one mistress, and no master" (qtd. in Weir 166), she once told the Earl of Leicester, Robert Dudley. Imperiled early on by events in her life that were out of her control, Elizabeth wasn't about to defer or relinquish control to a man once she gained it.

The granddaughter of Henry VII, the daughter of Henry VIII and Anne Boleyn, she was one step in front of Mary Stuart for the throne of England but two behind her half brother Edward (the son of Henry VIII and his third wife, Jane Seymour) and her half sister Mary (the daughter of Henry VIII and his first wife, Catherine of Aragon). When Henry had Anne beheaded on trumped-up charges of adultery and married Jane Seymour, who finally bore him a son, he declared both Mary and Elizabeth illegitimate only to reinstate them in the line of succession shortly before he died.

Elizabeth survived both the death of her brother and her sister's bloody reign by keeping a cool head, biding her time, sidestepping scandal, and studying. She had a "fantastic intelligence," Glenda Jackson recalled thirty years after her Emmy Award–winning performance in the six-part *Elizabeth R* (1971), which we discuss in chapter 7 (interview with Glenda Jackson). Jackson, who played Elizabeth again that year in *Mary, Queen of Scots*, remembered doing copious research for the role and thinking: "If you had been on her good side, she must have been the most fascinating, stimulating, exciting person to be around. Equally, if you had been on her bad side or caught her on one of her bad days, it must have been one of the most painful and brutal experiences. . . . She could curse and swear and destroy people with her tongue." She drove her nobles to near madness with her indecisiveness yet inspired their lifelong devotion and trust. She had an unwavering loyalty to her people, an unshakable belief in her God-given right to rule, and a shrewd diplomatic policy of keeping princely suitors dangling for years, thus preserving the peace between her country and foreign states while growing too old to marry or produce an heir. She kept religious factions in a relatively balanced state for forty-five years, slowly building England as a prosperous world power.

In a sense, Elizabeth wrote her own public narrative. Jane Dunn argues: "Her tenacity of mind and loyalty of feeling meant that she revisited many times in her speeches the trials of her past as well as the triumphs. In this way she involved her people in an act of sympathetic imagination and in her lifetime created her own biography for them to share" (30). But there was a private side to Elizabeth that no one knew. Jackson mused: "I don't think anyone ever knew what she was really like. . . . There was something inside her, hidden. Maybe formidable experiences in youth made her keep her center to herself" (interview with Glenda Jackson). Thus, as the Scottish queen's reign unfolded in a series of horrific personal choices, Elizabeth looked on, supportive, but scarcely able to comprehend a sister sovereign's inability to overrule "private desire" for the "public good" (Dunn 164).

Mary of Scotland (1936)

Even though history and biography highlight these distinctions in background, temperament, and governance, art can't seem to resist the temptation to canonize Mary and caricature Elizabeth, as evidenced in John Ford's 1936 film. Mike Vanderlan rightly suggests that, in Anderson's play, "Mary is idealized, but in Dudley Nichols' script and Ford's handling she becomes almost Christ-like" (1548). Though the title suggests that the film focuses on Mary (and it does for the most part), Ford constantly cuts back and forth between Mary and Elizabeth as a means of contrasting the two women. Elizabeth's temperamental, paranoid behavior comes off as monstrous compared with Mary's saintly victim, as the exposition of the film illustrates. Trumpets blare and announce "the Most High and Mighty Sovereign, by the Grace of God, Queen of England" as Elizabeth stomps through a line of guards and bowing nobles. "Get up. Get up. Are you glued to the floor?" she barks. Every inch the drama queen, she flops in a chair at the head of a long table in a huff and goes into a tirade about Mary: she's returning to Scotland from France, she refuses to acknowledge Elizabeth as queen of England, she throws Elizabeth's taint of illegitimacy in her face, she uses her personal charms to lure men to her. It goes on. At the end of it, she collapses across the table and asks Lord Throckmorton: "Suppose she lands. What then?" Elizabeth answers her own question. Her sea hawks must covertly attack Mary's ship and prevent her from reaching Scotland.

This Elizabeth is haughty, mean, conniving, jealous, and insecure. She sneers a lot and stares into mirrors—at one point looking from a beautiful miniature of Mary to her own aging reflection. Reveling in Mary's every misstep, she reminds us of the Wicked Queen in Snow White, whose mantra, remember, is "Mirror, mirror on the wall, who is the fairest of them all."

Perhaps Ford got a sneak preview of Disney's animated film, which came out one year after Mary of Scotland. As we see to a more pronounced effect in 1939's The Private Lives of Elizabeth and Essex, the English queen becomes a cartoon, a mass of conflicting exaggerations. After this introduction to Elizabeth, Ford cuts to Mary in a small boat, attended by her female companions. Mary of Guise, her regent in Scotland, has died, and Mary, suffering from the double loss of her mother and young husband, is

Mary of Scotland. John Ford loved Hepburn's angular face and spends much of the film shooting it in glorious close-ups. But he grew about as bored directing this costume romance as his star looks here. Hepburn would rather have played Elizabeth I. After all, Hepburn said, she was the powerful one. (Courtesy Jerry Ohlinger's Movie Material Store.)

returning to her homeland to take her place on the throne. Faithful servants paddle silently through the darkness and fog, a motif that reappears
later, suggesting Mary's uncertain future. Lilting Scottish music plays as
she steps onto her native soil, falls to her knees, and softly prays that she
will "rule with piety and wisdom." Ford holds a close-up on Mary's face,
bathed in light, as she lifts her eyes toward heaven. Casting the exquisitely
beautiful and photogenic Katharine Hepburn in this role ensures our own
rapt attention to her every move. Ford said that she was his first and only
choice as Mary (Sharpe 166). He watched all her movies, studying "every
angle of her strange, sharp face and chiseled nose, the mouth, the long
neck," and deciding "how best to light her features and what make-up to
use in order to achieve for her a genuine majesty" (Sharpe 333). Ford never
says how much time he spent studying and lighting Florence Eldridge. The
juxtaposition of these two opening scenes leaves no doubt that, whatever
the conflicts between the two women, Mary will emerge the victor even
though she goes to the block.

Unlike the barren vessel Elizabeth, Mary does her queenly, and womanly, duty by marrying Henry Stuart, Lord Darnley, and producing an heir
who will rule Scotland as James VI and, after Elizabeth's death, England
as James I. Never mind that the real queen acted rashly. Infatuated, she
rushed into marriage with Darnley against her nobles' wishes and without
dispensation from the pope, a necessary step since Mary and Darnley were
cousins and Catholics. At one point, Elizabeth herself had put Darnley
forth as a match for her cousin. Dunn posits that Elizabeth thought to use
Darnley (1) to threaten Mary, as he was a rival heir to the English throne
and a male one at that, (2) to distract Mary from marrying one of England's old enemies, Spain or France, or (3) to bind Mary to a weak, ineffectual, disastrous king and husband (214). Whatever her intentions, she
changed her mind and was furious at the match. Elizabeth also proposed
her own favorite, Robert Dudley, Earl of Leicester, as a possible marriage
partner for Mary, probably as a means of keeping someone she could actually trust next to Mary.

Mary exploded in anger, and we see this reaction in the film. Lord
Throckmorton (Alan Mowbray) conveys Elizabeth's idea, and an insulted
Mary spits fire: "Her favorite? Her leavings? And now she wants to cast
him off on me? Make me a laughingstock before the world?" The film has

Mary goaded into marrying Darnley (Douglas Walton) to spite Elizabeth when, in fact, she married him because she was besotted with him. However, she quickly became disillusioned with her spoiled, drunken, abusive husband. (The film shows her repulsed by him from the beginning.) She soon found herself embroiled in the plot to kill him and, with lightning speed, married Lord Bothwell, one of the men accused of his murder. In doing so, she lost the affection of her people and the support of some powerful nobles. However, as Antonia Fraser and others have argued, Mary was ill equipped to rule over a people she hardly knew or understood, she was exhausted and sick, and she was surrounded by treacherous, traitorous, ambitious Scottish clansmen (including her own illegitimate half brother James Stuart, Earl of Moray) with their own agendas.

Fraser suggests that Mary looked to the nearest, strongest man for help, that man being James Hepburn (a distant relative of Katharine Hepburn's), Earl of Bothwell. Fredric March plays Bothwell as a blustering, swaggering, but likable man's man. He's accompanied wherever he goes by his band of merry bagpipers and loyal dog. He affectionately teases Mary's ladies and challenges the bad guys. But Mary's announcement that she's going to marry the effeminate Darnley flips his kilt. He kicks a chair out of the way and says: "You can't. I'm a soldier, and I love ya." Mary protests—weakly. "Why didn't you pick a *man?*" he asks as he storms out the door. The film's tagline marketed the movie as "one of the greatest love stories of all time," but history and biographies have not been so kind. Fraser calls Bothwell boastful, violent, and bullying, "the last person to unite successfully that essentially disunited and suspicious body, the Scottish nobility" (263). A married man, a philanderer, an opportunist, he quickly divorced his wife, "abducted" Mary, and married her, some sources suggesting not against her will. Kirkaldy of Grange reported at the time: "'She has said that she cares not to lose France, England, and her own country for him, and will go with him to the world's end in a white peticoat ere she leave him'" (qtd. in Dunn 297). Bothwell, on the other hand, continued to keep his ex-wife as his mistress, which made for some stormy scenes with Mary. None of this appears in the film, which distills enough of the couple's bad characteristics to make them attractive and heroic.

Mary justified her speedy third marriage when she wrote: "This realm being divided in factions as it is, cannot be contained in order, unless our authority be assisted and forthset by the fortification of a man who must take upon his person in the execution of justice" (qtd. in Fraser 324). The statement reflects a pattern in Mary's life. She always sublimated her own will to that of the men in her life. She looked to men for guidance, protection, and adulation. The French King, Henry II, pampered her. Her young husband, François, adored her. The Ducs de Guise, her powerful French uncles, filled her with ambition and instilled in her the belief that she was not only queen of Scotland and France but also queen of England. None of these influential men helped develop the character of a queen, so Mary's refusal to relinquish this last claim, even entwining the arms of England and Ireland with her own, was an act of a child in queen's clothing. She also refused to sign the Treaty of Edinburgh (1560), under which the French withdrew from Scotland and recognized Elizabeth as the rightful queen of England, thus insulting the English queen and provoking the lifelong rift between them.

From the time Mary enters Edinburgh Castle in the film, we see a factious lot. The unruliness of her court compared with the orderliness of Elizabeth's evokes our sympathy. Mary's got her hands full. The nobles argue and cross swords. Even their dogs bark at each other while John Knox (Moroni Olsen) wanders the streets like a loose canon, lobbing "French Jezebel" over the castle walls. Mary confronts him. All she wants is to practice her religion and let him practice his. Knox is not impressed. Neither are most of her nobles. She sees through their veiled threats and stands up to them, yet she yields at critical moments. She won't be told what to do, yet she'll have no part in forming her Council. Beset by explosive, hostile forces, Mary crumbles.

In one scene, a frustrated Bothwell pleads: "You say you're a queen, so act like one." But we and Bothwell are doomed to disappointment. When some members of her Council decide that her Italian secretary and friend, David Riccio (John Carradine), has too much influence over her, they charge her with infidelity, burst into her apartments (with the help of her duped husband, Darnley), stab Riccio to death, and then force her to sign their full pardon. The film renders a truthful account of Riccio's brutal murder and the chaos of this court. It also renders Mary a victim instead of an impetuous, reckless monarch who caused a lot of her own problems. She thought that she could return to Scotland and take up the crown without knowing the nature of her country and her people and without building a firm support base as Elizabeth had with William Cecil, Francis

Walsingham, Robert Dudley, and others. Mary favored and promoted Riccio even though she knew that, as a foreigner, he would be in danger in xenophobic Scotland. Nothing and no one could prevent her from marrying Darnley, yet, after his murder, she raced headlong into marriage with Bothwell, implicating herself, and incurring the ire of not only her own country but Europe as well. Dunn writes: "Elizabeth at this time was alone among her fellow monarchs in offering human sympathy and moral support" (308). But Mary refused Elizabeth's advice to distance herself from Bothwell, insisting, as Lord Throckmorton wrote to Elizabeth, that she would "live and die with him" (qtd. in Dunn 309). Mary paid dearly for her personal folly. Scottish nobles forced her to abdicate in favor of her one-year-old son, James, whom she never saw again, and she lost the goodwill of her people.

In truth, Mary's public responsibility to her people was only a footnote in her private life. In the game of high-stakes politics, the woman overshadowed the queen. Often in the film, we see her embroidering while her nobles bicker about policy; or in her apartments surrounded by the four Marys (Fleming, Livingston, Seton, and Beaton), her devoted ladies-in-waiting and friends who had been with her for most of her life; or listening to Riccio's sorrowful tunes. In an ironic twist, she bounces the infant James on her lap, cooing, "He's going to grow up into a great big man and take care of me when I'm an old woman," something he never did. The Protestant James barely knew his mother and aligned himself with Elizabeth—and the throne of England. In thinking a man would save her, Mary was always to be disappointed.

It wasn't as if she lacked powerful female influences. Growing up in the French court, Mary was surrounded by female friends, especially Henry's daughters. Her mother, Mary of Guise; her mother-in-law, Catherine de Medici; Henry II's mistress, Diane de Poitiers; and her grandmother, Antoinette de Guise—all were strong women. But, as the darling of the French court, she had her every whim indulged, she was shielded from anything unpleasant, and she was encouraged to frolic, not to study, to charm, not to rule. Mary quickly learned that what she wanted could be gotten through men and not through her own volition.

Mary tells Bothwell of her life in France as they stand on the parapet of his Dunbar Castle. The moon and stars provide a romantic backdrop to the lovers' one moment of privacy. Dialogue entwines fact with fantasy.

While the details that Mary offers of her life in France dovetail with historical and biographical accounts, personal declarations of love ring purely fictitious: "From the very beginning I've always belonged to you. I know it. . . . Perhaps I didn't really exist until I met you." Not only the mise-en-scène but also Mary's words sublimate her to the man, the public to the private self.

Hepburn actually directed this love scene, her first and only foray behind the camera. In 1935, *Photoplay* wrote: "Like Garbo at MGM and Dietrich at Paramount, Hepburn is the 'prestige' star at RKO." But the article goes on to say that Hepburn's box-office pull was slipping (Baskette, "Is Hepburn Killing Her Own Career?" 51). She needed a hit. John Ford, who defined himself as "a director of Westerns" (Buscombe 288), seemed an unlikely candidate to direct a female-centered film like *Mary of Scotland*. As a literary work, the material appealed to him; as a romantic film, it did not. Berg tells us: "Long before shooting finished, Ford lost interest in the project. The sets, the staging, and photography were unusually good, but he offered no support for fleshing out the characters, all but reducing the actors . . . to pageanteers" (125). One day, he got up in disgust and told Hepburn to direct the love scene, but neither her directing nor her acting saved the film. It was a flop both critically and commercially. As Hepburn put it: "'It laid a great big egg'" (qtd. in Berg 125).

The love scene, however, paints a tender seduction of the manly Bothwell. "She draws people to her in gentle ways," Lord Randolph (Ralph Forbes) reports to the commanding Elizabeth. The real Elizabeth identified at least publicly with her father, Henry VIII, since her own mother was beheaded when she was three. She spent her childhood with male tutors and her early adulthood living under the fearful gaze of her paranoid sister, Mary. Elizabeth had many loyal female friends and servants, but, for the most part, she surrounded herself with men, brilliant men. Still, there was never any doubt as to who was ruling the kingdom. She'd had a long time to prepare for her life's career as queen and solidify her determination to do it without a man beside her on the throne. Randolph's very comment about Mary's gentleness reminds Elizabeth that she's the one who is not natural, not a "normal" woman. But as Jane Dunn writes: "A female monarch was in a different relationship with the world; she had a public, political and spiritual contract as ruler of her people, while her personal and private relationship as a woman made her naturally dependent on the male.

Mary, Queen of Scots. As a general rule, films about the Scottish queen paint her as the saintly, innocent victim of Elizabeth's jealousy and paranoia. Even this medium two-shot visualizes their relationship. Light bathes Mary, dressed in white, while a haughty Elizabeth, in head-to-toe red, looks on. (Courtesy Jerry Ohlinger's Movie Material Store.)

Elizabeth at least was able to counteract the perceived weaknesses of her sex with the certainty that as a queen she was divinely chosen above all men. . . . This confidence and certainty she could bolster with the knowledge that she had more intellectual and executive competence than almost anyone of her acquaintance" (21). The problem was that Mary could not say the same for herself. She leaned too heavily on charisma instead of intellect because that's what she had been taught to do.

Hepburn addressed her character's flaws in her own testy style. "I thought she was an ass," she told her biographer A. Scott Berg. "I would have rather played Elizabeth, who, after all, was the powerful one" (124). In fact, Hepburn tried to play Elizabeth *and* Mary in the film. The story goes that RKO was having trouble casting the "antagonist," Elizabeth, in *Mary of Scotland.* Both Ginger Rogers and Bette Davis wanted to play Gloriana, Rogers because she wanted to prove she could do more than sing and dance backward, and Davis because she was always fighting for better parts. It says something about the force of Elizabeth's character that all these powerful actresses saw her not just as a potent symbol but also as a complex woman of substance, one to whom they would be proud to attach their careers. Warner Brothers, however, wouldn't loan out Davis, and no one wanted to take a chance on Rogers for a historical piece, so Hepburn (or "Katharine of Arrogance," as she was called by some) suggested that she could play both parts, according to Berg's account. John Carradine, who plays David Riccio in the film, shot back: "But if you played both queens, how would you know which one to upstage?" (Berg 125). "Hepburn found nothing amusing about the comment at the time," Berg writes. "Years later she roared with laughter telling it" (125). In the end, it was Florence Eldridge, Fredric March's real-life wife, who won the part. Davis would end up playing Elizabeth in 1939's *The Private Lives of Elizabeth and Essex* and again in 1955's *The Virgin Queen,* while poor Ginger had to settle for playing the queen in Rodgers and Hammerstein's 1965 version of *Cinderella.*

If Maxwell Anderson's and, subsequently, John Ford's distilled portraits of the monstrous Elizabeth and saintly Mary distort our perception of these queens, then so does Ford's narrative squeeze. He evokes our sympathy for Mary's plight by collapsing nineteen years and two trials into what seems like days, a sham of a trial over trumped-up charges, and a hasty beheading. By eliminating critical details—like Mary's plots to overthrow Elizabeth over the years and Elizabeth's determination to safeguard a fellow sovereign prince against the advice of her councilors—Ford perpetuates Mary's innocence and Elizabeth's treachery. In the film, once Mary escapes from Lochleven Castle in Scotland (faithful servants, small boat, darkness, and fog) where her own nobles have imprisoned her, she flees to England and Elizabeth's protection. But the trusting Mary trades one prison for another. "How wonderful to be free again," she sweetly proclaims to Elizabeth's men, who take her to Sir Francis Knollys's castle, where she thinks she's a guest until they lock her in a great, drafty hall, her "apartment," the high windows lined with bars. The scale of the set towers over a vulnerable, defeated, isolated Mary.

It's difficult to know how much time she spends here because neither Mary nor Elizabeth age from the beginning to the end of the film. Ford, however, uses lighting to suggest some passage of time. Mary stands alone in the center of the room, the bars throwing shadows across her and the floor. Gradually, the light dims until most of the hall is in darkness. As Mary sits underneath the window, she seems to fade into the shadows and the stone walls of her prison. Ford then cuts to Bothwell, arms chained to a dungeon wall in a Danish prison where he has gone to gather support for his wife. His enemies in Scotland have made sure that the Danes arrest him on some pretense or other, and this is where he dies, raving madly to his servant about hearing his pipers and freeing Mary as a storm intensifies outside his cell walls. The storm rages across the sea to England, blowing through Mary's window, and she sits up in bed in wonder. The juxtaposition of these scenes not only underscores Mary and Bothwell's great and tragic love story but also assures their innocence and spiritual purity against the backdrop of brutal times and unspeakable cruelty.

Biographical and historical accounts paint a different picture. Freed from Lochleven by her supporters, Mary waged a battle against her brother, Moray. She lost and fled to England, putting Elizabeth and the stability of England in jeopardy. What to do with Mary became the question of the next two decades. Scotland refused to take her back, and Elizabeth did not dare risk the fragile alliance she had built with the Protestant lords in power there. To send her back to England's old enemy, France, was political suicide (besides, Catherine de Medici had washed her hands of her former daughter-in-law), as was keeping her in England, free to move about at will, a rallying post for every Catholic with designs on setting her on the English throne.

Elizabeth's solution, which really satisfied neither queen, was to keep Mary and her retinue of servants and attendants under the protection of various lords on their guarded estates. Though her movement was restricted, Mary lived according to her rank and status. Over the years, she won over admirers, smuggled out incriminating, coded letters to potential liberators, and involved herself in plots to overthrow Elizabeth while she waited for Bothwell to raise an army and save her. Bothwell's initial attempts to rally support met with little success. In the northern isles of Orkney and Shetland, he gathered some pirate ships, but Kirkcaldy of Grange quickly defeated them and drove Bothwell into Norway, where he was eventually imprisoned. Joyce Miller writes: "For a while King Frederick of Denmark held onto Bothwell in the hope that, in some way, he might be able to obtain the northern isles in return for his hostage, but by 1573 Bothwell was imprisoned at Dragsholm [Castle], where he went insane and died in 1578" (60). Like her husband, Mary was to eventually meet an unfortunate end.

For years Elizabeth refused to act against Mary. Against all advice and mounting evidence, she could not bring herself to execute a cousin and fellow sovereign. Finally, after the Babington Plot to kill Elizabeth and set Mary on the throne was foiled by Walsingham and his network of spies, the Council and Parliament had had enough and convinced Elizabeth of the danger of Mary's continued presence in England. The complex sequence of events that followed can be found in history books, correspondence, and biographies of both Mary and Elizabeth. Briefly and simply, confronted with charges of conspiring against Elizabeth and the realm as well as incriminating evidence in the case, Mary denied everything. England had no jurisdiction over her, an anointed queen. Others were culpable, not her. Faced with the choice of death or a pardon if she confessed and mended her ways, she opted for martyrdom.

The film's trial scene dramatizes Mary's position. The stark courtroom contains only two chairs. One is Elizabeth's empty throne, her crown symbolically placed on the seat to represent the absent monarch. The other is a smaller wooden chair for Mary. She prefers to stand, "symbolically." The elongated bench at which the judges sit stretches toward the ceiling, dwarfing Mary, who must crane her neck to speak to them. Ford's low angles on the judges reinforce their all-powerful presence. The effect of the set and the photography is menacing—a high row of robed and angry men against one lone woman. There will be no justice here. Mary holds her own, however, arguing that the court has no jurisdiction over her, denying most of the charges, condemning Elizabeth for inventing a "false trap"—until she learns that all who have helped her have been executed for treason. The final blow enters with Bothwell's servant, who is brought in to tell her that her husband is dead: "He said he'd be waiting for you with the bagpipes playing." At this point, Mary says: "Condemn me. Kill me. I don't care." It's a guaranteed tearjerker, but sympathy for the underdog is a trademark of many John Ford films. The heightened drama, the juxtaposition of scenes, the exaggerated sets, and Hepburn's acting talents serve to punch up sympathy for these two lovers so cruelly separated and wrongly accused.

Mary actually had two trials, one in York when she first arrived in England (to investigate her involvement, if any, in the death of her husband, Henry Stuart, the English Lord Darnley), the second at Fotheringhay Castle (to answer charges on her part in the Babington Plot), which Fraser describes so well in her biography of Mary. The hall was packed with lords, judges, solicitors, and onlookers. Far from being alone, Mary, "lame with rheumatism," entered with her surgeon, apothecary, and three of her attendants. She sat on a velvet chair with a velvet cushion for her feet and acquitted herself admirably during the questioning (Fraser 509–10). She admitted nothing, declared her innocence, and insisted that she was the injured party. She placed her "'cause in the hands of God'" (qtd. in Fraser 516).

After months of struggling with the decision, an uneasy Elizabeth signed Mary's death warrant, though she refused to confirm the sentence, still hoping for a way out of a no-win situation: continued intrigues if Mary lived, condemnation of the Catholic world if she died. She would be threatened by Spain, certainly, and censured by Scotland and France, fragile alliances at best. Furthermore, as Jane Dunn writes, Elizabeth had a "powerful sense of the inviolability of monarchy," to the point that "trespassing on God's territory in order to punish an anointed queen who, by definition, was above mere mortal intervention, filled her with dread" (404). In the film, Mary's words ring in her ears: "My blood will stain you. You'll never wash it off." This worried Elizabeth in life as well. In the end, Elizabeth's Council, under the leadership of Lord Burghley, took the matter out of her hands and quickly carried out the sentence—with or without her knowledge, depending on the source you read. As for Mary, she welcomed the guilty verdict and went to her death a martyr for the Catholic faith—having never met her cousin, Elizabeth.

Both Maxwell Anderson and John Ford, however, imagine a confrontation between the two queens in their adaptations. In the film, Elizabeth visits Mary after the trial to convince her to renounce her claim to the throne of England and, thus, save her own life. Mary refuses. Their dialogue resounds with accusations, focusing the private versus public, woman versus queen issue. "You're not even a woman," Mary flings at Elizabeth, who responds: "I am a queen. . . . I gave my love to no man but to my kingdom, to England." Mary tells her that she wouldn't trade one day with Bothwell for a century of Elizabeth's life. "What do you know of my life?" Elizabeth asks. And so they continue. In the end, it's Mary who gets the last word, privileging the idea that a woman's real happiness lies in the private realm, with a husband and child. She calls after Elizabeth: "My son will inherit your throne. Still, still, I win." But it's "a victory in defeat," as Vanderlan observes, "which can be found in many of Ford's films" (1548). It can also be found in Mary's epitaph: "In my end is my beginning."

Thunder claps, and lightning strikes across the sky on the morning of Mary's execution, equating her death with Christ's. The camera follows Mary as she prays and then shifts to a high-angle long shot as she climbs the scaffold stairs to meet her death. We hear the lilting Scottish music again as light bathes her face. Bagpipes softly fold in, suggesting that Bothwell is waiting. Mary clasps her hands in prayer, smiles, and looks up to the heavens as lightning streaks across the sky. Dramatic, yes, but not as interesting as the real-life stories of Mary's execution, which have become a part of the Marian mythology. Attended by her servants, Mary wore the color of martyrdom, a deep red. Courageous and calm, according to many accounts, she laid her head on the block. Here's how the biographer Jane Dunn characterizes Mary's death scene:

> All kinds of eyewitness reports replayed the ceremonial agony of the event and the rapt nobility of the Queen. Rumours became entwined with fact, inevitably embellished in the telling of something more awesome and traumatic than anything they would ever see again. The Queen of Scot's head was held up for all to see, her lips still moving for a further fifteen minutes,

it was said, in silent prayer; the lustrous auburn curls fell away in the execu-
tioner's hand to reveal the dead Queen's own grey hair cropped close, trans-
forming her from a beauty to an old woman in front of their eyes; one of her
favourite pets, a Skye terrier, smuggled in under her skirts, emerged howling
piteously and would not leave the severed head of his mistress. (409–10)

Dunn argues that Mary's "heroic death went a long way towards reconcil-
ing a less than heroic life" (395). It also assured her place among the martyrs
and inspired artistic renderings of a haloed queen that persist to this day.

Bothwell reportedly once said that Elizabeth and Mary together
wouldn't make an "honest" woman. His comment certainly applies to the
characters in this film. The monstrous Elizabeth and the saintly Mary ring
too hollow, too one-dimensional. One wielded power mightily, making her
less than a woman. The other threw away a kingdom, sublimating her power to men, making her less than a queen. The real queens, the real women,
warts and all, would have been far more whole—and far more exciting.

Mary, Queen of Scots (1971)

Biopics of Mary generally follow the screenwriter Linda Seger's conten-
tion that it's easier, and a lot less boring, to adapt one incident or slice of a
person's life than it is to attempt a "womb to tomb" story in two hours (*Art
of Adaptation* 52), picking up her story with her return to Scotland, and
ending it with her beheading. Her life in between packed a plotline of
conflict, intrigue, love, and betrayal—enough for ten lifetimes. Writers and
filmmakers, however, have focused their dramatic attention and rising action on Mary's conflict with Elizabeth. In doing so, they have skewed both
portraits, touching up Mary's blemishes while bringing Elizabeth's into
sharp relief, and perpetuating the myth that the Scottish queen was a victim of Elizabeth's hysterical paranoia.

The tagline of 1971's *Mary, Queen of Scots* trumpets how little had
changed in the thirty-five years since *Mary of Scotland* regarding depictions
of Mary and Elizabeth: "They used every passion in their incredible duel
. . . and every man in their savage games of intrigue!" Every word pits
woman against woman, privileging the private over the public, suggesting
that women wield power ruthlessly—with emotion, not intellect. Perhaps
our postfeminist reading of prefeminist copy sounds harsh and unfair, but,
at best, advertising for the film heralds what the critic Roger Ebert called

at the time a "historical soap opera," an unfortunate but honest assessment of a film that began with so much promise.

Hal Wallis, the producer, and Charles Jarrott, the director, were hot off their 1969 critical and commercial success *Anne of the Thousand Days*, starring Richard Burton as Henry VIII and the newcomer Geneviève Bujold as Anne Boleyn. The film won ten Oscar nominations, including Best Actor for Burton, Best Actress for Bujold, Best Supporting Actor for Anthony Quayle, and Best Picture for Wallis. It picked up only one statue—for Best Costume Design—but practically swept the Golden Globes with wins for Best Drama, Best Director, Best Actress, and Best Screenplay—all in all, an impressive showing for the Wallis and Jarrott team. Deciding to strike while audience interest in period films was hot, producer and director went looking for more historical material to adapt and found inspiration in the BBC's own triumphant six-part series *Elizabeth R*, starring the Oscar winner Glenda Jackson, and Antonia Fraser's 1969 best-selling biography *Mary Queen of Scots*. The time was right, they reasoned, to revive one of the most dramatic slices of Mary's life, her rivalry and power struggle with Elizabeth Tudor. It had been three decades since Hepburn's "egg," and a new adaptation couldn't miss, especially when two of Britain's stage and screen royalty agreed to play the iconic queens: Glenda Jackson and Vanessa Redgrave, who would eventually become as famous for their own politics as for the parts they played.

By 1971, both actresses were at the top of their game. Glenda Jackson had just received a string of Best Actress awards from the Variety Club of Great Britain, the New York Film Critics, and the National Society of Film Critics for *Women in Love* (Ken Russell, 1970), capping them off with an Oscar in 1971. According to the biographer Chris Bryant: "Apparently unconcerned by the outcome of her nomination, Glenda neither went to the ceremony in Los Angeles, nor stayed up to await the result, so John Mills' daughter accepted it on her behalf from Walter Matthau, and the movie mogul Hal B. Wallis came to Britain for a formal presentation" (99). Bette Davis, who had played Elizabeth I twice in her lifetime, rang Glenda early next morning to tell her the news. Reportedly, Jackson said: "'It was nice of her to call, but I could have done with the extra hour in bed'" (qtd. in Bryant 100).

The Oscar launched a busy year for Jackson. She spent seven months shooting the BBC series *Elizabeth R*, immersing herself in the part of the

Virgin Queen. Bryant writes: "Glenda was as rigorous as ever in her approach to the part. She learnt how to ride side-saddle for the opening sequence, archery, calligraphy and how to play the virginal. She endured hours of make-up every morning, allowing Dawn Allcock, her make-up artist, to build a suitably Tudor nose for her, and offered to have the pate of her head shaved . . . for authenticity's sake" (104).

Davis, one of the first actresses to take extraordinary steps to achieve physical oneness with her character, would have been proud. After seeing Jackson's work, the producer Roderick Graham made the comment: "'She can go from total woman to total politician in mid-sentence'" (qtd. in Bryant 104). Jackson, who had always insisted on portraying women with authenticity, took home two Emmys (Best Actress in a Series and Best Actress in a Single Episode) for her work in *Elizabeth R,* but, when Wallis tapped her almost immediately for Elizabeth in his feature film *Mary, Queen of Scots,* she balked. Character actors like Jackson have not only a horror of being typecast but also a low threshold for boredom. Money and a three-and-a-half-week shooting schedule brought her around, but Jackson regretted her decision. Bryant claims that Jackson was "ashamed" of the film, which was "a commercial star vehicle" rather than a "serious historical film": "The screenplay veered from the banal to the ludicrous; and the direction . . . was too lumbering to capture anything of value from the distinguished cast" (105). Jackson herself said: "'One really shouldn't do films like that, especially if like me you're a silly cow and talk about your artistic principles and then go blithely into productions which you know bloody well are going to make you compromise and betray them'" (qtd. in Bryant 105–6). Her assessment speaks to her artistic temperament but can't diminish her brilliant performance. Jackson steals the movie. She was prouder, however, of *Sunday Bloody Sunday* (John Schlesinger, 1971), for which she won another Academy Award nomination in a field that included Julie Christie in *McCabe and Mrs. Miller* (Robert Altman), Janet Suzman in *Nicholas and Alexandra* (Franklin J. Schaffner), her costar Vanessa Redgrave in *Mary, Queen of Scots,* and Jane Fonda, who won for *Klute* (Alan J. Pakula).

Both Jackson and Redgrave won Golden Globe nominations for *Mary, Queen of Scots,* and, though the film makes light of history, it remains highly watchable mainly because of their performances. In fact, the casting choices of Jackson and Redgrave offer an interesting parallel to the queens they play in at least one respect. Like Elizabeth, Jackson came up the hard way, experiencing years of struggle, hardship, and uncertainty before becoming Britain's reining queen of theater and film and eventually entering the political arena herself as a member of Parliament for Hampstead and Highgate. Vanessa Redgrave, on the other hand, was the daughter of Sir Michael Redgrave and Rachel Kempson Redgrave, already British stage and screen royalty. Her brother, Corin, and sister, Lynn, made the Redgraves the most famous acting family since the celebrated American Barrymores. As with Mary, the way was paved for Vanessa, her future set, though she had enormous talent under that tiara. In the 1950s, she trained at the Central School of Speech and Drama and won critical acclaim for her performances on the London and New York stage. She starred in her first film, Brian Desmond Hurst's *Behind the Mask,* in 1958 and went on to play Guinevere in *Camelot* (Joshua Logan, 1967) and Isadora Duncan in *Isadora* (Karel Reisz, 1968). By the time she made *Mary, Queen of Scots,* Redgrave had been married and divorced from the film director Tony Richardson (their daughters Natasha and Joely are also actors) and had a serious affair with her *Camelot* costar Franco Nero (Lancelot) that produced a son, Carlo. In her autobiography, *Vanessa Redgrave,* she mentions *Mary, Queen of Scots* only to reference more important things in her life—meeting Timothy Dalton, who plays Darnley in the film and who became her real-life romantic partner, and collecting money for the Upper Clyde shipworkers who were about to lose their jobs through company bankruptcy (176–77). Neither she nor Jackson mentions anything significant about the film itself or their roles in it. Their silence speaks volumes about this "historical soap opera."

The film rewinds Mary's life to give us a fragment of her life in France. It's early morning. A high-angle long shot picks up Mary and François (Richard Denning), still in their nightclothes, running along the palace walls, through elaborate gardens: laughing, talking, holding hands. Clearly, even at this distance, Redgrave at thirty-four is a bit old to play the eighteen-year-old Mary. She had married the dauphin on April 24, 1558, when she was only fifteen and he fourteen, but, with Henry II's sudden death from a jousting wound the following year, the young couple found themselves on the throne of France, forecasting the circumstances and rise to power of a later young couple: Marie Antoinette and Louis August. Totally unprepared for their new roles as king and queen, Mary and François left matters of state to his mother, Catherine de Medici, and her uncles de Guise, two parties locked in a power struggle for control of France.

Mary's long, loose blonde tresses (the real Mary's hair was auburn) and white, flowing shift suggest a freedom of movement and innocence as fragile as the fabric of her gown, but her happiness shatters when François dies. In the film, we see her weeping over her young husband's body while Catherine (Katherine Kath) flings accusations that her son's death is Mary's fault. (Interestingly, the real Catherine stripped Mary of all her jewels only one day after François's death and refused to entertain any suggestions that Mary wed her younger son, Charles.) Never a robust child, François suffered from chronic ear infections that eventually spread to his brain, and he died in 1560—the same year Mary lost her mother, Mary of Guise, who had been governing Scotland in her daughter's absence. Grief stricken, Redgrave's Mary is by turns dazed, confused, hysterical, lost. Powerful men begin to close in around her, taking up her space. For example, it's James Hepburn, Lord Bothwell (Nigel Davenport), who delivers the news of Mary of Guise's death and the state of affairs in Scotland. He leans in close to her face, almost crowding her out of the frame, saying: "Your brother is now regent. There's disorder in your land. . . . The clans fight for power. . . . You're needed in Scotland." After François dies, Mary's uncles sweep her aside and literally back her against a wall, hissing that she is the queen of Scotland by birth and the queen of England by right. The usurper Elizabeth is nothing but a harlot who dallies with her horsemaster, Robert Dudley (Daniel Massey). Mary must return to Scotland, take up her crown, and wait for the right moment to invade England. Cornered, all Mary can do is cry: "François! François!"

The exposition of the film, then, sets up immediately the conflict between Mary and Elizabeth over the throne of England, the issue of Elizabeth's legitimacy and her "dalliance" with Dudley, and Mary's misfortunes. A cut from a distressed Mary to an intimate moment between the "harlot" and her "horsemaster" confirms the world's opinion at the time that Mary was the saint, Elizabeth the sinner. The scene shows Elizabeth on a barge with Robert. The curtains are drawn. They're alone. He's singing a song while Elizabeth lies listening seductively on pillows, her flaming red hair hanging loose around her. As he finishes, Elizabeth asks about the song, and Dudley tells her that when a married Henry VIII sang it for her mother, Anne Boleyn, Anne boldly told him: "Go sing it to your *wife*." Elizabeth, always touchy about the subject of her mother, finds the story amusing: "By God, my mother had the courage of ten." Biographers suggest that, while identifying with and invoking the name of her father publicly, Elizabeth kept her feelings about her mother private. Jane Dunn says that, at some point in her life, Elizabeth began to wear a ring with a secret clasp that opened to reveal miniature portraits of mother and daughter side by side (64). For the most part, however, the scene sets up the romantic nature of Elizabeth's relationship with Robert Dudley—her friend, her suitor, her "eyes," her "Robin." Though the two bickered on and off over the years like an old married couple and supported each other until his death in 1588, scholars think it highly doubtful that they ever consummated their relationship.

A message from William Cecil (Trevor Howard) interrupts a passionate kiss between Elizabeth and Robert, shattering any possibility of eventual marriage between them (assuming that Elizabeth had wanted to marry him, which isn't likely). Amy Dudley, Robert's wife, has been found dead at the foot of the stairs in Cumnor Hall in Oxfordshire. Tongues are wagging, there's talk of murder, and fingers are pointing to Robert as the likely suspect. Jarrott cuts to Elizabeth in council with Cecil, discussing the situation. Cecil argues that there must be a public trial. Elizabeth must distance herself from Robert. "Now will the great scandal begin," an angry Elizabeth sputters as she smashes a lute over the table. The queen not only loves Dudley; she feels a sense of loyalty to him. "When I was in great danger during my dead sister's reign, he did not desert me," she tells Cecil. Elizabeth refers here to the financial and moral support Dudley gave her when she was imprisoned in the Tower by her sister, Mary Tudor. But, in life and art, Elizabeth realizes that Dudley must be publicly cleared of all charges before he can return to court and to her side.

In a slick bit of staging, Jarrott has Jackson turn her back to the camera, lower her head, and lean against the fireplace as she says to Cecil: "Bring him to trial in open court. Hide nothing." With this small staging turn, Jarrott gives us a snapshot of Elizabeth's duality: the woman hides her private feelings while the queen issues a public command. Unfortunately, Mary was always to lead with her feelings, lashing out right and left, rarely stopping to think about how her actions would affect her country or

150 ROYAL PORTRAITS IN HOLLYWOOD

her people or her own reputation. Neither of the film versions gives us a truthful account of her, though Redgrave's interpretation comes closer to the mark than Hepburn's.

As we point out in our chapter on Catherine the Great, it's never a good idea to begin a biopic about a woman the moment she meets "the Man," as if she had no life before him. Unfortunately, both Mary and Elizabeth here appear with men at their sides from the first frame. Why can't we ever see them as children (as so many male biopics begin), or young adults, or women ruling a kingdom? In the case of Mary, it's particularly distressing as showing us her childhood would explain so much about her later actions. Before Mary leaves France, Bothwell asks her: "Will you rule the Scottish lords, or will they rule you?" Of course, she won't rule the Scottish lords because she's never practiced self-governance, let alone governance of a kingdom. Biographies and history tell us this, but, without a context, the film Mary seems simply weak and childish. She echoes what her uncles have taught her, delivering lines like a Stepford queen—"I think I'll go to Scotland by way of England so that I can meet Elizabeth the Usurper and be friends"—and she's unable to see the contradiction here. Mary won't sign the Treaty of Edinburgh, yet she wonders why Elizabeth won't grant her safe passage through England. It's hardly surprising that her half brother, James Moray (Patrick McGoohan), treats her like a child from the moment she hits Scotland.

The trusting child innocently greets her brother "Jamie," a cool, calculating Scotsman who, as a bastard son of James V, lives by his wits, content to be the power behind the throne. She immediately makes him her chief minister, but his designs become clear as he walks Mary, like a lamb to the slaughter, to her tiny, spartan chambers in the castle. This is no French court. No frills here, he tells her. The Scots don't go in for flash and finery. The stairs narrow and the walls close in with every step she takes. From this point in the film, Mary is a virtual prisoner, first of her own lords, later of Elizabeth, but mainly of her own choices. In her chambers, James tells Mary that she can play and dance; he'll rule. "Be discreet, and consult me in all things," he cautions and leaves. Steaming over her brother's patronizing plans, Mary eagerly bends to an alternate plan presented by Riccio and her priest. To foil her brother, she must marry again—and quickly.

Redgrave's Mary seems more emotionally fragile than Hepburn's in many respects. She exhibits less control, swinging to extremes from cour-

age to collapse, which is probably the more accurate portrayal. Mary's letters to Elizabeth, many of which still exist, exhibit this same bipolar swing
from bravado to compliance. The story line differs in this later film, but
casting influences the portrait as well. The stainless steel spine, the bones,
the angles, the jutting chin, the aristocratic carriage and accent, the rapid
delivery of her speech, the force of her presence, all are part of Hepburn's
iconography, making her tougher than what Mary probably was in real life.
Yes, the historical Mary could rise to a challenge, especially in a fight, often
donning men's armor, but it was more about getting caught up in the moment than thinking a situation through. The blonde, blue-eyed Redgrave
looks softer, more malleable. She's stunned when John Knox calls her a
"Papist whore." What has she ever done to him? Her anger quickly dissolves into tears, and she can cry a river while Hepburn may release a single,
controlled tear. As the Scottish queen, Redgrave falls helplessly and believably into Elizabeth's trap to marry her off to Henry Stuart, Lord Darnley.
Like the real Mary, she is far from being repulsed by the tall, effeminate
English lord.

The juxtaposition of scenes in this film serves to contrast Mary and
Elizabeth, just as it does in *Mary of Scotland*. A shift from Mary's contem-
plation of marriage to Elizabeth's plot to set her up with that "weak, de-
generate fool" Darnley reinforces Mary's role as victim. Elizabeth schemes
to offer her own favorite, the exonerated Robert Dudley, Earl of Leicester,
and a promise to name Mary her heir if she marries him. Convinced that
Mary will reject Leicester, she prays: "May it please her to hate me as I hate
her. Then she will marry Darnley—and I have won." How sinister Elizabeth appears next to the hopelessly clueless, vulnerable Mary.

Back in Edinburgh, Mary has met and fallen in love with the handsome young Lord Darnley (Timothy Dalton). First we see them riding
together along the beach, Mary now in men's clothing, not unusual since
Mary did occasionally dress like a man when she traveled around Scotland
(shades of Queen Christina and Catherine the Great). When Henry falls
from his horse, she runs to fetch water for his brow. Tears of worry and
compassion fill her eyes. She's hooked. "I love him. . . . I must have him,"
she cries to Riccio, but a cut to Darnley in bed with David Riccio (Ian
Holm) shows us Henry's duplicity. Dalton's portrayal rings true to what we
know of the real Henry, who was spoiled, petulant, and cruel. Jane Dunn
says: "He hit people who could not return his blows and gained a reputa-

tion for being quick to pull a knife on anyone who displeased him" (232–33). Antonia Fraser describes him this way: "Throughout his short life he showed remarkably little interest in any matters of the mind, and a single-minded concern for the pursuit of pleasure" (222). In his "pursuit of plea-sure," he contracted what was most probably syphilis. When sores erupted on his skin, he covered his face in gauze. In the film, Bothwell warns Mary of Henry's condition: "He's diseased. He is poxed. He will rot with it."

Darnley and Mary shared a grandmother: Margaret Tudor, the daugh-ter of Henry VII and sister of Henry VIII. Margaret's first husband was James IV of Scotland, and they produced James V, Mary's father. After James IV of Scotland died, Margaret married Archibald Douglass, the sixth Earl of Angus. They had a daughter, Margaret Douglas, who married Matthew Stuart, the fourth Earl of Lennox, a Scotsman and descendant of James II. Margaret and Matthew were Darnley's parents. Darnley, like his cousin Mary, was a product of his parents' ambitions. His mother's aim was to set him on a throne, and Scotland would do for the time being.

We never see the Countess of Lennox in the film; instead, we witness the product of her aspirations. Against all counsel, including Bothwell's, Mary marries Darnley, but his impeccable manners slip away as soon as their wedding night to reveal his twisted soul. Lines like "As I mount you so shall I mount the throne" leave us in no doubt. It's a credit to Timothy Dalton's acting ability that Darnley emerges as more than a one-dimensional sicko in this film. He manages to evoke sympathy for this pathetic, misguided, fright-ened bully who was bred to be king but possessed no governing tools. Mary denies him the crown matrimonial. He's lost, he's hated, he's drunk, and he's out of his depth. In one scene, plotting Scottish lords close in around him as they trick him into helping them kill David Riccio (Ian Holm). As the cam-era pulls out to a long shot, we see him through the doorway, trapped, a tiny figure overshadowed by towering nobles.

Mary, Queen of Scots essentially replays the same key events in Mary's life as its 1936 predecessor: her power struggle with Elizabeth, her conflict with James Moray and the Scottish lords, her marriage to Darnley, Riccio's murder, Darnley's murder, her speedy marriage to Bothwell, their capture, her flight to England and imprisonment, her trial, and her martyr's death. Fantasy swims with fact in both portraits of the Scottish queen and the characters that swirl around her. We find it interesting, however, that the two films render Riccio and Darnley more truthfully than either Mary or

Elizabeth. In *Mary, Queen of Scots,* Jarrott throws a key light on Riccio and his murder, bringing the historical figure and his death into sharp focus, and, with faithful brushstrokes, he paints a vivid Darnley, complete with syphilis sores and white gauze.

At the same time, the film depicts James Moray as an ambitious sleaze-ball who masterminds the deaths of Riccio and Darnley and Bothwell's demise, while Bothwell comes across as loyal and wise, with an undercurrent of menacing ambition, and a scapegoat for Moray's scheming. Next to Moray, Bothwell looks like a saint. He saves Mary from her "poxed" husband and makes love to her himself while a drugged Darnley lies in the next room. Desperate and distraught, Mary needs Bothwell to protect her—to keep order in one kingdom and usurp Elizabeth, "the heretic," in the other. After Riccio's death, Bothwell helps Darnley and a pregnant Mary escape and takes them to his own Dunbar Castle, where one look at Bothwell's wife sends Mary into labor. The film never reveals how he disentangles himself from his wife in order to marry his queen, but it does show us his capture of James (whom an incredibly dim-witted Mary spares) and his implication in the plot to murder Darnley. His fellow conspirator James, however, throws all the blame on Bothwell. A shocked Elizabeth goes into mourning for her dead cousin and his widow, but, when the "murderer" absconds with the queen and then marries her, Scotland and England rise up in outrage. In fact, Mary's folly stunned the world and incurred the ire of monarchs throughout Europe. Today, her exploits would splash across tabloid headlines and feed the media for months.

Mary, Queen of Scots boasts no tender love scene on the castle parapet, just two lovers trapped by their need of each other and outwitted by a formidable foe incapable of showing them the mercy that they showed to him. Surrounded by Moray's men, and confronted with their own incriminating love letters (the "casket letters") to each other, Mary has no choice but to abdicate, sending Bothwell to Denmark with a tearful "I can't exist without you." But Mary recharges long enough to confront Elizabeth on the English border. It seems that no director can resist the temptation to dramatize a meeting that never took place, though the fact that the sister monarchs never met actually heightened the tension and misunderstanding between them.

The border scene begins on a hopeful note as Mary rides toward England, shouting: "I have my whole life before me!" Her meeting with Elizabeth, which begins with sweet exchanges, quickly sours, locking the two women in conflict, and playing to the tagline's "every passion," "incredible duel," and "savage games of intrigue." Mary demands an army, supplies, and money to defeat James. Elizabeth says no, and Mary explodes in anger. Elizabeth's response to Mary's tantrum rings true to what we know of the historical Mary: "This is the outpouring of a pampered woman demanding that all indulge her." But, because Elizabeth is portrayed as the antagonist to the saintly Mary, her words sound accusatory and hurtful rather than wise. By the end of this round, Elizabeth utters what Mary has made obvious: "I must keep her prisoner until the day of her death."

A cut to a middle-aged Mary in confinement, looking listless and sick, tells us that years have passed. Bothwell is dead, and all that's left for her is coded letters and plots. A cut to Elizabeth soaking her feet suggests her increasing age. As Lord Cecil tries to convince her that Mary has been plotting to kill her, a tired Elizabeth refuses to act. She will not have Mary killed, even though the pope has excommunicated her for keeping Mary prisoner and her Catholic subjects are "torn in two." Even when Cecil and Walsingham (Richard Warner) reveal Mary's part in the Babington Plot of 1586, Elizabeth won't sign Mary's death warrant. "If she begs forgiveness of me, she shall live," Elizabeth tells them, just as she told Parliament after both Lords and Commons "petitioned for Mary's immediate execution" (Pryor 89).

Seeking another solution to the problem (a testament to the real queen's reluctance to commit violence on any person, let alone an anointed queen), Elizabeth visits Mary at Fotheringhay Castle in a second meeting that reflects to some extent what they wrote to each other in their letters. "Despite your efforts, I am not dead," Elizabeth remarks as she enters Mary's room. "I have lived in fear of your assassins," she tells Mary as she bends down to light her fire. "I want to spare you, but you must beg my forgiveness." The years have taken the heat out of their passionate accusations, but, ultimately, Mary won't beg for forgiveness. "I long for the trial ... to defend myself. I will die a martyr to the Catholic faith." Not even the casket letters, which suggest that Mary and Bothwell planned Darnley's murder, will change her mind.

"For the first time in your life, put aside your personal desires and behave like a queen. Think of your son," Elizabeth pleads. But, once again, Mary taunts: "I have made my peace with God ... and now I must die...."

It's your destiny to kill me. . . . The judicial murder of an anointed queen. It will torment you always." She knows exactly where to wound Elizabeth. However, in this adaptation, Elizabeth gets the privileged line, one that resounds with truth should audiences actually listen: "Madam, if your head had matched your heart, I would be the one awaiting death." The line literally sums up the life of Mary, Queen of Scots, a monarch who always placed her emotions over her intellect, her personal life over her public reputation.

Yet this film is not kind to Elizabeth. As the ax falls on Mary's head, a cut to Elizabeth shows her alone on her throne, the folds of red velvet behind her signifying the blood of a sister queen. An extreme close-up of Elizabeth's eyes, knowing and tormented, and a cut to her hands holding Mary's Bible and cross complete the picture of a defeated queen, a repeated image in other biopics of Elizabeth. Jarrott's slow zoom-out supports Mary's prediction that Elizabeth would always be alone, as the title card reads: "Elizabeth ruled England for another sixteen years. She died as she had lived, unmarried and childless. The thrones of England and Scotland passed to the only possible claimant . . . a man. King James the First." Is this a blunt reminder that women who rule, women who put their public responsibilities above their personal lives, must pay an enormous price? Can the execution of justice be wielded only by a man? The questions beg other answers and other adaptations that positively focus on powerful women—and not as "rare and unnatural" phenomena whose "authority [must] be assisted and forthset by the fortification of a man." As Rosalind Miles puts it: "[Elizabeth] had everything that women want: She lived her life to the full. She knew the love of good men and a good country. And she died at peace in her own bed" (interview with Rosalind Miles).

At one point in Jarrott's film, Elizabeth tells Mary: "Your fate is linked with mine." This is perhaps the truest line in the film. The lives of Elizabeth Tudor and Mary Stuart were so tightly knotted together that even death could not fully separate them. Today, a visit to Westminster Abbey in London finds Elizabeth's tomb in the north aisle of Henry VII's Chapel, Mary Stuart's in the south. Their portraits hang next to each other in the National Portrait Gallery and Hatfield House. Bits and pieces of their lives crisscross the British Isles: Elizabeth's saddle encased in glass at Warwick Castle, Mary's death mask at Lennoxlove House, Hilliard's miniature of Elizabeth next to a silver memento of Mary and Darnley's wedding. History notes the blemishes of Elizabeth and revels in her triumphs. A new spate of biopics (discussed in chapter 7) attests to a renewed fascination with the Virgin Queen. Mary, on the other hand, has been restored to a state of grace in her native country. Scotland once again embraces its first queen, assiduously marking her every journey and visit on maps, in tour books, and on signposts. A chat with one of the guides at Stirling Castle, where Mary was crowned and later became a frequent visitor, assures us that all has been forgiven, clearing the way for yet another saintly screen version of the Scottish queen. The plotline of the upcoming *Mary, Queen of Scots*, written by Jimmy McGovern, directed by Phillip Noyce, and starring Scarlett Johansson, promises that little will change regarding film renderings of this monarch and her royal sister: "A chronicle of the life and reign of Mary I of Scotland . . . with a concentration on her strained personal and political relationship with her cousin, Queen Elizabeth I of England" (imdb.com).

Chapter Five

Queen Victoria

If they only knew me as I am.
—Queen Victoria, in *Queen Victoria: Evening at Osborne*

C losest to us in time of all our queens, Queen Victoria has become the emblem of her age. Mary Stuart's history can read like a hagiography, but even a casual mention of Victoria's life conjures up a more earthly record of day-to-day dedication to country and family: the child trained toward the throne; the eighteen-year-old girl becoming queen of England in 1837; the young queen falling in love with the German Prince Albert; the two marrying and producing nine children; their family life encouraging domesticity in England; darkness entering with Albert's death in 1861; Victoria's deep mourning, lasting for nearly ten years; the Golden and Diamond Jubilees demonstrating the British public's love for their venerable queen. Victoria ruled until her death in 1901, making hers the longest reign of any British monarch yet.

We dwellers in the twenty-first century think we get what it meant to be Victorian and often reduce Victoria's age, as well as her life, to a limited set of assumptions. Like the Puritans, the Victorians have receded into costumed figures embodying hypocrisy. We apply the adjective *Victorian* to wallpaper patterns, imperialism, stodgy morality, and hidden sexuality. Why else would Victoria's name—used as the softest-porn joke—front that home of racy, lacy underwear, Victoria's Secret, which trades on the idea that there *was* a Victorian secret, a volcano of passion ever ready to erupt? But never can we know another age, any more than we can experience the complete truth of another life.

To keep Victoria from becoming a decaying valentine, to record a life that contained more than highlights, biographers have mined the queen's

Queen Victoria. (Courtesy the Francis Frith Collection/Art Resource, New York.)

writings, as well as paintings, prints, photographs, and reams of records, to construct interpretive biographies. Revisionist views of Victoria began as early as 1921, with Lytton Strachey's groundbreaking psychological take on this royal life, *Queen Victoria,* a work that includes her sometimes irrational tenacity and her kittenish flirtations with her ministers. As he did to others in *Eminent Victorians,* Strachey gleefully chips away at the queen's imposing facade.

Before Strachey wrote *Queen Victoria,* the British director Will Barker had filmed a visual interpretation of the queen's life. Only a few minutes remain of *Sixty Years a Queen* (1913), the first film to be shot at Ealing Studios. Extant biopics of Victoria's life swing dramatically from the public to the private, from worshiping her facade to seeking the living woman beneath that tiny, sparkling crown. Herbert Wilcox's award-winning *Victoria the Great* (1937) delivers just the view its title promises, a tribute to the monarch. Sixty years later, *Mrs. Brown* (1997) focuses on Victoria's violent reaction to the death of her beloved husband. Willfully isolated in a haze of deep mourning, the queen tested the affection of her people. Only the attentions of a servant, John Brown, and the ministrations of Prime Minister Disraeli induced her to leave her cave of private despair. The most recent biopic, *Victoria and Albert* (2001)—a joint A&E/BBC project—retraces some of the ground covered by Wilcox's film. This time, however, the camera insists on an intimate perspective. Elizabeth Longford, one of Victoria's many biographers, says that Victoria "always insisted" that "true biography drives out false" (457). Rarely, however, can biographies be arranged so neatly into true and false versions. These three films give viewers an opportunity to construct a more complete, if not ever completely true, picture of Queen Victoria's life.

Victoria the Great (1937)

Herbert Wilcox's *Victoria the Great* is true in a Victorian way, providing positive, pivotal scenes from a long, productive life, sacrificing most glimpses of the person beneath the regal persona. The strength of the film lies in its almost archival visual accuracy and in its performances from Anton Walbrook as Albert and especially Anna Neagle as Victoria. A browse through engravings, paintings, and photographs shows the care paid to specific, physical details. For a glimpse at how specifically such detail has been reproduced, see the engravings of Victoria's coronation at Westminster Abbey (Strachey, *Queen Victoria*, 67); a sunbeam shines through a high window to light her youthful figure, just as one does in Wilcox's restaging of the scene. The physical similarity of the two leads to their royal characters fosters the tableau effect. The prince's hairstyle and clothing suit Walbrook, whose features are enough like Albert's to make him convincing. After the release of this extremely popular film, Neagle posed as Queen Victoria for Madame Tussauds. Neagle's costumes, hairstyles, and headdresses replicate those worn by the real queen, while her gliding walk recalls comments made by those who remembered Victoria's "genius of movement" (Longford 573). Neagle also played Victoria in *Sixty Glorious Years* (1938), a full-color sequel, also directed by Wilcox. Her re-creation of the queen earned Neagle and Wilcox (her husband as well as director) their entrée to Hollywood, where *Victoria the Great* was released by RKO in 1937.

There's an interesting parallel between Herbert Wilcox's public approach to the queen's life and Neagle's autobiography. Portraying Victoria was the pinnacle of Neagle's career: "It caused a furore" (Neagle 85). If it didn't make her a reigning queen of Hollywood, it did, literally, make her British royalty, garnering her a title. She was declared a DBE (dame of the British Empire) in 1969. In her autobiography, Neagle takes very little credit for her many strong performances—she also played Florence Nightingale, Nurse Cavell, and Nell Gwyn. Critics generally agreed that *Victoria the Great* was "a triumph of acting for Anna Neagle": "All the time a monarch—every inch a Queen" (qtd. in Neagle 73). Still, Neagle commented, "I've ruined the whole thing," after watching the film through for the first time (84). She credits others—all men—for her triumphs, and she asserts: "I was born a hero worshipper" (22). She delivers portraits of "heros"—her father, her brothers, and her romantic leads—as well as many tributes to her husband, to whom she says she owes most of her acting success (7). But it's difficult to find the private person speaking or to understand what her marriage to Wilcox was like from the inside.

Neagle's never angry, although she implies that the burden of raising her and her brothers fell on her "always fragile" mother (Neagle 38); although she had to wait ten years for a "Private Members Matrimonial Bill" to marry Wilcox, who was married when they met (62); although she and Wilcox experienced frighteningly diminished finances during their later years (188). When preparing to play Victoria, Neagle says she found the queen's diaries more helpful than the biographies, which often "carried the author's bias" (82). Readers of Neagle's autobiography might long for *her* diaries or even for a little bias to give this anecdotal account of parts played and stars met more of the flavor of its teller. Neagle turns her gracious, public face toward us, but that's the only face she reveals.

Wilcox uses a similar approach to Queen Victoria's life, turning away from personal narrative and toward public events, neat vignettes, identified by dates and titles. This gives the film the feel of a pop-up book with each page carefully ornamented. But aren't the important parts of the queen's life obvious and mandatory? It might seem that the screenwriters, Miles Malleson and Charles de Grandcourt, had little choice about which bits to tell and which to ignore. Anyone who shapes a life, however, does make choices, and Malleson and de Grandcourt omit some crucial realities. Phyllis Roses's caution to biographers applies to screenwriters as well. "If you do not appreciate the force of what you're leaving out," she says, "you are not fully in command of what you're doing" (qtd. in Heilbrun 30).

This big slice of Victoria's life—highlights from the sixty-five years of her reign—deletes her childhood, as do many biopics of queens. *Victoria the Great* begins with the night before and the morning of Victoria's accession to the throne. Interactions between the Duchess of Kent (Mary Morris) and her daughter quickly illuminate their relationship. "I do not wish you to walk down the main stairs alone again," the duchess tells Victoria, "not ever, under any circumstances." Circumstances change dramatically that very night, when cabinet ministers summon Victoria, who walks down the stairs, alone, to receive their news, a real-life event Wilcox replicates stunningly. The young queen's transfigured face deserves the bow it gets from the two elderly statesmen. Victoria's first action as queen is to demand her own room. Her second is to announce that she will see her ministers alone, making it clear that her mother's plan to be the power behind the throne has been thwarted.

But a little more of what brought Victoria to her mother's rapid dismissal would help develop both characters. The biographer Cecil Woodham-Smith details what the Duchess of Kent called "the Kensington system" (64), a plan short on affection and long on discipline, aimed at producing a perfect monarch. Little Victoria was "never allowed to be alone, day or night." She could never see a guest without a "third person present" (69). An hour-by-hour timetable of scheduled lessons consumed most of her day. When she was twelve, her mother made sure she was "enlightened" about her closeness to the throne, a revelation that made her cry and promise: "I will be good" (Strachey, *Queen Victoria*, 27–28). Sir John Conroy, a smarmy character, helped the widowed duchess implement her system, but he's not fleshed out in this film. Neither is Victoria's governess, the Baroness Lehzen, who directed her study and earned her friendship. This isolated, programmed existence continued until she was eighteen. No wonder power translated into freedom for the young queen. No wonder the possibility of being alone with Albert—or anyone, for that matter— seemed such a pleasure.

Wilcox's film charmingly documents the public progress of Victoria and Albert's romance. According to Victoria, her relationship with Albert (her first cousin) was the most important of her life (Woodham-Smith 210). But she had reservations about marrying, and her doubts—barely recognized in the film—involved losing power. She declared that she was "accustomed to having her own way," and any thought of the compromises that marriage must bring was unwelcome (179). Malleson and de Grand-court's screenplay details Victoria and Albert's courtship but suggests the queen's postmarital struggle with compromise in a single episode. Albert makes it clear that he wants to help Victoria in affairs of state, and she refuses. Angered by her rebuff, and bored by his position as man of leisure, he rebels. First, he plays "their" song, "On Wings of Song," surrounded by lovely court ladies. Next, he smokes, openly, sulkily, in violation of Victoria's edict that no one should smoke. Finally, he refuses to come when called. He demands that Victoria must come to *him*. Enraged, she complies, but Albert will not open his door when she informs him that "the queen" is on the other side. He still refuses when she identifies herself as "Victoria." Only when she becomes the meek petitioner, "your wife," will he let her in. Strachey includes this telling anecdote in his biography (*Queen Victoria* 84). The film hints at the truth about Victoria and Albert's initial power struggle. As the real Victoria did in life, Wilcox's Victoria makes Albert her full partner in all things. With this crucial merger, Victoria crossed a boundary, giving up individual control for shared governance. In life, she took the step gradually, reluctantly, but Wilcox plays Albert's rebellion and its outcome as a lovers' quarrel, funny and sweet, and the melodious sound track reinforces the idea that the compromise was easy and, on the whole, amusing.

In reality, the relationship between husband and wife was punctuated by the queen's towering rage, which occurred "at intervals over several years, embittering the life of the Queen and the Prince" (Woodham-Smith 335). Often Albert's response to Victoria's anger was to walk away, but sometimes he wrote notes to lecture her about it (334–35). Those notes raised our temperatures a few degrees, and we're just commoners. How must it have felt to be the queen of the British Empire and to be scolded for losing your temper? Considering the nature of this portrait, it's not surprising that Wilcox omits Victoria's anger, as he does a central source of Victoria's anguish, childbirth.

Anna Neagle portrays the physical changes that Victoria goes through as she travels from youth to age. In her autobiography, Neagle mentions looking in the mirror while wearing the heavy makeup of wrinkles, pouchy cheeks, and under-the-eye bags and seeing "the old Queen herself" looking back (83). The substantial changes of pregnancy, however, never appear in the film. In the 1930s and 1940s, Hollywood's notion of looking pregnant involved wearing loose clothes, donning a hair ribbon, and reclining on a divan, as Gene Tierney does in *Leave Her to Heaven* (John M. Stahl, 1945). Tierney hasn't even a suggestion of a baby bump like those that modern women flaunt. In *Victoria the Great,* there's not even a Tierney-esque scene to acknowledge that the queen was pregnant for *eighty-one months* of her life—a significant chunk of time. The film's single childbirth scene shows the queen lying next to the newly arrived Prince of Wales, as if he were a package delivered by post. It's triumphant and funny—Prince Albert finds his heir "very red"—but this glimpse erases the pain of delivery and the prior birth of a daughter. The subsequent seven babies never appear. Much later in the film, some kilt-wearing Scots watch the queen dancing a reel at Balmoral and comment, in amazement, that "the mother of nine" can turn such a light foot. The denial that producing such a large brood might have required a little effort fits the 1930s outlook that having children was just what women did, as it also fits the elevated status of the queen. Viewers are asked to assume that raising nine children made no ripples in Victoria's life.

Heilbrun identifies the tendency of male biographers to "reinvent" the lives of their female subjects (34), and, with regard to pregnancy and parenting, this is certainly true about Wilcox's film biography of Victoria. The real Victoria hated being pregnant and said that she feared having a large family (Woodham-Smith 206). She was horrified to discover that she was pregnant a second time; the Prince of Wales was born only eighteen months after his sister. The queen commented that the first two years of her marriage were "utterly spoilt" by pregnancy and wrote to her daughter Vicky to advise her to put off pregnancy if she could (224). Even a suggestion that her pregnancies were tiring or that she liked her children much better when they were no longer infants might have given female viewers a personal link to Victoria. Wilcox also deletes Victoria and Albert's substantial worries about their children—especially Bertie, the heir, on whom the queen placed partial blame for his father's death. Any hint of these realities would have shown that even monarchs cannot avoid the problems that come with progeny. While Wilcox does not hitch Victoria's destiny to her biology—a good thing—he does not acknowledge that, for much of her life, she was its captive.

Victoria is at her most human in Wilcox's film as she walks away from the camera after Albert's death, head bowed. The moving transition from this episode to the next, "The Widow of Windsor," shows the same hallway seven years later, with an aging, grieving Victoria walking toward the camera. Wilcox lets his audience glimpse Albert's room, frozen, as it was at his death, and he nods to the importance that Albert's servant, John Brown (Gordon McLeod), played in rejuvenating the queen. In Malleson and de Grandcourt's screenplay, however, one conversation with Prime Minister Gladstone (Arthur Young) about what Albert would have wanted her to do jolts Victoria from her seclusion. *Victoria the Great* doesn't linger on the darkness of the queen's mourning. Neither does it try to reimagine John Brown's impact on her.

Victoria's affection for her Highland servant, Brown, made her family anxious. She believed Brown to be an unflawed hero and had medals struck in his image. Public reaction to this relationship revealed the flip side of veneration. Some politicians, tired of the queen's monolithic mourning, found her behavior with Brown a "theme for ribald jest" (Strachey, *Queen Victoria*, 236), and London buzzed with jokes about the queen and her servant. This incident and other less-than-positive events don't jibe with Wilcox's portrait; Kara McKechnie points out that *Victoria the Great*'s "drive" toward mythology recognizes the climate outside the cinema in the years following King Edward's abdication (106). The skip past Brown's influence implies Wilcox's unwillingness to highlight an internal, or even an external, crisis. He deletes the Crimean War, although he does depict riots demanding the repeal of the corn laws and one of several assassination attempts on the queen, acknowledging that all was not always rosy. These included events contribute to the queen's heroism, whereas recognizing the venal criticism leveled at "Mrs. Brown," as her detractors mockingly called Victoria, would have changed the tone of this laudatory film. (John Madden's *Mrs. Brown* [1997] focuses on the Brown incident.)

At sixty-nine, Victoria recorded feeling "fresh and young," eager for more life (Longford 551), and she was extremely active, brokering royal marriages for her grandchildren, playing politics in the interconnected tangle of European states. In its resolution, *Victoria the Great* abandons action and embraces panoply. The two great celebrations of Victoria's Gold and Diamond Jubilees (the fiftieth and sixtieth anniversaries of her accession) are signifiers for the rest of her reign and life (no death or funeral scenes included). Shots of cheering crowds and grand processions through the streets of London capture the adoration of her people. Perhaps the film's love fests—incredible crowd scenes with London's landmarks in the background—come closest to the truth. In a diary entry, Victoria commented in amazement: "No one, ever, I believe, has been met with such an ovation as was given to me" (Longford 548).

Wilcox signals the import of the Diamond Jubilee by switching from black and white to color, and, even though the transition can't help but make modern viewers think of Dorothy's entry into Munchkin Land, the rich panorama of Neagle's elderly Victoria surrounded by Indian servants is made magical by those rainbow hues; the coming of color, an advancement in technology, also provides a fitting metaphor for a reign that saw many such changes. There's a lot to be said for a film that delivers exactly what's expected. "The Queen—she has arisen," one elderly innkeeper who had seen the real Victoria declared (Neagle 97). Indeed, Victoria might have liked this popular and financially successful film because it masks her private self.

Mrs. Brown (1997)

In our more intrusive, less laudatory time, the director John Madden lifts what Lytton Strachey calls the "veil" that "descends" over Victoria's life after the death of Albert (*Queen Victoria* 185). Madden's not the first director to find this period mesmerizing. Jean Negulesco imagined the end of the queen's mourning in his film, *The Mudlark* (1950), a fiction that identified a street urchin as the agent of the queen's turnabout. Madden's *Mrs. Brown*, starring Judi Dench as Victoria and Billy Connolly as her Highland servant, John Brown, mines biography in its more realistic rendition of Victoria's renewal.

Wilcox's earlier biopic, *Victoria the Great*, glides over the late 1860s, framing those years in a vignette that barely illuminates the depth and length of Victoria's isolation. Wilcox gives a glimpse of John Brown but places the responsibility of persuading Victoria back into public view solely on the prime minister, who reminds her that Albert would have expected her to resume her duties. The incident seems little more than a hesitation, a static moment on the path toward the euphoria of the jubilees. In reality, the queen's enforced seclusion—from 1861 to 1868—was a critical stumble, a detour that ignited dangerous critiques of her person, her reign, and the monarchy. "Where is Britannia?" read the caption beneath an 1867 cartoon depicting an empty throne. Antimonarchists repeated that question, capitalizing on the queen's absence and the record of her expenses to denounce a system that, they claimed, provided little return for its crippling cost.

Adding fuel to this blaze, half-humorous, half-horrified rumors about the queen's feelings for her Highland servant made her the object of ridicule. As the jokes and double entendres about "Mrs. Brown" (had she married him?) mounted, detractors began to suggest that the queen had gone mad or, at least, lost her grip on reality. Madden focuses on the Brown incident, a personal entanglement that attracted public attention. *Mrs. Brown* depicts a near symbiosis between the queen and the commoner in which the grieving queen drew energy from the increasingly drunken, paranoid, and ailing Brown. Although, like *Victoria the Great*, *Mrs. Brown* favors a carefully segmented structure—the screen fades to black between glimpses of dated incidents—it's the antithesis of Wilcox's public view. The audience sees Victoria's private, post-Albert hell from the inside and must learn to traverse that dark, ritualistic enclosure.

Dark perfectly describes the start of Madden's film. Before the credits run, black screens with white type offer three blunt blurbs that sum up the queen's life. "Queen Victoria came to the throne in 1837 at the age of eighteen," the first declares. The second tells us: "At twenty, she married Prince Albert of Saxe-Coburg. It was one of the happiest royal marriages in history." The third jumps to the end of the marriage: "When he died from typhoid in 1861, she was inconsolable." This last, context-creating statement might be expected to transition into something like Wilcox's shot of Victoria as a grieving widow, black garbed, coming toward the camera. Instead, Madden presents a visual non sequitur. Against a bright blue sky, the black bust of a bearded man falls in slow motion, end over end, through the air. Whom does the bust represent? How has it fallen? Why does the fall matter? A sound transition takes viewers from the crash of the bust to a roar of thunder. The camera races through a night forest with a disheveled, red-faced man who points a gun and spins as if surrounded by threats. "God save the queen," he shouts, discharging his pistol into the shadows. In *Mrs. Brown*, Madden uses a bookend approach, coming full circle to the point at which these enigmatic opening scenes make sense. At the end of the film, the black screens and white type appear again, this time bearing blurbs that sum up Victoria's post-Brown reign.

The opening scenes pose questions. The film proposes answers. *Mrs. Brown*, which juxtaposes natural and emotional landscapes, is much more like life: puzzling and fragmented, not at all like a Victorian pop-up book. Madden's view of Victoria evolves via telling scenes, scenes in which she is never alone. Placed in the same position as those who surround the queen, the audience must weigh her words and her expressions. The first glimpse of Victoria, dated 1864, comes from her chamber at Osborne House. A servant attends her, and the back of the queen's head centers the screen. Her face is reflected in the dressing-table mirror, a nice reminder that what we are seeing is an image—and a secondhand, reversed image at that. A close-up of her ravaged face reveals Victoria's state: dazed, in pain. It's often Judi Dench's face, more than the screenplay, that holds the key to relevance in *Mrs. Brown*. As von Sternberg used Dietrich's face in *The Scarlet Empress* as the coalescing image, John Madden makes Dench's face the speaking center of his elliptical film. Gradually, like a miraculous birth, light comes back to her eyes. Her vacant gaze refocuses. She begins, again, to see the world around her instead of the landscape within, but her renewal has a halting progress.

Providing some rare exposition, a voice-over glosses the first shot of the queen's face in the mirror, helping establish the in medias res situation—a servant named Brown has been called from Balmoral to help diminish the "unfettered morbidity" of Victoria's mourning. Although more comprehensible than its opening shots, *Mrs. Brown* continues to make visual demands on the audience. Only prior knowledge of Victoria's life can explicate the significance of the servants' actions during the voice-over. The clothing so carefully laid out and the steaming bowl of water are for Albert—just as if he were alive to shave and dress. Verbally demanding as well, the screenplay by Jeremy Brock insists that viewers grasp and synthesize bits of dialogue if they hope to identify members of the royal family, the household, and the government. Thrust into a game in progress, the audience must scramble to decode its rules. The critic Barbara Shulgasser believes that Brock's screenplay goes "nowhere," but we think that Roger Ebert's assessment that "the movie is insidious in its methods, asking us to see what is happening beneath the guarded surfaces," fits both images and words more accurately (rev. of *Mrs. Brown*). To modern eyes, all court etiquette looks like a minuet, but there's more going on in Osborne House (the royal summer retreat on the Isle of Wight) than the usual, formal dance. This is a grim caricature of that childhood game Mother-May-I, with its call and response. Victoria's silent arrival at the breakfast table and the comfortless meal that follows show how the game is going.

May anyone raise his or her voice? No. May anyone leave the house without the queen's permission? No. May anyone walk ahead of the queen? No. May anyone speak to the queen before being addressed? No. May anyone try to lift the queen's burden? No. May anyone do anything to dispel the gloom? No. May anyone acknowledge that the world might still hold interest? No. No. No. Victoria's secretary, Henry Ponsonby (Geoffrey Palmer), whose voice we first hear, understands that all of them are "prisoners of the queen's grief." The royal warden, however, barely acknowledges those around her. Judi Dench renders Victoria's intense, initial state and her slow recovery moving and real. Her powerful performance as Victoria brought her fresh recognition, including an Oscar nomination. Helen

Hunt won the Best Actress Oscar for 1998, but, a year later, Dench received a Best Supporting Actress Oscar for her brief portrayal of Elizabeth I in *Shakespeare in Love* (John Madden, 1998), an honor that many thought also recognized her excellence in *Mrs. Brown*. The award led her to quip: "I can only play Queens now" (Miller, *Judi Dench*, 297).

Dench was an acknowledged queen of the British theatrical world well before the release of *Mrs. Brown*. Her biographer, Johnathan Miller, notes: "By the 1980s Judi had scaled the highest pinnacles in the theater" (272). As a member of the Royal Shakespeare Company, the Old Vic, and the National Theater, Dench had played Ophelia, Juliet, Titania, Isabella, Portia, Lady Macbeth, and Cleopatra—almost every important woman in Shakespeare's oeuvre—and she had, by the age of sixty-one, won every award the British stage—or the nation—could give her, including being made a DBE (dame of the British Empire) in 1988. Certainly, she had nothing to prove when she took the role of M to Pierce Brosnan's Bond in *Goldeneye* (Martin Campbell, 1987), her first blockbuster film, or when she eagerly accepted the challenge of playing Victoria.

To prepare for the role of the queen, Miller says, Dench had long conversations with Madden "about the character of Queen Victoria," and she read "one biography of her, and her highland journals" (*Judi Dench* 276). Miller never elaborates on the content of those conversations, and he volunteers little about what Dench felt or thought of Victoria. He prefers describing Dench's good humor as well as practical jokes, horse farts, and muffed scenes he observed during filming.

Miller had amazing access to his subject, as all the on-set trivia shows. As more proof of his insider status, he begins the biography with selections from a journal he kept during the filming of *Mrs. Brown*. Yet his irritatingly opaque work settles for providing a bare-bones account of the main events in Dench's life that reads like a dated list. A record of her many roles and critical responses to them, anecdotes that demonstrate Dench's normalcy, and laudatory or amusing observations from her colleagues fill in the 313-page book, making it exactly the kind of biography Carolyn Heilbrun would hate. Almost everything that would be fascinating to know about Dench is missing. Her insights about the characters she has played, her specific memories of childhood and her parents, the nature of her marriage, her relationship with her daughter, her close friendships, her reaction to her husband's death, all are left unplumbed. Instead, readers must be satisfied with knowing that Dench likes to play word games while she waits on a set or that, as a gift for Billy Connolly, she embroidered a "wee" pillow that read: "To J.B. from V.R." (279).

Miller hints at one reason for the lack of personal or interpretive information. Dench, he says, was "initially very reluctant" to consider a biography. She dreaded "all that talking about [herself]" (1) but finally agreed to the project. A single, painful, personal incident explodes from these bland pages like a bomb when Miller explains that in 1997 Finty (Dench's only child) gave birth to a son and that neither parent knew she was pregnant. In the context of this revelation, Miller mentions Dench's "distress" at the media attention this "story" received, and he makes a trenchant comment: "As I observed over the months spent researching this book, she is outraged by intrusions into [her] privacy." He recounts Dench once saying: "I've made up my mind I'm not going to give any more interviews" (287).

Dench didn't follow that edict, but she grants very few interviews. When she does speak to the press, she usually mentions the difficulty of maintaining privacy. In 1981, she told a BBC interviewer that she and her husband, Michael Williams, made "a pact" to "never discuss" their work at home, acknowledging their compartmentalization of private and public lives (Dench, interview with Sonia Beesley). In 2004, during another brief interview, Dench was "appalled" by the demand: "Tell . . . everything that has been important in your life, everything that has made you happy and made you sad in the next thirty seconds." After reprimanding the interviewer, Dench responded: "My family. My family has always been the most important thing in my life, and after that, everything is secondary" (Dench, interview with Simon Hattenstone). Again nominated for an Oscar in 2007 for her performance in *Notes on a Scandal* (Richard Eyre, 2006), Dench consented to a telephone interview with two other "queenly" nominees, Helen Mirren and Meryl Streep. During the interview, the media's treatment of Lindsay Lohan came up.

"Now there's nothing you don't know about people," Dench commented. "You can find out everything about everybody, and I think that's rather an eroding thing" (Collis 28). It couldn't be clearer that Dench, with her repeated mantra that private life trumps everything else, insisted that Miller draw a line right at the threshold of her real life. Although this is disappointing for anyone seeking a picture of Dench, it's also an understandable reaction to a media-obsessed world that rarely differentiates between curiosity and exploitation.

Perhaps the careful guarding of her personal life gave Dench a strong connection to Victoria. Public exposure and political pressure were so wearing to the queen, Longford points out, that she often threatened to lay aside her crown. Instead, Victoria used her "routine retirements to Balmoral and Osborne" as "abdication-substitutes" (570). More than any other Victoria biopic, *Mrs. Brown* focuses on the tension between public and private worlds; it's not the queen's mourning for Albert's person alone that draws her increasingly into solitude, this film insists, but the loss of what Albert created for her, a space in which he kept the world at bay. Only Brown, of all the characters in the film (or in the queen's life?), understands this. Everyone surrounding her reads her woodenness as a refusal to provide what's needed. To her children, especially Bertie (David Westhead), she's an immovable object barring his path to power. To the servants, she has become a mawkish tyrant, limiting even their small pleasures. To the politicians, she's the "old girl," as Disraeli (Antony Sher) says, whom they can "winkle out" if needed. To the public, she's an unknown quantity, invisible and, apparently, unstable, no longer the familiar figure fronting national pageantry.

Into this seething circle of frustration strides John Brown, summoned from Balmoral by Harry Ponsonby, to help ease the queen back into normal—that is, public—life. Victoria called Balmoral "this dear Paradise" (*Leaves from the Journal of Our Life in the Highlands* 89) and identified Brown—whom Albert liked—as a central figure in its landscape: "He has all the independence and elevated feelings peculiar to the Highland race" (55). When it comes to Brown, Madden loves metaphor. He emphasizes the Highlander's foreignness by introducing him in a series of crosscuts between the tomblike interior of Osborne House and the windswept shore where Brown is landing. While all inside is stasis, a breeze ruffles Brown's kilt and lifts the ribbons of his cap. The opposition of nature and culture continues as Brown shows just how free he can be, how effectively he can disrupt the "rigid arrangement" of the enclosure (McKechnie 112). From the start, his "independence and elevated feelings" shape his interactions with the queen. Victoria was not the first queen to find solace in an unlikely person. Her affection for Brown recalls Catherine the Great's reliance on Potemkin, Mary of Scotland's connection to Riccio, and Marie Antoinette's attraction to Count Fersen. It makes sense that an outsider might be a welcome alternative to the stultifying protocol of court life.

Brock's screenplay emphasizes Brown's important differences. Unlike everyone else at Osborne House, Brown speaks plainly, dropping words like stones into the stagnant pool of mannered language. He calls Victoria "woman," as the real Brown did, when even she speaks of herself in the third person. Brown violates a major communications edict—one must not address the queen unless addressed—the first time he is brought into her presence. Horrified by her changed physical state, her querulousness, and her shaky gulp from a glass of water, he says: "Honest to God, I swear I never thought to see you in such a state. You must miss him dreadfully." His bluntness sparks Victoria's hysteria, but it also knocks her out of what Ponsonby describes as her "ferocious introspection." Brown's unique combination of fresh air and fresh speech energizes the languid queen. Before long she is riding, quoting Brown's health tips, and swimming. She even smiles; the normality of the environment Brown creates for her has cushioned her jangled nerves. But three years later, in 1867, the queen seems addicted to the Brown cure, and he manages her life. Can this be the same Victoria, visiting a Highland family, happily helping prepare the table, laughing at a joke?

Madden and Brock are interested in Brown's motives. Again missing the mark, Shulgasser insists that "Brock's interpretation" presents a Brown who "wanted nothing for himself; with fanatical loyalty he lived only for his Queen" (rev. of *Mrs. Brown*). Brock's screenplay, Madden's play of images, and Connolly's performance simply don't add up to such a simplistic characterization. Instead, Brown is a nexus of wanting. He begins his climb by appropriating the head seat at the servant's table. After suborning the staff, he moves on to humbling Ponsonby and, finally, to bullying Bertie, the queen's disappointing heir. Casting aids Brown's complexity; Billy Connolly's eclectic mix of Puckish charm, notoriously foul mouth, and varied experience as a physical laborer, stand-up comic, and Shakespearean actor makes him a good choice to play the quixotic Brown, "rough, handsome, intelligent" (Longford 325). From his first appearance, Connolly shows he's up to the part. His walk toward Osborne House establishes Brown's cocky confidence. In *Mrs. Brown*, the Queen's Highland servant acknowledges his ambition, telling his brother, Archie, who also serves the queen, that he doesn't intend to remain a "wee sprat." He pursues the queen's interests, even asking a maid what Victoria is reading. Brashly, he accrues power, and, brashly, he uses it, wielding the queen's favor as he climbs. "There's no stopping me now," he declares as he and his brother dash naked into the cold sea, another example of Brown's hardy physicality.

Brown demonstrates his closeness to the queen most openly at Balmoral Castle during a dance for the family and the staff. It's 1868, and the queen grasps Brown's hands for a prolonged swing at the end of a reel. The camera follows her motion. No longer in stasis, no longer the colorless, querulous old woman who disintegrated at Brown's first words, she's blooming, pretty, relaxed; Brown bows to her, happy in her gaze. In contrast, close-ups show the grim expressions and raised eyebrows of Victoria's advisers and family, demonstrating that they appreciate the queen's new attachment as little as they did her perpetual sorrow. The film suggests their less-than-regal response, depicting a violent beating, a choreographed attempt to characterize Brown as a drunkard—Victoria despised smoking and drinking. "You're a servant," Brown's brother reminds him. "She doesn't give a damn about you." The queen, however, acts as if she does. When Brown tries to resign to prevent more rumors, Victoria refuses. "Without you," she tells him, "I can't find the strength to be who I must be." In this moving, central scene, an invention that feels real, they kiss each other's hands.

But, as the queen regains her strength, the balance shifts, and Brown begins to fade. Glimpses of his drinking and his fanatic raving about the queen's security illuminate his descent. The servants—no longer cowed by his rough ways—now ridicule him. But he has yet to meet his most serious adversary. If Brown represents the pull of nature, Benjamin Disraeli represents the pull of culture. Madden builds this opposition by developing Disraeli's character in careful crosscuts between the queen's pastoral retreats and London, where the political situation escalates. Brock's dialogue shows that, like Brown, Disraeli can be both funny and plainspoken, a master of all forms of language. Although he gives moving speeches in Parliament about the value of tradition, he privately calls the queen "the old girl" and wonders whether she's needed. When his party is threatened by the antimonarchists, he reads public sentiment well. Victoria's Highland journal, he notes, has sold "more copies than Dickens." Buoyed up by this display of the queen's popularity, he acts.

Mrs. Brown. John Brown had better savor this precious moment with the queen. *Mrs. Brown* traces the Highland servant's healing effects on the grieving Victoria. His ministrations enable her to resume her role, but his triumph signals the end of his power. (Courtesy Jerry Ohlinger's Movie Material Store.)

Madden imagines a showdown between Prime Minister Disraeli and the queen's Highland servant—a verbal skirmish on a mountaintop. In 1868, when Disraeli realizes that he must drag "the old girl" back, he visits Balmoral. Brown tries to break the effete city dweller by taking him on a punishing hunt, through rain, and up impossible slopes. Disraeli, in obvious discomfort, soldiers on and recovers enough to challenge Brown to another, more difficult climb. This time Disraeli beats Brown on his own terrain. It's Brown—holding his heart—who is suffering.

At the pinnacle, the men sit together, and Disraeli asks Brown's aid in encouraging the queen to return. He acknowledges Brown's power but "winkles" the Highlander into a difficult position. If he cannot, or will not, convince the queen to return, his failure will be seen as a lack of control. If he counsels her to return, however, the queen will group him with those who oppose her wishes. When Brown agrees, Disraeli, literally and figuratively, wins the high ground.

From this point on, Brown is out of his element. Angered by Brown's insistence that she return to public life, and galvanized into action by her son's recovery from typhoid, the queen goes to London. Brown's kilt, cap, and sporran, so suited to mountain life, look like a costume at Buckingham Palace. Victoria increases her exposure, beginning with a ride to St. Paul's in an open carriage (which Brown counsels against). Ever vigilant, Brown stops an assassination attempt, but he gradually recedes into the ranks of the many who serve. Madden measures the increased distance between Victoria and Brown at a palace dinner. Bertie, flushed, happy, a little drunk, makes light of Brown's "heroic" actions. The queen, however, praises Brown, vowing to have a medal struck of him.

Their physical separation defines their positions. The queen sits at the head of an opulently appointed table, speaking about Brown in the third person, while Brown stands against the wall, in the shadows, still on guard. Queen Victoria doesn't look at Brown, but the care with which she avoids doing so telegraphs her sensitivity to his presence, even if her total dependence on him has ended. When the scene in the dark woods appears again, now dated 1882, viewers recognize an aging, ailing, delusional Brown as the man with the gun, and they see how this piece fits into the context of the narrative. After his death, Ponsonby explains, Bertie smashed a bust of Brown—the one we saw fall—and now it's clear why even his image might arouse the heir's anger.

The physical showdown on the mountaintop between Brown and Disraeli may be fiction, but all who surrounded the queen acknowledged a point at which the "Brown crisis" was over. "The thing runs smoothly, and we wonder there was ever a row about it," Ponsonby wrote in 1871 (qtd. in Longford 333). While *Mrs. Brown* cites no specific biographical source, fancifully alluding to Brown's "missing diary" as a treasure trove of truth, it parallels Elizabeth Longford's account, even in some of the language that makes its way into Brock's screenplay, including Victoria's insistence that "the Queen will not be dictated to" about anything concerning Brown (qtd. in Longford 329). Victoria wrote these words to her equerry when she discovered a plan to keep Brown away from a public event. In the film, her family has written her a letter asking her to relinquish Brown. She responds, using the same phrase. In this scene, Madden underscores the queen's separation from her children, and vice versa. Since they have not addressed her personally, she responds similarly, ordering Ponsonby to read them her reply while they stand in her smoldering presence.

In *Victoria the Great,* Wilcox treats the queen's temper playfully; Madden does not. *Mrs. Brown* isn't hesitant to fill the anger gap that Heilbrun identifies in *Writing a Woman's Life*. Reading Miller's biography might make you think that Judi Dench has rarely had an angry moment, but her performance as Victoria implies her understanding of that emotion. In one scene, Victoria plays the sprightly "Highland Man" for Disraeli's entertainment (surely a loaded choice). In contrast to the song's gaiety, her eyes flash, and her fingers pound the keys with rage. Dench uses physical cues like this one, as well as voice and expression, to describe a self swept away by sorrow and anger. A misreading of *Mrs. Brown* could validate the jokes contemporaries made about the queen and Brown, boiling their relationship down to an outlet for anger, a nervous flirtation. The ugly supposition inherent in this view is that the queen (like any woman?) simply needed a real man—the rougher, the better—to get over her sorrow.

But Dench, Connolly, and Madden work toward a subtler conclusion. *Mrs. Brown* says that, while Victoria appreciated being seen as an attractive woman, a person as well as a head of state, she needed the balm of human connection and, most of all, a friend. Why did Victoria find this intimacy with an outsider only? Elizabeth Longford attempts an answer, first asking a Heilbrunian question: "Where was [her] female friend?" She guesses that Victoria, trained from childhood to hold a "princely" view of herself, could never have imagined intimacy with her ladies-in-waiting or with anyone else in the stratified group surrounding her (371). *Mrs. Brown* emphasizes the strict conventions that Victoria's ladies-in-waiting followed. They trail along in the queen's wake. Never do they converse with her, speaking only when she asks them a question. Immersed in a system designed to breed sycophants, the queen must have often longed for a real companion.

Mrs. Brown acknowledges Brown's importance to the queen, interpreting their relationship, imagining them alone together. Brock creates a final scene in which Victoria visits Brown on his deathbed, apologizing for her long absence, assuring him that "even now" she is "feeling desperate at the thought of losing [him]." History too reveals Victoria's lifelong affection for her Highland servant. Before she died, Victoria carefully prescribed the contents of her coffin. In this last act, she strove to maintain control, designing a final resting place that included a secret compartment. She depended on trusted retainers, not her family, to place many private mementos beneath her body. One of these faithful servants was to have been

Brown, but his death preceded the queen's. Among the objects placed in the secret space were "favorite shawls," an "alabaster" sculpture of Albert's hand, "the Prince consort's dressing gown," and "a robe . . . embroidered . . . by Princess Alice, the first of the Queen's children to die" (Packard 200). This bottom layer was covered before the queen's sons entered the room to lift their mother's body into the coffin. After her family left the room once more, the servants performed Victoria's final commands. They "put Victoria's wedding veil over her face and upper torso," placed a photo of John Brown in the queen's left hand, and laid "a lock of Brown's hair, wrapped in tissue paper," among the flowers (201).

Victoria and Albert (2001)

Mrs. Brown, with its intimate focus on human need that transcends the most extreme class difference, has an unlikely resonance with Titanic, John Cameron's big, record-breaking picture that debuted in the same year. Titanic tells the tale of Jack Dawson (Leonardo DiCaprio), a steerage passenger, who fixes his gaze on the first-class beauty Rose DeWitt (Kate Winslet) and sacrifices his life for her. The tale brings Rose's memory to life, and her retelling of events gives the treasure hunter Brock Lovett (Bill Paxton) a human context for what he has seen as a distant, historic event.

Victoria and Albert isn't the least bit interested in attraction between high and low, but it pays homage to memory as the key to unlocking the past. The title of this joint A&E/BBC production promises a focus on the shared life of the royal couple, but Victoria's name comes first in the title; and, most of the time, her perception is privileged in the made-for-television miniseries starring Victoria Hamilton and Jonathan Firth. According to the opening device, the queen's memory orders all events. The narrative begins when a retainer wheels the aged queen (Joyce Redman) into Albert's carefully preserved room at Windsor, and, here, among his things, Victoria hears voices from her past. She recalls her coming of age, her courtship, her marriage to Albert, and their years together. At the end of the film, the camera returns again to the queen, the framer of what has transpired. In recounting these events, John Erman, the director, and John Goldsmith, the screenwriter (he also cowrote A&E's rampage through Catherine the Great's life), cover some of the same material as Wilcox's 1937 Victoria the Great, and, after its starting flashback, this most-current version of the queen's life favors a similar chronological approach, dating and labeling most episodes, as did its 1937 predecessor. *Victoria and Albert* can't claim the intensity of *Mrs. Brown,* but it attempts more than an updated rehash of the significant events in Victoria's life. This twenty-first-century biopic takes an inside look at Victoria's early life and her relationship with Albert. In every event selected, in every line uttered, it pursues the private, not the public, view.

Generally, the memory catalyst and the close-up approach work. *Victoria and Albert* explores new film ground when it examines Victoria's early influences: the Duchess of Kent; her secretary, Sir John Conroy; and the Baroness Lehzen, Victoria's governess/confidante.

Madden's *Mrs. Brown* covers Victoria's prolonged period of mourning, starting three years after she had lost both her mother and Albert. Wilcox's biopic begins with the night before Victoria's accession—the event that delivered her from a stultifying existence. Erman and Goldsmith rewind to provide some context for Victoria's first commands: that she would have her own bedroom and that she would see her ministers alone.

Starting when Victoria was a teen, *Victoria and Albert* clarifies the lay of the land at Kensington Palace. Victoria spent her childhood here, sequestered, far from her uncle, King William IV, whom her mother, the Duchess of Kent, abhorred. (The king returned her dislike.)

A recent trip to the palace allowed us to imagine the pastoral atmosphere it had when mother and daughter shared its grounds and dark interior spaces. The duchess did not want her daughter tainted by the court's corruption, and she preferred to be Princess Victoria's single influence. Consequently, she rebuffed any overtures from the king. In *Victoria and Albert,* their joint animosity crackles in a tense scene based on history. The king (Peter Ustinov) has ordered Victoria (Victoria Hamilton) and her mother (Penelope Wilton) to attend him at Windsor Castle for his seventy-first-birthday dinner, where he takes the opportunity to berate the duchess publicly for keeping her daughter away from his court.

Lytton Strachey describes the "flood of vituperation" that flowed from the king at that dinner (*Queen Victoria* 46), some of which Goldsmith's dialogue re-creates. Although everyone knew of whom he spoke, the king never named the duchess, venting his wrath on "a person now near him," while the duchess sat at his right, trembling with rage. In her attempt to control Victoria's thoughts and actions, the duchess was assisted by Sir

John Conroy, equerry to Victoria's late father, who hoped for grand rewards. Virtually locked in their airtight environment, Victoria had only her mother and Sir John to provide her with political information. Their ministrations strained the definition of protection. Once, when Victoria was ill, "Sir John, abetted by the Duchess, . . . tried to wring a signed promise" that Victoria "would appoint him to the key position of her private secretary" (Marshall, *Life and Times of Victoria*, 21). This was one of many affronts that made Victoria, who refused to sign the document, despise Sir John.

Wilcox must have thought Sir John too shady a character to be included in *Victoria the Great*, but *Victoria and Albert* does a nice job of revealing his selfishness. Most important, his portrait colors Victoria's, for hangers-on are the lot of monarchs, and a biopic that erases them (and all such excrescences) sacrifices dimension. Victoria's repugnance for Sir John demonstrates her ability to judge him for herself, even though the duchess encouraged her to think well of him. When Conroy (Patrick Malahide), brusk and peremptory, tries to browbeat young Victoria into compliance, it's obvious that he cares only for the power she will hold, not for her. In a key scene, Sir John looms over her, repeating his favorite mantra: "Your mother is your best friend and your wisest counselor." Victoria is putting together a puzzle and has only the last few pieces to place, a visual signifier for the crucial "pieces" she lacks. When she attains her majority, and when the king dies, she will be lifted beyond Sir John's reach. High-contrast lighting clarifies Sir John's character—and hers. Dressed in white, Victoria sits in a beam of sunlight while Sir John circles her, literally in the dark—a perfect metaphor for the situation, which came to an "abrupt conclusion" (Strachey, *Queen Victoria*, 54). When Victoria became queen, she quickly rid herself of Sir John. This beginning section of Victoria's life is shot in shadowy half light. On the morning of her uncle's death, after she has been told that she is queen, Victoria opens a tall window to flood the room, and herself, in sunlight, ending her shadow life.

Stanley Weintraub describes Conroy and the Duchess of Kent as "two figures who might have been conceived by the Brothers Grimm" (97), but *Victoria and Albert* gives the Duchess of Kent a more nuanced position than Sir John's. Wilcox granted the duchess a theatrical hauteur, but, after the opening scenes of *Victoria the Great*, she disappears. Erman and Goldsmith more adequately represent the recriminations and reconciliation between mother and daughter. After she became queen, Victoria had little desire to see her mother, who had dominated her world at Kensington Palace. The Duchess of Kent found herself "shut off from every vestige of influence, of confidence, of power" (Strachey, *Queen Victoria*, 53). Victoria placed her full trust in the prime minister, Lord Melbourne, an important figure in *Victoria and Albert*. Even though the Duchess of Kent could no longer filter the queen's reality, Victoria felt that her mother's continuing presence in the palace was a "torment." Marriage offered her another escape from maternal pressures (Woodham-Smith 178). As the young couple's family began to grow, Albert—who liked the duchess—pushed for, and helped achieve, a rapprochement.

Victoria and Albert offers the only extended examination of a mother/daughter relationship in the royal biopics we discuss. With her narrow, angular face, sharp elbows, and rigid posture, Penelope Wilton creates a duchess who's difficult to like. She's firmly in the grip of the despicable Sir John, but she's truly disagreeable on her own as well. She demonstrates this in a scene that takes place shortly after an assassination attempt against her daughter. Even though Victoria has just been attacked by a madman, barely escaping injury, the duchess chooses that tense moment to seize Albert's arm and whine about her living arrangements—hardly a maternal impulse. Yet Wilton makes it equally difficult to despise the duchess. With every unblinking stare and angry, flouncing exit, she makes it clear that she has been damaged by difficult financial and political circumstances and has suffered acutely.

"I have sacrificed everything for you," she scolds her daughter, speaking the truth. The pain in young Victoria's eyes answers that such bald sacrifice has eaten every chance of normalcy, easy affection, or fun that could have made the difficult early years bearable for both. A chastened duchess—now freed from dreams of power—appears at Victoria's side after her first child is born. Much more at ease, she remembers the "delight" she and her husband felt at Victoria's birth, and her words break through the young queen's shell of hostility. A little more than a year later, after Victoria has given birth to Bertie, she and her mother look comfortable together; Victoria says that they must forget "the past" and be "great friends." In these and later family scenes, *Victoria and Albert* gives evidence of their growing warmth, and the interpretation isn't an exaggeration. During the duchess's last years, Victoria stayed "in the closest touch with her mother either through daily visits or letters." After the Duchess of Kent died in 1861 with "her hand in her daughter's," Victoria "suffered a nervous breakdown" and a feeling that she had been "abandoned" (Longford 290).

Although she came to care for her mother, Victoria felt much closer to her governess, the Baroness Lehzen, during her childhood. *Victoria and Albert* often shows the princess literally between the two women, who felt little affection for each other. Probably because Lehzen too occupied an ambiguous position in the queen's life, her role is nearly erased in *Victoria the Great*. *Victoria and Albert*, with its focus on private life, establishes her importance, especially during the dark years at Kensington Palace. Diana Rigg, a DBE and a queen of stage and screen, won an Emmy for her performance as Lehzen, an interpretation that equally displays her admirable and her detestable qualities, making her a character as rich as Wilton's duchess. The good Lehzen girds the young Victoria for every challenge and promises to be with her "forever." "Remember who you are," Lehzen reminds the princess. Her constant support reflects reality; Baroness Lehzen dedicated herself to her charge, always considering the ramifications of her actions. Lehzen avoided anything "imprudent"; she would not even keep a journal during her years with the princess for fear that it might be used to harm Victoria in the future (Longford 30). Victoria's marriage, however, altered the relationship between the queen and her governess. Prince Albert's secretary, Mr. Anson, noted that Lehzen "meddled and made mischief" whenever she could do so at Albert's expense (Woodham-Smith 222–23).

Lehzen was jealous of the prince, and he had less than warm feelings about her. Albert believed that Victoria had been poorly educated and blamed Lehzen. He also disliked her approach to palace housekeeping. As the controller of the household, she could have instituted much-needed reforms. Instead, she relied on the existing system with its waste and graft. *Victoria and Albert* capitalizes on the acrimony between the baroness and the prince. With every jealous glance and barely suppressed smirk, Rigg's Lehzen telegraphs her dislike of Albert. Not content simply to harbor that emotion, she tries to undermine him, to "meddle" at every opportunity. In one scene, she draws Victoria's attention to Albert's choice of companion. He's in conversation with Sir Robert Peel, whom Victoria detested. Trying to provoke Victoria, Lehzen comments that the two men look "thick as thieves" when they are simply exchanging small talk. Lehzen jealously guards her power as keeper of the royal household and bristles at Albert's attempts to untangle the knot of staff duties. A childish tattler, she runs to the queen, complaining that the prince is overstepping his bounds; Lehzen practically sneers at Albert as she leaves the queen's rooms. She even jumps into verbal combat with the prince. In a scene that takes place after the assassination attempt, Albert argues that the certifiably insane man who attacked the queen should not be executed. Angrily, Lehzen accuses Albert of "defending" the assassin against his own wife.

In life, the queen's decision to end Lehzen's service came after several troubling incidents. The first involved Princess Vicky's care during a childhood illness; the prince favored more modern, scientific treatment, while Lehzen relied on aging palace doctors and home remedies. *Victoria and Albert* includes the nursery scene, complete with the shrieking princess, the scowling Lehzen, and an angry Albert stalking from the overheated room. In matters of palace security, Lehzen also followed the status quo, and the miniseries recounts the famous case of "breaking and entering" that ended Lehzen's rule. In 1840, a working-class teen, "the Boy, Jones," broke into Buckingham Palace more than once. When he was finally discovered, he explained how easily he had entered and wandered the halls, undetected— a feat that screams CODE RED to our security-sensitive post-9/11 world. His comments proved that he had come close enough to the royal family "to hear the Princess Royal cry" (Longford 155). Not too long after this security breach, Lehzen left, at the queen's bidding. She received a pension and retired to a small German village. The biographer Stanley Weintraub feels that, had Lehzen "made any conciliatory gestures towards Albert," she could have kept her place or, at least, stayed in the palace, near Victoria (160). Years later, Victoria asked that "not only [Lehzen's] mistakes" be included in a biography of Albert. Lehzen's belligerence, the queen insisted, had come, not from "personal ambition," but from her insistence "that no one but herself was able to take care of the Queen" (Woodham-Smith 236).

As Lehzen leaves, light and sound underscore Victoria's turn away from her childhood adviser and toward Albert. Unable to halt the changing order, Lehzen watches from the shadows as servants carry Albert's desk into Victoria's brightly lit study, where he will share her work. In her last interview with the queen, an unrepentant Lehzen insists that, although she did her best, "nothing was good enough for Prince Albert." A clock chimes, and this auditory marker of passing time acts as the transition to Lehzen's departure. On a gray morning, she rides away, taking with her the last vestiges of Kensington Palace. Neither the Duchess of Kent nor the Baroness Lehzen were completely admirable characters, but both were strong women, focused on training the young queen and on fighting for their own survival. It's satisfying to see them as full characters in this biopic, granted their importance to Victoria, radiating the passionate intensity that they shared.

As a parallel to Victoria's early years, *Victoria and Albert* offers a similar, if briefer, look at Prince Albert's youth, a period colored by his potential to be Victoria's bridegroom. These scenes of Albert's private life, which the queen could not have witnessed, violate the "memory" format of the miniseries, even if they flesh out the "*and Albert*" part of the title. Baron Stockmar (David Suchet), lost in the background of *Victoria the Great,* jumps into high relief here, especially during the crucial nuptial negotiations. Stockmar acted as an emissary for Leopold, king of Belgium—played with panache in *Victoria and Albert* by Jonathan Pryce—who was uncle to both Victoria and Albert, and who desired the obvious political benefits of a union between his niece and nephew. The miniseries illustrates Stockmar's importance as one of the "other forces" in the lives of the young royal couple (Strachey, *Queen Victoria,* 55). Tirelessly, he buzzes around Victoria and Albert, encouraging the reluctant princess to invite Albert and his brother, Ernst, for a visit, inspiring the reluctant prince to accept the position of royal consort. "What would I be?" Albert worries. "A nothing, a cipher, two steps behind the queen of England, like a pet dog." Stockmar convinces Albert that he can attain enough power to do some good. "There is only one ability a man needs to make himself a master," he assures the prince, "to wait." In *Victoria and Albert,* Albert follows that advice in politics and romance.

At first, Victoria believed that Albert—after all, a foreigner—should have no influence on policy. In matters of state, she consulted her prime minister, Lord Melbourne, only. Both *Victoria the Great* and *Victoria and Albert* illustrate the queen's changing view. This event, like others depicted in both biopics—the visit, the proposal, the wedding ceremony—demonstrates a pervasive difference in tone. Wilcox plays the predicament as a lovers' quarrel culminating in the prince locking Victoria out of their private rooms. After she petitions to enter, not as "the queen," but as his "wife," Albert unlocks the door. The next scene shows the result—the royal couple working happily together, their desks facing each other.

Victoria and Albert depicts the queen's change as a series of painful steps that led her to share her political burden with Albert. The "locked-door" scene is repositioned to take place after Albert's visit to Lehzen's nursery. Victoria's appeal to enter as the prince's "wife" comes after an angry showdown between them. The change in the timing of the scene and the inclusion of Lehzen-induced tension make this moment a dramatic turning point instead of a cute, sentimental spat. And there's no quick dissolve to the two, at companion desks, happily signing bills. Albert "waits," gently pointing out just how helpful he could be. Miserable, in the last months of her second pregnancy, the queen still resists him, although she accepts many of his suggestions. After Lehzen leaves, Victoria finally relinquishes her tight hold on all things political. She hands Albert an important object, a signifier of her transfer of trust. A close-up shows the key, bound with red cord, that will unlock the top-secret dispatch boxes. The key gives Albert entry to those urgent documents, but it also delivers a message from Victoria that, as far as she is concerned, the last barrier is down between them.

Such complete surrender comes less easily to Albert, who waits for the key that will open his heart. Erman and Goldsmith's script shapes the prince's search for love into a quest, starting with the lines Albert says to Stockmar after he has accepted Victoria's proposal. "I don't love her," the prince tells his adviser. "I feel a great affection, warmth for her, but I don't love her. That frightens me." Biographers agree that, although Victoria had been pleased with Albert during his 1836 visit (glimpsed in *Victoria and Albert*), she fell in love with him passionately immediately on his return in 1838. "Albert's *beauty is most striking,* and he is amiable and unaffected—in short, very fascinating," she wrote in her diary (Longford 133). Biographers also agree that Albert's feelings were measured. "He was not in love with her," Strachey baldly asserts (*Queen Victoria* 90). Dorothy Marshall phrases the same content more gently: "Whether Albert was as lyrically happy as his wife . . . has been questioned by contemporaries . . . and by subsequent biographers" (76).

Erman and Goldsmith ask us to consider the possibility that the prince came to love his wife with something better than immediate passion. In the miniseries, Albert "researches" the matter of romance. He attentively watches Sheridan's comedy *The Rivals*, in which a character recommends "a little aversion" as a good way to begin a marriage. "Were you in love?" he questions his private secretary, and Mr. Anson replies that he married for money but found "something more lasting" in building a home and family. All this questioning seems a little demeaning to Victoria, a reminder that we have moved beyond the window of her memory. How would such a private person as the queen have felt about the prince's revelations to Stockmar and Anson? These scenes do underscore the loneliness of Albert's life, summarized neatly by Sarah Ferguson, the Duchess of York, who points out that Albert was "virtually alone in a foreign country, with no companions from his old life" (19). Perpetually a boarder in his wife's castles, surrounded by her staff, what choices of confidants were available to him?

Often, Victoria tells Albert how much she loves him, but, because he is entirely truthful, the prince withholds the phrase "I love you" until he can mean it. Finally, he speaks, in an imagined scene set in 1851, right after the opening of the Great Exposition, the prince's pet project. Both Victoria and Albert are regally dressed for a state dinner. (*Victoria and Albert* won an Emmy for costume design.) Before they go to their guests, Albert says: "I want you to know how deeply I love you." The kiss that follows has more warmth than the one that sealed their engagement. A reality check quickly halts any lapse into sentiment. After all, there were those nine—*nine*—children. The real Albert *may* have anguished over the nature of his feelings for Victoria, but his contemplations didn't hamper his libido. Still, it's a nice moment, an antidote to all those stock Cinderella endings in which just-joined couples merge into perfect embraces. Instead, viewers get a chance to see a condition rarely depicted on the screen, an example of mature love.

According to *Victoria and Albert*, the prince was a highly principled, studious, reflective man, and his desire for meaningful occupation was sincere, not a disguised grab for political power. The miniseries sums him up as a devoted husband and an affectionate, concerned father, jumping ten years to show him bringing the custom of the Christmas tree to England and romping with his children. There's also a brief look at Bertie's escapades with a showgirl and Prince Albert's reaction to this upsetting behavior. The quickly aging, ailing, overtired prince travels to Cambridge to lecture, but he apologizes instead. "The fault is mine," he tells his son. "I've expected too much of you."

Most biographers paint Albert in similar hues. His flaw, they imply, was his drive for perfection. Was he too focused? Too moralistic? Too industrious? Too humorless? Too rigid? Too patient? Erman and Goldsmith don't answer these questions. They follow Albert's quest for true love, and they show a few outbursts of temper to give him a hint of internal turmoil, but he's still a saintly figure. Some of the scenes of Albert's life subvert the controlling device—that trip through the queen's memory—but the interpretation of Albert seems exactly right if the queen's consciousness is the filter. It makes perfect sense that Albert is an animation of the queen's own words: "unlike anyone who ever lived" and "an angel gone before me" (*Queen Victoria: Evening at Osborne*). Handsome, lithe Jonathan Firth gives this prince without blemish grace and a loose-limbed elegance.

Passion. Anger. Fear. Curiosity. Distress. Frustration. Obsession. A perfect foil for the angelic prince, Victoria Hamilton's completely human queen experiences all emotions. Many see Hamilton as Judi Dench's heir. Trained for the stage, she too has played Cordelia and Rosalind as well as Queen Victoria. Recognized for her acting ability, she got great reviews for supporting parts in film adaptations of Jane Austen's novels *Pride and Prejudice, Mansfield Park,* and *Persuasion,* but she has also played modern women, and, as an interviewer points out, she's "more than a period face" (Hamilton, interview with Aleks Sierz). Like Dench, Hamilton knows how to give a character layers.

While working on *Victoria and Albert,* Hamilton discovered that she is the same height as the queen, five foot four, and that her tiny waist measurement is the same as young Victoria's. Hamilton calls this correspondence "freaky" (Hamilton, interview with Aleks Sierz), but it seems significant to us that she's a near physical match for the real thing. Neagle's grace perfectly centered Wilcox's laudatory biopic, but Hamilton's quirkier, edgier presence better fits a screenplay that privileges the queen's private life. Her performance can be read as a bridge to Dench's isolated queen. Hamilton illustrates Victoria's yearning for a soul mate, and watching the young queen seek stability helps us better understand her later overwhelming sense of loss. Besides adding the important first act of Victoria's youth, *Victoria and Albert's* three hours provide time for exploring her anger. Most important, however, is the view that *Victoria and Albert* gives of the queen's physical life. Hardly a bodice ripper (à la the Catherine Zeta-Jones vehicle *Catherine the Great*), the miniseries attempts a reality sidestepped in *Victoria the Great*.

Young Victoria's costumes reveal her slender neck and small frame; soft and drooping, crafted of sprigged muslin and pleated white lawn, these dresses emphasize her fragility. But there's nothing drooping about her physical carriage. Sprightly and upright, taking quick, small steps, Victoria reads energy in motion. Her dynamism makes a nice contrast to the half-trusting expression in her eyes and to her tremulous smile. Contrast also dominates her first, very successful meeting alone with her ministers.

The real Victoria was dressed in mourning for this occasion; after all, the king had just died. Anna Neagle's costume replicated her black gown. The designer Maria Price, however, chooses an almost Grecian, draped white dress for Hamilton's Victoria, following the lead of the artist David Wilkie. In Wilkie's painting of the crucial coming together of monarch and ministers, he deliberately changed Victoria's garb from black to white, "to emphasize the innocence of the young queen" (Marshall, *Life and Times of Victoria*, 38). Clad in white, touched with light, the young Victoria speaks with humility and poise (Hamilton reads the queen's actual statement), and her presence moves one of her jaded ministers to exclaim at her "dignity." "I think she'll do," he tells his colleague. Hamilton adds a physical conclusion to the scene. As she returns to her rooms, Victoria skips down the hall, childishly, joyfully.

When she becomes queen, Victoria's encased in stiffer, richer fabrics, and she sports sparkling ornaments and more elaborate hairdos. Although she wears the signifiers of a queen, she's still a child and still incredibly innocent, *Victoria and Albert* insists. In a fictional scene set in front of Victoria's dollhouse, the queen reveals just how innocent she is. Albert has accepted her proposal of marriage. (She had to make the offer because of her exalted rank.) Victoria runs to Lady Hetty (Rachel Pickup). *Victoria and Albert* combines Victoria's ladies-in-waiting into this single figure and paints Lady Henrietta Standish as the closest thing Victoria had to a friend. With hesitation, Victoria asks the married Lady Hetty about the physical side of the union. Lady Hetty, also looking incredibly innocent, haltingly repeats the wildly insufficient advice given her by her mother to "let the man . . . take charge." Lady Hetty and the queen continue to play with the dollhouse while they speak, an Ibsenesque reminder that young

Victorian women were as uninformed as children when it came to physical reality and that even married women were embarrassed to communicate the truth.

But why create a scene like this when a real incident reveals more? Because of its insistence on intimacy, it's significant that *Victoria and Albert* leaves out the strange story of Lady Flora Hastings (a lady-in-waiting to the Duchess of Kent), which demonstrates that, if "the Queen's knowledge of the reproductive processes was sketchy," she did know that "impregnation required a man" (Weintraub 119). Biographers from Strachey on relate the events summarized here. In 1839, Queen Victoria and Lehzen (still constantly beside the queen) thought that they perceived a significant change in Lady Flora Hastings's figure. The unmarried Lady Flora was a friend of Sir John Conroy's and had shared a coach with him on a visit to Ireland. The queen's reckless comments about the cause of Lady Flora's plumpness sparked rumors. Was Lady Flora pregnant? Was Sir John the father?

Enraged and humiliated, Lady Flora first denied such stories, but, when speculation persisted, she submitted to a medical examination by the palace physician. He didn't believe that Lady Flora was pregnant, but he wouldn't rule it out entirely. The queen too refused to give up her suspicions. Lady Flora retaliated by asking two impartial, highly respected doctors to reexamine her. (Pelvic exams were hardly the norm for unmarried women.) They declared her still a virgin. Disgusted by the queen's insinuations, Lady Flora's powerful family made the affair public, and sentiment turned against Victoria. Things worsened when Lady Flora died and an autopsy proved that a tumor had caused her weight gain. Wilcox never would have considered including this episode in *Victoria the Great* because of its obvious sexual import, but it certainly would have fit the intimate focus of *Victoria and Albert*. The exclusion of this mean blunder demonstrates that, while *Victoria and Albert* keeps a zoom lens on the queen's life, pretending to mine the queen's memory, the close-up is largely an empathetic portrait and, in this case, an effort to keep Victoria "Victorian." The Hastings affair, however painful, would have been a better choice than the dollhouse scene because it reveals that, on some level, the queen was preoccupied with sex before her own marriage confronted her.

Victoria and Albert deserves credit, however, for having the chutzpah to go where no one has gone before: right into Victoria's and Albert's bedroom. This isn't as voyeuristic a trip as it sounds. On their wedding night, Albert gently sponges the forehead of the nervous queen, who says her head is "splitting." A loving embrace and a dissolve worthy of a 1950s romance follows his ministrations, and the next shot shows the royal couple, apparently naked, nestled in each others' arms. *Victoria and Albert* follows sexual pleasure with the pain of birth—yes, this version includes pregnancy and labor. Anna Neagle, slim and glamorous for most of *Victoria the Great,* never wears anything identifiable as a maternity gown, and none of Victoria's nine children (except for a single shot of Bertie as an infant) ever appear with their parents. In Wilcox's film, a single scene announces the arrival of a child. The queen lies in an orderly room, apparently alone with the baby prince, while ministers and Albert wait outside. Albert enters, hesitantly, and takes her hand as if it is made of glass. We hear her voice and see the top of her head—with every hair in place—but we never look farther, as though her body, as well as her ordeal, has been placed beyond our gaze.

Victoria and Albert fills in Wilcox's muted sketch of motherhood. Ungainly, exhausted, dressed in voluminous gowns of silk and lace, Victoria Hamilton's Queen Victoria—hugely pregnant—goes on with the affairs of state, regardless of her condition. The delivery scene in the miniseries is as realistic as Victoria's maternity wear, offering a complete contrast to Wilcox's serene fiction. Red faced and in pain, Hamilton's Victoria moans, cries, and paces the room. She's disheveled and sweaty, no longer the head of state. Instead, she has become a female body, straining to complete its most painful task; her agony acts as a potent reminder that neither rank, nor wealth, nor legions of minions can lift the burden of delivery from a mother-to-be or erase the peril involved. This graphic scene, which even shows the queen with her knees bent, panting, right before the child emerges, has to stand for the eight other births she endured, but it's enough. Victoria feared producing a large family, and this view of her experience, repeated again and again in her life, tells us why. In our age of designer delivery drugs, it's easy to forget the indignities every woman—even the queen—had to face and the danger every birth—even the birth of a crown princess—entailed. By 1853, when her eighth child, Prince Leopold, was born, doctors had finally discovered the benefits of chloroform, an advancement the queen praised (Woodham-Smith 328).

Prince Albert shines during the arrival of his daughter. While a crowd of influential politicians (all men) mill around outside the birthing chamber, smoking and waiting for news of an heir, Albert stays with the queen, as he did in life. After Albert died, Victoria recalled that "during her confinements ... no one [but Albert] ever lifted her from her bed to her sofa," and she remembered how he would "come instantly" when he knew she needed him (Marshall, *Life and Times of Victoria*, 77). The members of Parliament lounging outside mock Albert's tenderness. One of them jokes: "When your wife's about to pop, you don't moon about the place making a damn fool of yourself. You go to your club." We, however, feel nearly ready to canonize Albert, as this miniseries does, on the strength of this single scene and the truth it represents.

A biopic that privileges the private life of a queen should feel complete, shouldn't it? Hamilton gives Victoria a powerful, physical presence in *Victoria and Albert*. She's surrounded and supported by a prestigious cast, and Erman and Goldsmith's coherent screenplay works. But, for all its worthwhile efforts, *Victoria and Albert* violates its own premise—that these scenes occur in the queen's memory—and, consequently, it's slightly muddy. More significant than the break in the memory frame, however, is the lack of context.

For all its stiffness, *Victoria the Great* keeps one eye on the public; Wilcox frequently cuts to the crowds to show their reactions to the queen. They cheer at her coronation. They storm the palace during a period of economic hardship, demanding her help. They wait outside palace gates for the birth of the heir. They throng to cheer Victoria during her jubilees. Wilcox's film mentions—but doesn't fully treat—some of the crucial political events of Victoria's reign, like the repeal of the Corn Laws and a flare-up with the United States. Even though *Mrs. Brown* selects a thin slice of the queen's long life, John Madden keeps referencing the situation in London, taking the temperature of Parliament, gauging the power of the antimonarchist movement.

Victoria and Albert acknowledges only a few public events: the royal wedding, an assassination attempt, the change of prime ministers, and the Great Exposition. The memory device deletes other public contexts. Would Queen Victoria leave her coronation out of a string of memories stretching back to her youth? Would she never pause on the Crimean War? Would she forget that she had planned her eldest daughter's wedding to Prince Frederick William of Prussia before Albert's death? It's also disturbing that the queen has few memories involving the welfare of her subjects—a lack that seems out of character for this highly empathetic queen, to whom the public always wore a human face. Marie Antoinette and Mary of Scotland might be best served by films that describe their enclosure. The comfort of staying inside the royal bubble may have soothed a traumatized post-9/11 audience. (*Victoria and Albert* was released in October 2001.) But the ephemeral presence of the outside world in *Victoria and Albert* isn't enough to illustrate the bond between Victoria and her people, who came to love her as a queen, a mother, and a grandmother.

Indelible public demands shaped Victoria's private self; a biopic that neglects the overlap of the two worlds is still a sketch, not a portrait. Overwhelmed and humbled by the affection of her subjects, Victoria said: "If they only knew me as I am" (*Queen Victoria: Evening at Osborne*). The wish to show her as she was drives these three ambitious but very different biopics, each one a reflection of its own cultural moment as well as hers.

Chapter Six

❧

Marie Antoinette

How lucky we are, in our position, to win the friendship of an entire people so cheaply. Yet there is nothing so precious; I felt it deeply and will never forget it.
—Marie Antoinette

There's a roundness to Queen Victoria's life, a resounding satisfaction in the knowledge that all—or nearly all—had been spoken and done. No one could say the same about the life of Marie Antoinette. When she was fourteen and a half, the Austrian princess was sent, like a living treaty, to France. She married the dauphin in 1770, watched him ascend the French throne in 1774, and reigned as queen of pleasure in the splendor of Versailles. After the long-delayed consummation of their marriage, she bore Louis XVI four children, two of whom died. Marie Antoinette spent her happiest days at the Petit Trianon, the tiny chateau that Louis gave her as a gift. Temporarily freed from the rigid protocol of Versailles, she aspired to live simply, pursuing her goal with the gusto and expense only the super rich can rationalize.

Outside the royal enclosure, revolutionary fervor mounted. The queen became the primary symbol of royal extravagance swirling at the center of the storm, the target of slander and hatred. After the fall of the Bastille in 1789, a mob stormed Versailles. The volatile crowd watched as the royal family was arrested and transported to Paris. Imprisonment at the Tuileries, also a palace, included elaborate meals served by a staff, but, as the urge to obliterate members of the aristocracy along with the old ways grew, Louis, Marie Antoinette, and their two children became the prisoners of increasingly hostile jailers. The king was tried and executed in 1793, and Marie Antoinette followed her husband to the guillotine ten months later.

Marie Antoinette. (Courtesy Rèunion des Musèes Nationaux/Art Resource,
New York.)

194 ROYAL PORTRAITS IN HOLLYWOOD

Of all the queens featured in these chapters, Marie Antoinette suffered the most devastating—indeed, fatal—reversal of public favor. When, in 1773, she wrote the words to her mother that serve as this chapter's epigraph, the dauphine was the toast of Paris, hailed for her charm and style. Who could know how dramatically the political and economic weather would change or how quickly she would find herself reviled by those who once adored her? Like a mirror image of Cinderella in her fall from grace, Marie Antoinette lost a "delicate high-heeled slipper with ruched ribbon trim" as she ran from the Tuileries in 1792 (Weber 249).

The queen's gruesome finish, perhaps the best-known thing about her, may overshadow the life lived, but the riveting details of that life—her youth, her glamour, her hunger for beautiful things, her long unconsummated marriage—provide multiple reasons for the enduring fascination she holds over us. Beginning with Edmund Burke's observations of Marie Antoinette, her biographers have been legion. Interpretations of her life range from *Marie Antoinette: The Portrait of an Average Woman* (1933), in which Stefan Zweig dubs her "a tepid creature" who would have died "without ever having lived in any true sense of the term" if not for the Revolution (xiii), to the more empathetic *Marie Antoinette: The Journey* (2001), in which Antonia Fraser attempts to consider the queen's life without "the somber tomb" always in mind (xix).

Not as diametrically opposed as the two biographies that inspired them, two Hollywood biopics, nearly seventy years apart, perfectly complement each other. *Marie Antoinette* (1938), starring Norma Shearer and directed by W. S. Van Dyke, travels sequentially through the public drama of the queen's life, from her engagement to Louis Auguste, to her last moments at the guillotine. *Marie Antoinette* (2006), starring Kirsten Dunst and directed by Sofia Coppola, covers a narrower slice of life beginning with the princess's journey to Versailles, and ending with her departure from that palace on the day that marked the start of the royal family's imprisonment. For most of its two-hour run time, Coppola's film stays in the intimate circle of the queen's day-by-day existence at Versailles and the Petit Trianon.

Each of these films works to "unravel the cruel myths and salacious distortions" that cloud the queen's memory (Fraser, *Marie Antoinette*, xix). One of those "cruel myths" concerns the remark, "Let them eat cake." Marie Antoinette never said that, and it seems fitting to place something she did say before our analysis of the films that portray her life. On the day of her husband's coronation, she wrote this: "In seeing the people who treat us so well despite their own misfortune . . . we are more obliged than ever to work hard for their happiness" (qtd. in Fraser, *Marie Antoinette*, 135).

Marie Antoinette (1938)

Marie Antoinette does not say "Let them eat cake" in W. S. Van Dyke's 1930s biopic, which cites Stefan Zweig's biography as its source. Van Dyke's film covers the queen's life, from her engagement to her death, in a series of events you would expect to see, with a few notable exceptions. The screenplay by Claudine West, Donald Ogden Stewart, and Ernest Vadja softens Zweig's tone to take an empathetic, generally public look at the French queen.

Zweig begins the introduction to his biography with a reference to the trial that came near the end of the queen's life. He describes the "calumny" that carried Marie Antoinette, "a mediocre, an average woman," to the guillotine (xi). The film too presents an introductory portent of what is to come. The first, disturbing image initiates a series of literal shadows that darken the queen's life. A fanciful clock with animated figures strikes the hour, and a high-angle shot (a perspective that often signals the working out of fate) shows young Marie Antoinette hurrying through a grand hall in her Austrian castle. Above her hangs the shadow of a tilted battle ax. The visual referents—the effete clock, the innocent girl, the shadowy ax—collapse the tale into expected themes: wealth, time, youth, death. Marie Antoinette has been summoned by her mother, who announces that she will marry Louis. The princess says, with anticipation: "I shall be queen of France." At the film's conclusion, a flashback returns viewers to this close-up of the princess's glowing face, superimposed over the figure of the prematurely aged queen emerging from La Force prison, ready to ascend the steps of the guillotine. But *Marie Antoinette* is more than a grim march to the beheading. From this ordered depiction of Marie Antoinette's life, a person emerges.

Norma Shearer's performance helps give the queen warmth and specificity. At thirty-four, Shearer was more than twice Marie Antoinette's age at the time of her engagement, the film's starting point, but a ribbon around her hair and a buoyant walk help her transmit an aura of youthful innocence. As Anna Neagle does in *Victoria the Great,* Shearer must age in *Marie Antoinette;* it's a less radical transformation than Neagle's, however, since Marie Antoinette died at thirty-eight. An unsuccessful candidate for the role of Scarlet O'Hara, Shearer's better suited to play a princess born to rule than a conniving Southern belle. As she develops from a frothy coquette into a grief-stricken prisoner, Shearer's Antoinette has a consistent sweetness and majesty that refuses a one-dimensional reading.

Extant portraits of Marie Antoinette and written accounts of her physical presence suggest that casting the glamorous Shearer was much less of an exaggeration than choosing Garbo to play Queen Christina. Zweig explains that Louis XV (the dauphin's grandfather) sent the French Abbé Vermond to tutor the princess. Vermond reported that she had "a most graceful figure" and that "her character, her heart [were] excellent" (Zweig 5). Yet Empress Maria Teresa, who planned her fifteenth child's marriage, found her appearance only "satisfactory enough" (Fraser, *Marie Antoinette,* 30). Carolyn Heilbrun asks: "How does [a woman] cope with the fact that her value is determined by how attractive men find her?" (27). We don't know whether Marie Antoinette was aware of Vermond's comments or how she reacted to her mother's less than flattering assessment of her charms. We do know that she got a makeover.

Even though she embodied a political prize and hardly needed extra attractions to increase her value, the princess's charms were embellished. Antoinette's forehead, the empress decreed, was too high, her bust too small, her shoulders uneven, and her teeth a little less than straight (Fraser 30–31). Undaunted, Maria Teresa set improvements in motion. Maire Antoinette got a new hairdo from "a real Parisian" hairdresser, padding to disguise the uneven shoulders, and primitive braces (36–37). The empress prepared her daughter for the royal marriage as if she were a starlet auditioning for a big part.

Contemporary reviewers agreed that the "big part" of Marie Antoinette suited Norma Shearer, and many rated the picture "frankly second in importance" to its female star, who "surpassed the Queen, herself" (rev. of *Marie Antoinette*). Bosley Crowther's 1938 interview with Shearer, "The Queen Was in Her Parlor," demonstrates yet again the conventional wisdom that one queen was playing another. Crowther claims that Marie An-

htps://

toinette would probably "envy" Shearer, who was, after all, a queen "of Hollywood," a much more prestigious position than Queen of France." *Marie Antoinette* paralleled a shift in Hollywood's royal alignment. By 1938, the new monarchs of MGM were ready to depose Shearer, one of a stable of female contract stars they were looking to replace with younger models. Shearer had lost her greatest fan and mentor, her husband, Irving Thalberg, and she would soon abdicate her throne and retire in 1941. *Marie Antoinette* was Thalberg's last project (he died before it was filmed) and one of Shearer's last—and best—performances, for which she received an Oscar nomination.

The queen remains at the center of the two-and-a-half-hour film, appearing in almost every scene, disappearing only when the camera visits King Louis XV's chambers or when it cuts to the impending revolution. Her childhood is deleted, so the film never lets us see that the little Antoinette loved her sister Charlotte and desperately wanted to please her mother. Nor do we learn that Marie Antoinette hardly knew "the history of her own country," let alone that of France (Fraser, *Marie Antoinette*, 38). She preferred music and charmed those who taught her, even if she complained that studying, especially history, was taxing. She was bred to strengthen her family's position.

After she tells her daughter about the engagement, Empress Maria Teresa vanishes from the film. There's only one glimpse of the long-distance hold she had over her daughter when Count Mercy—the Austrian ambassador to France and the empress's minion—brings the dauphine reprimands from her mother. That single letter stands for a substantial whole. Mother and daughter never met again, but the empress's presence occupied a prominent place in her daughter's consciousness. Fraser explains that the empress sent a series of letters that could be described as "lethal missives," directing Marie Antoinette's behavior in all things, especially her marriage, from afar (*Marie Antoinette* 98).

Several scenes illustrate Marie Antoinette's relationship with Louis Auguste, and these help develop her character, while Robert Morley's portrayal of the king—which also netted him an Oscar nomination—keeps Louis from being a caricature. At thirty, Morley looked less like a teen than Shearer did (Louis was fifteen when he met his bride), but his body language communicates awkwardness and yearning, a combination that fits biographical portraits of the king who, by all accounts, was neither graceful nor confident. Van Dyke introduces Louis to the audience and to Marie Antoinette at the same time. After stepping out of the coach that brought her from Austria, the princess floats down the aisle of a huge salon, plumes waving. She lifts the skirt of her delicate gown and daintily runs the last few steps to bow before Louis XV (John Barrymore). Next, she looks around for her husband-to-be. Heavy, doltish, and nervous, belittled by his royal grandfather, the poor dauphin chokes out fragments of his welcome speech. When Marie Antoinette tries to help him—supportive of him from the start—he silences her, insisting: "There's some more to my speech." Morley's halting delivery and his expression—like that of an anxious child—disappear by the end of the film, when he bravely faces his fate.

The real dauphin and his bride-to-be had a first, more private meeting, chaperoned by the king, but it makes sense that this MGM production opted for a grander setting. Louis Giannetti uses *Marie Antoinette* as an example of the "lavish spectacle pictures" that MGM favored in the 1930s, a genre that found life at Versailles an ideal subject. The background shots of the palace are the real thing, but the studio built the impressive interior sets. The Hollywood version of the palace ballroom, for example, was twice as big as the Versailles original. The public meeting of the princess and the dauphin is one of many glittering larger-than-life scenes in *Marie Antoinette*, as is their marriage ceremony (Giannetti and Eyman 122). At their wedding, Marie Antoinette and Louis kneel together, but he avoids her touch, pulling his hand away after placing the ring on her finger. Someone divides the couple in every shot: the priest, the king, members of the court. Their on-screen separation reflects the truth that, at its start, the marriage was a merger, not an affectionate partnership, as Victoria and Albert's marriage was. Neither was it a train wreck, like the collision of Catherine and Peter. In its depiction of Marie Antoinette's marriage, Van Dyke's film offers a more nuanced portrait than Zweig's biography does.

Sections of Zweig's work, a product of its time, read like a case study composed by a naturalist observing an unusual insect. In his short afterword, Zweig explains why he chose to ignore most extant, personal texts written by those who knew the queen. He characterizes these memoirs and diaries as "unconditionally, touchingly, inviolably loyal," politically expedient, and "hopelessly untrustworthy" (470). In a 1938 interview preceding the release of *Marie Antoinette*, Zweig claimed to have given "equal measure of all facets in [her] personality" ("History and the Screen"), yet, in his biography, "all facets" devolve into a pseudo-Freudian pronouncement. There's diminishment in the way in which Zweig sometimes refers to Marie Antoinette; no current biographer would describe his or her female subject as a "fascinating flapper" (16), or "our lassie" (41), or, especially, as so "luscious a morsel" (170). Such reductions reinforce Zweig's central belief that the queen was, above all else, "an average woman," a member of a subordinate group, not an individual. As an average woman, Zweig implies, Marie Antoinette makes an especially interesting specimen since she was placed in a situation that could hardly be described as average. The realities of the royal marriage bed, for example, could only be considered abnormal.

Zweig obsesses over sexual details, admittedly a high-interest topic. Biographers believe that inexperience and awkwardness kept Louis and Marie Antoinette from fully consummating their marriage for seven and a half years. In the incestuous French court, the dauphin's difficulties could hardly remain secret. Zweig blames sexual malfunction for the weak performance of all the king's duties, conflating private and public failures: "Because he had been unable to play the man in his sleeping apartment, he could not play the monarch in public" (2). His analysis of the queen reduces every action to the absence of orgasm. Zweig asserts: "One hardly need be a neurologist or a sexologist to recognize that her superlative liveliness, her persistent and unavailing search for new satisfactions, her fickle pursuit of one pleasure after another, were typical outcomes of unceasing sexual stimulation by a husband who was unable to provide her with adequate gratification" (27).

Paradoxically, while he lumps her with all "average" women, unable to function minus orgasms, Zweig also blames Marie Antoinette for allowing the Revolution to triumph. Although she was just a "mediocrity," he thinks that, had she paid attention or tried harder, "all the threads of French diplomacy would have been in her hands." After all, he asserts, "Europe was governed by three women: Marie Theresa, Marie Antoinette, and Catherine of Russia" (89). Weigh his words against the reality of the French system, in which power passed exclusively through the male line. French queens rarely even attended coronation ceremonies since they "did not participate in government" (Lever 72). Under Salic law, the queen had "no authority whatsoever," according to the French historian and biographer Evelyne Lever. A queen was to be "completely submissive" to the king, forget about her own country, and "never express an opinion" (56). She ranked even lower than a lover, as Caroline Weber points out in this summing up: "Three things were important at Versailles—the king, his mistresses, his court. A queen was nothing" (84).

Heilbrun defines power as "the ability to take one's place in whatever discourse is essential to action and the right to have one's part matter" (18); by this definition, Marie Antoinette had little chance of becoming the dominant figure that Zweig imagines. Constantly pressured by her mother, her brother, and partisan royals to push political agendas, Marie Antoinette usually failed. Like Mary, Queen of Scots, she had neither the wisdom nor the instinct to succeed at such manipulation, and to imagine that a little effort would have made her as powerful as Maria Teresa or Catherine of Russia greatly exaggerates her status and her capabilities.

Van Dyke's film generally avoids the topic of the queen's attempts at political influence. Instead, it interprets Marie Antoinette's behavior as a quest to satisfy average desires; she yearns to cement her marriage, to find her place at Versailles, and to discover true affection. *Marie Antoinette* downplays Zweig's Freudian monomania without sidestepping the couple's sexual problems. One telling long shot shows the royal pair finally alone on their wedding night, teetering on opposite edges of the frame, perched on gilt chairs. A high console table divides them, and, above the table, an enormous mirror reflects back their ornate marriage bed, which looks more like a sarcophagus than a site of passion. Dwarfed by the ornate bedchamber, the husband and wife are miniatures in a room designed for giants. Marie Antoinette keeps trying to bridge the gulf, inching her chair closer and closer to Louis's. Gently, she questions him about himself, then runs to the window, excited by the fireworks that celebrate their union. The dauphin, who has no small talk, makes it clear that there will be no pyrotechnics inside, naming his impotence with this dialogue: "There'll never be an heir because of me. There. Now you know. I'm glad. Glad it's over." He's wrong, of course.

The film links Louis's ascent to the throne with his sexual success. The first scene after his coronation shows the queen giving birth to the heir, an obviously Freudian (and, thus, Zweigian) touch. The consummation of the marriage did happen after Louis became king, but the catalyst—not depicted in the film—was a visit from Marie Antoinette's brother, the Emperor Joseph, who provided Louis with some much-needed advice. Even before the "great act," the teenaged dauphine had conquered Paris, the behavior Zweig indicts as the "fickle pursuit" of pleasure caused by sexual frustration. It's hard to imagine that Marie Antoinette—or any young person—would have turned down the enticing joys of that seductive capital or would have been indifferent to the thrill of feeling the crowd's affection, which Fraser describes as "popular ecstasy, the worship of the true goddess" (*Marie Antoinette* 132). Van Dyke offers a neat visual parallel to Marie Antoinette's ascent. She literally becomes what the Duc D'Orleans (Joseph Schildkraut) describes as "the brightest, highest figure" in the court in a shot that shows her poised at the top of an ornate palace staircase on the arm of the smarmy duc.

The Duc D'Orleans entices the queen to "become alive" and attends her as long as he thinks he can use her. *Marie Antoinette* exaggerates his importance as the queen's potential love interest to provide a signifier for the political turmoil surrounding her. His presence also underscores the film's view of the queen as a woman searching for affection. As he does in the film, the real Duc D'Orleans, always expedient, removed his powdered wig, renamed himself Philip Egalite, joined the revolutionaries, and cast the deciding vote for the execution of Louis XVI, his cousin. After she poses at the top of the duc's staircase, a series of scenes describe Marie Antoinette's life as the spoiled darling of the court, playing blindman's bluff, attending an artists' ball, and gambling at a gaming house. Her daring behavior draws negative comment. The film hints that Marie Antoinette encouraged men, including Louis's brother, to attempt intimacy with her. Most biographers agree that the queen did herself profound damage by welcoming casual behavior, but most share her brother's view about her character. Joseph believed that she remained "innately chaste," despite the pleasure-mad lifestyle he chided her for (Fraser, *Marie Antoinette*, 145).

One of Marie Antoinette's greatest sources of pleasure, the Petit Trianon, does not appear in Van Dyke's film. There, in the little chateau that Louis gave her, the queen escaped from Versailles, where protocol "poisoned her daily life" (Lever 88). At the Trianon, she thrived on informal behavior, simpler food, close friends, and abundant nature. Paradoxically, a simpler life, as the queen envisioned it, devoured francs; Marie Antoinette satisfied every whim as she embellished her minipalace and garden, and the Trianon became one of the symbols of wretched excess that inflamed the revolutionary mobs. As Lever points out, however, the queen's spend-

Marie Antoinette. With her mask at the ready, the last queen of France looks flirty and full of *je ne sais quois.* For the most part, Norma Shearer's Marie Antoinette radiates innocence. The splendor of Versailles, she quickly discovers, masks a strong undercurrent of pettiness and jealousy. (Courtesy Jerry Ohlinger's Movie Material Store.)

ing wasn't the primary financial drain. Court expenditures (including dec-
orating the Trianon) constituted "a mere 6 percent, plus 2 percent for pen-
sions," while the real "strain on the budget" came from supporting
America's revolution against England (185). Marie Antoinette's retreat,
embellished with expensive details meant to replicate rural life, provided
convenient visible proof of decadence (like Tyco CEO Dennis Koslowski's
$6,000 shower curtain), a target of anger more accessible than a war con-
ducted on another continent.

Her insistence on a private life also cost the queen the support of many
nobles. Those excluded from the intimate circle at the Petit Trianon later
found little reason to defend Louis and his queen. Oblivious to the complex effects of her attempt to live simply, Marie Antoinette was inspired to
make her clothing fit her more natural lifestyle. She abandoned elaborate
hairdos and court gowns for unpowdered hair and lighter dresses, and
women of fashion followed her. Adrian, who won an Oscar for the film's
glittering gowns, doesn't acknowledge Marie Antoinette's dramatic fashion shift; the queen wears her towering poufs and court robes throughout.
The absence of the queen's favorite place, in which she said she tried to
look and live "like a private individual" (Lever 136), again stamps this film
as an external view of her life.

Marie Antoinette's treatment of the royal children confirms that perspective. After Louis's accession in 1774, the film jumps to the birth of the
little dauphin, heir to the throne, in 1780. The earlier birth of the princesse
royale is barely mentioned, and the two children who followed the dauphin, Louis Charles and Beatrice, are deleted. If the film were your only
source of knowledge, you'd think that Marie Antoinette and Louis had
only two children. Anyone who adapts a full-length biography into a two-
hour film must compress events and combine characters, but ignoring the
sorrow that descended on Marie Antoinette's family before the Revolution
dramatically alters her portrait. Beatrice died as an infant, and, more tragically, Marie Antoinette's first son, the dauphin, died when he was twelve
after a short life of illness and pain.

The queen's life-altering personal loss is missing, but *Marie Antoinette*
does include the most disturbing and very public scandal associated with
her, the diamond necklace caper. "Because of this unfortunate affair," Lever
says, "Marie Antoinette would be seen as a perfidious and debauched

woman who squandered the coffers of the kingdom for her personal plea-sure" (182). The film gives a simplified account of the costly hoax. Greedy con artists use a forged note to convince Cardinal Rohan, currently out of royal favor, that the queen has selected him to act as her agent in purchas-ing an ostentatious diamond necklace. Hoping for increased intimacy with Marie Antoinette, the cardinal carries out the transaction. On a dark night, he even delivers the necklace to the "queen," a heavily veiled imposter, who meets him in the gardens of Versailles. When the jeweler's bill arrives at the palace, the queen questions the cardinal, and the truth is revealed. By that time, the thieves have sold the diamonds, and the onus of buying such an extravagant thing in a time of famine remains with Marie Antoinette.

Biographers agree on the queen's innocence in this affair but identify her extravagance and love of informality as enabling factors: "Though . . . Marie Antoinette . . . was . . . blameless, she remains blameworthy that so gross a swindle could have been attempted and victoriously achieved under cover of her name" (Zweig 186). Even though the swindlers were punished, the cardinal (who belonged to a powerful noble family) was exonerated, and the queen's popularity plummeted, a reaction depicted in a dramatic scene at the Paris Opera. When the queen enters, another aristocrat, drip-ping with jewels, sneers: "I wonder that she'd dare to show her face." The camera closes in on the queen as a man shouts the verdict to the glittering throng. The crowd cheers the cardinal's vindication while Marie Antoi-nette's look of horror and comprehension says everything.

Zweig calls Marie Antoinette's involvement in this affair "giddy-pated" (165). In the film, the queen's refusal to buy the necklace springs from her realization of conditions outside Versailles. She is shocked that a jeweler would offer her such a piece. "With people starving?" she asks. When the necklace plot is revealed, she—not Louis—quickly sees the gravity of the situation and demands action. "I don't think you realize how serious this is," she tells the king. "It could destroy me." Her remarks echo Fraser's claims that, by 1785, Antoinette's motherhood had given her "new steel" to address challenges. Fraser explains that the queen's high point correspond-ed with a low for the king, who would "fall asleep in Council meetings," and who would visit the queen's chambers and cry (*Marie Antoinette* 250–51). But, by this time, slumbering tensions had escalated into open defi-ance. It's shocking to realize what isolated lives the king and queen led at Versailles. When the queen's brother, Emperor Joseph, visited France, "in a few weeks he [did] more to acquaint himself with [France] than Louis XVI would do in several decades" (Lever 108). Finally, however, the danger of the royal family's position penetrated the royal bubble. The film shows their removal from Versailles to the Tuileries and includes a telling detail from their failed escape attempt. As their coach heads for the border, Louis excitedly follows the route on a map, a tourist in his own land.

No one could call either Louis or Marie Antoinette informed, intuitive, or forceful. Neither was trained to lead; Louis XV—who had little interest in his heir—never included him in counsel meetings or political discussions, and Marie Antoinette failed at most attempts to influence policy, the only power she held. But, had they been the most politically skilled, enlightened, and charismatic of monarchs, it's hard to imagine how they could have halted the revolt against a system so riddled with corruption and decay. *Marie Antoinette*'s mise-en-scène suggests the scope of royal atrophy: the too-lavish, too-insular world of Versailles with its bevies of attendants, its fickle courtiers, its self-consumed (and greedy) family members. Who could loosen such a tangled knot?

Marie Antoinette's friendships with women added to the tangle. As they marched toward the Revolution, mobs accused the queen of nymphomania and lesbianism as well as extravagance. Pornographic cartoons showed her having sex with the women she chose as her intimate friends. When women get too powerful, similar smut still appears in gossip rags—fast-forward to the charges made against Hillary Clinton during the Monica Lewinsky scandal. Fraser points out that romanticized female friendships were part of the culture and that having female friends at court was a necessity "for support" (*Marie Antoinette* 930). In contrast, Zweig scolds the queen for being a "dilettante" in friendship, unaware that lavishing favors on her favorites, the princesse de Lamballe and the princesse de Polignac, could have serious repercussions (147). Along with these friendships, Zweig characterizes the "curious results" of the queen's loneliness as inappropriate. He is amazed that Marie Antoinette once begged for a puppy, and he is astounded that she romped with the servants' children (41). Such behavior seems more revealing than curious. If Marie Antoinette always "felt herself a stranger" at Versailles (Zweig 41), she must also have felt an overwhelming need for affection.

Versailles offered complicated female alliances, not friendships, to the newly arrived teenaged dauphine. King Louis XV's sisters, one of whom nicknamed Marie Antoinette "the Austrian," longed to increase their power by enlisting her in their war against the king's mistress, Madame Du Barry (Lever 33). Du Barry, who flaunted her influence over the king, loathed the dauphine but craved her recognition. Van Dyke accurately portrays Du Barry's jealousy but inaccurately portrays Marie Antoinette's response in an interesting example of the way a biopic bends events to rachet up tension. In *Marie Antoinette,* the dauphine impulsively insults Du Barry in front of the king, and this plot device sparks a fantastic climax. On the night of the insult, the king tells Marie Antoinette that he will punish her by annulling her marriage and sending her back to Austria. At this news, the Duc D'Orleans drops the dauphine. Still on the same night, the despondent dauphine connects with her soul mate, Count Axel Fersen, who voices his deep love for her. This chance for romance reverses Marie Antoinette's slide into despondency. Now she's ecstatic that she will soon be an unmarried Austrian princess. Later, on that extremely busy night, Marie Antoinette returns to Versailles, only to discover that King Louis XV's death has made her queen of France. She will not return to Austria in disgrace, but neither will she be free to love Fersen.

Marie Antoinette would have relished speaking that insult to Du Barry publicly, so the scene of their encounter has the satisfying feel of wish fulfillment. The less dramatic reality demonstrates the hold that Maria Teresa had over her daughter, even from afar. Pressured by her mother, the dauphine gave in and spoke civilly and briefly to Du Barry (Lever 38). Marie Antoinette's capitulation angered the aunts, but it appeased the king and satisfied Du Barry. Because she was the target of such intense social and political pressure, Marie Antoinette's desire for amusing friends hardly seems surprising. One of the women she chose, the princesse de Polignac, doesn't appear in *Marie Antoinette,* but the other, the princesse de Lamballe (Anita Louise), stands beside the queen, literally, in most of her endeavors.

Instead of questioning Marie Antoinette's choice of friends or indicting her careless (and lavishly demonstrated) affection for them, as Zweig does, the film suggests the part her friends played in her life. There's little dialogue between the queen and the princess, underscoring the more public nature of this portrait, but body language helps define the relationship. When the Duc d'Orleans first visits her chambers, Marie Antoinette and the princess clasp hands and giggle like teens (which they were), anticipating chatting with someone so "distinguished" and "wicked." During the conversation, the princess sits in the window seat, reacting with pleasure to every compliment paid to Marie Antoinette, gasping in horror when the duc suggests that the dauphine do battle with Du Barry. She often repeats this bystander role, mirroring Marie Antoinette's reactions, or providing responses that help viewers read situations. As the real princesse did, she refuses to leave Marie Antoinette, even when ordered to do so in the interest of her own safety. She underscores the queen's reactions to the mob and dies, horribly, at their hands. This portrait simplifies Marie Antoinette's relationship with Lamballe, but it's good to see this not-so-average woman included in *Marie Antoinette.*

"You want to be my friend in my disgrace?" Marie Antoinette asks the Swedish Count Axel Fersen, another faithful ally and, perhaps, lover. This breakthrough role for the glamorous, young Tyrone Power got him top billing (above Shearer's), Crowther notes, on some theater marquees. Although the count sounds like a screenwriter's dream, the polar opposite of the doltish Louis, Fersen's character springs from reality, not some inflamed pen. Many felt that Fersen, whom Marie Antoinette met at a Parisian Ball in 1774, "looked like a hero from a novel"; he was "tall and slim, with a narrow face, intense dark eyes . . . and a slightly melancholy air" (Fraser, *Marie Antoinette,* 110). On the strength of one of Fersen's diary entries, "reste la" (I stayed with her), and on the basis of other comments culled from a cache of letters, some biographers—Zweig, for one—think the relationship may have been physical as well as emotional (339–40). Lever cautions that the only thing we can be sure of is that "the Queen and the Swedish count loved each other" (163).

Graceful editing allows the audience to judge the nature of the affair. The screenplay gives Fersen the unselfishness to place Marie Antoinette's role as a queen before his personal satisfaction, and it cooks up a Sydney Cartonesque scene in which Fersen relinquishes his freedom to visit her in prison before her death. The especially romantic detail of the ring that Marie Antoinette gave Fersen—inscribed "Everything leads me to you"— is based on history; the real Fersen treasured it. Fersen helped carry out the failed escape accurately detailed in the film, and, during the royal family's imprisonment, he lobbied in foreign courts for the deposed French monarchs. On the subject of Fersen and the queen's "enduring love" (Zweig 237), *Marie Antoinette* and Zweig's biography are in accord; both find the count "a sincere, an upright, a virile and courageous friend" (Zweig 236).

It would have been simple for post-Code, late-1930s screenwriters to condemn this extramarital romance. *Marie Antoinette* chooses not to do that. Instead, it presents the affair as well as the strong relationship between the queen and Louis. The film attempts a similar ambiguity with regard to the Revolution. After the birth of the heir, the camera begins a series of crosscuts that show the escalating horror of everyday life outside Versailles, where children cry for bread and adults rail at their spendthrift queen. The assault on the real queen involved more than the budget, and it came from many factions. Slighted members of the court, as well as peasants and revolutionaries, found Marie Antoinette an easy mark, a nexus for rumor. Why had it taken so long for her to have a child? Was the king really the father? Was she a lesbian or a nymphomaniac or, perhaps, both? Did the queen ever think of France, or was she concerned with Austrian interests only? Was she a spy? Why must she squander money? Hadn't she built an entire faux village at the Trianon? Short on bread and francs, the once-adoring public, their anger fed by pornographic pamphlets, vilified the queen.

In *Marie Antoinette,* the crosscuts to the suffering masses delete the brutality of the personal attacks on the queen; hunger and justice are the rallying cries of the mob. What American audience wouldn't be for liberty, fraternity, and equality? In these rousing scenes, Van Dyke indicts the monarchical system, but not the royal family. The king and queen demonstrate bravery when confronted with mob violence and nobility during the travesties of their trials. Even though the system had gone awry, the screenplay suggests, the personal behavior of the king and queen was admirable. Perhaps this "all-good" approach to French independence and to the royals reflects America's pro-France stance prior to World War II. The stirring playing of "Le Marseilles" over beginning and ending credits reinforces the idea that the French Revolution, the frame for the queen's life, was inevitable; the scenes of Marie Antoinette's final, lonely days, when all had been taken from her, are accompanied by a haunting dirge that transitions, very slowly, into the French national anthem.

Zweig credits the queen for nobility in her suffering, and so does Van

Dyke, who juxtaposes her initial joy at the prospect of becoming queen of France with the last shot of her face. Gender stereotyping typical of his time colors Zweig's acknowledgment of Marie Antoinette's development. He equates her strength with masculinity, claiming that tragedy carved this average woman into something more like a man. In her last letters, Zweig points out, "one might almost describe her writing as virile" (443). Many biopics of queens reach similar resolutions, demonstrating that powerful women often find themselves alone and stripped of their femininity. *Marie Antoinette* transcends that formula to show a girl growing into a mature woman, wiser and more beautiful, despite extreme pressure and disappointment. Successful in its own time, this still-engaging view of Marie Antoinette and the French court was recalled to life in the fall of 2006, when cable channels aired the classic film as a prelude to Sofia Coppola's updated version.

Marie Antoinette (2006)

The main character in Edith Wharton's short story "The Fulness of Life" compares a woman's "nature" to "a great house full of rooms." Public life goes on in the outer rooms, but in "the innermost room, the holy of holies, the soul sits alone and waits for a footstep that never comes" (14). Van Dyke's biopic treats Marie Antoinette empathetically, but it looks *at* her, not *with* her, rarely acknowledging that she might have a private self, an innermost room. Details from Marie Antoinette's quest for privacy resonate with Wharton's metaphor. When a former page visited a deserted Versailles after the Revolution, he was astonished to find "a host of little apartments connected to the Queen's apartment, whose existence he had never suspected." Evelyne Lever notes: "The Queen protected her privacy better than anyone imagined" (189).

Sofia Coppola, who wrote and directed the most recent biopic of the French queen's life, shot her film at Versailles, that "great house full of rooms," where Marie Antoinette woke and slept and dined and walked the grounds. Coppola says that she imagined the young queen "passing from her grand public bedroom into her small private apartments" (*Marie Antoinette*, screenplay). In *Marie Antoinette*, a faithful adaptation of Antonia Fraser's biography, Coppola dares to look beyond Versailles's incredible facades and interiors to the queen's "innermost room." The most visually beautiful film of its year, *Marie Antoinette* got mixed critical reception and a single Oscar nomination—and win—for costumes.

Many reviewers waxed lukewarm; some, like A. O. Scott and Caryn James, cheered Coppola's idiosyncratic vision. Scott points out an important "paradoxical" theme in the film, that "the pursuit of sensual delight is trivial compared with other undertakings," but continues: "Pleasure is also serious, one of the things that gives life shape and meaning." James, too, sees Coppola's "visual extravagance and candy-colored palette" as more than frilly, frenetic excess. She links *Marie Antoinette* to today's "celebrity culture" dominated by Hollywood royalty. International news grants film and rock stars a special status, demonstrated in headlines like "Brangelina Takes Namibia" or "Madonna Gets Malawi," but, although they are recognized around the globe, James points out, they "travel the world" in a bubble, surrounded by "their loyal retainers," almost as isolated from reality as was Marie Antoinette.

Negative criticism for *Marie Antoinette* began with some boos from the partly French audience at its Cannes Film Festival premier. Coppola took this in stride. A colder, meaner, print response followed the film's October 6 American opening. Next, in the October 22 "Week in Review"—a section of the *New York Times* that rarely concerns itself with film—Eric Konigsberg railed about Coppola's ahistorical take on this historical figure. He characterized *Marie Antoinette* as a dangerous misreading perpetrated on an ignorant audience, a call to materialism, a wish to flip the queen's persona into the guise of a revolutionary. In his article "Marie Antoinette and the Ghosts of the French Revolution," Alexander Zevin mounts a more detailed charge. He complains that the film lacks precise language, historical context, traces of the Revolution, and, most of all, depth. In his fervor to point out what *isn't* in Coppola's film, Zevin provides a convenient starting point for examining what *is*.

In the politically incorrect, unrepentantly ethnocentric 1940s, few in W. S. Van Dyke's American audience would have expected his cast to have French accents. Even fewer could have imagined that an American director might, someday, script an entire film in the language of the culture it depicted instead of in English. In an increasingly global environment, auteurs do struggle with authenticity of language. Globalization has sharpened even American ears. Nearly every reviewer mocked Kevin Costner's attempts at Old English in *Robin Hood: Prince of Thieves* (Kevin Reynolds, 1991), demonstrating how risky faking it had become by the end of the century. More recently, Mel Gibson amazed Hollywood by scripting his controversial film *The Passion of the Christ* (2004) in Latin and Aramaic and his blood-splattered *Apocalypto* (2006) in Mayan dialects. Gibson attracts mass-market audiences—not the usual foreign-film afficionados— suggesting that the visual language of gore trumps subtitle trauma.

Coppola could have made the Costnerian choice, to have actors fake French accents, or she could have chosen the Gibsonian method—to have all the characters in *Marie Antoinette* speak French and deliver the dialogue via subtitles. Instead, she opted for what she felt was a more natural approach. Some actors, including Kirsten Dunst (Marie Antoinette) and Jason Schwartzman (Louis XVI), speak American English. Others, like the French Aurore Clement (the Duchess of Char), speak French-accented English. As the Duchesse de Polignac, Rose Byrne speaks with a British accent, and Lauriane Mascoro, who plays two-year-old Marie Teresa, speaks French. Whatever the accent, Zevin complains that the dialogue is "barely audible" and that the actors are "inarticulate" (32), but it isn't only language choice or clarity that offends him. He sneers that Coppola uses "resolutely contemporary" dialogue (32) and that she "has made a new kind of period film, which is not interested in accuracy of speech" (35), claims he doesn't bother to document.

Even in her use of natural sounds, Coppola follows a cue from history. English visitors to Versailles after Louis XV's death commented on the "loud sound of birdsong in the garden" (Fraser, *Marie Antoinette,* 116). In *Marie Antoinette,* amplified birdsong plays an important part in creating the atmosphere; it punctuates the film, as does the rock music many have commented on. The spoken word often springs from Coppola's source. *Marie Antoinette* is hardly a talky film; snippets of conversation, not long discourses, dominate the screenplay. Unidentified off-screen voices whisper gossip, and, as Zevin claims, sections of dialogue, especially in party scenes, are less than audible. *Marie Antoinette,* however, far surpasses Van Dyke's 1938 film in "accuracy of speech." Anyone who has read Fraser's work, or any biography of the French queen that quotes primary sources, can hear the care with which Coppola has blended historically accurate dialogue into what seems to be casual discourse.

When Empress Maria Teresa (Marianne Faithful) sends her daughter off to France, she warns that "all eyes" at the French court will "be fixed" on her. Those words come from a letter Maria Teresa sent to Versailles with Marie Antoinette (Fraser, *Marie Antoinette*, 48). To ensure that the instructions stayed fresh, the empress required her daughter to reread the letter monthly. As a nice contrast to Maria Teresa's emphasis on propriety, Coppola uses Louis XV's own words to introduce the sixty-year-old king (Rip Torn), whom she describes as a "noble and handsome old lion" (*Marie Antoinette*, screenplay). "How is her bosom?" he wants to know, right before meeting the Austrian princess. The king actually asked this question of a blushing Comte Mercy, and, when Mercy answered that he hadn't noticed, the king responded: "Oh, didn't you? That's the first thing I look at" (Fraser, *Marie Antoinette*, 64). Coppola works that last remark in as well. Historical discourse also helps illustrate the rivalry between King Louis XVI and his brothers. When the Comte de Provence takes his wife off to bed, bragging "four times last night wasn't enough," he's repeating a boast (probably a lie) that the wily comte made to taunt Louis Auguste and Marie Antoinette (Fraser 96–97).

The queen's dialogue too combines fictional and historical speech. After her journey from Austria to France (it took two and a half weeks), Marie Antoinette asks the question all children ask during any trip: "Are we there yet?" But the words she speaks to the Duc de Choiseul as she exits the coach to meet her husband-to-be—"I shall never forget that you are responsible for my happiness"—are the words the real Austrian princess uttered as she first stepped on French soil (Fraser, *Marie Antoinette*, 57). Coppola illustrates the rigid protocol of Versailles by repeating scenes of the lever—the elaborate rising ceremony that greeted Marie Antoinette every morning. The words that Kirsten Dunst speaks as she waits, naked, for ladies of the court to dress her sound contemporary. "This is ridiculous," she complains to the Comtesse de Noailles. "This is odious," the real Marie Antoinette said in the same situation, shivering, while one noblewoman deferred to another with a higher rank (Fraser, *Marie Antoinette*, 75; Weber 65). In the film, Marie Antoinette greets the arrival of her daughter with this passage, taken from the queen's first recorded words after the birth: "Poor little girl, you are not what was desired, but you are no less dear to me. . . . A boy would be the son of France, but you, Maria Teresa, shall be mine" (Fraser 168).

Sometimes Coppola transposes the speakers of historical dialogue. As

Louis and the queen ride away from Versailles, he asks her if she is "admir-ing" her "lime avenue." She answers: "I am saying good-bye." Louis's sister, Elizabeth, spoke these words to him as they left Montreuil. Fraser includes the quotation at the end of the section entitled "Hated, Humbled, Morti-fied," which describes escalating revolutionary tension during the royals' last summer at Versailles (*Marie Antoinette* 297). Coppola, who ends her careful adaptation of Fraser's work exactly at that point, places the evoca-tive answer to Louis's question on the queen's lips.

Coppola has said, again and again, that it was never her intent to create a historical document, so she might agree with Zevin that, in a sense, her film is "ahistorical." She describes it as a "gold-plated Versailles hangover of the memory of a lost girl, leaving childhood behind, to the final dignity of a woman" (*Marie Antoinette,* screenplay). Clearly, she isn't aiming for mimesis, the approach that Martin Scorsese favors for trapping the past. In *The Age of Innocence* (1993), he anguished over each period detail, making sure that even the newspapers his characters read were the real things, antiques, not just set decorations. His obsession led James Berardinelli to call *The Age of Innocence* a "time capsule." Coppola doesn't ignore or disre-spect history—a primary document even appears in *Marie Antoinette.* A shot replicating the dauphine and dauphin's famous marriage contract, with her childish writing and the ink blot after her signature, follows the lavish wedding scene (*Marie Antoinette,* screenplay). Versailles, the primary location of *Marie Antoinette,* is the setting that the real French court tra-versed, and the film's dialogue features historical content, but, from the start, *Marie Antoinette* signals that audiences shouldn't read what follows as a time capsule. The term *postmodern* best fits its intriguing blend of past and present.

Many films open with an establishing shot that announces the time, place, mood. In contrast, *Marie Antoinette*'s first image is a "disestablishing" shot. After Kirsten Dunst's name appears in the credits—hot pink against a black background—a scantily dressed "queen," half reclining on a chaise, appears. (Articles about and reviews of the film often reproduce this shot without mentioning its ironic intent.) A maid adjusts her shoe while the queen swipes a finger through the pink frosting on a cake next to her. She turns and looks knowingly at the audience. "I am exactly who you expected to see, right?" she seems to say. But this *isn't* the "real" Marie Antoinette, nor is she the one Kirsten Dunst plays in the film. Coppola calls this image the "evil fantasy Queen" (*Marie Antoinette*, screenplay). An anachronism underscores her "evil fantasy" identity. It's not a lady-in-waiting who adjusts her shoe but a maid, and this maid wears a costume different from all the other servers glimpsed in the backgrounds of the lush interior shots. They wear pastel, Watteauesque gowns, not black dresses with white aprons and matching black-ribboned white caps. This maid's uniform recalls *that* French maid, the archetypal one who says, "Oui, oui, Monsieur!" in all the French-maid jokes. She's a stereotype of a maid waiting on the stereotype of a queen. The credits continue after this thirty-second shot. The film's "real" opening shot presents a perfectly balanced contrast—an unanticipated view of the queen. An extreme close-up shows Marie Antoinette, a young girl with tousled hair, waking up in her own bed. In the background, an Austrian maid opens a shutter to let in the light of the day on which the princess will travel to France.

By the time the evil fantasy queen returns to say, "Let them eat cake," other anachronisms have shown that *Marie Antoinette* is, indeed, a "new kind of period film," an impression of the way in which things might have been in the now of the late eighteenth century with an overlay of the way things are in the now of 2006. There's the rock music, part of a multitemporal score, which mixes pop hits and eighteenth-century opera. There's the dancing at a masked ball, which ranges from minuet to rave. There's the powder-blue high-top tennis shoe, lying, untied, amid the vivid assortment of court shoes that Marie Antoinette and her ladies have been admiring. There's Coppola's pastel pallette, which glows with lighter, brighter tints than the more saturated colors popular at the French court.

Compare Coppola's layering of times to Stephen Soderbergh's more clinical approach to the past in *The Good German* (2006). Seeking the "truth" of the 1940s—the time period in which his film noir is set—Soderbergh used only techniques available to 1940s directors and shot in black-and-white. He even embedded film from the 1940s in his footage. Some applauded his craft, but words like *curious*, and *self-conscious*, and *mechanical* cropped up in most reviews. Some reviewers, like Mick LaSalle and Manohla Dargis, just plain hated the film. LaSalle found *The Good German* a "bloodless, academic exercise," while Dargis claimed that trying to make such a "genre pastiche" drained "all the air, energy and pleasure from [Soderbergh's] own film making." Coppola's reluctance to mimic the past in every detail or to erase the present via technique yields a much different result that could, more legitimately, be called a *pastiche*. The reverse of *The Good German*, *Marie Antoinette* plays on the friction between realities. The film vibrates with energy; it's a reminder that, in every era, youth has distinctive sounds, fashions, and colors.

In her impression of Marie Antoinette's life, Coppola begins with history, choosing scenes from the first four sections of Fraser's biography, but she finds her own rhythm in imagining the queen's most personal moments. Antonia Fraser says that she adores "the look of" *Marie Antoinette*, and she laments that writing "could never do" what film can, with "just a look" (*The Making of Marie Antoinette*). Coppola uses film's visual power to create Marie Antoinette's private world, a secret space never entered before. Van Dyke's film begins with a long shot of Marie Antoinette running through the corridors of her Austrian palace. Coppola starts with an extreme close-up on Marie Antoinette as she wakes up in her own bed, in her own room, on the morning of her journey to France. Van Dyke shows Marie Antoinette stepping from her gilded coach into the palace of Versailles. Coppola puts the audience inside the coach for the two-and-a-half-week trip. Lined with cerulean blue tapestry, the white-and-gold coach is both a moving jewel box and a cage in which the princess and her ladies play cards, look at a miniature of Louis, eat, and sleep. Along the way, we sometimes share Marie Antoinette's point of view as she gazes out the window, usually at ranks of trees.

Van Dyke skips the "handover" at Schuttern, where French noblewomen, led by the Comtesse de Noailles, helped Marie Antoinette shed her Austrian clothing and replace it with French court attire. Coppola includes this ritual, which demonstrated that even Marie Antoinette's body was no longer her own but the property of France. Mistaking the handover for a personal welcome, Marie Antoinette hugged the comtesse (played by Judy Davis in *Marie Antoinette*). As she does in the film, de Noailles stiffened at Marie Antoinette's embrace, stressing the symbolic, public nature of the ceremony (Lever 18). Even though he is leery of almost every aspect of *Marie Antoinette*, Zevin acknowledges Coppola's formalist eye when he says: "There is something painterly in [her] style" (33). A blend of composition and content is especially striking in the shot of Marie Antoinette exiting the handover pavilion. Centered, to show that forest surrounds it, the pavilion's dark interior is lit, improbably, by a crystal chandelier. In this temporary outpost of Versailles, culture ignores

Marie Antoinette. Nearly a child, like the little nobles who trail her, Marie Antoinette walks through the halls of Versailles toward her bridegroom. Filmed on location at the palace, Sofia Coppola's film follows the young queen's reach for a respite from the pomp that surrounds her here. (Courtesy Jerry Ohlinger's Movie Material Store.)

nature. Symmetry signals Marie Antoinette's entry into the pattern of the French court. A triumph of artifice, the new dauphine emerges and pauses, perfectly framed in the doorway, while guards stand at attention on each side of the draped enclosure. Marie Antoinette's Austrian ladies, her playful dog, her hair ribbon, and her looser gown have been left behind, scraps of her little-girl identity. A curled and corseted confection, she has been processed into a sexy French fashion plate, fit to be seen and desired by the dauphin.

Editing, too, adds to the impression that Marie Antoinette has entered an insular world where everything, even time, bends to French custom. In Van Dyke's more public film, Marie Antoinette goes from her coach directly into the state salon where she meets her husband. Coppola follows her into her suite of rooms at Versailles, the scene of a choreographed ballet performed by servants who are delivering her perfectly hued trunks and placing her beautiful accessories. Trailed by a string of solemn, elegant royal children, Marie Antoinette glides across her white, blue, and gold salon, which perfectly complements the color of her new French gown. Not only has she been dressed to fit her new position, but she has also been dressed to match these fantastic surroundings, rooms out of a fairy tale. Like a music box, the tinkling melody of "Jeynweythek Flow" repeats while jump cuts confuse the rate of the dauphine's progress and the orientation of the space she travels through, creating déjà vu moments. Hasn't she passed that fireplace? Hasn't that serving man bowed to her, or is that another, identically dressed servant? Hasn't she entered the doorway of the state bedroom? A trip to Versailles reveals that these rooms, which appear to open into each other, are not even contiguous, as Coppola's scene makes them seem. Real time awaits Marie Antoinette only in the private boudoir reached via a hidden door. We look with her into a charming room, smaller in scale, empty of swarming attendants. Might this be a place where she can pen a letter, lounge in comfort, escape the public gaze?

Complete escape from the clutches of protocol was, of course, impossible. Zweig describes the queen's ineptitude as she floundered in the powerful court web; Van Dyke's film uses the dauphine's duel with Du Barry and her involvement in the necklace scandal to stand for the whole. In contrast, the new *Marie Antoinette* lingers on the texture of the dauphine's day-by-day life at the heart of Versailles. Coppola called repeating scenes of the morning ceremony the "Groundhog Day wake-up montage" (*Marie Antoinette*, screenplay), and that's what they look like. Only the colors of the ladies' gowns signal that these are different mornings. Similar, circular views of Marie Antoinette's attendance at daily mass, her public meal with her husband, her preparations for bed, and night after night of chaste sleep in the great marriage bed illustrate the looping nature of court existence. But daily ritual was a minor source of stress compared to the major pressure on Marie Antoinette to become pregnant.

Van Dyke cuts from the coronation to the birth of the little dauphin—a transition that says *voilà!* Coppola spends more time illustrating Marie Antoinette's anguish over the tenuous state of her marriage. In one scene, Marie Antoinette reads a "lethal missive" from Austria (based on a real letter) in which her mother declaims: "Nothing is certain about your position there, until an heir is produced." A long shot shows that she is standing against a wall of pink, blue, and gold wallpaper patterned with large, beribboned bouquets of flowers and peacock feathers. She wears a dress with a slightly smaller, similar pattern in pastel tones. She could, literally, be part of the wallpaper. This shot offers a visual response to a question that Heilbrun wishes biographers of women would answer: "How does the process of becoming, or failing to become, a sex object operate in the woman's life?" (27). In her letter, the empress scolds her daughter for failing to entice the dauphin: "Remember, everything depends on the wife, if she is willing and sweet." As Marie Antoinette reads, she slides down the wall, slowly, and the camera moves in, slowly. The dual motion makes the pattern look alive, like twisting vines eager to entangle her. Finally, she sits on the floor, staring hopelessly at the audience. Since Coppola's film contains countless shots like this one that juxtapose the beauty of the setting with the strangling effects of the system, it's hard to imagine how anyone could interpret *Marie Antoinette* as a text "dripping with nostalgia for what appears to be the *ancien regime*" (Zevin 33) or how Coppola could be accused of giving her material a surface treatment.

Surfaces do intrigue her. Each of her three films, *The Virgin Suicides* (1999), *Lost in Translation* (2003), and *Marie Antoinette* (2006), features an evocative setting essential to its meaning. The lush lawns and carefully maintained houses of the 1970s neighborhood in *The Virgin Suicides* mask the underlying landscape of lust, where men are free to act on sexual impulses but a single tryst turns a virgin into a slut. No exceptions reverse this formula, and Lux Lisbon and her sisters understand that death alone can trump the rigid pattern. Coppola won an Oscar for the screenplay of *Lost in Translation,* in which the flashing neon facade of Tokyo stands in contrast to the serenity of a Buddhist temple. How can these wildly different manifestations be part of a coherent whole? Charlotte and Bob, the central characters, both insomniacs, can't speak the language or negotiate the culture, and, while they struggle to interpret the external terrain, they try to understand their attraction to each other. Sex could provide them with easy, nonverbal comfort and maybe the path to sleep, but they choose to remain companions. Their decision not to translate their warm intimacy into physicality seems a revolutionary choice for modern protagonists. *Marie Antoinette* turns on similar tensions between setting and character. Transported to the calculated unreality of Versailles, Marie Antoinette labors to create a personal context in the midst of an edifice ripe for the toppling. In this trio of texts, the protagonists are tested by Coppola's bête noire—alienation. Their only defensive weapons are connection and self-knowledge.

You can feel Coppola's personal connection to Paris and to all things French even in the fluffy "Sofia's Paris," in which readers get to "[tag] along" with "the director" on a shopping trip in "the city of light" (Hirschberg 103). Coppola's face is on the cover of the fall 2006 *New York Times* travel supplement, and, in that shot, a neon-pink plastic Eiffel Tower earring swings from her visible earlobe, a vampy, campy allusion to the title. Apparently, Sofia wears Paris like a bauble. The body of the article is dotted with photos of colorful window displays, glimpses of Parisian streets and parks, and informal snapshots of Coppola. For the most part, the text glosses the illustrations, describing what's available to someone with taste and euros: "bouquets that are organized by scent rather than color" (105), shoes to die for, pastries like jewels, and, if you're incredibly lucky, a little personal tailoring by Azzadine Alaia. These rich spoils are enough to cause shopper's envy in those—like us—forced into the more quotidian suburban American choices of Macy's, Target, Old Navy, or—double shudder—Wal-Mart.

Coppola's words—even in this frothy piece—make it perfectly clear that the whole Eiffel Tower earring thing is a joke. She's never arrogant, has very little lust for acquisition, and harbors more than a soupçon of affection for things French. Parisian shopping, she says, is "not so much about buying": "Whether you get something or not, when you go in a store, you see what Paris is like" (Hirschberg 105). She speaks of always loving Paris. "We came here a lot when I was really little," she explains. As a teen, she interned at Chanel (104), and she remembers admiring adult Parisians. "I would look at my parents' French friends and think: 'That's what you're supposed to be like when you grow up'" (104). An "emotional" stop in the Jardin du Luxembourg—a park she finds calming and restorative—prompts her to remark that her father was "so taken with the place that he built a little fountain in Napa based on the fountain here" (108). Her first inspiration for making *Marie Antoinette* came from a Parisian dinner conversation with the designer Dean Tavoularis, who told her about the young queen. "Everything about France influenced [*Marie Antoinette*]," Coppola comments. "The light here is different, the way the French hold themselves is different. . . . Here, they have lifestyle priorities" (106). The

author of "Sofia's Paris" agrees: "In many ways, the finished film is an homage to all things Francais" (Hirschberg 106). "Sofia's Address Book," a list
of shopping and dining establishments, and "Sofia's *Marie Antoinette*," a
map of shooting locations for the film, accompany the eight-page article,
conflating the director's life, her work, and the setting.

Van Dyke's film shows the dauphine's swerve toward Parisian pleasures:
she wears glittering gowns and fantastic accessories, she revels in elaborate
games, and she whirls at a bohemian costume ball. *Marie Antoinette,* too,
acknowledges the pull of beautiful objects and the power of immersion in
lovely places, but Coppola reads them as reflections of change in the queen's
beneath-the-surface self. Marie Antoinette's awakening has a catalyst: the
recognition that she can make *some* choices. Her entry into the luxury of
choosing follows a scene that illustrates her lack of control. She has just had
to congratulate her sister-in-law, the Duchess of Provence, for giving birth
to "the first Bourbon prince of his generation." As if she needed more reminding that she has not produced an heir, a group of fishwives, who have
gathered at Versailles (anyone who was decently clothed could enter), taunt
Marie Antoinette crudely as she returns to her chambers.

When she reaches the semiprivacy of her rooms, she bursts into tears.
In a corner of the gold and white room, she slides to the floor, weeping. She
has not chosen to live her life in public. She has not chosen her marriage.
She does not choose to remain childless. What's the remedy for such a
profound malaise? "Princely" thinking might have provided an option, but
Marie Antoinette was neither an Elizabeth I nor a Victoria, conditioned to
command. Caroline Weber believes that she sought to control a realm she
could affect by making "bold, stylistic experiments" (3). Coppola links the
queen's love of beauty and her "experiments" in style to self-development.

"Candy's just what the doctor ordered," counsels the sound track. And
candy is exactly what follows the scene of a weeping Marie Antoinette,
alone, at a literal and psychological low. The bright, kinetic montage that
comes next is meant to spark a beauty-induced high in the audience; it
could be a live-action companion piece to "Sofia's Paris." In this incredible
home shopping spree, the enticements of Paris are offered up to the dauphine: gorgeous flowers, incredible objets d'art, shoes to die for, pastries
like jewels, and, because Marie Antoinette's really lucky, a private session
with the A-list hairdresser Leonard. By placing a powder-blue high-top

among the court slippers—which aren't that different from Candies slides—Coppola slips in a reminder that teen spirits have always been lifted by material things and that lavish retail therapy hardly died in the eighteenth century.

But the montage is more than a feast for viewers or an enactment of Marie Antoinette's elevation to fashionista. The sweet princesse de Lamballe (Mary Nighy) and the saucy Duchesse de Polignac (Rose Byrne) experience the heady rush of fabric and feathers with Marie Antoinette. She has chosen their friendship over isolation and has shed her heavy sorrow like an old shoe. From this point on, her two friends are often at her side, as they are through the montage. Artistically grouped, the three make the best of the private boudoir, exclaiming at the riches before them while they spoil their lapdogs, sip champagne, and eat bonbons. Coppola gives Marie Antoinette's choice of friends (whether wise or foolish) a sense of inevitability. Would you prefer to maintain protocol with the stiff-necked Comtesse de Noailles, to conspire with the double-dealing aunts, or to shop with affectionate, amusing friends? It's a no-brainer.

A fall—a metaphor in motion—signals another phase of the queen's development. Finally, the queen's deflowering—marked by her surprised "Ooooh!"—takes place in the dark. The next brightly lit shot shows a glowing Marie Antoinette literally falling back onto a flower-strewn lawn, arms spread, face raised to the sun, in complete abandonment. Pain, glimpsed in the quick cut to her daughter's delivery, isn't the only payoff, for her fortunate fall brings her the perfect gift; Louis hands her the key to the Petit Trianon, tied up with a blue ribbon, a transaction that actually took place in 1774, just after Louis became king (Weber 130). Van Dyke never mentions Marie Antoinette's tiny, personal palace, but Coppola makes it the heart of her film—it's the innermost room—and stamps it with Marie Antoinette's cipher. A close-up of the cipher, M and A intertwined, introduces a scene in which the queen performs at her minitheater. Was she wise or foolish to flee "the rituals of the court" for her signature world (Weber 134)? Instead of pontificating, Coppola imagines the charm of life at the Petit Trianon, from the inside out. Form reinforces content in this section of *Marie Antoinette;* as the queen abandons herself to simplicity, the camerawork becomes looser, more realistic, and the lighting—often the sun or flickering candles—dapples and softens the atmosphere.

In a scene that begins with a shot of a relaxed Marie Antoinette gazing from a window, we hear her request for "something simple, to wear in the garden," mirroring the real queen's fashion change to the *gaulle,* a "white muslin shift," the garment that quickly became de rigueur for women of style (Weber 150). Her preference for lighter fabric and a less restrictive cut triggered a violent reaction from the French silk industry, whose fortunes waned as court dresses fell from favor (Weber 137). Revolutionaries used the change from silk to muslin as more evidence of the queen's anti-French leanings. The film shows the almost complete insulation that separated Marie Antoinette from their charges. The queen keeps to her Eden; gathering eggs, playing with her daughter, entertaining her friends. A visit to the Petit Trianon, its grounds, and its attendant village confirms that the sense of enclosure still belies the presence of Versailles, so near by. Coppola holds the audience inside the garden, where each of Marie Antoinette's choices feels right.

In that affirming environment, the screenplay suggests, Marie Antoinette abandoned herself to passion for nature and to passion for Axel Fersen. When it comes to their affair, Van Dyke includes most available historic information and fictionalizes when that runs out. Things heat up in the new *Marie Antoinette,* where Fersen (Jamie Dornan) gets less screen time than Tyrone Power did, but his every scene—including his meeting with the queen at a masked ball—crackles with sexual energy. At the Petit Trianon, Marie Antoinette poses for him, dressed in embroidered stockings and little else, a decorative fan shielding her body from the audience. Later, when Fersen embraces her in the garden, the turn and stretch of his beautifully muscled legs and slender waist imply a world of pleasure. In Coppola's version of the queen's life, romance speaks the language of young bodies more than words. These scenes trap the moments before or after lovemaking, evoking the anticipation or the memory of love, not its full embrace. When Fersen leaves, the queen and her friends return to Versailles, as if exiled from the garden, and the tone of the film changes.

Now comes the end of choice. Coppola uses vignettes to signify the darkening mood: a funeral with a tiny coffin; the queen embracing her two remaining children, the comment "Queen of Debt" scrawled on a banner across Élisabeth Vigée–Le Brun's portrait, the evil fantasy queen uttering, "Let them eat cake." The reviewer Daniel Mendelsohn feels that too little visual information documents this turn of events; its absence is one reason that *Marie Antoinette* is "ultimately . . . horribly, fatally truncated" (3). A key scene, which Mendelsohn doesn't mention, illustrates that Marie Antoinette understands, fully, with whom future choices lie. After the fall of the Bastille in 1789, things came to a head when a mob marched from Paris, demanding a confrontation with their monarchs. Wakened by their shouts, Marie Antoinette dressed quickly and joined her husband and children. When the mob demanded that she stand before them, alone, the queen appeared on a palace balcony. She crossed her hands over her chest and made a "deep curtsy" (Lever 230). Paradoxically, the mob cheered her courage. "Long live the queen," they cried.

Coppola alters this gesture, increasing its portent. As Marie Antoinette faces the mob, she inclines her head and slides her hands out, along the balustrade. When she stops, her head is lowered, and her arms are outstretched. Her posture recalls the moment before a beheading on the block, like that of Mary, Queen of Scots: "She laid her head down . . . [and] stretched out her arms and legs" (Fraser, *Mary Queen of Scots*, 538). Before Marie Antoinette steps onto the balcony, you can hear the accompaniment to her action, the high wail a wine glass makes when its rim is rubbed with a finger. In a previous scene, the queen and her friends giggle like children, making this sound during a candlelight picnic at the Petit Trianon. As it becomes the eerie undertone for billowing torch flames, shouted epithets, and the queen's graceful capitulation, it sings that such moments have passed.

Coppola's portrait of Marie Antoinette at the Petit Trianon, reveling in her faux simplicity, might invite comparisons to today's spoiled princesses, like Paris Hilton. In her turn toward a private world, however, Marie Antoinette seems the antithesis of the media-savvy Hilton, who inserted herself into "The Simple Life" for the exposure and the profit. The talented Kirsten Dunst, Coppola's pick for Marie Antoinette, is no Paris Hilton. In her bubbly biography of Dunst, written for a teen audience, Anne E. Hill unintentionally highlights what must be an ongoing issue for Dunst, who began her career at three, and who played the child vampire, Claudia, in *Interview with a Vampire* (Neil Jordan, 1994), at the age of ten. On the one hand, Hill diligently tries to characterize Dunst's life as normal, "much like [the lives] of other teenagers" (35); on the other hand, she cheerfully points out that, at twenty-four, Dunst is worth millions and, already, has had a career that spans "decades" (10). Fascinating too is Hill's insistence that Dunst is different than "teen stars of today, like Lindsay Lohan" (35), as if Dunst—four years older than Lohan—comes from another time and generation.

In the more insightful article "Kirsten," Marshall Heyman connects Dunst's life with the life of the French queen: "*Marie Antoinette* . . . cannily paralleled the life of a young celebrity in Hollywood, not far, one would imagine, from Dunst's own" (258). In her talk with Heyman, Dunst voices some ambivalence about her position as one of Hollywood's acknowledged princesses: "When you get to be 17, 18, you realize, Oh, I'm famous . . . and maybe that wasn't my choice completely" (266). One focus of the piece is Dunst's wish to make smart choices and to guard her innermost room. She mentions taking an art class but will not "talk much about" it or "reveal where it is." "It's so private, and I love it so much," she says, "it's like a little secret in my heart" (266). It's hardly a secret that Dunst was disappointed by the weak box-office response to *Marie Antoinette*, but she hesitates to elaborate, for fear of sounding "weird." Instead, she jokes about becoming an "old lady," remembered for her role as Spiderman's flame, Mary Jane. After *Marie Antoinette* flopped at the box office, Dunst says, "I was feeling that I had to prove myself. . . . I didn't prove myself enough." She has faith, however, in the staying power of the film: "It'll live on" (262).

Marie Antoinette will "live on" because Coppola directs her modern, intimate focus at a narrow slice of the queen's life, refusing to retrace a narrative dependent on "the houses and stories of men" (Heilbrun 47). With this film, she places herself in the chain of "female chroniclers" of Marie Antoinette (Fraser, *Marie Antoinette*, xx). Zevin devalues Coppola's beautiful film because she dares to present a multitemporal, very personal view. He bemoans the absence of the expected story, the one that would include footage of revolutionary mobs and antiroyalist figures like Robespierre. Perhaps Zevin knows of some arcane biopic rule of inclusion kept secret from most of us. It seems more likely, however, that, in his zeal to watch the storming of the Bastille, the imprisonment, and the beheading, Zevin— mired in the realm of the literal—simply does not recognize the harbingers of the revolution breathing from the screen. The physical agents of change are, as he points out, nearly absent. The approaching, seismic shift is not.

The revolution is present in the total isolation of the royals. It's present in the cold, sated faces of the aristocrats who "welcome" Marie Antoinette. It's present in the ominous tinkling of chandelier crystals, like wind chimes, signaling the approaching storm. It's present in the silly stasis of life at the palace. It's present in the fall breezes that lift the skirts of the royal women trailing back from the Petit Trianon to Versailles. It's present in the queen's symbolic beheading on the balcony. It's present in the ominous whine from the rim of a wine glass. It's present in the final shot of the shattered state bedroom. *Marie Antoinette* never neglects the "blustery wind" that ended the last summer at Versailles (Fraser, *Marie Antoinette,* 297–98).

We find something disturbing and wrongheaded in the implication that Coppola's careful adaptation aids those who would silence any evidence of class injustice. *Marie Antoinette* emphasizes the dehumanizing effects on any life lived by class designation alone. Also upsetting is the assertion that this film could be made "right" (read: left) only if Marie Antoinette's beheading—"she must be killed again" (Zevin 35)—were its visible conclusion. In its tone and content, *Marie Antoinette* follows Antonia Fraser's inspiration that "the elegiac should have its place as well as the tragic" (*Marie Antoinette* xix). But make no mistake; *Marie Antoinette* is never a lament for a corrupt system. It's a potent reminder that, in all times, isolation dooms every fragile human construct.

In our blasé world, where shopping is a hobby, niche marketing is a given, and lavish material goods dangle at our fingertips, it's not surprising that you can purchase Marie Antoinette's perfume. A historian "unearthed" the formula for "Sillage de la Reine," the "Trail of the Queen," and a perfumer reproduced the "intensely floral" scent, which debuted as an upscale souvenir at Versailles in 2006, the year *Marie Antoinette* was released ("Marie Antoinette Perfume Revived"). Some paid an astounding €8,000 for deluxe, twenty-five centiliter crystal bottles of the perfume, available to less affluent shoppers at €350. As does this souvenir, so personal to its original wearer, both these ambitious biopics try to trap Marie Antoinette's elusive essence. In their empathetic frames, as in the gardens of Versailles, her complex scent—rose, iris, jasmine, orange blossom, sandalwood—still tantalizes.

Chapter Seven

❧

Queen Elizabeth I

I will have but one mistress and no master.
—Elizabeth I

Images of the Virgin Queen fast-forward across film history, unforgettable, iconic images: the stately bearing; the red wigs; the high forehead; the long, aristocratic nose; the alabaster makeup; the pearl-drop earrings; the stiff, ornate ruffs; the fingers dripping with jewels; and the gowns, with yards and yards of white satin, purple velvet, gold, and silver ornamented and sparkling with rubies, diamonds, and more pearls. Even a schoolchild would be hard-pressed to mistake her for any other monarch.

As a case in point, this past fall, on one of our many visits to the National Portrait Gallery in London, we were strolling through the Tudor Rooms, contemplating the familiar faces of Elizabeth I and her entourage—Henry VII, Henry VIII, Mary Tudor, Robert Dudley, Francis Walsingham, William Cecil, Christopher Hatton, Sir Walter Raleigh, Sir Francis Drake, Robert Devereux, and others—when we happened on a primary school teacher and her class. The children, maybe seven or eight years old, all dressed neatly in their navy blue school uniforms, were sitting cross-legged on the floor in front of Elizabeth I's coronation portrait. The teacher asked: "Now, who is this?" Twenty hands shot into the air. "Queen Elizabeth the First," one child confidently answered. "Who was queen before Elizabeth?" Tiny voices in unison responded: "Her sister, Mary." And so it went as the teacher took the children through a visual history lesson, moving from portrait to portrait of the Virgin Queen, her kindred, her courtiers, and her counselors. Their answers came swiftly, with a kind of assurance that only the very familiar breeds. How many times in their short lifetimes had they seen the imprint of that famous face? we wondered.

Queen Elizabeth I. (Courtesy Victoria and Albert Museum, London/Art
Resource, New York.)

Mesmerized, we followed the group until at last, two by two, in a quiet, orderly queue, they left the gallery, images of Gloriana sealed forever in their minds.

Elizabeth carefully constructed her image to impress on her people and her courtiers alike that she ruled by divine right and that she, who answered to no one but God, walked on the earth solely to watch over England and its people. Lytton Strachey, examining the icon from his Victorian lens, wrote: "The form of the woman vanished, and men saw instead an image—magnificent, portentous, self-created—an image of regality, which yet, by a miracle, was actually alive" (*Elizabeth and Essex* 10). She refused to marry, bear children, or share her throne with a man. She sacrificed her personal life and desires for her public duty and demanded the same of her closest advisers, like Robert Dudley, Frances Walsingham, Christopher Hatton, and William Cecil. Magnanimous and tempestuous by turns, she lifted men up with titles and favors and cast them down if they betrayed her. She kept her court off balance, filling up a room with her big, bawdy laugh, or sucking all the air out of it with a flash of her temper. In short, she was larger than life.

No wonder actresses vied to play her on the stage and in films and television miniseries. Sarah Bernhardt, Flora Robson, Florence Eldridge, Bette Davis, Agnes Moorehead, Irene Worth, Catherine Lacey, Jean Simmons, Glenda Jackson, Anne-Marie Duff, Helen Mirren, and Cate Blanchett have played Elizabeth I over the years, some—like Robson, Davis, Jackson, and Blanchett—more than once. A role this powerful garnered Oscar and Emmy nominations. In 1998, Dame Judi Dench won an Academy Award for Best Supporting Actress for her eight-minute, four-scene portrayal of Queen Elizabeth I in *Shakespeare in Love* (John Madden, 1998), in the same year that Cate Blanchett received a nomination in the Best Actress category for her role in *Elizabeth*. In 2006, Helen Mirren walked off with an Emmy for her spot-on performance in the HBO miniseries *Elizabeth I*, which costarred Jeremy Irons as Robert Dudley, the Earl of Leicester. And, most recently, Blanchett won an Oscar nomination for her role as Elizabeth I in *Elizabeth: The Golden Age*, making her the only actor ever to receive nominations for playing the same character.

While audiences revel in these rich images, multiple portraits of Elizabeth Tudor across the last century make it difficult, at best, to do her justice in a single chapter. Some of Elizabeth's background we address in chapter 4 since any discussion of Mary, Queen of Scots, necessitates a treatment of Elizabeth, her cousin, her sister queen, her defender, and her jailor—the two forever entwined in history, in literature, and in cinema. And, while Elizabeth I makes appearances in fiction films like *Fire over England* (William K. Howard, 1937), *The Sea Hawk* (Michael Curtiz, 1940), *Seven Seas to Calais* (Rudolph Maté and Primo Zeglio, 1963), and *Orlando* (Sally Potter, 1992), the focus here is on films exclusively about her life, beginning with the last of the 1930s queen biopics: *The Private Lives of Elizabeth and Essex* (1939), starring Bette Davis. With this film as our touchstone, we then turn to seven other important works: *Young Bess* (1953), *The Virgin Queen* (1955), *Elizabeth R* (1971), *Elizabeth* (1998), *Elizabeth I: The Virgin Queen* (2005), *Elizabeth I* (2006), and *Elizabeth: The Golden Age* (2007).

The Private Lives of Elizabeth and Essex (1939)

Hollywood hit its peak in 1939, turning out a record number of critical and commercial successes. *The Private Lives of Elizabeth and Essex* wasn't one of them. *Gone with the Wind* (Victor Fleming), *Stagecoach* (John Ford), *Mr. Smith Goes to Washington* (Frank Capra), *Dark Victory* (Edmund Goulding), *Of Mice and Men* (Lewis Milestone), *Ninotchka* (Ernst Lubitsch), *The Women* (George Cukor), *Wuthering Heights* (William Wyler), and *The Wizard of Oz* (Victor Fleming) simply overshadowed the Warner Brothers adaptation of Maxwell Anderson's play *Elizabeth the Queen*. Perhaps it's just as well. As Robert Morsberger once wrote: "Historical accuracy and consistency were never Anderson's chief concern" (1386). In fact, Anderson made fast work of the truth in all three of his Tudor plays: *Elizabeth the Queen, Mary of Scotland,* and *Anne of the Thousand Days.* Consequently, subsequent movies based on them only perpetuated his twisted royal portraits.

    Elizabeth the Queen opened on Broadway in 1930 and starred Lynn Fontanne as Elizabeth I and Alfred Lunt as Robert Devereux, the Earl of Essex. Hoping to capitalize on its long run as well as a decade-long string of successful female royal biopics, Warners bought the rights to the play and quickly cast their reigning queen, Bette Davis, in the role of Elizabeth. Davis, a two-time Oscar winner by 1939, had fought her way to the top, demanding "better scripts, more varied roles, more sensitive directors, and stronger co-stars" (Giannetti, 10th ed., 275). Along the way, she acquired the reputation of being difficult. But her "fight against slavery" (Allen 551), as she put it, and the injustices of the studio system ultimately netted her juicier parts and the respect and gratitude of her fellow actors.

During her lengthy career, Davis picked up a total of ten Oscar nominations and the American Film Institute's Life Achievement Award, the first female star to be so honored (Katz 337). She built her reputation on roles that nobody else wanted and turned them into tour de force performances, like the cruel, conniving Mildred in John Cromwell's 1934 version of Somerset Maugham's play *Of Human Bondage*. Nobody in Hollywood wanted to play the part. Not glamorous enough. Besides, the public, ever prone to confuse the star with the on-screen character, might forever link Bette with the malicious Mildred. Bette didn't care. She saw it as an opportunity to show Hollywood—and, more specifically, Warner Brothers, where she was drowning in a sea of romantic schlock—what she was made of. When she didn't even receive an Oscar nod for her standout performance, the industry trades, the Hollywood minions, and the fans "raised a hullabaloo" (Baskette, "The Girl They Tried to Forget," 120). Bette didn't care, or, if she did, she didn't respond to the general outrage. She just walked off the next year with the Best Actress statue for Alfred E. Green's 1935 *Dangerous*.

Davis never considered herself "glam" or shied away from doing what was necessary for the part (witness her Charlotte Vale in *Now, Voyager* [Irving Rapper, 1942]), so we can only guess what she must have thought (or said) if she read Sylvia of Hollywood's beauty and personality advice to her in *Photoplay*: "If you're going to continue to play unsympathetic roles . . . you've got to show me—and the rest of the world—that you're not like that in real life. That you're not actually hard and bitter and cynical." Later in the piece, after detailing Davis's physical flaws, including her neck, eyes, and jaw line, Sylvia boldly writes: "God gave you intelligence. I can see that in your expressive forehead. But it isn't always wise, in Hollywood (or anywhere else in the business world), to show it too pronouncedly. So make that intelligent forehead look softer by bringing your hair forward, over it" (Sylvia of Hollywood 189). One wonders if it was this humble advice that inspired Davis to shave two inches from her hairline for her role as Elizabeth I to imitate the monarch's baldness under those elaborate red wigs.

The producer Hal Wallis tried to veto Bette's interpretation of Gloriana. Stop her from making herself look like "a female Frankenstein," he told the director Michael Curtiz (qtd. in Leaming 155). The truth is that neither Wallis nor Curtiz cared about the truth. Wallis made that clear when he said: "We have a story that we are going to try and make into a great love story, and this is not going to be possible if we try to do it with Flynn, as handsome as he looks in his clothes, in love with an ugly woman" (qtd. in Leaming 155). Most biographies of Elizabeth suggest no "great love story" here. As Alison Weir points out: "She seems to have regarded [Essex] as the son she had never had rather than as a lover or suitor. There is certainly no evidence that she had any real sexual attraction to him" (385). Lytton Strachey's 1928 biography, *Elizabeth and Essex*, suggests otherwise. Strachey writes: "He [Essex] had betrayed her in every possible way—mentally, emotionally, materially—as a Queen and as a woman—before the world and in the sweetest privacies of the heart" (262–63). But then Strachey is writing from that Victorian perspective about a queen so very different from the one he knew, a devoted wife and mother of nine. As Sarah Gristwood aptly states in her excellent treatment *Elizabeth and Leicester:* "The Victorians—while relishing the brave and beruffed ruler as an icon of empire—were troubled by the whole question of Elizabeth's sexuality." They couldn't reconcile the "unwomanly" icon, the eternal virgin, with the flesh and blood sexual, unmarried creature (365). It's understandable why Strachey would think Elizabeth and Essex were lovers.

Elizabeth enjoyed Essex's company. He was tall, handsome, and charming with a little flirty danger around the edges. He flattered her, and Elizabeth liked keeping up the pretense that she was still youthful and beautiful. She favored him with honors and titles and property. She also tried to protect him from himself, his own worst enemy. His noble line stretched back to the Plantagenets, but Essex was egotistical, extravagant, impetuous, ambitious, and greedy for military glory when he had little facility of command. Neville Williams in *The Life and Times of Elizabeth I* calls him "a spoilt child, utterly self-centered, petulant and unpredictable" (193). Essex wanted more and more of everything, especially power and authority, and, when Elizabeth wouldn't concede, he took them. He defied the queen at every turn: marrying Frances Walsingham (Sir Francis Walsingham's daughter) without Elizabeth's permission, dashing off to Cadiz when she forbade him to go, whipping up conspiracies where there were none, and badgering her for the Irish command. He was, in a word, ungovernable.

With access to Hatfield's Muniment Room, a treasure trove of the Cecils' private and public documents, including some of Elizabeth's letters, Lord David Cecil came across a letter from William Cecil to his son Robert. In it, the father lays out ten guidelines for a good life. In number 8, William writes: "I advise thee not to affect or neglect popularity too much. Seek not to be Essex; shun to be Raleigh" (Cecil 82). The wise man of court and council smelled disaster coming. But Elizabeth was no fool. In *The Cecils of Hatfield House*, David Cecil writes that Elizabeth, "born normally susceptible to male charms . . . , had learned that anyone in her position must be very cautious about yielding to them" and "saw to it that her head ruled her heart" (45–46). She would always put the good of the realm and her people above her personal, private desires. Her speeches usually included some form of the following: "Though you have had and may have many mightier and wiser princes sitting in this seat, yet you never had nor shall have any that will love you better" (Weir 474).

Elizabeth put up with Essex for as long as she did because he was the stepson of Robert Dudley, the Earl of Leicester, "Sweet Robin," "My Eyes," the one man Elizabeth favored above all others. Gristwood argues: "The Queen's long, her extraordinary, indulgence toward Robert Devereux was her long lament for Robert Dudley" (337). Many biographies suggest that Elizabeth and Robert Dudley's childhood friendship ripened into genuine love, which, though probably never consummated, bound them steadfast to each other—through political and personal tempests—until his death in 1588. Grief-stricken, and perhaps out of loyalty, Elizabeth turned to a hollow substitute, even granting Essex Leicester House on the Strand, which he promptly renamed Essex House.

Elizabeth was thirty-three years Essex's senior, and, at the time the movie takes place, she would have been in her sixties, Essex in his thirties. She was balding. She did wear outrageous costumes and red wigs laced with pearls. She did prevaricate, a strategy that probably helped her keep her head, her crown, and her independence for forty-five years. But, when Essex led a rebellion against her, she signed his death warrant without hesitation. As Strachey tells us: "She saw plainly that she could never trust him, that the future would always repeat the past" (*Elizabeth and Essex*

261). This is the history we seldom glimpse in *The Private Lives of Elizabeth and Essex*. Though the characters and even some of the speeches are essentially true to history, the core of the film—scenes depicting "the private lives" of the queen and the earl—are sheer speculation, and events are tweaked to favor Essex.

Barbara Leaming's biography of Bette Davis suggests that, preferring male action movies, Warners wanted to shift the focus from Elizabeth to Essex. Studio executives tried to change the title to *The Knight and the Lady*, which, of course, undercut the queen's role and significance. Bette objected. She wanted to stick with the original title, *Elizabeth the Queen*. Errol Flynn objected. It diminished his role in the film. Since Strachey's biography of the queen and her courtier was already titled *Elizabeth and Essex*, the compromise became *The Private Lives of Elizabeth and Essex*. Unfortunately, Warners managed to keep the spotlight on Flynn in more subtle ways.

Opening the film with Essex's heroic exploits in Cadiz assures Flynn's importance over Elizabeth's. The canons fire at the Spanish, and, before long, we witness his triumphant homecoming through the streets of London, throngs of people shouting his name. Casting the handsome, athletic Errol Flynn assures Essex our attention and sympathy. He smiles and waves. Hearts melt. What a contrast to Elizabeth's first appearance. Curtiz cuts to her in shadow. She's dressing behind a screen while talking to one of her advisers. As her shadow primps in a mirror, she speaks of putting Essex in his place. "His ambition has jeopardized the prosperity of the English people." Though this is, in fact, true, the juxtaposition of scenes makes her seem jealous and petty. As Essex marches with his men into the throne room, we see only him and the back of the throne until the camera crosses the 180-degree line and tilts up dramatically to an angry Elizabeth. Instead of praising, she chastises. She has taxed her poor people heavily to raise the money for the Cadiz venture, and he returns empty-handed, no promised Spanish treasure in tow. Her tongue-lashing in front of the court and her promotion of Lords Howard and Raleigh (actually the real heroes of the expedition) are more than he can bear. He explodes and turns his back on her. She boxes his ears. Putting his hand on his sword, he says, "I wouldn't take that from your father, the king, and I won't take it from a king in petticoats," and stalks out.

The scene, emblematic of most scenes in the film, makes Essex look

The Private Lives of Elizabeth and Essex. The composition of this shot tells us whose movie this really is. Bette Davis may play the queen, but the charming Flynn steals the film. Here, he looms over her, taking up the intrinsically heavy, right side of the frame where the viewer's eye is naturally drawn. We get the feeling that, if he stood up straight, he'd pop right out of the frame. But note how Davis's Elizabeth checks his advances with her pointed ruff and cocked elbow. (Courtesy Jerry Ohlinger's Movie Material Store.)

justified in his actions. The ear-boxing incident actually did take place, but much later, during the Irish debate. Elizabeth and Essex had been arguing over who to send to Ireland as lord deputy when, not getting his way and "with gross disrespect," he turned his back on her. She boxed his ears, shouting: "Go to the devil!" He reached for his sword and was about to strike her when Lord Nottingham stepped between them. Weir writes: "Too late, Essex realised the enormity of what he had done" (434–35). In the aftermath of the quarrel, the film has her sitting behind her desk gazing up at a portrait of the handsome favorite, sighing: "Robert, Robert. I don't know which I hate the most: you for making me love you or myself for needing you so." The portrait towers above her, a technique employed in several queen films to indicate the place that men occupy in the lives of female monarchs. We see it first in *Queen Christina* (1933) as she works beneath a wall-size painting of her father, who cast a long shadow over her short reign. Later, in *Elizabeth* (1998), a larger-than-life-size portrait of Henry VIII looms over the queen as she berates herself for a mistake her father would never have made. Sixty-five years have not diminished the significance of this shot or its meaning.

For much of *Elizabeth and Essex,* Davis stomps around in a state of agitation, her body jerking about, her hands in a constant twitter. When not bemoaning her aging self, her fading beauty, and breaking mirrors, she's erupting in shrewish, jealous rages at Lady Penelope Gray (Olivia de Havilland), who has her beautiful, young eye on Essex. Though the real queen had many loyal female friends, here women emerge as mostly rivals as she storms and strikes, fidgets and fingers fruit and candies from the nearest bowl. Davis's mannered performance distracts, and we see only glimpses of the brilliant, charismatic stateswoman and intuitive, wise ruler. For this early portrait, we must watch Flora Robson in *Fire over England* (1937) and again in *The Sea Hawk* (1940), two films based on novels but, in many respects, far superior to *The Private Lives of Elizabeth and Essex.* Robson gives a nuanced performance in these cameos, given what we know of Elizabeth, and her scenes with Errol Flynn, who plays a dashing swash-buckler in *The Sea Hawk,* reflect their genuine affection and respect for each other. Davis and Flynn, on the other hand, loathed each other. Davis once told Charlotte Chandler: "Errol Flynn liked to put his tongue in your mouth after he'd been out drinking all night. Ugh! I always kept my lips tightly closed" (262). This explains the many tight-lipped kisses in the film and the lack of chemistry between the two leads. But, ultimately, Flynn's natural charm and seemingly effortless acting style tip the balance in favor of his portrayal of Essex over Davis's affected portrayal of the queen.

If we didn't know better, we'd think that Essex was a paragon of virtue instead of a warmonger. Like Queen Christina, Elizabeth hated war. Too wasteful. "My policy has always been peace," she tells Francis Bacon, a tough thing to maintain when the men around her clamor for war with Spain, with France, with Ireland. She warns Essex, who dreams of another military command, about playing into the hands of his enemies at court who would welcome his ruin and shame, enemies who would goad him into taking on the near impossible task of subduing the rebel Tyrone in

Ireland. But, of course, he doesn't listen to her, and events play out as she predicts—in life and in the film. He's easily duped by his enemies at court and by Tyrone in Ireland. He totally botches the Ireland campaign, leaves what men he has left there, and rides home in shame. The film, however, throws blame for his loss on Elizabeth, who didn't support him enough, and on Robert Cecil (secretary at the time) and Walter Raleigh, who have intercepted the queen's and Essex's letters to each other.

No letters were intercepted in real life. In fact, Strachey writes: "Unable to bring himself to admit that he had muddled away his opportunity, he sought relief in random rage and wild accusations, in fits of miserable despair, and passionate letters to Elizabeth" (*Elizabeth and Essex* 206). The queen, in turn, kept close account of events and told him to stay the course. When he, muddy and disheveled, burst in on her in the process of dressing, it wasn't long before she put him in custody and cut off his income. Enraged, he led a rebellion against her, thinking that he had the people of England behind him. He was wrong again. Advised to stay indoors on the day Essex marched his men into London, they obeyed their queen, displaying no divided loyalties. The film reflects her decree. Streets empty and shutters close as Essex and his gang thread their way through the city in treason, not triumph. Realizing quickly that they could not rally Elizabeth's subjects, many of Essex's men slithered off into the shadows; others, captured with him, suffered the fate of traitors. Essex was sent to the Tower and beheaded shortly thereafter. Before he died, he implicated all his co-conspirators, including some of his family members.

Toward the end of the film, Elizabeth explains to Essex why he would have made a poor king: "For the greater glory of Essex you would make war upon the world, drag your country down, and drown her in a sea of debts and blood." Though she's absolutely right, the staging of the final scene and embroidered history dilute her message and paint Elizabeth as a needy, clinging, desperate queen. Earlier in the film, in one of their private moments, Elizabeth gives Essex a ring and tells him that, if he's ever in need, he's to send it to her and she will forgive him anything—a romantic but fictitious story. We see Essex in the dungeon, gazing on the ring, too proud to send it. Taking the room above his cell, Elizabeth breaks down and sends for him. As her guard opens the trap door in the floor, Essex emerges through beams of light while the queen sits in darkness. We've come full circle. He stands before her as charming and handsome as ever, refusing to request her pardon. After her wonderful speech about loving England and her people more than anything else, he privileges his private feelings over her public concerns with these words: "Perhaps you're right. I'd have made a sorry king. So then it's better this way. But this I'd have you know. If things had been different—you simply a woman, not a queen, and I a man with no crown between us—we could have searched heaven and earth for two perfect lovers and ended the search with ourselves. Of all the things on this earth that I'm now to leave, I care about leaving none of them but you." He leaves her clinging and clutching and crying out: "Robert, take my throne. Take England. It's yours." This film replays the story that an older woman who loves a younger man is always pathetic and ridiculous, even when she's a queen. The reverse is rarely true.

At the block, we see Essex kiss her ring and die a noble death in the clear morning light. A cut to Elizabeth on her throne, alone in the dark, a solitary tear sliding down her cheek, visually illustrates what happens when a queen puts her realm before love. Though the *New York Times* critic Frank Nugent wrote, "It's Queen Bette's picture" (1657), Flynn's Essex trumps Davis's Elizabeth, despite the character's intelligence and strength, with charm and a nobility the real Essex never possessed. In real life, no one trumped Elizabeth, who, throughout her reign, refused to share her power with or live her narrative through a man.

Young Bess (1953)

In *The Private Lives of Elizabeth and Essex,* we see an aging Elizabeth, moving toward the end of her reign. *Young Bess,* directed by George Sydney, rewinds that life, taking Elizabeth from cradle to coronation. Released to coincide with Elizabeth II's coronation (2 June 1953), *Young Bess* offers a slice of the monarch's life we seldom see enacted on screen, and for that reason alone the film merits inclusion in our discussion. Adapted from a historical novel by Margaret Irwin—part 1 of her Elizabeth trilogy, which includes *Elizabeth, Captive Princess* and *Elizabeth and the Prince of Spain*— the film boldly speculates about Elizabeth's relationship with her father, Henry VIII; her stepmother, Catherine Parr; her brother, Edward VI; and her first crush, Thomas Seymour, the lord high admiral of England. But the opening scroll heralds Tudor fact, not myth, proclaiming that Elizabeth was born "at a time when heads were falling around her like cabbage stalks. To grow up at all was an achievement; to grow up to greatness was a miracle." As David Cecil states: "To read about Elizabeth's early life is to enter the world of Jacobean tragedy, sensational and spectacular, gorgeous and bloodstained" (34).

The story, told in flashback, bookends with Elizabeth's servants Thomas Parry (Cecil Kellaway) and Katherine "Kat" Ashley (Kay Walsh) on the eve of their mistress's ascension to the throne, 16 November 1558. Sitting by the fire, they raise their glasses to the young Bess and reminisce about the "ups and downs" along that twenty-five-year journey. Mary is dead. Long live Queen Elizabeth, they toast, beginning their tale with words Elizabeth herself would have approved: "We were our father's daughter. . . ." A cut finds the proud, corpulent Henry (Charles Laughton) showing off the infant Elizabeth to an admiring court while his huge hands caress Anne Boleyn's (Elaine Stewart) neck. Who needs to see her head roll when this gesture says it all?

Henry was actually in a rage when Elizabeth was born, according to Carolly Erickson's biography, *The First Elizabeth*. The child's grand entrance into the world at Greenwich Palace on 7 September 1533 was a cosmic disappointment to both parents. Anne had promised Henry a son. Astrologers and soothsayers had predicted a boy. Henry had waited six years, tearing court and country apart, to divorce Catherine of Aragon and marry Anne. He broke with Rome and the pope, he appointed himself head of the church, he executed those who would not bend to his will, and he suffered the slings of gossipmongers who whispered that he was bewitched. And for what? A girl? Henry felt betrayed and angry: "He lashed out at everyone within range, first driving out the astrologers . . . and then swearing at the physicians and midwives until he reduced them to submissive self-reproach. Even the horse master and grooms of the stables felt the bite of his rancor when he summoned them to cancel the carefully planned jousts" (Erickson, *The First Elizabeth*, 19). Anne was terrified, with good reason. Eric Ives, in his *The Life and Death of Anne Boleyn*, contends: "With a daughter in the cradle, Anne had still to establish her claim to the throne. The birth of Elizabeth undid much of what the coronation had set out to achieve; Anne Boleyn remained a pretender. If she had had a son in September 1533, her position would have been beyond challenge" (186). In Justin Chadwick's 2008 film adaptation of Philippa Gregory's *The Other*

Boleyn Girl, Natalie Portman eerily renders Anne's fear and desperation during her dizzying slide in Henry's affections after Elizabeth's birth.

Most biographies of Elizabeth concur with Ives's assessment. Anne was never popular with the court or the people. Too shrewd, too pushy, too temperamental, they thought. She was the one who had found the loophole for Henry's divorce. Hadn't he married his brother Arthur's wife, Catherine, after Arthur's early death? Didn't that defy the laws of God and nature, even though they received permission to marry from the pope? Catherine was a saint compared with Anne, who taunted a smitten Henry with her virginity until he risked his mortal soul to marry her. This was the general belief at the time, though centuries of research reveal a more sympathetic portrait of Anne and another side of the story.

Henry liked the hunt. He'd already taken Anne's sister, Mary, as a mistress. She bore him a son, as did Bessie Blount. Illegitimate, they didn't count as heirs. Biographers offer evidence that, even before Elizabeth's birth, Henry was growing tired of Anne and looking in a new direction—Jane Seymour. A few miscarriages later, Anne's fate was certain. She was beheaded on trumped-up charges of adultery and took five "lovers" with her. "The Great Whore" went to her modest grave denying the accusations against her while Henry went hunting—literally. Then he scrambled over to Jane Seymour's house and married her ten days later. As Erickson writes, his conduct was "below reproach": "Leaving aside the unfathomable issue of how any man, king or no, could in cold blood send a woman he had once worshiped to her death, there was the additional scandal of his grotesque rejoicing over it, and of his hasty third marriage" (*The First Elizabeth* 35).

How these events worked on the psyche of a princess, biographers can only speculate. What she heard, from whom, under what circumstances, we can only piece together, as she must have had to do. We do know that she asked: "How haps it? Yesterday my Lady Princess, today but my Lady Elizabeth" (qtd. in Cecil 37). What was her reaction to news of her father's latest conquests and behavior? Did she know that people called her "The Little Whore," Anne Boleyn's "bastard child"? When and how did she process the details of her mother's death? Elizabeth rarely spoke of her mother, but she carried her image in a ring and appointed Boleyn relatives to positions of power when she felt they deserved it. Outwardly, she identified with her father. In *Elizabeth: The Struggle for the Throne,* David Starkey suggests: "For her, he was not the wife-murdering monster, but a loving parent, a formidable ruler and model to which she aspired" (32). It took a while, however, before that father/daughter bond kicked in.

Ives suggests that the king and queen rallied from their initial disappointment and put on a good show of pomp and ceremony for Elizabeth's christening. They established Hatfield as their daughter's main household and visited occasionally. On special occasions, Henry would trot out Elizabeth and show her off. A scene from *Young Bess* mirrors his actions in January 1536 on the death of Catherine of Aragon. Relieved to have his first wife out of the picture (a pattern he establishes here), Henry dressed himself in bright yellow, called for his daughter, and "carried her about for some time, holding her out to each of his courtiers, smiling at her, talking about her" (Erickson, *The First Elizabeth*, 29). The film shows him with an infant Elizabeth, though she would have been about two and a half at this time.

Henry's relationship with his daughter after Anne's death drives the exposition of Sydney's film. While Henry plays out the drama of his marriages to Jane Seymour, Anne of Cleves, Catherine Howard, and Catherine Parr, we see Elizabeth at Hatfield in the care of Catherine "Kat" Champernon, her governess from the age of four and the mother figure in her life. Kat became a relative when she married John Ashley, a cousin on the Boleyn side and a servant in Elizabeth's household. The film nicely captures the genuine affection between Kat and her charge as she shuffles a young Bess (Noreen Corcoran) back and forth between Hatfield and Hampton Court to meet her succession of stepmothers. Elizabeth is simply a walk-on part in the soap opera of her father's life, and she knows it. When her father takes a fifth wife, she's had enough. A seven-year-old Elizabeth spits on the floor and says she won't go.

The film goes to great lengths to make the point that Elizabeth is her father's daughter. Her coloring is Henry's. She stands like Henry, hands on hips, legs apart. She's precocious, intelligent, and stubborn. In one interesting scene, she stands silent, glaring, before the table where Henry sits tearing into the mountains of food before him. Finally, he notices her and with a full mouth says: "You dare defy me. Yes, I'm beginning to like you." Later in the film, a teenaged Elizabeth (Jean Simmons) bravely stands up to him when he bellows at sixth wife, Catherine Parr (Deborah Kerr), for sanctioning an English translation of the Bible. Elizabeth intercedes, so he threatens to send her back to Hatfield. "I will not go back to Hatfield," she bellows back. "You would shape the world as it suits you," he chastises. "Why not? Didn't you?" Silence. People swirling around them freeze until Henry suddenly laughs and shouts: "You're my daughter!" On his death-bed, the room filled with his advisers and his children—Mary, Edward, and Elizabeth—it's Elizabeth he singles out. She's the one to watch, he tells everyone. "Keep an eye on *her.*" Then, beckoning her forward, he whispers: "I wish you were a boy." And so he dies, the dramatic fade to black a final blessing on Elizabeth, his unlikely successor.

David Starkey carefully lays out the occasions on which father and daughter actually met in real life. For several years after her mother's death, Henry saw little of Elizabeth, but, as he aged, he gathered all three of his children around him more frequently. Some of this togetherness had to do with Catherine Parr, a kind and conscientious stepmother to all Henry's children. The king married Catherine, who had been married and widowed twice before, in July 1543. Mary was twenty-seven, Elizabeth almost ten, and Edward five. Elizabeth and Edward, especially, responded to her warmth and her attempts to bring them together with their father. They came to court. Henry dined with them at Whitehall. The family was to-gether at Leeds Castle after Henry's defeat of the French at Boulogne. Evidence indicates that Elizabeth adored him, and he seems to have taken "a warm, fatherly pride in her" (Starkey 30). There's a hint that she did something to displease him at one point and was banned from court for about a year, but no one knows exactly what happened. In the end, how-ever, Elizabeth must have exceeded Henry's expectations. Tutored by the best scholars in England, Roger Ascham and William Grindal, she proved herself a serious scholar. Here's what Alison Weir has to say in *The Life of Elizabeth I:* "She had a formidable intelligence, an acute mind and a re-markably good memory. Ascham declared he had never known a woman with a quicker apprehension or a more retentive memory. Her mind, he enthused, was seemingly free from all female weakness, and she was 'en-dued with a masculine power of application'; he delighted in the fact that she could discourse intelligently on any intellectual subject. There were many learned ladies in England, but Ascham was not exaggerating when he claimed that 'the brightest star is my illustrious Lady Elizabeth'" (14). In 1544, three years before he died, Henry restored Elizabeth to the succes-sion, after Edward and Mary. He left his daughter one of the richest women in the realm in property and titles. Like Mary, she received an annual income of £3,000 and a dowry of £10,000. The hitch was that neither she nor Mary could marry without the Council's permission, else they forfeited their place in the succession. It was a stipulation that some would argue saved Elizabeth from an early, potentially disastrous marriage.

Though *Young Bess* is based on a novel, it unveils a somewhat truer tapestry of Elizabeth Tudor's life than later, more popular biographical films, like *Elizabeth* and *Elizabeth: The Golden Age*. But then Irwin was noted for her knowledge of Elizabethan England and celebrated for her historical accuracy and attention to detail, and Sydney's film reflects that. It follows the life of Elizabeth after her father's death and focuses on her relationship with her younger brother, now king, Edward VI; her stepmother, Catherine Parr; and Thomas Seymour, Catherine's husband.

By all accounts, Elizabeth loved Edward (Rex Thompson). They didn't meet often, but there existed between them a bond of blood, education, religion, and pride in being Henry's children. The film paints a close, almost conspiratorial partnership between brother and sister as they team up against the "bad guys" here: Edward "Ned" Seymour (Guy Rolfe), his wife, Ann (Kathleen Byron), Robert Tyrwhitt (Alan Napier), and Lady Tyrwhitt (Norma Varden).

Elizabeth's feelings for Catherine, interpreted largely from her letters, also appear to have been affectionate and respectful. Deborah Kerr plays Catherine in *Young Bess*. MGM initially tapped Kerr to play Bess, after deciding against Greer Garson for the role, and then settled on Simmons. But both Kerr and Simmons seem a strange choice to play Elizabeth, who was only ten years old when Henry married Catherine and fourteen when Catherine married Thomas Seymour. The younger Simmons, however, was far more likely to convincingly play Elizabeth as a teenager, and Kerr's own regal persona was a better fit for the thirty-one-year-old Catherine. Beautiful, kind, virtuous, majestic, and maternal, the film Catherine reaches out to her wary stepdaughter, gently saying: "We've got you, and we're going to keep you." Elizabeth responds to her instantly. And what's not to like? Having no children of her own, Catherine treated Henry's children as if they mattered. She supervised their education, tended to matters of state when Henry was fighting in France, and modeled her own life as a living testament to the new religion, Protestantism. In many ways, she became a role model for Elizabeth, especially with regard to her religious beliefs.

Catherine's position thus established in the film, it's all the more poignant when we see her relationship with Elizabeth begin to crack as Thomas Seymour becomes the romantic goal for both women.

Though the historical frame remains intact, the film posits several important questions: What if Seymour wasn't the ambitious, power-hungry charmer that history painted him? What if he really did love both Catherine and Elizabeth? What if we got him wrong? What if Elizabeth actually had romantic feelings for him? Though he's never the main event in the film, Elizabeth's feelings for him are—and that's the speculative, dramatic focal point of the story. The real story, documented by virtually every biographer of Elizabeth, goes like this.

After Henry's death, Edward Seymour (the brother of Jane Seymour, Henry's third wife and the young Edward's mother) quickly seized control of the Council of Regency, promoting himself to the position of lord protector over his nephew, the young king. Apparently, Edward was as sour and stern as his brother Thomas was handsome and charismatic. But both brothers had something in common: ambition. Nothing was ever enough. While Edward took the king, Thomas made a bid for the queen; future queens or ex-queens, it didn't matter. Anyone who moved him closer to the throne was fair game for Thomas. Not content with his wealth and status, he first tried for the hand of Mary Tudor. Not going to happen, brother Edward warned. How about Elizabeth? Don't even think about it. Thomas looked outside the inner circle. Anne of Cleves was still around. She had been Henry's fourth wife briefly. That didn't work out either. Finally, he settled on Catherine Parr, Henry's widow, and this time he didn't ask for permission. They married just months after Henry's death, in secret, and Catherine's vast fortune transferred to Thomas.

For Catherine, at least, it was a love match. She and Thomas had courted before Henry spotted and claimed her for his sixth wife. Free to finally choose for herself, Catherine quickly agreed to Thomas's proposal. She had been living in Chelsea with Elizabeth, and now Thomas joined them. It wasn't long, however, before he began to pay a little too much attention to Elizabeth. Most of her biographers recount the now familiar stories of how Thomas would come into her bedchamber early in the morning, usually before she had arisen. He teased and tickled, striking her "'on the buttocks familiarly'" (qtd. in Erickson, *The First Elizabeth*, 69). David Starkey even suggests that he might have sexually abused her (*Eliz-*

abeth: The Acclaimed Saga of England's Virgin Queen). To avoid his advances, Elizabeth arose earlier so that she would be dressed when he arrived, but the consensus is that she fell for him.

We know about these incidents largely because of Kat Ashley's testimony. She liked Seymour and chided him good-naturedly about his attentions to Elizabeth until he began coming into her chamber half dressed. Rumors flew about Elizabeth and Thomas. Catherine herself was involved in one still inexplicable episode that took place in the garden. Thomas cut Elizabeth's somber dress to shreds with a pair of scissors while Catherine held her down. Why? This is the question that echoes over history. We may never have the answer, but we do know that Kat interceded. Her lady's reputation was on the line. Catherine too, now in her midthirties and pregnant with Thomas's child, was growing uncomfortable with, and perhaps a little jealous of, the turn in her husband's relationship with Elizabeth, especially after she witnessed them in an embrace. Finally, she sent Elizabeth to live with Kat Ashley's sister, who had married Sir Anthony Denny.

Sydney's film reflects its times, the 1950s, when showing on-screen a schoolgirl's crush on an older man was one thing, scandalous acts between a stepfather and his fourteen-year-old charge quite another. Thus, there's no hint of Seymour's visits to Elizabeth's bedchamber and certainly no reenactment of the dress-cutting scene. There's no mention of Catherine's pregnancy and no deathbed rants about how Thomas had done her wrong. Instead, the film binds the three characters by honor and self-sacrifice, victims of the cunning Ned Seymour. Casting seals their noble portraits.

Jean Simmons was already a veteran actress, though she was only twenty-four when she played young Bess. With no biography of her own, her story is told through biographies of important men in her life: Stewart Granger, Laurence Olivier, Burt Lancaster, Kirk Douglas, Howard Hughes, Marlon Brando, and others. Tim Wallace does a nice job of piecing together her story, however, in his 2000 online biography. Born in the poor end of London, Simmons was discovered at fourteen, and, by sixteen, she was playing the native girl Kanchi to Deborah Kerr's Sister Clodagh in *Black Narcissus* (Michael Powell and Emeric Pressburger, 1947). Several films later, including a bit part in *Caesar and Cleopatra* (also starring Stewart Granger), she made her breakout film—Laurence Olivier's 1948 adaptation of *Hamlet*. At eighteen, she found herself acting Ophelia opposite Laurence Olivier. Her performance won her an Oscar nomination and international fame. The parts came in quick succession. In 1953 alone, she starred in *The Robe* (Henry Koster), *The Actress* (George Cukor), and *Young Bess*. Playing a young Elizabeth I didn't make Jean Simmons a star; she already was one. What it did was solidify her status as Hollywood royalty. Sophisticated and stately beyond her years, she developed a regal screen persona, not unlike Deborah Kerr's or Liz Taylor's. The camera caught her delicate mouth, flawless skin, and wide eyes, framed in thick, dark hair, in stunning close-up. Though she was not physically right for the role (too petite, too dark, too old), there's something fragile but steely about her beauty as though underneath that luminous, gorgeous exterior lurks a smoldering passion and a will of iron—an Elizabeth in soft focus.

Jean Simmons and Stewart Granger had been married for two years by the time they starred together in *Young Bess*. He was fifteen years her senior, perfect in age and attitude for the role of the handsome, impetuous Thomas Seymour. It would be nice to think that Seymour had as much class as Stewart Granger, but it's doubtful that's the case. We meet him in the film when Bess locks herself in her room at Hatfield. Henry has just married for the sixth time, and a frustrated, angry Elizabeth refuses the trek to London to meet Catherine. What's the point? she thinks. She'll invest her feelings in another stepmother only to have her father erase her too. Henry insists. He sends his favorite Seymour brother to persuade his daughter to join him, a task Thomas acquits so admirably that, by the time he and Elizabeth reach the palace, her crush is full-blown.

Kat is not the only one watching Elizabeth's feelings for Thomas play out. Ned and his wife, Ann, are just waiting for Thomas to slip up. He's too popular with the people, and he's too popular with the young king. Edward likes his Uncle Tom, who affectionately tosses him in the air, twirls him around, brings him gifts, and slips some extra cash under the carpet for him. When Ann sees Elizabeth running from Thomas's room one night, she and Ned practically hiss with anticipation. Seduction of a royal princess is grounds for treason and beheading. Desperate to tell Thomas of her feelings for him, the naive Bess sneaks into his room at night. A high-angle shot signals that fate is about to be played out here. "I'd rather die than be lonely all my life," Bess tells Thomas, boldly kissing him. Thomas, at least, realizes that their union would mean disaster for both. It's Kat Ashley who finally tells Bess that Thomas is in love with another woman, Catherine.

Young Bess forwards the theory that Elizabeth pulled back only after hearing this news. She loved Catherine. She loved Thomas. If they loved each other, she would make the sacrifice and step out of the picture. The film also suggests Elizabeth's influence on her younger brother. She goes to Edward, encouraging him to sanction Thomas's marriage to Catherine. We see them conspiring together in the garden, cuddling together in her bedroom, and chatting together about court politics. Simmons looks every bit the older sister to Rex Thompson's Edward, though Elizabeth was only four years Edward's senior. It's the affection between them that matters, and we see that clearly in one of the later scenes in the palace where they desperately try to save Thomas from the block. Elizabeth and Edward are writing a letter of pardon for Thomas, but it's too late. The drums roll, and so does his head. The camera sweeps up to high, mullioned windows, their chilling slits of blue light splattering on the despairing brother and sister below. The shot reminds us that they too are victims of Ned Seymour's jealousy and ambition. Edward's bedchamber echoes with his soft whimpers as Bess tucks him into bed. "Why didn't they let you see me?" he cries. "I liked my Uncle Tom."

The on-screen chemistry between Granger and Simmons sizzles, ensuring our sympathy with Thomas and Elizabeth's plight. At one point in the film, Elizabeth tells Kat that she and Thomas "match." We could well say the same about Granger and Simmons. They do *look* beautiful together, their attraction for each other obvious in every scene. Thomas's attentions toward Elizabeth begin innocently enough. She's just a kid, an important one, but a kid nonetheless. Standing on the staircase, Thomas kisses Catherine passionately while an anguished Elizabeth looks on from a distance. She's smitten with him, but he's not going to cross that line. Yet those eyes, those glances, are hard to ignore. Home from one of his pirate-hunting expeditions, he grabs Elizabeth in a bear hug and kisses her on the lips. It's enough to make Kat nervous: "I'm not sure he realizes that she's no longer a child." It's enough to send Catherine into denial: "It has always delighted me to see them together." All Elizabeth can do is wax on about Thomas and ships and spending eternity together. On one outing, Thomas asks Bess what she would do if she were queen. Her answer sparks a visible turn in how he sees her. "And you'll be with me, Tom, always, always." It's not enough to wrest him away from Catherine, however.

Elizabeth tries to make him jealous. First, at a banquet hosting a Danish envoy who seeks her hand for his prince, she calls attention to herself

Young Bess. As the title suggests, this film, based on Margaret Irwin's novel, serves up a slice of Elizabeth I's life seldom seen on-screen, unfolding the events—from cradle to ascension—that shaped the monarch's life. The concentration in the film is on the Thomas Seymour affair, here romanticized to showcase the golden off-screen couple Jean Simmons and Stewart Granger. In this shot, Simmons's Bess flirts a little with Thomas's page, Barnaby (Robert Arthur). (Courtesy Jerry Ohlinger's Movie Material Store.)

with her loud, artificial laugh (reminiscent of her mother's at the beginning of the movie). The scene jars not only because it points up Bess's uncharacteristic phoniness but also because it shatters Simmons's own quiet, reserved screen persona. Thomas and we glare in disapproval. Later, Bess flirts with Thomas's page, Barnaby. When she accuses Thomas of being jealous and laughs at him, he slaps her, then kisses her. "I love you, Tom. . . . I can't stop loving you, Tom," she cries, as she melts into his arms. Historical fiction meets the romance novel in this scene of pure fabrication.

In real life, and in the movie, Catherine finally intervenes. Things have gone too far. She says she's not strong like Bess. She needs and loves Tom. "He means my whole life to me." Elizabeth leaves. Catherine must have said something to this effect to Elizabeth before she left for Mistress Denny's. Accounts of their encounter describe Elizabeth as listening quietly, but their letters to each other after Elizabeth's departure suggest a still-loving bond. "Elizabeth thanked the Queen for the 'manifold kindnesses' she continued to show," Gristwood writes. "'Thank God for providing such friends for me,'" Elizabeth told her stepmother (qtd. in Gristwood 42). Just months later, at Sudeley Castle, Catherine and her new baby girl died, leaving Thomas a rich widower. The film doesn't mention that Catherine dies after giving birth. There's no reference to why she's dying. It's a mystery. Tom cradles her and carries her around, and the saint-like Catherine dies, saying: "You're not the first man to be in love with two women at the same time." She leaves the world with her blessing on his future with Elizabeth.

It doesn't work out that way on film or in reality. Thomas still could not marry Elizabeth without the permission of the Council, and Edward Seymour wasn't about to let that happen. Marrying Elizabeth would have given his brother too much power. In *Young Bess,* the young Edward tells Elizabeth: "My Uncle Tom loves you very much, and that's why Ned wants to kill him." Nothing was so simple in real life. Accounts of this period in all the major biographies imply doubt that Thomas really loved Elizabeth, but who knows? The truth is that, whether he was in love with her or not, marriage to her would have answered all his dreams of power. He talked to Kat Ashley, who sanctioned his suit. He asked the cofferer Thomas Parry about Elizabeth's estates and income. Elizabeth, wisely, remained uncommitted, perhaps sowing the seeds of her "no master" strategy. But, thwarted at every turn by his brother, Thomas made a foolish move to gain physical control over the young king's person. With a small group of armed men, he broke into the king's chambers, running Edward's barking dog through with his sword, and waking the whole household. Thomas was quickly apprehended and sent to the Tower.

Kat Ashley and Thomas Parry soon followed. They buckled under pressure but miraculously managed not to destroy Elizabeth in the process. They spilled the stories about Thomas's visits to Elizabeth's bedchamber and confessed to encouraging Elizabeth to marry him—but not without the permission of the Council. Meanwhile, Edward Seymour sent Robert Tyrwhitt and his wife to deal with Elizabeth. She didn't buckle. Today, we're still amazed at her mettle and grace under fire. She gave away nothing but what Kat and Thomas Parry had already admitted. "They all sing one song," Tyrwhitt said in frustration. Though Kat and Parry eventually were released and reunited with Elizabeth, Thomas was executed on 20 March 1549.

The film paints Elizabeth in shades of her feisty father as she faces Tyrwhitt, Lady Tyrwhitt, and the Council members who tell her that Thomas has been arrested and taken to the Tower. At first she looks small and fragile, standing to the left side of the frame. She collapses into a chair, dropping the arrest orders, but quickly rallies, accusing Ned of killing his brother, and striking him with a whip that happens to be lying conveniently on the table before her. Her strength is, perhaps, exaggerated here for the sake of a good love story. Before Thomas dies, Barnaby visits him in the Tower and tells him: "She was their judge." Whether Elizabeth loved Thomas Seymour remains the stuff of movies and speculation. Starkey makes an interesting observation that many portraits support: "Almost all the men that she subsequently loved, or pretended to love, resembled Seymour" (76).

Where fact and fiction merge is in showing that Elizabeth was a survivor, a theme that later biopics would foreground. After Thomas Seymour's death, she retreated to Hatfield and buried herself in intellectual pursuits. She kept a low profile, dressing so conservatively that her brother called her his "Sweet Sister Temperance." Erickson suggests that Elizabeth deliberately cultivated "an image of innocent, sober piety both to counteract the recent slanders against her and to align herself unmistakably with the new, zealously Protestant tone of Edward VI's court" (*The First Elizabeth* 92). She would later use a similar strategy to create the iconic image we know today, the Virgin Queen. In this somber guise, she managed marvelously to navigate her life until Mary's reign and the Wyatt Rebellion—another story. The film dissolves finally to the "present." Kat and Parry have been talking all night. "She'll be queen of England," they marvel. We never hear their musings about Edward's death, Ned's own execution, Mary's "bloody" reign and demise. Instead, time collapses, and we see Elizabeth, dressed in deep blue velvet, standing alone on her balcony, crowds cheering while Kat and Parry bow to her. *Young Bess*, like so many film adaptations of Elizabeth, ends with that solitary shot, as if all her moments summed to one image: she ruled alone.

The Virgin Queen (1955)

The Thomas Seymour affair marked the rest of Elizabeth's narrative. David Starkey suggests that it was a defining moment in her life, a turning point, coalescing the danger of "adult politics and adult sexuality." Perhaps it only strengthened her resolve not to marry, a rare personal confession she made to Robert Dudley when they were only eight years old. After the Seymour incident, she trusted almost nobody, her trademark defense against a hostile world (*Elizabeth: The Acclaimed Saga of England's Virgin Queen*).

By the time she met the virile Devonshire rogue Walter Raleigh in 1581, Elizabeth was a seasoned politician, maintaining the delicate balance of her court and courtiers like a vaudeville plate spinner. Sir Christopher Hatton; Sir Frances Drake; Sir Philip Sidney; Edward de Vere, the Earl of Oxford; Robert Dudley, the Earl of Leicester; William Cecil, Lord Burghley; Robert Cecil, his son; Sir Frances Walsingham; and Robert Devereux, the Earl of Essex—all strong, ambitious, opinionated men, they swarmed sometimes jealously round her. From time to time, they bared their teeth, challenging and provoking each other as they jockeyed for power and position. A word, a look, a blast of that famous temper could send them simpering off into their respective corners until, chastened, they crawled back to lick the hand that fed them. It must have been exhausting keeping them all in check, though her inner circle of senior advisers—Leicester, Burghley, Hatton, and Walsingham—learned how to get along with and support each other after many years in her service. There were times, however, when a younger, handsomer hunk caught her eye, and the snarling and posturing began anew. Capturing this culture of the court remains the one strength of Henry

Koster's *The Virgin Queen,* an adaptation that spotlights the relationship between Elizabeth and Walter Raleigh.

Raleigh was the latest cock of the walk. Strachey calls him "a dangerous and magnificent man" (*Elizabeth and Essex* 30). Big, bold, blunt, and beautiful, he quickly became the queen's favorite. He was twenty-nine; she was forty-eight. Maybe that cloak-over-the-puddle incident clinched her interest, but their attraction was certainly more complicated than this gallant gesture, now thought to be apocryphal. Raleigh, a relative of Kat Ashley's, was a man of action with an impressive seafaring record. He had already commanded his own ship, the *Falcon,* and fought with the Huguenot army in France and against the rebels in Ireland. We might think of him today as a swashbuckler: daring, fearless, proud.

Walter Raleigh knew who he was and what he wanted. By the time he was finished, he had fought the Spanish in Cadiz, founded the colony of Virginia in the New World, and introduced the potato and tobacco to the old one. After Elizabeth's death in 1603, King James tossed Raleigh in the Tower on some manufactured charges of treason. Some sources suggest that Robert Cecil, in his correspondence to James VI of Scotland, had already whipped up anti-Raleigh sentiment. Unsure of Raleigh's allegiance, James maneuvered him out of the way when he became James I, king of England. Raleigh, for his part, made good use of his time in the Tower, working on his *History of the World.* James released him in 1617 to command an expedition to Guiana in search of gold that ended in a tussle with some Spanish settlers. The Spanish ambassador, Gondomar, called for Raleigh's head, and James gave it to him on 29 October 1618. Winston Churchill in his *History of the English-Speaking Peoples* argues that Raleigh was executed "to please the Spanish Government" and that "this deed of shame" left a permanent rift between King James and his people (160).

Raleigh wasn't wildly popular while he lived, but, like Elizabeth, he could fill up a room. He was the kind of man who made women swoon, and Elizabeth was not unaffected by his dark, good looks and brilliant mind. She loved to wrangle with him, and Raleigh was a great wrangler. He could convincingly argue that the sun circled the moon, and, though he was a bit rough around the edges, he had the soul of a poet. (One has only to read his "Nymph's Reply to the Shepherd," written in response to Marlowe's "Passionate Shepherd," to imagine his quick wit in action.) Queen and subject simply clicked intellectually. Elizabeth quickly dubbed him Sir Walter Raleigh, her "Water." He called her his "Cynthia." Estates, ships, and enormous wealth followed, and, while his quick temper and lack of diplomacy kept him from the Privy Council, Raleigh became captain of the guard, a special legion of men who protected the queen's person. Raleigh, however, wanted action, not guard duty. He yearned for the sea, not court. He once wrote: "'Go tell the court it glows and shines like rotten wood'" (qtd. in Weir 255). Raleigh knew too well the habits of the court vultures. While they circled, he dreamed of ships and the New World.

Richard Todd plays Raleigh in Koster's film. In Charlotte Chandler's Bette Davis bio, *The Girl Who Walked Home Alone,* Todd says that the title of the film was originally *Sir Walter Raleigh:* "'When Bette agreed to be Queen Elizabeth, the film took on a whole new aspect. She was a great star. The title changed'" (qtd. in Chandler, "Bette Davis Sighs," 213). Rewind to 1939's *The Private Lives of Elizabeth and Essex,* and the words have a familiar ring. In a war over top billing, Davis always came out the winner. Todd remembers that he wasn't upset: "'I thought it was an honor to work with Bette. . . . She had a rather imperious quality, wonderfully appropriate to her queenliness'" (qtd. in Chandler 213). Ultimately, the shift in title did not shift the focus of the story. It's still Sir Walter Raleigh's story. The film privileges Raleigh as he effortlessly leaps over a railing in the local inn, challenges a patron to a sword fight, destroys the furniture in the process, sweeps a serving wench out of harm's way with one arm, and then digs Lord Leicester, Robert Dudley's carriage out of the mud—all in the first scene. Whew! What a man. When Lord Leicester, here portrayed as a kindly old courtier, offers Raleigh money for his efforts, Raleigh refuses, saying: "To serve my queen is reward enough."

Written by Harry Brown and Mildred Lord, *The Virgin Queen* scans like a bad stage play with its painted backdrops and overblown acting. Even its Oscar nomination for Costume Design cannot lift the film from its B-movie status. (It lost to *Love Is a Many-Splendored Thing* [Henry King, 1955].) Davis, in the trough of her career in 1955, should never have repeated her performance as Elizabeth. She cavorts through the court like a stiff-legged drama queen, waving her fans and tossing wine at Raleigh. The same jerky gestures that punctured her performance in *Elizabeth and Essex* morph into parody here as pirate-like commands tumble forth: "Take me to me chamber" (matey?). We have to wonder where she did her research on Elizabeth and what Koster was thinking to recast her in this role. Davis might have been imperious, but this is a clear case of poor fit between actress and character. What does come through in her performance we find in a classic Davis remark: "'One must live in the present tense, but I have always lived in the present tensely'" (qtd. in Chandler 5).

Physically, Davis never fit Elizabeth's profile. She was too short, too round. Elizabeth was taller, lithe, athletic, graceful. Perhaps it was Davis's *will* to play such a meaty part that made her hammer herself so unnaturally into the character, and the effect disappoints, especially since we know that Davis was no prima donna when it came to acting. She would do whatever it took to authenticate her characters. And, though she shaved her head again for this 1955 film, later confessing that it never all grew back, her attempt at authenticity fails here. She never loses her Massachusetts accent or her clipped speech patterns. Those iconic, elaborate red wigs bedecked with jewels come off looking simply clownish. Actress and monarch never merge into a complex whole.

The Virgin Queen picks up the action roughly ten years before *The Private Lives of Elizabeth and Essex*. Raleigh and the younger Essex hit court about the same time and were rivals for the queen's affection. Part of the new generation of courtiers, they came charged with boundless energy, vitality—and testosterone. Their clamor for titles, gold, ships, and war with Spain must have made the queen's head spin. At one point, she tells Raleigh: "If I gave each man in the court everything he wanted, I would have to give away half the world." Elizabeth had her hands full just keeping them away from her ladies-in-waiting, not always successfully.

In the film, we see her giving, taking, conceding, and demanding—keeping everyone off balance and unsure of where they stand with her. She chastises Raleigh and then promotes him. She humiliates him by making him sit at her feet on a pillow, her new "lap dog." Then she knights him, gives him one ship, the *Golden Falcon,* and sanctions his voyage to the New World. No sooner does he happily go hence to Plymouth to renovate his ship than Elizabeth calls him back. She's changed her mind. He can't go. She needs him too much at home.

Sir Christopher Hatton is beside himself with jealousy. Robert Douglas plays him as a mustachioed villain, an odd choice since Hatton was reputed to be kindly and sweet of disposition (Gristwood 223). We see him here rubbing his hands with glee when he discovers that Walter has "dal-

The Virgin Queen. Though Bette Davis played the Virgin Queen twice in her career, it was not a good fit between actress and role. Davis hammered herself into Elizabeth I's persona, even shaving her head to create the aging queen. Unfortunately, she could never shake the mannerisms that made her a personality star. (Courtesy Jerry Ohlinger's Movie Material Store.)

lied" with one of Elizabeth's ladies-in-waiting, the beautiful Elizabeth "Bess" Throckmorton (Joan Collins). Raleigh has not only "dallied" with Bess; he's impregnated her, secretly married her—an act of treason—and plans to take her to the New World with him. He's even included a double bed in his renovations. When Hatton visits Raleigh in Plymouth, he notices that it's "not the bed of a single man" and tells Elizabeth. How much of a hand Hatton had in Raleigh's fall from grace in real life is questionable. Raleigh was a ladies' man. Regardless, furious with both Raleigh and his new wife, the queen threw them both in the Tower, where they stayed for several months. Elizabeth felt betrayed again. After all, Robert Dudley had done the same thing with Lettice Knollys behind her back. She eventually released them, but Raleigh never again tasted the same kind of favor he knew before this slip.

While making the film, Joan Collins complained that Bette Davis didn't like her. Collins was young and beautiful; Davis was on the wane. That probably had something to do with Davis's behavior toward her, others advised. Collins thought that it was something more, and it made her nervous. In Chandler's biography of Davis, Collins tells the story of having to put the queen's shoes on in one scene. Davis, evidently, "made it hard for her and criticized the young actress" (Chandler, "Bette Davis Sighs," 214). When Davis later found out what Collins had thought, she said: "'How absurd. The poor girl was confused. Of course I didn't like her character. She wanted to take Sir Walter away from me, and as Elizabeth the Queen, I resented that. It was essential that an air of hostility exist between us'" (qtd. in Chandler 214–15). The comment says everything about Davis's acting method, style, and attitude toward her work.

Color marks Elizabeth's mood in the film. The sets become a gaudy blend of reds, signifying Elizabeth's perverse passion for Raleigh, as well as her anger, as the story concludes. In the climax, she visits Raleigh in his Tower cell. She has played nemesis to Raleigh's hero through two acts. It's she, not Hatton, who has stood most in the way of what he wants: his ships and a life with Beth. The queen enters the dark cell wearing a brilliant red gown. Instead of pleading for what he wants, Raleigh surprises her. Someone else must sail to the New World, he tells her. "You'll forget a dead man whose eye wandered." Never one to mince words with the queen, he bids her leave his presence. They argue. Elizabeth wails: "Walter, Walter. I needed you, and you betrayed me." He doesn't see it that way. "I loved you, Madam, as a man loves a great queen. And that love you betrayed." Elizabeth plays her gender and age cards. She is, after all, just a woman "and not too young." Raleigh kisses her hand. In a dramatic moment, Elizabeth turns to leave, changes her mind, and tells Raleigh that he must sail himself. "I will not forgive you or the slut you married. I want the world you promised. I don't want to dream of a brat crying as I dreamed last night." She puts her hands on her hips in a familiar gesture. "Those cargoes you bring back had better be rich and rich." She walks out.

But wait a minute. Rewind. Did we just hear Elizabeth say "slut"? How did that make it past the Production Code? Earlier, Elizabeth referred to Beth as a "strumpet," and, as the queen and Dudley watch the *Golden Falcon* sailing down the Thames in the film's resolution, her own scarf flying high on the mast and Raleigh and Beth canoodling on deck, her only comment is this: "A puking wench and some waves. I must go on with the business of state." It makes Elizabeth seem mean and petty—and, of course, alone. The final shot gives us Elizabeth at her desk, surrounded by a sea of red—walls, drapery, carpets—the color of passion and danger. The camera pulls back and up to a high angle as Elizabeth lowers her head in grief.

Raleigh once said that Elizabeth was a "'lady whom time hath surprised'" (qtd. in Weir 229). We can interpret the remark in a couple of ways. The older Elizabeth got, the more she clung, desperately, to the illusion of youth and beauty. Perhaps today she would opt for plastic surgery, as so many celebrities do, but, in the sixteenth century, no amount of powder, rouge, wigs, fine fabric, or jewels could hide the fact that she was aging. She hunted, she danced, and she flirted. She kept her mind sharp and agile. She was the sun; she dazzled the court. But in her innermost chamber, at night, it must have surprised her to see the tired, wrinkled, balding woman staring back at her in the mirror. It might have been even more difficult for a queen to acknowledge physical change. Who else was so flattered and cosseted? Who else was told that she was eternally divine? Davis gives us a glimpse in *The Virgin Queen*. In one scene, Elizabeth is in bed when Bess Throckmorton enters to plead Raleigh's case. Elizabeth removes her nightcap to reveal a bald head, a hag in a nightgown. "Men have loved me," she moans. And, indeed, they did. As Raleigh says at one point: "I admire the woman, not the wrappings."

The men in the real Elizabeth's life, those whose love and loyalty she counted on, were fast disappearing as the new century approached. In 1588, following England's triumph over the Spanish Armada, Robert Dudley died. Elizabeth was so devastated that she locked herself in her chamber and wouldn't come out for days. In April 1590, Walsingham died. Hatton followed close after him in November 1591, Drake in 1596. Her beloved Cecil, Lord Burghley, died in 1598 after a long and productive life of service. Essex was executed in February 1601. In a little over a decade, Elizabeth had lost them all. For the first time, she was truly alone.

Elizabeth R (1971), *Elizabeth I: The Virgin Queen* (2005), *Elizabeth I* (2006)

The Miniseries

Only a book-length study of Elizabeth films alone could fully treat all the visual versions of her life. Here, we briefly acknowledge three excellent Elizabeth I miniseries, first identifying the privileged content that their extended length permits, and then considering the character actresses who play the monarch: Glenda Jackson, Anna-Marie Duff, and Helen Mirren. Celebrated for their extraordinary talent—and not necessarily for their box-office-ringing physical beauty—these women are perfectly cast as the brilliant but less-than-stunning sixteenth-century monarch who was, in many ways, ahead of her time. This is what all three miniseries, made thirty-five years apart, get right. In each case, they place the emphasis squarely on Elizabeth, the private woman and the public monarch, not her leading man of the moment. Jackson, Duff, and Mirren anchor each miniseries, threading hours of small-screen time together with the force of their performances. While moving the historical plot forward, they draw out elements of Elizabeth's character that appeal to modern women with regard to politics and war, romance and marriage, presenting a queen who's as real today as she was over four hundred years ago. In sum, within the episodic format, these actresses offer finely drawn, intimate representations of Elizabeth, as brilliant as any Hilliard miniature.

Elizabeth R runs a total of nine hours. Glenda Jackson created the historical persona over six episodes and seven months of filming with the same cast and crew, praising them for their extraordinary talent and dedication. The costume designer Elizabeth Waller and the makeup artist Dawn Alcock researched for months, studying portraits and existing sixteenth-century dress, to re-create the queen's elaborate ensembles and makeup down to the finest detail. As the series progresses, Elizabeth's gowns get more intricate. One in particular stands out: the gorgeous white frock with deep blue sleeve inserts that she wears to meet the Duc d'Alençon. Although stunning, it looks a bit sad and out of place, like a wedding dress for a marriage that never comes off. Glenda Jackson describes most of the costumes as "desperately uncomfortable" until she had to act, and then they worked their magic, snapping actress and queen, life and art, together into a tailored fit. For Jackson, it was an "extraordinary privilege" and "unique experience" not only to work with that kind of honesty to the period but also to sustain a performance over such a length of time, taking Elizabeth's life from youth to death (interview with Glenda Jackson).

The historian and author Alison Weir calls *Elizabeth R* "the one that rings true, the one that really clicks." With a few exceptions where time has been telescoped and certain characters combined, the film is, Weir says, "sumptuous and incredibly accurate," with "superb acting" and dialogue taken "directly from original contemporary sources" (interview with Alison Weir). Given the luxury of time and casting that doesn't depend on a billion-dollar name, the series delivers what no feature film can. It pulls up the smaller moments of a life, moments that fill in the historical time line. Instead of epic, we get up close and personal, witnessing private exchanges between characters we don't normally see or hear. Their conversations provide plot details and background information, giving us insight into pressing problems and issues of the period. Sets are smaller, shots are tighter, suggesting psychological drama that peels back the inner landscapes of courtiers and queen alike. The entire series lingers over beautifully written little scenes, full of wit and humor and angst, revealing what it means to be human. By the end of *Elizabeth R*, we, like Jackson herself, feel like we know this world and this woman—as much as anyone ever knew Elizabeth.

The consistency of *Elizabeth R* remains remarkable given that it's actually a series of six different plays, written and directed by six different teams. Hollywood is littered with examples of what happens when too many writers and directors get their hands on a script, but none of that applies to this project. Written as a follow-up to the BBC's *Six Wives of Henry VIII*

(1970), each episode highlights a different phase of Elizabeth's life and segues seamlessly into the next. Characters age naturally, and their relationships build and develop over time, as they would in real life. The nucleus of the whole, however, is Glenda Jackson's Elizabeth, whose story picks up with the Thomas Seymour affair in "The Lion's Cub," written by John Hale and directed by Claude Whatham.

The first episode sets up the intrigues surrounding Elizabeth before she ascends the throne, simultaneously focusing on the danger of being an heir, providing possible reasons for Elizabeth's later actions, and establishing her as a survivor. It begins with Thomas Seymour (John Ronane) killing Edward's dog and trying to kidnap the king. Elizabeth, caught in the web of Seymour's plans to marry her, flashes back to her "games" with her stepfather. The odd bit of first-person camera gives us Elizabeth's perspective only as Thomas approaches her (the camera) in bed, shreds her dress with scissors, and declares his love for her in front of the pregnant Catherine Parr (Rosalie Crutchley). This telling doesn't sanitize Seymour's ambitions, Elizabeth's feelings for him, or Catherine's attitude about her husband's philandering. Depicting Elizabeth by Catherine's deathbed distorts history to dramatize the moment, but it doesn't rankle.

The plot plays out with Seymour's beheading, the Wyatt Rebellion, Elizabeth's imprisonment, Mary's reign and death, and Elizabeth's ascension. Scenic jewels weave throughout the episode, such as the conversations between Elizabeth and William Cecil (Ronald Hines), a man she admires and respects, an intellectual, political, and religious soul mate. He steadies the frightened young woman with his advice and constant support. "I serve the good of this land, the proper order of things," he tells her. "You are the hope of the people." Both must act a part under Mary's reign; both put the good of the order above themselves; both are survivors. In one scene, after being brought face-to-face with Thomas Wyatt (Robert Garrett), Elizabeth drops to the floor, whispering: "I will survive." In another scene, Elizabeth visits her godfather, Archbishop Thomas Cranmer (Bernard Hepton), in his cell, a tender moment we never get in any feature film. The plot moves and develops through these conversations. For example, we understand how unpopular Mary's marriage to Philip is from a dialogue between Kat Ashley (Rachel Kempson) and Elizabeth. But perhaps the most heartening aspect of this miniseries is the realistic way in which Elizabeth is presented. We see her fears and her flaws along with her more appealing characteristics. This Elizabeth is ambitious. She denies any implication in the Wyatt Rebellion, yet we're left with some doubt as to her involvement. No facile moral judgments here, and the story is the better for it.

"The Marriage Game," written by Rosemary Anne Sissons and directed by Herbert Wise, highlights the beginning of Elizabeth's reign, fixing her desire to be a "monarch for use," not a baby breeder. Shaped by circumstances in her youth, the new queen doesn't take long to develop the maneuvering tactics and political acumen she needs to deal with her Council, unwanted marriage proposals, and scandal in her backyard. She deftly sidesteps the issue of marriage, but the haranguing takes its toll. Flashing that famous temper, she yells, "Enough!" about the Archduke Charles. Another scene exhibits Elizabeth's acting skills honed at the feet of her sister, Mary. The queen's feigned surprise at Philip of Spain's marriage proposal, which she already knew was coming, strikes a comic chord. "If I ever consider marrying outside this kingdom, I will think of Philip," she cleverly informs the confused Spanish ambassador.

The heart of the episode lies in Elizabeth's becoming a monarch to be reckoned with. She flexes those power muscles while she flirts with Robert Dudley (Robert Hardy). A pan around her bedchamber reveals the incredulous reactions of her ladies-in-waiting as they witness a passionate kiss between Elizabeth and Robert, "still the most handsome man in the kingdom," as she tells Kat Ashley. Part of Dudley's charm for Elizabeth must have been that he was already married. Scenes between Robert and his wife, Amy (Stacey Tendeter), point up the difficulty of being the queen's favorite as well as Dudley's ambition. He can't spend much time with Amy, who suffers from a "lump" in her breast (most probably breast cancer) and begs him not to go back to court. Sorry, can't stay. He's got a job to do and a position to protect. Besides, he knows Elizabeth better than anyone. "Whoever sits beside her on the throne must know that I helped put him there," he tells his wife on the way out the door. Amy's not getting it. A husband should stay with his wife. "Do you want to destroy me?" he cries. The living Amy can't, but the dead one sends Dudley on a downward spiral. Elizabeth casts him out of the court until the investigation is over. Another privileged glimpse into private lives reveals Cecil and Robert conversing in Robert's home. We could have found out that the jury brought in a verdict of accidental death some other way, but this moment seems so poignant because Cecil delivers the news and these two servants of the queen haven't always gotten along. When will she let me return to court? Robert wonders aloud. True to his nature, Cecil advises patience.

Neither the rumors surrounding Amy's death nor Dudley's later, secret marriage to Lettice Knollys shake the lifelong bond between Elizabeth and her "Eyes." She names him lord protector when she thinks she's dying of smallpox and swears that nothing improper ever passed between them. *Elizabeth R* spins their relationship into the climax of the episode with the question: Will she marry him now that he's free, or won't she? Robert delivers an ultimatum: "Meet me at 11:00 at St. Swithin's Church. I won't wait a minute longer." He waits; he leaves. She dithers; she comes. Their exchange is priceless, however. He: "You came, but too late." She: "You waited, but not long enough." What's important is the end of the scene when Elizabeth explains why she will never marry. Her father, her stepmothers, plots, accusations, the Tower—how dangerous her life was. "As I am now," she reveals, "I owe my life to no man's goodwill, except the goodwill of the people—and I've always known how to keep that." He understands. The episode ends with Elizabeth climbing back into her coach. "Robin?" He replies: "I am here." Elizabeth counted on that for the rest of his life.

Robert's "secret" marriage to Lettice, the problem of Mary Stuart, and Elizabeth's courtship with François, the Duc d'Alençon (who later becomes the Duke of Anjou), dominate the third episode, "Shadow in the Sun," written by Julian Mitchell and directed by Richard Martin. Though these are weighty matters, this chapter resounds with humor, wit, and sexual innuendo. By this time in her reign, Elizabeth's Council began working like a well-oiled machine. Her councilors didn't always get along perfectly, but they understood each other—and they knew the queen. All committed themselves to governing the state and serving Elizabeth. In this, Elizabeth was perhaps the most fortunate of our queens. She had a firm base in her councilors. They disappointed her from time to time, and she, in turn, drove them crazy with her dithering and prevaricating and "answers answerless," but she ruled more easily with their support. This episode takes us behind the scenes, so to speak, into the Privy Council, where Cecil, Dudley, Hatton (Bernard Horsfall), and Sussex (John Shrapnel)—with excellent comic timing—debate about who's going to tell the queen about Robert's marriage to her cousin, Lettice Knollys, and what they think Elizabeth wants them to do about Duc François, her "frog."

The scenes point up the difficulty in which Elizabeth found herself. If she married Spain, the French would be angry. If she married France, she would upset Spain. If she married either, her xenophobic people would abandon her. If she married an Englishman, she would stir up jealousy among her lords. And then there was her constant refrain: "I have no wish to marry." Despite some funny scenes with the duc (Michael Williams) and Elizabeth's claim to "have him," *Elizabeth R* lingers over the desperation the queen must have been feeling at this time. Her biological clock is ticking, and she knows it's the last chance for marriage or an heir. "I want to be young again. I want to feel happiness again. I want not to feel time like a dead child in my womb," she tells one of her ladies. Later, she confides to Sussex that she hates the idea of marriage, she's afraid, she has her reasons, but she means never to marry. The miniseries format allows time to include scenes like this, scenes that leave us, like her Council, her biographers, and historians, wondering about those reasons. What was she afraid of? Death? Childbirth? Losing control? Was she toying with the duc? Would she have married Robert Dudley? How did she really feel about her mother? Her father? Her childhood? We'll never know, so we're left with the enigma of Elizabeth, which *Elizabeth R* argues in its own leisurely way.

There's little levity to be had in "Horrible Conspiracies," written by Hugh Whitemore, as Mary Stuart's sordid fate plays out. In fact, the director Roderick Graham's episode seems spare indeed compared to the other five. It begins in 1585 with a death mask and ends in 1587 with the Scottish queen's beheading. The costumes are bleak and black for the most part, even Elizabeth's, making Mary's martyr-red shift a shock by the end of the chapter. There's no gaiety in this court—and barely anyone in it except for Elizabeth and Francis Walsingham (Stephen Murray). The rest of the lords must have gone on holiday. But, though Mary Stuart (Vivian Pickles) figures prominently in the story, the episode belongs to Elizabeth—her indecisiveness, her reluctance to kill her cousin and sister queen, and her own fear of death.

Jackson mesmerizes here, her face a kaleidoscope of fear, anger, resignation. Elizabeth tries to skirt the issue of Mary's plots against her, pretend they're not a threat, but Walsingham keeps the pressure on. When the Babington Plot, and Mary's obvious involvement in it, surfaces, she can no

Elizabeth R. Elizabeth R offers what no other feature film or miniseries before or since has ever done: it plays out the major events in Elizabeth's life over a nine-hour span. Filmed as a series of six plays, written and directed by six different teams, the piece revels in rich details, quiet moments, and brilliant performances with Glenda Jackson as the golden thread. The makeup may look stagy at times, but the acting is spot on. (Courtesy Jerry Ohlinger's Movie Material Store.)

longer ignore the evidence or the consequences. Still, she hems and haws over signing Mary's death warrant. Once she does, Walsingham and Cecil, now Lord Burghley, act swiftly. Elizabeth is apoplectic. She lashes out at Walsingham, calling him a "piss bowl of self-righteousness," and sends Secretary Davison (John Graham) to the Tower. "Horrible Conspiracies" unfolds the circumstances and details that lead to Mary's execution, especially, Elizabeth's conflict over killing a sovereign queen. "I am innocent of this death," she cries. But, in the end, she realizes that the blame lies with her. It doesn't sit easy. Her conversation with Walsingham at the end of the episode sends shivers down the spine. This is not the cozy relationship between queen and councilor of Shekhar Kapur's later films. Walsingham hopes Mary is at peace. Elizabeth strikes. "There is no peace for the dead," she tells him, proceeding to describe, in vivid detail, how even now Mary's body is being "invaded by a legion of gray flesheaters." Death is a busy, fearful business.

Gory and grisly, the episode is permeated with fear and death as the rackmaster, Topecliff (Brian Wilde), explains to a tortured Babington how—exactly—he will die. Elizabeth kneels, praying that her enemies will "perish in great agony . . . their bodies torn apart and their souls damned to everlasting torment." The miniseries doesn't shy away from showing us the flip side of the queen's persona: vengeful, treacherous, and vindictive. In spite of her flaws, however, Elizabeth comes across as smarter than those who bow and swirl around her. Jackson makes us feel that almost instinctively in her intelligent stare. We get the sense that she's always assessing, always several moves ahead of the poor sots who serve her. She's fully aware of the long-term ramifications of Mary Stuart's death, while others can see only an immediate fix. We are grateful that *Elizabeth R* never panders to dramatic license in that there's no devised scene between these two women who never actually met each other. The series makes clear in their separate, juxtaposed scenes the disparities in their personalities. One bit of dialogue bears repeating here because, of all that's been written on Mary, Queen of Scots, it best encapsulates who she was, the antithesis of Elizabeth. In this scene, Mary reveals herself to Gifford (Bernard Holley), Walsingham's spy who pretends to be Mary's supporter and friend:

> I regret nothing. I know my faults and my virtues. I know that I am a crea-
> ture of impulse seldom thinking before I act, driven on by passions, delight-

ing in the unexpected, and bored by sensible caution, and disliking all who are not of my humor. This is my alchemy, and I rejoice in it, even though it has brought me much unhappiness, even though it has led me here. I would not have been created differently. And this is not self-love, Gifford, merely an acceptance of what I am and what I ever shall be. God made me thus, and I am glad he did so.

Never one to think even a step ahead, all Mary can do is play out her destiny as Catholic martyr while Elizabeth cries out in agony at the senselessness of it all.

In the aftermath of Mary's execution, Philip of Spain unleashes his armada, a debacle from start to finish, as the episode "The Enterprise of England," written by John Prebble, illustrates. While we deal with the Spanish Armada elsewhere in the chapter, a brief mention about the way in which the incident was handled in *Elizabeth R* by the director Donald McWhinnie is in order. Crosscutting the action between Elizabeth and Philip, showing what's happening simultaneously in both courts, McWhinnie points up the reluctance of the two monarchs to plunge their countries into a costly war. At one point, Elizabeth's prayer "defend my people from all of our enemies" dissolves into Philip's same prayer. Neither ruler has the resources, in money or manpower, to engage the other. Besides, they have a grudging respect for each other. Philip calls Elizabeth "that remarkable woman." Elizabeth feels some obligation to her former brother-in-law, who saved her from the Tower. Both are aging, both freely dispense advice on physics and restoratives to anyone in range, and both are surrounded by advisers clamoring for war. These are interesting conjunctions of the Protestant and Catholic rulers who are caught up in forces beyond their control. Philip, urged on by the pope—who calls Elizabeth the "greatest prince in Christendom" but still wants her dead—feels a duty to revenge the Catholic Mary, while Elizabeth, after denying the threat, prepares to defend her realm.

They are a couple of paradoxes. Philip can barely walk; he wears a patch over his ailing eye, yet he's dictating ever-changing strategies to an inept and unwilling Duke of Medina-Sidonia (Gordon Gostelow). The king has scraped the bottom of the military barrel, enlisting untrained Portuguese and Italians into service while insisting on two hundred friars and a prayer regimen to accompany them. He turns a deaf ear to greater wisdom to break off the attack. Meanwhile, Elizabeth chastises Walsingham for whipping up anti-Spanish sentiment and dismisses the navy. She's more afraid of a mistake in her Latin than she is of Philip. But the armada comes, and she no sooner makes her inspiring speech to the troops at Tilbury, promising to reward all who would fight for her, than she reneges, leaving the victors victims of disease and poverty. For the most part, it's a true and accurate account of events and behavior, on both sides of the Channel.

Jackson calls the Armada script one of the best. The editing reveals character, the dialogue crackles, the plot moves, and the acting holds the audience transfixed. Major players of the court reappear, with some new faces, like Drake (John Woodvine), Howard (Peter Howell), and Essex (Robin Ellis), Dudley's stepson and Elizabeth's new favorite, who is always lurking in the background. Elizabeth's interactions with them ring true as well. Her final scene with Dudley, the Earl of Leicester, at Tilbury and his subsequent death erase her triumph at the English victory over Spain. She locks his last letter to her in a drawer, tosses an irreverent Essex out of her chamber, and weeps, not in agony this time but in pure grief.

Elizabeth R never whitewashes what happens in the final chapter of Elizabeth's life. "Sweet England's Pride," written by Ian Rodger and directed by Roderick Graham, pays careful attention to detail in the chain of events that mark the rise and fall of Robert Devereux, the Earl of Essex. This is not Errol Flynn's romanticized hero. Ellis plays Essex with all his warts, and, of all the Essexes, he is possibly the most perfectly cast. Tall and strapping, he is, as Elizabeth says, "the sun in splendor." "He is all our pride." Essex says of himself: "We are the sun shining on a dark court." (Note the royal *we.*) But this queen has no illusions about her favorite. She knows that he's a spoiled, selfish, arrogant whiner. After he fails miserably in Ireland, disobeys her every order, and bursts into her bedchamber while she's sans wig and soaking her feet, she tells Robert Cecil (Hugh Dickson): "I will not again play guilty parent to his hurt child." Miscalculating his own popularity with the people, he marches on London. That fails too. Elizabeth doesn't dither or flinch this time. He goes to the ax.

Glenda Jackson's performance as the dying Elizabeth crowns the entire miniseries. Silence permeates the court. Dialogue, what there is of it, is delivered in whispers. Elizabeth's musicians are barely perceptible, as are Captain of the Guard Sir Walter Raleigh's usually heavy footsteps. A series of dissolves marks the passage of time. Days pass. Elizabeth stands for fifteen hours, but she's lucid enough to tell Robert Cecil that "the word 'must' is not used to princes" when he urges that she must go to bed. In her last moments, he asks about England's heir. Is it James VI of Scotland? No. Yes. No. Yes, again? Maybe. We're not sure. She dies quietly, sucking her finger. A pull-out shot shows her clothed in her golden robe, red wig falling about her shoulders as her hair did in her youth, surrounded by her closest friends and advisers. The doorway frames the shot. Another portrait.

As Michael Dobson and Nicola J. Watson observe in *England's Elizabeth*, Jackson's is "the canonical face of Elizabeth for the last quarter of the twentieth century" (246). No one replaced that face until Cate Blanchett came along in the 1998 feature film *Elizabeth*, ushering in a new wave of interest in the monarch that spawned two more miniseries: *Elizabeth I: The Virgin Queen* (2005) and *Elizabeth I* (2006), different but nevertheless excellent adaptations in their own way.

Elizabeth I: The Virgin Queen, made for Masterpiece Theater and released three decades after *Elizabeth R*, is technically superior to its predecessor, but, then, it should be. A lot changed during those thirty-four years. *Elizabeth R*, shot in the early days of VHS, can't compare to the slick production values of film stock, the beauty of location versus studio sets, and the impressive special and visual effects. Advancements in lighting alone allow the director, Coky Giedroyc, and the cinematographer, David Odd, to create the mood of darkness and confusion (a recurring motif) during Mary Tudor's reign for the small screen. The atmosphere stifles and oppresses. Anonymous eyes spy through peepholes. Danger lurks everywhere. Dressed in black, and sporting an armored breastplate, the threatened, paranoid Mary (Joanne Whalley) spews venom about her fair sister. Torches flicker and flare, casting a menacing glow over the Catholic queen's guards as they summon Elizabeth (Anne-Marie Duff) to the Tower, where tortured men scream in agony in the cell next door. The lighting shifts, signaling a transition from this dark, gritty, brutal world to a more civilized one once Elizabeth learns she is queen. She runs through dark corridors into the garden and the sunlight to a magnificent oak tree, where she delivers those famous lines: "This is the Lord's doing; it is marvelous in our eyes."

The director also utilizes distortions of movement, like slow motion, throughout the miniseries. Though probably overused here, it's a technique that can effectively slow the action down, calling attention to particular events and characters. There's a beautiful slow-motion shot of Elizabeth as she's reunited with her female companions in a sunlit garden and another memorable one as Elizabeth and Robert Dudley (Tom Hardy) dance the volta. The slow motion wraps them in their own romantic fantasy as hundreds of greedy eyes and gossiping tongues look on. Toward the end of the series, when Essex marches on London, the camerawork mimics the madness and chaos of his actions. Yet, though interesting, the overhead shots, high angles, low angles, pans, swish pans, and other technical wizardry sometimes get in the way of more basic elements of storytelling.

Elizabeth I: The Virgin Queen, for example, is a life on fast-forward. It follows the same episodic trajectory as *Elizabeth R* but tries to cover essentially the same ground in just under four hours. It begins with the Wyatt Rebellion and ends with Elizabeth's death, but it scans like a series of tableaux. The emphasis is on the visual rather than plot detail. One scene leads to what seems like the middle of the next and so on, with the result that viewers not familiar with the life of Elizabeth might find themselves a bit lost and confused. Dreams play a vivid role, blurring the line between fantasy and reality. Elizabeth dreams of Robert making love to her. Is it really happening? In her recurring dream, she's walking through her father's court, all eyes on her, mouths whispering "bastard" as she approaches the throne. Henry strikes a terrifying figure for the small child, his roaring laugh blending with Elizabeth's scream as she wakes.

Like the 1963 adaptation of Cleopatra, *Elizabeth I: The Virgin Queen* splits into two parts, the first infinitely superior to the second. Perhaps we're drawn to the youthful Elizabeth, the Elizabeth who beats the odds but realizes that power demands sacrifices. Perhaps part 1 simply unfolds in a more leisurely way than part 2, where time seems even more compressed. The leap from 1588 to 1598 particularly jars. The makeup, excellent for the most part, is inconsistent at best in the second episode. In one scene, Elizabeth's wrinkled face looks a bit over-the-top while her hands remain youthful and smooth. One moment she appears every bit her age; in subsequent scenes she appears more youthful, which upsets the chronology of events. The music too, a fusion of contemporary and Elizabethan sounds and note patterns, while intriguing and fresh at first, becomes more and more insistent, invasive, and irritating as the miniseries plays out.

In spite of these relatively minor defects, the writer Paula Milne's

Elizabeth I: The Virgin Queen succeeds as a biopic. It aims for authenticity, using bits of dialogue taken from Elizabeth's speeches and contemporary sources. Instruments of torture and gynecological exams seem equally real and chilling. No, it doesn't get everything right, but it hits the mark enough. We get a real sense of Elizabeth's genuine fondness for her female friends, especially in her relationship with Kat Ashley (Tara Fitzgerald). Many of the characteristics we've come to associate with Elizabeth—her intelligence, loyalty, fury—come through in her interactions with both her inner circle and her people. In a flash, she puts the puffed-up Norfolk (Kevin McKidd) in his place as she raises Robert Dudley to one of the most pre-eminent peers in the land out of love and loyalty. Milne's script gives us an ambiguous Dudley that seems more believable and in keeping with the real man. He's torn between his affection for his wife, his love for Elizabeth, and his own ambition. In one scene, he has a tender conversation with Amy, and, as he leaves, he tells one of his servants to take care of her because "she might well be the best part of me." After Elizabeth names him lord protector when she thinks she's dying of smallpox, he sits on her throne, an enigmatic smile crossing his lips. He loved Elizabeth, but he also loved power, and that comes across here. Though he fell in and out of her favor, Elizabeth remained deeply attached to him, as Duff's grief-stricken scene at the news of his death illustrates. "Not this. Anything but this," she cries as she slides to the floor.

One of the things that this miniseries does better than either of the others or the feature films is depict the relationship between Elizabeth and her "Sprit," William Cecil, Lord Burghley (Ian Hart). He began as Princess Elizabeth's surveyor in charge of her estates. She quickly recognized a kindred spirit and man of extraordinary talent, faith, and loyalty.

Immediately on becoming queen, Elizabeth appointed him her chief minister and charged: "This judgment I have of you. That you will not be corrupted by any manner of gift and that you will be faithful to the State and that, without respect of my private will, you will give me that counsel which you think best" (65). Done. She created him Sir William Cecil, Lord Burghley, Knight of the Garter, Secretary of State, and Lord High Treasurer. For forty years, he ran the business of government and held the queen's unwavering loyalty.

The miniseries renders a faithful account of Elizabeth and Burghley's bond. "You are the rock upon which I built my reign," she proclaims when he wants to retire. At his deathbed, a scene that would wring a tear from the eye of even the toughest viewer, she tells him: "You are my alpha and my omega. No prince ever had such a counselor." A slight mutation of the original ("No prince in Europe hath such a counselor"), but just as effective. With his passing, Elizabeth feels lost and alone, and Giedroyc's production, again, works this point where others fail. In a previous scene, the queen and Cecil talk about the upcoming generation, its self-interest and ambition. Giedroyc visualizes this in a couple of telling scenes. Echoing what happened in real life, Elizabeth's court begins to break down, the old ways giving way to the new. Young people show little to no respect for their aging Gloriana. Essex (Hans Matheson) is able to muster the restless young bucks, while Elizabeth's own ladies laugh and make fun of their mistress as she dances alone in the cloister. They disrespectfully rummage through her most private things, including Dudley's last letter and miniature. Robert Cecil (Daniel Evans), William's son, writes to her successor, the unnamed James VI of Scotland, with unbecoming callousness. She rallies for her last address to Parliament, but, sensing that her time is over, she virtually wills herself to die.

This version of Elizabeth's life takes us into dark corners of the human soul. While Giedroyc re-creates the brutal world of sixteenth-century politics, economics, medicine, and religion, Anne-Marie Duff holds her own with perhaps more famous names that have played Elizabeth I. She's done extensive work in television, including miniseries such as *Amongst Women* (1998), *Aristocrats* (1999), *The Way We Live Now* (2001), and *Charles II: The Power and the Passion* (2003), in addition to a number of British television series like *Shameless*. Duff knows the medium, but she was little known in America until *Elizabeth I: The Virgin Queen* in 2005, which has since launched her into the world of film. In 2006, she costarred in *Notes on a Scandal* with two other members of the Elizabeth I club: Judi Dench (*Shakespeare in Love*) and Cate Blanchett (*Elizabeth* and *Elizabeth: The Golden Age*).

In *The Virgin Queen*, Anne-Marie Duff looks the part with her lithe figure and flaming red hair. She's bewitching rather than beautiful. Fiery and passionate, she leans into a challenge with her whole body, whether dressing down Norfolk or Dudley or Cecil or flailing away at Lettice Knollys (Sienna Guillory). Duff unwraps Elizabeth with gusto: jealous, brilliant, vengeful, gracious, demanding, and merciful by turns. In one scene, she dictates her own image to the artist. Immortal is the look she's after. Lots of jewels and a thousand eyes on her gown so that her people will always know she can see them. No shadows on her face or neck. Hair free and flowing over her shoulders. Hands slender and youthful. Virginal. "Divinity, if you can so render it," she demands. "Henceforth, when my people think of their queen, this is the image they must see." The result is the *Rainbow Portrait*. It's a novel way to visualize the "becoming-an-icon" scene. Playing Elizabeth in later life, Duff moves inward. She becomes less physical and more pensive. We almost see the joints stiffen and her desperation to stop time as she, now an old woman, dances alone in the cloister. Life and loss have taken their toll, but she's got just enough spirit left to orchestrate one more scene—her own death. The series ends with Robert Cecil opening Elizabeth's ring, the one containing the portrait of her mother, a reminder of how remarkable the events that conspired to create the life and reign of Elizabeth I.

When Dame Helen Mirren, best known for her role as Detective Superintendent Jane Tennison in the long-running PBS series *Prime Suspect*, was offered the part of Gloriana in the HBO two-part series *Elizabeth I* (2006), she accepted immediately, explaining: "There are so few truly great roles for women, and this is one. This is the mother lode. And anyway, it's great to be queen" (Mirren 33). She should know. She's played Queen Cleopatra at least three times on the stage, Queen Charlotte to Nigel Hawthorne's King George III in *The Madness of King George* (Nicholas Hytner, 1994), and, most recently, Elizabeth II in Stephen Frears's *The Queen* (2006). Mirren's list of stage, film, and television credits and awards is long and impressive, so *Elizabeth I* was no breakout performance for the sixty-one-year-old actor, but it might possibly be the most hypnotic, stirring portrayal of the Virgin Queen to date. The historian and author David Starkey calls it "the best film that has been made on Elizabeth" (*Uncovering the Real Elizabeth*), and we would have to agree.

There's something magic about Helen Mirren, how she disappears into her characters, making it all look so effortless and believable. She wears the mantle of Elizabeth as if it were her own skin. We can never be sure where Mirren leaves off and Elizabeth begins. The director Tom Hooper says: "When she acts, it feels incredibly real and truthful and natural, and I think that's one of her great gifts" (*The Making of Elizabeth I*). In *Elizabeth I*, there's little of the icon and much of the woman. Mirren shuns the white, garish makeup that lifted Elizabeth above mere mortals for a more natural look, making the queen more accessible to those around her as well as the audience. In one scene, Elizabeth returns to London from one of her progresses and walks casually among the people who have gathered to greet her. She smiles, jokes, shakes hands; anyone would think she was a politician today working the crowd. Mirren's Elizabeth is a working monarch, and we see that in the elegant but less formal gowns she wears. Hooper and Mirren agreed that this would be a very personal story, and to achieve that Mirren had to get beyond the familiar icon. "Costumes are marvelous because they obviously make the statement for you, but then you have to start fighting your way out of the costume and out of the makeup, so it's both a tool and a liability because you want to make this person a living, breathing person and not just a painting," Mirren says (*The Making of Elizabeth I*).

The opening shot forecasts the unwrapping of Elizabeth. A medium shot from the neck to the thighs of a woman in rich, green brocade, arms outstretched, being undressed by anonymous hands. Busy fingers detach the sleeves, then the bodice, the skirt insert, and so on until the queen stands in only her shift. She's getting a gynecological exam, a most private moment. The Council must know whether she's still able to bear children. After all, she's forty-six when the film opens, and France has come acourting. With her bedchamber right next to the Council's meeting chamber (an arrangement that Henry VIII introduced and Elizabeth kept), the good news is received by her Privy Council in a matter of seconds. Thus, the credit sequence sets up the intention of *Elizabeth I:* the juxtaposition of the personal and the political.

This HBO film may step in and out of history, blending fact and fiction at will, but it works. Hooper and the screenwriter Nigel Williams must have their credit, but most of the miniseries' success lies at the feet of Mirren and her costars: Jeremy Irons (Robert Dudley, the Earl of Leicester), Ian McDiarmid (William Cecil, Lord Burghley), Patrick Malahide (Sir Francis Walsingham), Toby Jones (Robert Cecil), and Hugh Dancy (Robert Devereux, the Earl of Essex).

So powerful are the interactions and relationships between Elizabeth and her advisers that Alessandra Stanley of the *New York Times* dubbed the miniseries "a buddy film disguised as a Renaissance costume drama"—

which is precisely what makes *Elizabeth I* one of the most human and modern portraits of the queen. The exchanges between Elizabeth and her privy councilors reveal character and plot details. Elizabeth's own intelligence, wit, humor, strength, vulnerabilities, and uncertainties surface, as do her concern for, respect for, and, at times, frustration with her advisers. They, in turn, treat her with admiration and a little awe. Theirs is an intricate relationship, long-standing and familiar after twenty years of working together.

The life of this Elizabeth picks up in 1579, and Secretary Burghley, William Cecil, sits opposite his middle-aged monarch like a sixteenth-century Merlin. Good humor abounds as they discuss marriage negotiations between Elizabeth and the Duc d'Anjou (a.k.a. Duc d'Alençon), a Catholic. Catholic? No problem. Walsingham "eats Catholics." The duc? No problem. He's accommodating enough. "He will pray in a corner if you ask him," Elizabeth jokes. Robert Dudley, the Earl of Leicester, puts his head down on the table with humorous impatience. He, of course, opposes the match. Nigel Williams strikes just the right balance between contemporizing the language and using dialogue taken directly from the original sources, and the actors, despite their period costumes, at times move and gesture with an informality that we recognize. These people are like us—well, sort of. They exhibit the same feelings and frustrations, happiness and despair. This queen reads like the chair of a corporate board, and its members are people anybody might know. Suddenly the four-hundred-year gap between our centuries closes. These are people we can connect with.

Establishing this kind of intimate working relationship with her advisers immediately in the film also makes Elizabeth's grief and sense of isolation more believable as she loses those closest to her one by one. "The whole world mourns your father," she tells Robert Cecil on Lord Burghley's death. She understood the importance of Walsingham too, though she could never warm to him. Leicester's death, so soon after the Spanish Armada's defeat, came as a stunning blow and turning point in her life. Part 1 of the miniseries focuses on that relationship. If Mirren is the definitive portrait of Elizabeth, Jeremy Irons is the quintessential Leicester. Their scenes together—representing acting at its finest—help unravel what they must have felt for one another. Irons once said: "Working with Helen is like watching a Bentley purr on the road: you know if you put your foot down, there's going to be a lot of power" (Griffin 54). Watching both actors is like taking a private tour of the castle, getting to see the nooks and crannies, the secret rooms, the innermost chambers of the human heart.

David Starkey believes: "There's no doubt that Elizabeth and Leicester were passionately in love. It may even have been quite physical." Elizabeth was, however, probably still a "technical virgin" (*Uncovering the Real Elizabeth*). This is the version that *Elizabeth I* delivers. In one scene, they kiss passionately, and we get the sense that they might have been lovers when they were younger. Now middle-aged, they still kiss and cuddle and take comfort in each other's companionship. She banishes him from her sight when she finds out that he has been secretly married to Lettice Knollys for a year, but, when crises arise, it's Leicester Elizabeth wants. Trying to avert disaster, Elizabeth has him arrange a secret meeting between her and Mary Stuart (yes, the obligatory meeting that never was, but at least it's presented in a plausible way here). Elizabeth tries to reason with Mary, but Mary is not one to be reasoned with. In the end, it is Leicester's counsel she listens to: "Bess, I cannot lie to you. The Scottish queen must die." And he's the only one brave enough to witness Mary's execution and tell Elizabeth about it. Candlelight bathes their faces as he kneels beside her and begins. She interrupts: "What is there between you and I? What's a crown when love's voice speaks to us? None of the others would have dared do what you have done." When she's anxious about what she should say to the troops at Tilbury because she's an "unwarlike woman," Leicester says: "Not so. I could have sworn Your Majesty had the heart and stomach of a king." Elizabeth delivers these lines, lines actually set down in her speech, and turns to nod in thanks to Leicester. It's possible he suggested them to her. Who knows? Moments like this one, as well as Leicester's death scene, knot their relationship.

Leicester was seriously ill when he left Tilbury for his castle, Kenilworth. He never arrived. He died alone in a manor near Oxford. Williams wrings every emotional drop from Dudley's death in *Elizabeth I* as Elizabeth sits by his side. She loves him. He'll be with her always. He, in turn, delivers the lines that sum up the real Leicester: "There were those who said I was the calculating kind. But what I felt for you I could not help. Sometimes it did not help my cause at all. But, truth be told, it was as constant as the heavens." He dies after making Elizabeth and his stepson, Essex, promise to take care of each other. Hooper then cuts Essex out of the frame, except for his hand, which remains on his stepfather's shoulder, and moves to an overhead shot of Elizabeth, weeping on the breast of her dead lover. The tableau serves as a visual reminder of the significance of each man in her life. What the scene, and, indeed, the entire miniseries, clearly shows is Leicester's ability to fulfill both the personal and the political needs of the queen. He recognized the shifting line between the woman and the monarch and treated her accordingly, something Essex never learned to do.

Though he never takes center stage, without Leicester and Jeremy Irons, part 2 of *Elizabeth I* loses something, and maybe that's the intent because we and Elizabeth feel his loss as the episode chronicles Elizabeth's fixation with Essex, a much younger man and, in many ways, a much lesser man. At one point Elizabeth realizes: "The same name [Robert], but not the same." Nancy Griffin writes: "Mirren prepared by immersing herself in historical research, and she discovered a monarch who veered between shrewd political strategist and flamboyant fool in love" (124). At one point, after a frisky romp with Essex, she says to herself: "I am a hopeless fool for love." In this story, she struggles with her duty and her desire, one moment chastising Essex, "Men like you must be ruled," and the next doling out the living from sweet wine tax and giving him Leicester's apartments in the palace. She flirts with Essex. She toys with him, like a cat with a mouse. She calls him "our marvelous boy." She indulges virtually his every whim—and he has a lot of whims. Her jealousy of younger women, especially the beautiful Frances Walsingham, is not attractive. "Eyes on me, Robin. And, Frances, also eyes on me," she commands as Essex and Lady Frances eye each other.

A low point comes when, to gain her favor, he accuses the faithful Dr. Lopez of conspiring to murder the queen on the basis of information he extracted from men under torture. She believes Essex and sends Lopez to his death, and death permeates *Elizabeth I*. Plots, assassination attempts, scenes of disemboweling, racking, the severing of seditious hands—all punch up the ever present physical danger of Elizabeth's world. Only later does she realize that Lopez was most probably innocent. "This was a man's life, Robin. . . . You act without thinking. That is not service," she tells him in one breath; in the other she forgives him. Elizabeth's folly and Essex's inevitable doom play out with all eyes watching. Having witnessed Mary, Queen of Scots's grisly beheading, he can't help but envision his own fate at the block, but he pulls himself together and goes to his death a noble Essex. He's such a wily, despicable character that his death is a relief.

More interesting aspects of part 2 depict the humorous exchanges between Lord Burghley and his son, Robert, whom he carefully groomed to take his own place as the queen's first in command. Here we're privy to Elizabeth's growing closeness with the younger Cecil, perfectly played by Toby Jones. Because of his small frame and slightly misshapen shoulder, Elizabeth nicknamed Robert Cecil her "Pygmy," sometimes her "Elf," but she recognized his worth and came to depend on him as she did his father. In Hooper's miniseries, their conversations are the stuff of speculation, but, again, they underscore the humanness of these figures, some of whom have slipped through the folds of history and all but disappear in the film versions of Elizabeth's life. The only other biopic to visualize such private moments and thoughts is *Elizabeth R*, but it does so in less detail. Hooper's adaptation even treats the queen's death with a slant to the private possibilities, positing the theory that Elizabeth felt that she had reigned too long for the good of her people. She *wants* to die. The doctors can find "no cause" for her malaise. In the end, the queen's final command reveals her purpose: "Fetch me a priest. I am minded to die."

Jeremy Irons explains that Helen Mirren "wanted to play the beating heart beneath the icon" (*The Making of Elizabeth I*). Hers is the living, breathing portrait, the one with skin warm to the touch. *Elizabeth I* and our next film, Shekhar Kapur's *Elizabeth*, starring Cate Blanchett, offer two very different representations, as different as the *Darnley Portrait* and the *Rainbow Portrait* of the queen herself. The *Darnley Portrait* attempts to envision the woman apart from her title, as Michael Dobson and Nicola Watson point out in *England's Elizabeth* (pl. 3). Crown and scepter lie visible but *behind* her on the table. Kapur's film, like the *Rainbow Portrait*'s stylized, idealized image, offers the most ethereal vision. With Mirren, then, we get details of a life; with Blanchett, we get an *impression* of the woman.

Elizabeth (1998)

Watching *Elizabeth*, Shekhar Kapur's first foray into the Elizabethan world, we're reminded of a critic's lament about *Elizabeth: The Golden Age*, the director's second venture forth. "The film is far more interested in romantic intrigue," Ebert wrote. "It undervalues the ability of audiences to get involved in true historical drama, instead of recycled action clichés" (rev. of *Elizabeth: The Golden Age*). Released almost ten years earlier than *Elizabeth: The Golden Age, Elizabeth* creates the template for action over accuracy, compressing almost twenty years of history into a two-hour story that is so far-fetched at times that it leaves us baffled. The film bookends with two rebellions. The first, the Wyatt Rebellion in 1554, a Protestant plot to depose Mary Tudor and set Elizabeth on the throne, leads to the arrest, torture, and execution of Thomas Wyatt. The second, the Northern Rebellion in 1569, a Catholic plot to depose Elizabeth and set Mary Stuart on the throne, results in the beheading of Thomas Howard, the Duke of Norfolk, in 1572. Beginning and ending with these two revolts begs the conclusion that, no matter who sits on the throne, navigating religious and political factions is precarious business but that she who puts the good of the state above self-interest earns the favor of both history and art—an interesting premise. But in between the two revolts lies a hodgepodge of events and combined characters.

Why? Why, when Elizabeth's real life was so full and rich and interesting, would the writer, Michael Hirst, and the director, Kapur, bend and twist and distort details beyond recognition? The lavish sets and costumes of both films, awash with Kapur's stunning Eastern/Indian color palate, provide a visual feast that almost satisfies, while Cate Blanchett, in her breakout role, is so right—physically, intellectually, spiritually—that she seems to be channeling Elizabeth. Her hypnotic performance and the director's stylistic bravado make *Elizabeth* a triumph of art over history.

But then Shekhar Kapur never claimed to be a historian. He tells a story in wide brushstrokes. He is a poet, an artist, and his films are expressionistic places where dialogue and historical details often bend to the will of style and form, where grand musings meet human limitations. "Neither prejudiced by the past, nor in fear of the future. The moment, only the moment," headlines his blog, telegraphing a philosophy of life—and making movies. He and Hirst fearlessly fracture the truth as we know it in *Elizabeth* until what we're left with is a kind of filmic pointillism. Up close, nothing makes sense, but, if we stand back, shapes snap into place, and we get a historical pastiche, not *the* truth, but *a* truth of Elizabeth, the woman and the monarch. Kapur wills us into Elizabeth's world by the sheer force of his talent, presenting moments that are transcendent, like the *Rainbow Portrait,* echoing Picasso, who called art "the lie that told the truth."

In *The Making of Elizabeth*, Kapur tells us that his film is an interpretation, not of history, but of personality. He uses his art to explore larger questions about Elizabeth: What would it have been like for a twenty-five-year-old woman to rule a country in times of political and religious chaos? What part did destiny play in Elizabeth's journey from what Cate Blanchett called "girlhood to statehood" (*Making of Elizabeth*)? How did Elizabeth become the Virgin Queen? What went into the making of an icon? What part of her personal self did Elizabeth sacrifice to become an absolute monarch and an icon for her people? What happens when power becomes absolute? In effect, one woman's journey allows Kapur to address more universal concerns: What does it mean to be human? Does choice or destiny hold sway? How do we reach the divine?

Hirst himself cautions that writing a screenplay and writing a history book are two different things. "You have to push things [with film]," he explains. "I needed to push the piece forward; I needed to push the drama and the tension and the love" (*The Making of Elizabeth*). Hirst often plays with circumstantial evidence in Elizabeth. For example, one of the debates in Elizabethan scholarship is whether Elizabeth and Robert Dudley were lovers. Maddeningly for some, no proof exists one way or the other. Would it have made any difference if they were? That's a question Hirst examines here. In the film, there's a beautiful scene shortly after Elizabeth becomes queen in which she and Robert (Joseph Fiennes) make love, her ladies-in-waiting both standing watch and watching through an elaborate stone carving. Our point of view is their point of view as together we watch the lovers shielded only by the sheerest silk curtains, printed with eyes and ears, like Elizabeth's gown in the *Rainbow Portrait*. Others, like Renée Pigeon in "'No Man's Elizabeth,'" note the connection and explain that, while the original intent of the imprinted gown was "symbolizing her advisors who supply her with the information, or 'intelligence' that allows her to rule effectively," in this scene "the original iconographic force of the image is thus reversed" (16). With one brushstroke, Hirst and Kapur make us all guilty of voyeurism, making the queen's most private moments meat for public thought. Hirst also argues that "putting them in bed together" hasn't "changed the course of English history . . . nor proved that Elizabeth slept with the historical Dudley": "It was just a small nudge in the direction of romanticism" (*The Making of Elizabeth*).

Cate Blanchett calls Hirst and Kapur's approach to the film a "what-if perspective"; the producer, Alison Owen, considers it "an imaginative inter-pretation" (*The Making of Elizabeth*). Roger Ebert says that the film "re-writes history at its own convenience, which is the rule anyway with En-glish historical romance" (rev. of *Elizabeth*). While we can appreciate the motives behind this telling of Elizabeth, still we yearn for art and life to mingle. As Sarah Gristwood says: "The more attractive and convincing the recent fictions have been, the more one's curiosity is sparked for the real story" (1). And that may be the guiding tenet for Kapur's revisionist adapta-tions of the Virgin Queen. The image that emerges of Elizabeth draws fire and spirit, igniting our passion to know the real woman and what really happened during her reign. Kapur does his art and places the burden of proof squarely on the audience to uncover whatever truth historians have pieced together. As Mark Carnes reminds us in *Past Imperfect*, we should regard historical films "as an invitation for further exploration" (10).

The film opens in 1554. Mary Tudor sits on the throne of England, and her world is dark and dangerous. Low-key lighting and tight framing cre-ate a stifling, claustrophobic atmosphere where every shadow threatens, every whisper poisons. Protestant heretics burn slowly at the stake. Delu-sion masquerades as hope as Mary announces her pregnancy. A cut to Elizabeth at Hatfield, dancing with her ladies in a sunlit field of lush green, sets up the juxtapositions of light and dark in the film, of good and evil. Elizabeth dances and laughs. Mary worries and moans.

Kapur continues this same light/dark representation to distinguish be-tween Elizabeth's court and Philip of Spain's in *Elizabeth: The Golden Age*. Here, Elizabeth often fades into or out of blinding white light, foreshad-owing her transformation to religious icon and, ultimately, celestial being.

In *Elizabeth*, Kapur plies his exposition with conflict. As Elizabeth dances with her ladies, Robert Dudley joins her, immediately introducing the notion of their friendship and romance, which, for the rest of the film, will be tested, threatened, and torn apart by external forces. Their sensual dance of love crosscuts with Mary's soldiers, armed and mounted, hooves pounding, coming to arrest her for complicity in the Wyatt Rebellion. "Re-member who you are," Robert whispers as they part. This whisper serves as the catalyst for the film's narrative arc, Elizabeth's becoming, from heir to icon.

Thus, in the first few moments of the film, Hirst and Kapur tweak his-tory to favor romance and drama. Mary is already married to Philip of

Spain when the film opens, but the Wyatt Rebellion happened early in Mary's reign, *before* her marriage to Philip. Public opinion opposed the union with Spain, and subjects from all corners of the realm revolted against the marriage negotiations. Most uprisings were quickly suppressed, but one attempt almost succeeded. The son of the poet Thomas Wyatt, who had been accused of being Anne Boleyn's lover, Thomas Wyatt the younger led the rebellion in Kent. His letters to Elizabeth, outlining his plans to overthrow Mary and place Elizabeth on the throne, were intercepted and his march on London quashed by Mary's troops. Some sources suggest that, with better timing and a different route into the city, he might have won the day. As it turned out, he was arrested, taken to the Tower, and tortured. Even on the scaffold, Wyatt refused to implicate Elizabeth. And, though she spent several months in the Tower (in the royal residence, not the dungeon), there was never enough evidence to try her. Mary sent Elizabeth to Woodstock under house arrest for a time and later permitted her to return to Hatfield. People in London celebrated her freedom.

Screenwriters know that, if you want to evoke sympathy for a character, you must make her a victim—immediately. In *Elizabeth*, Mary whisks her sister off to the Tower before we can say *opening credits*. A series of overhead shots signals Elizabeth's unhappy fate. She looks small and vulnerable as she falls to her knees before Mary and protests: "I cannot confess to something I did not do." How lovely and fair and regal she looks next to the short, dark, half-Spanish Mary.

No confession? OK, then how about a promise to uphold the Catholic faith? Elizabeth will act according to her conscience, thank you. The story goes that Philip secretly watched this exchange. It was he who insisted that Mary meet with her sister, and he liked what he saw in Elizabeth. If Mary died, he would marry Henry's younger daughter, continuing Spain's alliance with England—a logical plan, but one that didn't factor in Elizabeth's iron will. Mary understood it, and here, angry as she is with her sister's stubborn refusal to embrace the Catholic faith, she cannot bring herself to sign Elizabeth's death warrant.

Kapur makes not Mary but the Duke of Norfolk (Christopher Eccleston) the villain of the piece. The force of the north, he glowers and bullies and swaggers through court corridors with one hand on his sword hilt. He skulks around in dark corners with his band of brooding supporters, including the Earl of Arundel (Edward Hardwicke) and the Earl of

Sussex (Jamie Foreman), or dallies with his mistress. Aligned with Spain and the Catholics, he thinks of Elizabeth as a bastard heretic, unfit to rule. When, after her audience with Mary, Elizabeth bravely walks through waves of courtiers, who bow before her in silence, Norfolk screams: "She is just a child, and still you piss yourselves!" On Mary's death rattle, he rips the royal ring from her finger and sends it to Elizabeth at Hatfield, all the while his busy brain planning her ruin.

Before she's comfortable in her royal robes, Elizabeth finds her mettle tested by Norfolk. Suspecting that she's spent the night with Dudley, he crashes into her bedchamber, throws back the curtains, and summons her to Council. Mary of Guise and the French in Scotland are threatening the northern borders. They must be stopped, immediately. He pushes an inexperienced young queen into attacking against her better instincts. "I do not like wars. They have uncertain outcomes," Elizabeth frets, but she bends to his pressure. It's a disaster for England. Norfolk has sent unprepared soldiers, including children, to their deaths. Elizabeth is blamed, naturally. The mad, bad, and dangerous to know Norfolk won't quit. He plots with the pope (John Gielgud) and his priest (Daniel Craig) to assassinate the newly minted queen. In one dream-like sequence, barges drift along the Thames while fireworks light up the night sky. Masks lend an air of appearance versus reality. Robert and Elizabeth float, time suspends, filmy curtains rise and fall with the breeze as he recites poetry, professes his love, and proposes to Elizabeth. Norfolk and his supporters menacingly watch from one barge, the scheming Spanish ambassador, Alvaro de la Quadra (James Frain), from another. Suddenly, two arrows rip through the moment, pinning Elizabeth, frightened but unharmed, beneath the silky net.

Kapur clearly sets up the factions and the conflict that will play out in the rising action, but all Norfolk's designs work as a counterpoint to Elizabeth's growing strength. Norfolk is much more of a threat on film than in real life. True, he was the most powerful peer in the land next to the queen, but his plot to marry Mary Stuart and set her on the throne cost him his life and the lives of his supporters. Elizabeth, who knew of his plans, offered him several opportunities to confess, but Norfolk, a bit of a wimp, wouldn't come clean. At the end of the film, Francis Walsingham—Elizabeth's superspy, hit man, and guardian angel—arrests Norfolk, telling him, "You had not the courage to be loyal," one of the most accurate lines in the script.

With every misstep and assassination attempt, Elizabeth's force gath-
ers. No poison dress or papal bull can bring her down. She learns whom to
trust and how to listen to her inner voice. From the time the ascension
bells ring and she walks into the light of her coronation, Elizabeth weaves
a spell on her courtiers, her subjects, and the audience. This is Blanchett's
doing. As Jenny Comita observes in "Queen Cate," a title trumpeting the
enduring cord between movie royalty and real royalty, Blanchett has built
a reputation on "shape-shifting in front of the camera" (344). From Katharine Hepburn in *The Aviator* (Martin Scorsese, 2004), for which she won
an Academy Award, to Bob Dylan in *I'm Not There* (Todd Haynes, 2008),
Blanchett fuses the line between actress and character. In 1998, however,
few people in America even knew who she was. Her first feature films,
Bruce Beresford's *Paradise Road* and Gillian Armstrong's *Oscar and Lu-
cinda*, had come out only the year before. Born in Australia, graduating
from Sydney's National Institute of Dramatic Art in 1992, the actress won
raves for her work in theater and television in her own country, but she was
no name in Tinseltown until *Elizabeth* sent her shooting through the Hollywood cosmos. Over thirty films later, she's still spellbinding, even as the
villainess Irina Spalko in *Indiana Jones and the Kingdom of the Crystal Skull*
(Steven Spielberg, 2008).

Looking eerily like Elizabeth in her coronation robes, red hair flowing,
Blanchett ascends the throne and turns to face us. We gasp as the image
and actress become one. We see her wear her power haltingly at first as she
steadies her crown while Norfolk towers over her in the upper-right-hand
corner of the frame. We also watch as Elizabeth tests her personal and
political authority. For example, there's a funny moment at the beginning
of her reign when she's practicing her speech to Parliament. Dressed in
only her night shift, grasping for the right words, she fumbles and fumes,
finally breaking down in frustration. The scene neatly transitions into the
actual speech. Seated uncomfortably, she rubs the arms of the throne ner-
vously and adjusts herself. Her brilliant red gown and sunbeams that bathe
her in light set her apart and above the sea of black robes before her. She's
asking Parliament to pass the Act of Uniformity. Shouting over their din
of objections, Elizabeth makes her argument with wit and humor. She
wants a single Church of England with a common prayer book and purpose. It's best for her people and the peace of the realm. In the end, however, a calm, self-assured Elizabeth tells them they must vote with their

Elizabeth. A spiritual and physical fit, Cate Blanchett seems to be channeling Elizabeth I as she prepares to dance the volta in Kapur's expressionistic rendering of the queen's early years. The film may fracture history, but it launched Blanchett's career into the Hollywood galaxy. As her position in this frame indicates, Blanchett's performance was central to the biopic's critical and box-office success. (Courtesy Jerry Ohlinger's Movie Material Store.)

conscience. She wins the vote, but Walsingham has ensured it. He has locked the dissenting bishops in the dungeon below so that they can't influence the decision, buying the new queen time to solidify her authority.

Walsingham becomes Elizabeth's guiding conscience in Kapur's film. William Cecil (Richard Attenborough), her real mainstay, is reduced here to a dotard with a one-note song: Get married and produce an heir. He sends her ladies-in-waiting into titters when he insists on inspecting the queen's sheets each morning. "Her majesty's body and person belong to the state," he reminds them. By the end of the film, Elizabeth puts him out to pasture, when in fact the queen never let Cecil retire. She fed him soup with her own hand when he was too ill to come to Council and allowed him to sit in her presence when he was too feeble to stand. David Starkey writes: "Their lives were indeed intertwined like body and soul" (caption to plate of Sir William Cecil). She survived him by only five years. Kapur has her dismiss him with a title, Lord Burghley. His services are no longer needed. An Englishwoman first, Elizabeth doesn't like his policies, which would make England part of either France or Spain. But how will she manage without him? She's just a woman, Cecil points out. "I am my father's daughter. I am not afraid of anything," she says, easing him out the door.

Kapur and Hirst elevate Geoffrey Rush's role as Walsingham to chief adviser and bodyguard. Kapur explained the character to Rush as a kind of Krishna, the Hindu deity, "a very wise man who can kill people whilst smiling" (*The Making of Elizabeth*). As Robert Dudley's star falls, it's Walsingham's voice Elizabeth begins to trust. He watches from the shadows with a growing respect and admiration, a little in awe of and a little in love with this young queen. His timing is impeccable. He knows just what to say and when to say it. In one scene, after Mary of Guise roundly defeats the English army, an emotional, guilt-ridden Elizabeth falls to the stone floor in a crouched position below her father's portrait. The angle shifts to Henry's perspective, as if to suggest that he's watching, judging her from his lofty position. The portrait towers above her, a technique employed in several queen films to indicate the place that men occupy in the lives of female monarchs. We see it first in *Queen Christina* with Greta Garbo as Christina works beneath a wall-size painting of her famous father, who cast a long shadow over her relatively short reign. Sixty-five years have not diminished the significance of this shot. Walsingham enters her space. "The bishops don't respect you and have no fear of you," he warns. "They do not expect you to survive." She rises to his veiled challenge, but it doesn't hurt that he locks up the bishops during the Uniformity vote and kills Mary of Guise (Fanny Ardant) after a wonderful scene of witty verbal foreplay.

When Walsingham tells Elizabeth about the priest assassin with letters from Rome and Norfolk's growing power in court, the queen realizes that she must act on his information and trusts him enough by now to do it. "Find the priest and all who harbor him," she commands. The real Elizabeth, the great prevaricator, usually didn't act so swiftly. The scene sequence in which Walsingham rounds up and destroys all Elizabeth's enemies resounds with shades of *The Godfather*. While Michael Corleone prepares to become godfather to his sister's child, he stands before the baptismal font and the priest taking oaths to renounce Satan. The director, Francis Ford Coppola, cuts back and forth between Michael in church and his hit men bumping off the heads of the five Mafia families. In *Elizabeth*, the queen kneels in prayer while Kapur cuts to Walsingham killing those who would threaten the safety of her or her realm. In one fell swoop, henchmen make Michael Corleone's and Elizabeth's power absolute. (In his article "The Godmother," Richard Alleva finds other connections between *Elizabeth I* and its iconic, 1972 predecessor.)

The sacrificial lamb of the film seems to be Robert Dudley, who genuinely loves Elizabeth and is innocently drawn into the plot to murder her. Their foreplay is a beautifully choreographed and edited volta. The more she favors him, the more dangerous he becomes to Norfolk, Spain, and even Cecil, who wants the queen to marry the French Duc d'Anjou (Vincent Cassel). Cecil tells her finally that she cannot marry Robert because he is already married, and so begins Dudley's descent. The court shuns him; Elizabeth belittles him. Their second volta is a disaster. He tries to explain what happened and ends with: "You are still my Elizabeth." Wrong thing to say. "I am no man's Elizabeth," she shouts. "If you think to rule here, you are mistaken. I will have one mistress here and no master." She exits, leaving him standing alone to face a hostile court. The Spanish ambassador moves swiftly to take advantage of Dudley's situation and recruits him to speak on behalf of her marriage to Philip of Spain, who would protect her from "great danger." Robert warns her, and, though the two are still connected by their black and ivory costumes, the thread is tenuous. Elizabeth isn't buying his "I did it out of love" explanation. "You love me so much you would make me your whore," she tells him. Elizabeth in the full flex of her power cannot forgive Robert, but she cannot kill him either. She simply leaves him a broken man, a reminder of how close she came to danger.

As with Cecil and Walsingham, the real Dudley's devotion to his queen was lifelong. He seemed to be able to reason with her when no one else could break through. A friend since childhood, he supported Elizabeth through her trials with her sister, and she, in her turn, made him master of the horse immediately on her ascension. Through the years, she favored him with property, power, and the title of Earl of Leicester. They behaved like lovers whether they were or not. She certainly knew about Amy Dudley, his wife, whose mysterious death in 1560 destroyed any hopes of their own union, always considering, of course, that Elizabeth really wanted to marry him. In 1578, Dudley did marry Lettice Knollys without Elizabeth's knowledge or permission, but in the film Kapur conflates the two marriages and makes Dudley's first marriage seem like the big secret, thereby punching up the drama. They fought, they fell out, other handsome courtiers came and went, but always Elizabeth and Dudley came back together. She kept his last letter by her bed until her own death. "You are everything to me," the future queen tells Robert in the beginning of the film. And so it was in life.

Elizabeth proffers that Walsingham ushers the queen through her transformation. It's difficult to know how much time has elapsed in the film, but, by the end, kneeling now beneath a statue of the Virgin Mary, she talks with her adviser about how to consolidate her power:

ELIZABETH: "I have rid England of her enemies. What do I do now? Must I be made of stone? Must I be touched by nothing?"

WALSINGHAM: "Aye, Madam, to reign supreme."

ELIZABETH: "She had such power over men's hearts. They died for her."

WALSINGHAM: "They have found nothing to replace her. All men need something greater than themselves to look up to and worship. They must be able to touch the divine here on earth."

The camera suddenly tilts down on Mary and up on Elizabeth as the scene shifts to Kat Ashley (here a young woman) cutting off Elizabeth's beautiful, long red hair. It falls to the floor silently and in slow motion. Her ladies mix the white paste that will become her new skin, and Elizabeth flashes back through her life as though she's committing to memory her very humanness. The camera holds on Elizabeth's face, a portrait of despair: "Kat, I have become a virgin."

Kapur cuts to an icon walking. Dressed in a fantastic gown of white and silver satin and an elaborate wig, all laced with pearls, her skin glowing ghostly white, Elizabeth seems to float out of the white light into the court. Her subjects now kneel before her. Elizabeth stops only once, before

William Cecil, and extends her hand. "Observe, Lord Burghley. I am married—to England," she informs him in a voice that seems deeper, almost otherworldly, shades of Galadriel in *Lord of the Rings* (Peter Jackson, 2001–2003). She moves toward the camera and her throne. Someone kisses the hem of her gown. Her ladies, dressed in white and wearing veils like brides, kneel in the left-hand corner of the frame. Kapur moves in to a close-up of Elizabeth's face and freezes the frame, leaving us with an image of loneliness, almost emptiness, a metaphor of personal sacrifice. Her eyes, like those of a statue, have seen their full destiny, which does not include love or personal indulgence. Is this what it means to be queen? Is this the price of power?

Shekhar Kapur once said that he used a lot of stone in making *Elizabeth* "to signify the ultimate power of destiny" (*The Making of Elizabeth*). Stone lasts. Human flesh does not. Shooting in cathedrals and castles around England, Kapur ensures his theme. While he introduces Elizabeth dancing in a green meadow against a backdrop of trees in full bloom and wearing simple gowns in earth tones that attach her to the natural world, he moves quickly to interior sets once she becomes queen. His overhead shots and wide angles visualize Elizabeth surrounded, dwarfed, virtually imprisoned by stone floors and walls. Her costumes—silver, gold, white, black—become more and more ethereal, elaborate, restricting her movement until, in the end, she can barely lift her arms. To survive, to reign supreme, Kapur argues in this film, she must become stone.

Elizabeth: The Golden Age (2007)

Shekhar Kapur manipulates reality for the sake of his own spiritual and psychological truths, for the sake of theme, and one of his favorite themes is, in his own words, "the search for Divinity through the haze and maze of human desire" (Kapur). What better manifestation of this quest than Elizabeth Tudor, whose sense of her public divine image and personal human desires frequently conflicted? In *Elizabeth: The Golden Age*, Kapur again uses lush, erotic colors, high angles, shifts in lighting key, crosscutting, slow motion, out-of-focus shots, and swirling camera moves to tell his story of Elizabeth's transformation from monarch to madonna. If we read Kapur's film with expectations of historical accuracy, we're destined to be disappointed, for, as Roger Ebert says, the film is "weighed down by its own

splendor," placing Elizabeth "in the center of history that is baldly simplified, shamelessly altered, and pumped up with romance and action" (rev.
Elizabeth: The Golden Age). If we read it, as with *Elizabeth*, as a formalist
text, an impressionist canvas, it works.

For Kapur, the question driving the film was "What do you do with
power when it becomes absolute?" (*The Making of Elizabeth*). Elizabeth,
the film argues, took it to the next level. She aspired to be divine. So, on
one level, there's a mystical wind blowing throughout the movie with
scenes like Elizabeth, barefooted with her white nightgown billowing
around her, standing high on a cliff as she looks down at her ships and
soldiers battling the Spanish Armada in the Channel below. Like a sixteenth-century Hera, she stands guard over her subjects, her spirit willing
their victory. In an earlier scene, encased in shining silver armor and
mounted on a high-spirited white steed, Elizabeth, looking every inch like
the saintly Joan of Arc, addresses her troops before battle. She shimmers,
untouchable, above mere mortals. For Cate Blanchett, on a more earthy
level: "This was a woman confronting the ageing process but also confronting her past. . . . She was moving through to a point of acceptance in
the film and part of that is accepting where you've been, who you are, how
old you are and the choices you've made in order to move forward" (Camevale). Only the most complex character could give director and actress
this kind of room to maneuver.

The film opens in 1585 and, even with the scrambled chronology, covers a period of about eight years, though no other time markers indicate
that. For the record, here's a handy time line of events:

1578	Raleigh first sails to America.
1581	Raleigh arrives at court and meets Elizabeth.
1584	Elizabeth knights Raleigh.
1585	Raleigh sponsors the first English colony on Roanoke Island, which fails. He does introduce tobacco to the English court.
1586	The Babington Plot unfolds.
1587	Elizabeth appoints Raleigh captain of the guard. Mary Stuart is executed at Fotheringhay Castle.
1588	England defeats the Spanish Armada. Raleigh, in charge of land forces on the coasts of Devon and Cornwall, sees no action.
1590	Walsingham dies.
1592	Raleigh's secret marriage to Elizabeth Throckmorton is revealed.

We're led to believe in the film that all events unfold in the same year, but time is not important to Kapur here. He's trying to visualize the essence of the events, of the woman, and what they mean.

Captions over a pan left of beautiful stained glass tell us that Spain is the most powerful empire in the world, that Philip has plunged Europe into a holy war, and that only England—ruled by a Protestant queen—stands against him. Kapur zooms in to a stained-glass image of Elizabeth: light, pure, divine. He then cuts to Philip (Jordi Mollà), shrouded by darkness, relieved only by pinpoints of candlelight. Priests surround him, singing an ominous note. From the opening shot, Kapur establishes the two opposing forces: one enlightened, the other evil and ignorant. This juxtaposition of light and dark continues throughout the rest of the film as we witness Elizabeth (Cate Blanchett) beset by political problems and her own personal demons.

The pressing issue is Mary Stuart (Samantha Morton). The Privy Council is calling for her head. She's too dangerous. She's plotting against their queen. She's rallying the Catholics to her cause. A tolerant Elizabeth insists: "I will not punish my people for their beliefs, only for their deeds." A cut to the Spanish court shows a scheming Philip: "England is enslaved to the devil. We must set her free." Back to Elizabeth, who says: "I'm assured that the people of England love their queen. My constant endeavor is to earn that love." Another cut gives us Mary (in one of the only non-saintlike film portraits) at Fotheringhay Castle; low-key lighting signals that she's up to no good as she unfolds a message that has been smuggled in to her from Babington. Now Philip's legions are cutting down trees in the dark forests of Spain (think Orcs killing the Ents in *Lord of the Rings*) to build his armada. Back and forth, back and forth, between the kingdom of good and the dens of evil, Kapur weaves the net of intrigue around Elizabeth until the audience has no choice but to see her as the sole beacon of hope in the world. Only Philip sees it differently: "Elizabeth is the darkness. I am the light."

As if Elizabeth doesn't have enough to worry about, Walsingham (Geoffrey Rush) is hounding her about an heir. Now, in 1585, Elizabeth would have been fifty-two and having an heir a moot point. But Cate Blanchett, for all her efforts to have "a greater sense of history and maturity" on-screen (Carnevale), still looks thirty, so Walsingham's pressure seems real and urgent enough. Elizabeth laughs it off. She is one calm,

Elizabeth: The Golden Age. Ten years after her breakout performance, Blanchett reprised her role as a middle-aged Elizabeth in Kapur's meditation on divine power. The out-of-focus shot of Francis Walsingham (Rush) befits his shadowy station as Elizabeth's adviser and superspy, while the queen, front and center and in sharp focus, contemplates the approaching Spanish Armada. In her butterfly-shaped wig, light bathing her face, Elizabeth looks ethereal, otherworldly—a foreshadowing of her celestial transformation. (Courtesy Jerry Ohlinger's Movie Material Store.)

controlled, controlling queen. A glance, a word, a gesture, and courtiers scurry to line up. This is not Bette Davis's court. There's no chaos here, and there's definitely no doubt about who's in charge. Elizabeth is the center around which the camera, and everyone else, spins in an orderly fashion. Bird's-eye angles depict her as the lead goose in the formation. At one point in the film, Raleigh tells her: "You eat and drink control." In this telling, Elizabeth may control the court, but she cannot control the heart.

Raleigh (Clive Owen) swaggers into Elizabeth's picture, throwing his cloak over a puddle, and captivating the queen with his stories of the New World and gold, compliments of Philip's Spanish ships. "The more gold I take from him, the safer your majesty will be," Raleigh reasons. In high Mae West style, Elizabeth returns: "Well, well, a political pirate." He's dashing and frank and different from other men. At one point, he asks the queen: "Why do you speak like a fool when you're anything but a fool?" In a court filled with sycophants, Elizabeth finds his honesty irresistible, and she is as hooked as her favorite lady-in-waiting, Bess Throckmorton (Abbie Cornish).

And so a strange love triangle begins. Suddenly, Elizabeth is staring into her mirror bemoaning the lines in her face and galloping across the countryside with Raleigh. She's struggling with her intellectual and sexual attraction to him and standing at the intersection of her public and private selves. "I envy you, Bess. You're free to have what I can't have," Elizabeth sighs. Does she then live the romance through Bess? In one scene, a jealous Elizabeth makes Raleigh dance the volta with Bess. Like a puppetmaster, Elizabeth works the strings while she watches from her throne. What she sees is herself, a young woman dancing the volta with Robert Dudley. The same shade of blue links master and marionette in this scene, as if mirror images of each other. In another surreal sequence of shots, Elizabeth, in her chamber, disrobes. We see her naked from the back, and suddenly we're looking at her face full front—no makeup, no wigs, no jewels. She's staring, her expression hard to read, at something almost beyond her immediate space. A cut to Raleigh and Bess making love snaps in the connection. Is Elizabeth really watching them? Is she experiencing the moment vicariously through Bess? Or is she simply alone, wondering if her body's still youthful enough to attract the likes of Raleigh, and imagining what it would be like to be touched by him. It's simultaneously sensual and voyeuristic.

In *Elizabeth: The Golden Age*, Kapur allows us to see Elizabeth by turns unadorned, vulnerable, yearning, volatile, jealous, proud, weak, vain, forgiving, resigned, and sublime. This is neither Essex's nor Raleigh's film by default. This time, the title reflects the character, and, though it is largely a work of imagination, director and actress capture the spirit of Gloriana in a kaleidoscope of scenes. During Mary's beheading, Elizabeth races frantically through the palace, unable to shake off the enormity of killing an anointed queen. We see her suppress her fear when, dressed in a bride-white gown, she turns from her prayers to face Babington's gun. Moving toward him, palms upward, she appears every inch the madonna, though he calls her "whore." Babington fires, but the gun's not loaded. The divine cannot die. In another scene, Elizabeth rises up fierce when the Spanish

ambassador threatens her: "Go back to your rathole. Tell Philip I fear neither him, nor his priests, nor his armies. . . . I have a hurricane in me that
will strip Spain bare when you dare to try me." The hurricane is unleashed
when she finds out that Bess is pregnant. Her voice thunders through the
air. When Bess confesses, the queen strikes her over and over, screaming:
"My bitches wear my collars." This is Elizabeth at her lowest. She knows it,
and Raleigh knows it. He intercedes: "This is not the queen I serve and
love." The queen sends Raleigh to the Tower and casts Bess out of the
court.

Elizabeth feels betrayed. In a vulnerable moment, she let her guard
down and bared her soul to Raleigh. They sit before a fire, that eternal
signifier of passion, and talk about love and death. The camera zooms in
close as Elizabeth asks: "In some other world, in some other time, could
you have loved me?" Raleigh responds: "I know only this world, and in this
world I have loved you." Kapur keeps the fire between them until the queen
asks Raleigh to kiss her—just for this once and then never to speak of it
again. On cue, the fire moves to the foreground of the shot. Afterward,
Elizabeth kisses Raleigh's hand and lays her head on his lap. It's a beautiful
moment, one a virgin queen might treasure—until she finds out that Bess
is carrying Raleigh's child. Not without remorse and mercy, Elizabeth releases Raleigh before the Spanish Armada attacks. "He is forgiven, as I,
too, long to be forgiven."

From this point in the film, Kapur focuses on Elizabeth's transformation from "the haze and maze of human desire" to the divine. She sets aside
her love for Raleigh, a hero in the film's reenactment of the battle, for her
country and her people. Her speech at Tilbury camp and her "Pre-
Raphaelite image of Joan of Arc" (Camevale) send waves of worship and
awe through her troops. Through the night, above the battle, she watches
over them, an angel in white commanding the winds to rise against the
enemy. An iconic shot of Elizabeth marks the end of Spain and the beginning of the "Golden Age." Kapur's camera swirls around a mannequin-like
figure of the queen, palms up and Christlike, dressed in a fabulous gown of
white, hooped wings attached at her shoulders. A fade to white finds the
angel of mercy at Walsingham's deathbed and then at Raleigh's estate,
where her divine image is solidified. She comes to give Bess and Raleigh's
son her blessing. The baby stops crying when Elizabeth takes him in her
arms. They lock eyes. Kapur bathes them in white light, sealing the mo-

ment and the message, virtually chiseling madonna and child into our memory. The camera sweeps directly above them, abstracting the image, Elizabeth's sleeves billowing out like angel wings.

"I am called the Virgin Queen," Elizabeth tells us in her final voice-over. "Unmarried, I have no master. Childless, I am mother to my people. God give me strength to bear this mighty freedom. I am your queen. I am myself." The monarch's last words signify that the public and personal selves have merged into the divine being, the ultimate sacrifice of a queen for her people. She has fulfilled the prophecy of her astrologer, Dr. John Dee (David Threlfall), who earlier tells her: "When the storm breaks, each man acts in accordance with his own nature. Some are dumb with terror. Some flee. Some hide. And some spread their wings like eagles and soar on the wind."

Certainly, few monarchs soar through the popular imagination with as much force and frequency as Elizabeth I. The power of that iconic image holds over decades of tellings and retellings of her unconventional life and reign. It doesn't seem to matter whether the biopics run traditional or re-visionist, artistic or realistic. Some dazzle with technical wizardry; some drip with romantic schlock. From Bette Davis to Helen Mirren, every interpretation enthralls. What is it about this life? What fascinates us? So much of her life is tantalizingly left to our imaginations. We long for evidence that will fill in those shadowy corners.

Yet we do know a great deal about her. For all that iconography, there's a tangibleness about Elizabeth. Joy, anger, frustration, jealousy, sorrow—we can all relate to that. Unfulfilled love, fear of aging, we get that too. The answer that echoes, however, is this: Elizabeth Tudor wrote her own narrative, and the truth of that provides comfort for modern women. Here's an example of what we mean. It's a passage from the autobiography of Jill Ker Conway, the first female president of Smith College and a historian who specializes in the experience of women in America. Conway writes: "After I discovered Shakespeare's sonnets, I began to bombard my teachers with requests for references to read about the Dark Lady of the Sonnets, and moved on from these to any book I could find about Tudor England. J. B. Black's detailed histories of the Elizabethan Parliaments were just coming out, and I hung upon the appearance of the next volume as though I were reading a popular serial. These brought me to the character of Elizabeth I and my first model for a woman leader. It was a new and comforting idea—greatness in a woman. I had not been conscious of hunger for such an image, but it was immensely satisfying to read about this woman with 'the heart and stomach of a prince'" (140).

Elizabeth navigated power in a man's world. At times vilified, criticized, even grudgingly respected for wielding that power alone, she coalesces the problems and concerns of today's female leaders. True, she had the help of excellent advisers, but, ultimately, she had to come to terms with her private and public selves on her own. Periodically, then, we must tell her story, like a barometer that measures our own value and place in the world.

Conclusion

The world has changed.
—Elizabeth II to Tony Blair in *The Queen*

Feeling sheer gratitude at not being born royal is one effect of studying the lives of queens. Heads that *don't* wear the crown can rest, if not always easily, at least without that particular weight. Recognizing the benefits of being common, however, doesn't quench our thirst to peer inside if a palace gate opens a crack. *The Queen* (2006), directed by Stephen Frears and written by Peter Morgan, satisfies what must be a universal urge to experience the British royal enclosure and mind-set, to walk through Buckingham and Balmoral straight into the private quarters. This intriguing addition to royal biopics, the first made during the reign of a living queen, focuses on the narrow slice of Elizabeth II's life following the death of Diana in 1997, imagining the sequence of inner and outer events that motivated her shift from private to public mourning for the people's princess—allowing us a public glimpse of the private woman.

The Queen throws down a postmodern card that 1930s directors like Rouben Mamoulian and Herbert Wilcox simply wouldn't have considered playing. It quickly announces its status as art, not life. *The Queen* opens to news coverage of Tony Blair (Michael Sheen) and his family on the election day that will make him the youngest prime minister in British history; the camera pulls back to show that we've been seeing the same television screen the queen, dressed in full royal regalia, is watching as she poses for an artist, who is observing her. He dabs at his portrait, unfinished, sketchy, its background dark while he discusses politics with her. A toe-to-crown tilt-up follows the name *Helen Mirren* in the title sequence, and, when the camera reaches Mirren's crowned head, the title *The Queen* appears. Turning from her fixed, three-quarters portrait stance, Mirren looks straight out at the audience. Louis Giannetti points out in *Understanding Movies:* "The more we see of the actor's face, the greater our sense of privileged intimacy; the less we see, the more mysterious and inaccessible the actor will seem" (11th ed. 81). Lost in her own thoughts, the queen rotates her remote position to an intimate, full frontal one, surely an invitation to read her facial landscape. This single turn foreshadows the entire plot of the film, as the queen allows us controlled access to the mind of a monarch.

Recent similarly nonconventional biopics make us hope for more. Shekhar Kapur likes to explode the narrative as he does in *Elizabeth* (1998) and *Elizabeth: The Golden Age* (2007) with portraits that pop Elizabeth I's image out of its context or that dissolve it in flashes of white radiance. Sofia Coppola begins *Marie Antoinette* with a shot that sums up the stereotype of the French queen and with reminders, like rock music and a blue high-top, that her film, also a product of 2006, isn't a period piece. Coppola and Kapur like to loop time, although they can hardly edit in news clips of the French Revolution or the Spanish Armada. *The Queen,* a more realistic work, uses this technique to continue the motif of watching and being watched, mingling real footage of Princess Diana with shots of Mirren as Elizabeth in bed, drawn to the screen.

The first film to consider the life of Elizabeth II, *The Queen* constructs the queen's persona with care. Critics lauded Helen Mirren's "unsentimental" performance as a display of "brilliant technique" (Dargis, "However Heavy It Gets"). Casting has, does, and will alter the flavor of a film about the life of any queen. Personality stars like Bette Davis, Greta Garbo, and Elizabeth Taylor may fight to be one with their characters, but they are never really meant to merge. Instead, the two icons coexist in a sometimes shaky juxtaposition that marries box office and historical realities. Character actors like Glenda Jackson, Cate Blanchett, and Helen Mirren, however, seem to be channeling their characters.

Costuming and makeup in *The Queen* aid Mirren's transmission, pushing the constant juxtaposition of what might have happened inside the royal family and what did happen outside. While others in the cast—Alex Jennings as Prince Charles, for example—evoke their characters without the benefit of striking physical likeness or extensive cosmetic assistance, Consolata Boyle and a team of makeup artists enhance every similarity between Mirren/Elizabeth and Michael Sheen/Tony Blair, designating the pair as real and central—or, in the case of the queen, almost more than real. Boyle understands that each gray wave on the queen's head, each round-toed pump, each opaque stocking, each odd hat, each tweed skirt, will be evaluated by viewers who can see the breathing reality on television and in the press, but Mirren, noted for her extensive research, fretted about how she would move beyond the externals. Who was the inner woman? Nancy Griffin reports that Mirren "immersed herself in books and news-reel footage" but that "something clicked" when she began studying paint-ings of the queen: "'I suddenly thought, That's it: you are just doing a por-trait. . . . It's never a perfect reproduction; it's a perception. You are like a portrait painter'" (qtd. in Griffin 124). Like Mirren's portrait of Elizabeth I, this film reveals the human side of Elizabeth II and probably did more for the queen's public image than any public relations wizard.

The difference between living *for* the public and living *before* the public lies at the heart of *The Queen*. Morgan and Frears's decision to focus pri-marily on the emotionally charged six-day period between Diana's death and her funeral avoids "highlights of a famous life" blandness and displays a willingness to view internal change as material riveting enough to be-come a screenplay. We like the way *The Queen* couches the public/private issue in generational terms, not a common approach for royal biopics. To the Queen Mother (Sylvia Syms), or "Mummy," as Elizabeth calls her, the vow that her daughter took is unambiguous and inescapable: "I declare that my whole life, whether it be long or short, shall be devoted to your service." At the start of the film, Elizabeth II agrees that, as a figurehead, she must live out that pledge without public displays of emotion; one hugs one's grief to oneself. "That's the way we do things in this country," she tells Tony Blair. "Quietly, and with dignity." Her certainty, unlike her mother's, is shaken by the mass reaction to Diana's death. As *Mrs. Brown* examines Victoria's critical shift from mourner to ruler, *The Queen* traces Elizabeth's realization that "the world has changed." The setting for both these inte-rior shifts, the landscapes around Balmoral Castle, reduce Victoria and Elizabeth to human scale while emphasizing their privileged isolation. Victoria and Elizabeth II come down from the mountains and reenter the city.

Frears and Morgan present the face and voice of the real Diana, the next generation, as an emblem of the pain and pleasure that result from living in public. She too looks out at us, but hers is a haunted, hunted sidelong gaze. "To be a queen of people's hearts," as Diana puts it, to leave the enclosure behind, is to bask in adoration and risk destruction. To represent this equation on a symbolic level, Frears and Morgan use a stag, a rare, beautiful creature that has been sighted at Balmoral. The queen's epiphany about Diana and about her own position parallels the stalking and killing of the animal. When Elizabeth looks at its headless body hanging in a game house, she has decided against her preference for stoicism. She gives a live, televised statement, speaking "as a queen and as a grandmother" (additions from Tony Blair's staff) about Diana. Tony Blair, portrayed as a master of the media, has encouraged her to do so, to connect with her public.

Method mimics meaning in *The Queen*. Too often royal biopics seek the sensational only, translating *personal* as *sexual*. Others turn to the ubiquitous fade to black to mask intensely private (or Code-busting) moments in the lives of queens. Although *The Queen* places its camera squarely inside the queen's space, it creates its own parameters for acceptable observation. An incredibly private view of Elizabeth standing in a hallway, watching through a doorway as Prince Charles tells his sons their mother is dead, leads us to conjecture about the barriers between her and her children. (Princess Anne is never mentioned in the film.) Although the queen speaks about comforting her grandsons, no scene shows them together, and never does the camera reveal the faces of the young princes. Only their figures, in half light, shot from the side or from the back or from a far distance, aid the telling. When the queen is brought to tears by the stress of events, Frears allows Elizabeth the privacy of that moment, keeping the camera behind her. We wish more directors would trust their audiences, as Frears does, to read import in small things. Quiet, angled shots of the queen thinking in her lovely sitting room, thinking in the wilds of Balmoral, thinking while her assistant, Robin Janvrin (Rogen Allam), counsels her, add up to a powerful whole.

The queen changes. "That's the way to survive," Blair confirms as he watches news coverage of Elizabeth viewing tributes to Diana outside Balmoral's gates and then wading through the sea of flowers and cards at Buckingham. Those of us who lived through that time watched the queen's actions. How much more painful it is to view those scenes, to read those cards inscribed with messages like, "Diana was better than the lot of you," after Frears and Morgan's guess at what brought her outside the gates.

Mirren's portrait of Elizabeth I illustrates the Virgin Queen's talent for taking the pulse of her people; her Elizabeth II acknowledges the alteration in rhythm. *The Queen* doesn't end there, however, and the final scenes evoke a feisty, canny person, someone like the Elizabeth II Fran Leibowitz photographed in 2007. Unlike the many biopics that depict a female ruler as masculine and alone, power having destroyed her femininity, *The Queen* leaves us with the familiar persona. Elizabeth wears a royal purple dress, vaguely like a bridesmaid's, with a carefully placed brooch, one of those getups we recognize as true, as she meets Tony Blair two months after Diana's death. Blair has come to respect the woman who has spent "fifty years doing a job she never wanted." He has changed too.

Their conversation, which moves from personal to political, from indoors to outdoors, marks a shift in their relationship and a new beginning for them as well as for the country. If the queen has earned her prime minister's respect, he has earned her trust. He has gently pulled the queen into a new technological age that demands immediate and visible communication from the world's powerbrokers. "I can see that the world has changed and one must modernize," she admits to Blair. Status quo risks not just the queen's reputation or sense of privacy. The survival of the monarchy is at stake. She must reclaim the goodwill of her people. A scan of a crowd of mourners outside Buckingham Palace, their tears turning to shy smiles and awkward curtseys as she walks by, suggests the powerful influence of the monarch's mere presence, assures us of their reconnect, and reminds Elizabeth of what she almost lost. Deeply marked by the summer's events, she lets Blair know that he has no immunity to such reversals, which happen "quite suddenly and without warning."

Elizabeth's next gesture virtually sums up a life. She rises from her chair across from Blair's. Never one to sit around talking and dwelling, she asks: "Shall we walk? A good walk and fresh air sort everything out." She might have been "just a girl" when she became queen, but Frears leaves no doubt that we are witnessing a woman who is equal to the challenges of leading. He leaves us with the queen and Blair strolling through a sunlit garden discussing matters of state. She's not alone; she has her prickly family, her loyal staff, this young man, and, right outside the palace, her grudging, needy people. This, finally, isn't a gender thing; the queen wrestles with the interior and external pressures that consume any woman, or any man, with power. The biopic has spent its time helping us imagine the person behind the crown. The result is a merger of private and public selves, a portrait of a modern queen.

The satisfaction of watching a perfect composition conclude shouldn't distract audiences from the democratizing vibrations that position *The Queen* on a new biopic frequency. The film enacts a final fusion of royal status and celebrity. We demand full disclosure from a queen in the palace and a queen on the screen. Queen Elizabeth II's invitation to Helen Mirren for tea and Mirren's polite refusal owing to a prior engagement engendered equal curiosity. We were just as interested in whether Helen Mirren went as in the extended invitation. The queen's open gaze is also an invitation. If we look back, acknowledging her humanness, does it mean that she's just like us? She seems to be. *The Queen* places her actions closer to now than any "once upon a time." Temporal distance no longer softens the image of a monarch; our age of easy access won't grant any queen, or president, or prime minister that filter. We've reached the end of a technological gap between reign and revision. The modern eye recognizes no barriers to full exposure, not even the gates of Buckingham Palace.

Bibliography

Alexander, John T. *Catherine the Great: Life and Legend.* Oxford: Oxford UP, 1989.

Allen, Robert C. "The Role of the Star in Film History." *Film Theory and Criticism.* Ed. Leo Braudy and Marshall Cohen. New York: Oxford UP, 1999. 547–61.

Alleva, Richard. "The Godmother." *Commonweal* 18 Dec. 1998: 14–15.

Bach, Stephen. *Marlene Dietrich: Life and Legend.* New York: Morrow, 2002.

Barthes, Roland. "The Face of Garbo." Trans. Annette Lavers. *Mythologies.* New York: Hill & Wang, 1997. 56–57.

———. "The Romans in Films." Trans. Annette Lavers. *Mythologies.* New York: Hill & Wang, 1997. 26–28.

Barzini, Luigi. *The Italians.* New York: Touchstone, 1964.

Baskette, Kirtley. "The Girl They Tried to Forget." *The Talkies: Articles and Illustrations from a Great Fan Magazine, 1928–1940.* Ed. Richard Griffith. New York: Dover, 1971. 120–21, 278.

———. "Is Hepburn Killing Her Own Career?" *The Talkies: Articles and Illustrations from a Great Fan Magazine, 1928–1940.* Ed. Richard Griffith. New York: Dover, 1971. 50–51, 276–77.

Berardinelli, James. Rev. of *The Age of Innocence,* dir. Martin Scorcese. 1993. *Reelviews: Berardinelli Sees Film.* http://www.reelviews.net.

Berg, A. Scott. *Kate Remembered.* New York: Putnam's, 2003.

"Bergner, Elizabeth." *International Dictionary of Films and Filmakers, 3: Actors and Actresses.* Ed. Nicholas Thomas. London: St. James, 1992. 99–101.

Brodsky, Jack, and Nathan Weiss. *The Cleopatra Papers.* New York: Simon & Schuster, 1963.

Bryant, Chris. *Glenda Jackson: The Biography.* London: HarperCollins, 1999.

Buckley, Veronica. *Christina Queen of Sweden: The Restless Life of a European Eccentric.* New York: HarperCollins, 2004.

Burton, Elizabeth. *The Pageant of Elizabethan England.* New York: Scribner's, 1958.

Buscombe, Edward. "John Ford." *The Oxford History of World Cinema.* Oxford: Oxford UP, 1996. 288–89.

Byrne, Bridget. "HBO Series Elevates Dame Mirren's Status." Associated Press 17 Apr. 2006. hbo.com.

Camevale, Rob. "Film Interview—*The Golden Age;* Cate Blanchett Interview." 11 Feb. 2007. http://www.orange.co.uk/entertainment/film/26963.htm.

Carnes, Mark C. *Past Imperfect: History according to the Movies.* New York: Henry Holt, 1995.

Cartmell, Deborah, I. Q. Hunter, and Imelda Whelehan. *Retrovisions: Reinventing the Past in Film and Fiction.* Vol. 6. London: Pluto, 2001.

Castelot, Andre. *Queen of France: A Biography of Marie Antoinette.* New York: Harper, 1957.

Cecil, David. *The Cecils of Hatfield House: An English Ruling Family.* Boston: Houghton Mifflin, 1973.

Chandler, Charlotte. "Bette Davis Sighs." *Vanity Fair* Mar. 2006: 256–70.

Churchill, Winston. *History of the English-Speaking Peoples.* New York: Dodd, Mead, 1956.

The Collected Screenplays of Bernard Shaw. Ed. Bernard F. Dukore. Athens: U of Georgia P, 1980.

Collis, Clark. "Silver Streak: The Oscar Race Is On." *Entertainment* 19 Jan. 2007: 24–30.

Comita, Jenny. "Queen Cate." *W* Oct. 2007: 342–48.

Commanding the Winds: Creating the Armada. Elizabeth: The Golden Age DVD Special Feature. Universal, 2007.

Conway, Jill Ker. *The Road from Coorain.* New York: Vintage, 1989.

Crittenden, John. "Liv Ullmann: Ingmar Bergman Star Talks about Life and Art." *Liv Ullmann Interviews.* Ed. Robert Emmet Long. Jackson: UP of Mississippi, 2006. 55–61.

Crowther, Bosley. "A Power in the Movies." *New York Times* 7 Aug. 1938. *The New York Times Encyclopedia of Film.* Ed. Gene Brown. New York: *New York Times* Books, 1984. Unpaginated.

———. "The Queen Was in Her Parlor—at the Waldorf." *New York Times* 21 Aug. 1938. *The New York Times Encyclopedia of Film.* Ed. Gene Brown. New York: *New York Times* Books, 1984. Unpaginated.

Custen, George. *Bio/Pics: How Hollywood Constructed Public History.* New Brunswick, NJ: Rutgers UP, 1992.

Dargis, Manohla. "However Heavy It Gets, Wear a Crown Lightly." Rev. of *The Queen,* dir. Stephen Frears. *New York Times* 29 Sept. 2006. nytimes.com.

———. Rev. of *The Good German,* dir. Steven Soderbergh. *New York Times* 15 Dec. 2006. nytimes.com.

———. "Now, Warrior." Rev. of *Elizabeth: The Golden Age,* dir. Shekhar Kapur. *New York Times* 12 Oct. 2007. nytimes.com.

Deans, Marjorie. *Meeting at the Sphinx: Gabriel Pascal's Production of Shaw's "Caesar and Cleopatra."* London: Macdonald, 1946.

de Madariaga, Isabel. *Catherine the Great: A Short History.* New Haven, CT: Yale UP, 1990.

Dench, Judi. Interview with Sonia Beesley. BBC, London. 3 June 1981.

———. Interview with Simon Hattenstone. *The Guardian* 13 Apr. 2004. http://www.guardian.co.uk/film/2004/apr/13/theatre.whoswhoinbritishtheatre.

Dobson, Michael, and Nicola J. Watson. *England's Elizabeth: An Afterlife in Fame and Fantasy.* New York: Oxford UP, 2002.

Dunn, Jane. *Elizabeth and Mary: Cousins, Rivals, Queens.* New York: Vintage, 2003.

Ebert, Roger. Rev. of *Elizabeth,* dir. Shekhar Kapur. *Chicago Sun Times* 20 Nov. 1998. rogerebert.suntimes.com.

———. Rev. of *First Knight,* dir. Jerry Zucker. *Chicago Sun Times* 7 July 1995. rogerebert.suntimes.com.

———. Rev. of *Mrs. Brown,* dir. John Madden. *Chicago Sun Times* 25 July 1997. rogerebert.suntimes.com.

———. Rev. of *Elizabeth: The Golden Age,* dir. Shekhar Kapur. *Chicago Sun Times* 12 Oct. 2007. rogerebert.suntimes.com.

Elizabeth: The Acclaimed Saga of England's Virgin Queen. Hosted by David Starkey. The History Channel, 2002.

Elizabeth R Documentary. Elizabeth R DVD Special Feature. A&E, 1996.

Erickson, Carolly. *The First Elizabeth.* New York: St. Martin's Griffin, 1983.

———. *Great Catherine.* New York: Crown, 1994.

———. "The Scarlet Empress." *Past Imperfect: History according to the Movies.* Ed. Mark C. Carnes, Ted Mico, John Miller-Monzon, and David Rubel. New York: Henry Holt, 1995. 86–89.

———. *The Hidden Diary of Marie Antoinette.* New York: St. Martin's, 2005.

Ferguson, Sarah. *Victoria and Albert: A Family Life at Osborne House.* New York: Prentice-Hall, 1991.

Franzero, Carlos Maria. *The Life and Times of Cleopatra.* London: Redman, n.d.

Fraser, Antonia. *Mary Queen of Scots.* New York: Delta, 1969.

———. *The Wives of Henry VIII.* New York: Knopf, 1993.

———. *Marie Antoinette: The Journey.* New York: Anchor, 2001.

Frewin, Leslie. *Dietrich: The Story of a Star.* New York: Stein & Day, 1967.

George, Margaret. *The Memoirs of Cleopatra*. New York: St. Martin's, 1997.

Giannetti, Louis. *Understanding Movies*. 10th ed. Upper Saddle River, NJ: Pearson/Prentice-Hall, 2005.

———. *Understanding Movies*. 11th ed. Upper Saddle River, NJ: Pearson/Prentice-Hall, 2008.

Giannetti, Louis, and Scott Eyman. *Flashback: A Brief History of Film*. 3rd ed. Englewood Cliffs, NJ: Prentice-Hall, 1996.

Gordon, Mary. Interview with Terry Gross. *Fresh Air*. National Public Radio. 31 Jan. 2005.

Grant, Michael. *Cleopatra*. Edison, NJ: Castle, 2004.

Griffin, Nancy. "Mirren, Mirren on the Wall." *AARP* Mar./Apr. 2007: 50–55, 124.

Griffith, Richard, ed. *The Talkies: Articles and Illustrations from a Great Fan Magazine, 1928–1940*. New York: Dover, 1971.

Gristwood, Sarah. *Elizabeth and Leicester: Power, Passion, Politics*. New York: Viking Penguin, 2007.

Guthmann, Edward. "*Sabrina* Still Irresistible: Ormond Carries Remake of 1954 Hepburn Film." Rev. of *Sabrina*, dir. Sydney Pollack. *San Francisco Chronicle* 15 Dec. 1995. http://www.sfgate.com/cgi-bin/article.cgi?f=/c/a/1995/12/15/DD15264.DTL.

Hall, Leonard. "Garbo-Maniacs." *The Talkies: Articles and Illustrations from a Great Fan Magazine, 1928–1940*. Ed. Richard Griffith. New York: Dover, 1971. 4, 270.

Hall, Mordaunt. "Elizabeth Bergner and Douglas Fairbanks Jr. in the British Production, 'Catherine the Great.'" Rev. of *Catherine the Great*, dir. Paul Czinner. *New York Times*, 15 Feb. 1934. *The New York Times Encyclopedia of Film*. Ed. Gene Brown. New York: *New York Times* Books, 1984. Unpaginated.

———. Rev. of *Cleopatra*, dir. Cecil B. De Mille. *New York Times* 17 Aug. 1934. *The New York Times Film Reviews, 1913–1968*. 7 vols. New York: *New York Times*/Arno, 1970. 2:1087.

Hamilton, Victoria. Interview with Aleks Sierz. "Long Live Queen Vic." 25 Apr. 2004. http://entertainment.timesonline.co.uk/tol/arts_and_entertainment/article830186.ece.

Haskell, Molly. *From Reverence to Rape: The Treatment of Women in the Movies*. 2nd ed. Chicago: U of Chicago P, 1987.

Haslip, Joan. *Catherine the Great*. New York: Putnam's, 1977.

Heilbrun, Carolyn G. *Writing a Woman's Life*. New York: Ballantine, 1988.

Heston, Charlton. *The Actor's Life: Journals, 1956–1976*. Ed. Hollis Alport. New York: Dutton, 1976.

Heyman, Marshall. "kirsten." *W* Apr. 2007: 256–66.

Hibbert, Christopher. *The Virgin Queen: Elizabeth I, Genius of the Golden Age*. Reading, MA: Perseus, 1991.

Hill, Anne E. *Kirsten Dunst.* Detroit: Thomson, 2005.

Hirschberg, Lynn. "Sofia's Paris." *Travel: New York Times* Fall 2006: 102–9.

Hopkins, Charles. "Cleopatra." *Magill's Survey of Cinema.* Ed. Frank N. Magill. Vol. 1. Hackensack, NJ: Salem Press, 1980. 466–71.

Inside Elizabeth's World. Elizabeth: The Golden Age DVD Special Feature. Universal, 2007.

Interview with Alison Weir. *Elizabeth R* DVD Special Feature. BBC, 2001.

Interview with Glenda Jackson. *Elizabeth R* DVD Special Feature. BBC, 2001.

Interview with Rosalind Miles. *Elizabeth R* DVD Special Feature. BBC, 2001.

Ives, Eric. *The Life and Death of Anne Boleyn.* Oxford: Blackwell, 2004.

James, Caryn. "Royal P.R.: People's Princess Obliterates the Stiff Upper Lip." Rev. of *Marie Antoinette,* dir. Sofia Coppola. *New York Times* 11 Oct. 2006: B7.

Kapur, Shekhar. "Golden Age/Divinity/History/Desire." 24 Nov. 2007. http://www.shekharkapur.com/blog/archives/2007/11/golden_agedivin.htm.

Katz, Ephraim. *The Film Encyclopedia.* 3rd ed. New York: HarperPerennial, 1998.

Kissel, Howard. "Bergman's Everywoman Speaks." *Liv Ullman Interviews.* Ed. Robert Emmet Long. Jackson: UP of Mississippi, 2006. 52–54.

Konigsberg, Eric. "A Looking Glass: Marie Antoinette, Citoyenne." Rev. of *Marie Antoinette,* dir. Sofia Coppola. *New York Times, Week* section, 22 Oct. 2006: 5.

Landy, Marcia. *Cinematic Uses of the Past.* Minneapolis: U of Minnesota P, 1996.

LaSalle, Mick. "Here's Looking at You, Kid (Nudge, Nudge, Wink, Wink)." Rev. of *The Good German,* dir. Steven Soderbergh. *San Francisco Chronicle* 22 Dec. 2006. http://sfchronicle.us/cgi-bin/article.cgi?f=/c/a/2006/12/22/DDGNRN3 GFQ1.DTL&hw=good+german+lasalle&sn=008&sc=390.

Leaming, Barbara. *Bette Davis.* New York: Cooper Square, 2003.

Lever, Evelyne. *Last Queen of France.* Trans. Catherine Temerson. New York: Farrar, 2000.

Long, Robert Emmet, ed. *Liv Ullmann Interviews.* Jackson: UP of Mississippi, 2006.

Longford, Elizabeth. *Queen Victoria: Born to Succeed.* New York: Harper, 1964.

Loos, Ted. "Leonor Varela: Brief Article." *Interview.* Mar. 2001.

Ludwig, Emil. *Cleopatra.* Trans. Bernard Miall. New York: Bantam, 1957.

Lurie, Alison. *The Language of Clothes.* New York: Holt, 2000.

Lyall, Sarah. "Ever Backward into the Royal Future." *New York Times* 11 Nov. 2007, 12 Dec. 2008. http://www.nytimes.com/2007/11/11/weekinreview.

Mackenzie, Faith Compton. *The Sibyl of the North: The Tale of Christina, Queen of Sweden.* Boston: Houghton Mifflin, 1931.

The Making of Elizabeth. Elizabeth DVD Special Feature. Universal, 1998.

The Making of Elizabeth I. Elizabeth I DVD Special Feature. HBO, 2006.

The Making of Marie Antoinette. Marie Antoinette DVD Special Feature. Columbia, 2006.

Mann, William. *Behind the Screen: How Gays and Lesbians Shaped Hollywood.* New York: Viking, 2002.

Marie Antoinette. Screenplay by Sofia Coppola. New York: Rizzoli, 2006.

"Marie Antoinette Perfume Revived." BBC News: 13 Dec. 2006. newsvote.bbc.co.uk.

Marshall, Cynthia. "*Antony and Cleopatra:* A Modern Perspective." *Antony and Cleopatra.* Ed. Barbara A. Mowat and Paul Werstine. New York: Washington Square/Pocket, 1999. 297–307.

Marshall, Dorothy. *The Life and Times of Victoria.* New York: Praeger, 1974.

Maslin, Janet. "Smilla's Sense of Snow: Intrigue amid Lonely Vistas of Snow." Rev. of *Smilla's Sense of Snow,* dir. Bille August. *New York Times* 28 Feb. 1997. nytimes.com.

Maybury, John. Special features. "De Patre Vostro." Episode 22. DVD *Rome: Second Season.* HBO Home Video, 2007.

McKechnie, Kara. "Mrs. Brown's Mourning and Mr. King's Madness: Royal Crisis on Screen." *Retrovisions: Reinventing the Past in Film and Fiction.* Ed. Deborah Cartmell, I. Q. Hunter, and Imelda Whelehan. London: Pluto, 2001. 102–19.

The Memoirs of Catherine the Great. Trans. Mark Cruise and Hilde Hoogenboom. New York: Modern Library, 2005.

Mendelsohn, Daniel. "Lost in Versailles." Rev. of *Marie Antoinette,* dir. Sofia Coppola. *New York Review of Books* 30 Nov. 2006. nybooks.com.

"MGM's 'Marie Antoinette,' in Terms of Norma Shearer, at the Astor." *New York Times* 17 Aug. 1938. nytimes.com.

Miller, Johnathan. *Judi Dench: With a Crack in Her Voice.* New York: Welcome Rain, 2000.

Miller, Joyce. *A Wee Guide to Mary, Queen of Scots.* Musselburgh, Scotland: Goblinshead, 2005.

Mirren, Helen. Guest Columnist. *TV Guide* 17 Apr. 2006: 33.

Morsberger, Robert E. "The Private Lives of Elizabeth and Essex." *Magill's Survey of Cinema.* Ed. Frank N. Magill. Vol. 3. Hackensack, NJ: Salem Press, 1980. 1383–87.

Neagle, Anna. *Anna Neagle Says, "There's Always Tomorrow": An Autobiography.* London: Futura, 1979.

Neale, J. E. *Queen Elizabeth I: A Biography.* New York: Doubleday, 1957.

Nugent, Frank S. Rev. of *The Private Lives of Elizabeth and Essex,* dir. Michael Curtiz. *New York Times* 2 Dec. 1939. *The New York Times Film Reviews, 1913–1968.* 7 vols. New York: *New York Times*/Arno, 1970. 3:1657.

Packard, Jerrold M. *Farewell in Splendor: The Passing of Queen Victoria and Her Age.* New York: Dutton, 1998.

Paris, Barry. *Garbo.* Minneapolis: U of Minnesota P, 1994.

Picardie, Justine. "Cate Shines." *Harper's Bazaar* Aug. 2005: 144–50.

Pigeon, Renée. "'No Man's Elizabeth': The Virgin Queen in Recent Films." *Retrovisions: Reinventing the Past in Film and Fiction*. Ed. Deborah Cartmell, I. Q. Hunter, and Imelda Whelehan. London: Pluto, 2001. 8–25.

Plowden, Alison. *Elizabeth Regina: The Age of Triumph, 1588–1603*. London: Sutton Pub., 2001.

Powers, John. "A Woman of the People." *Vogue* May 2006: 268–71, 302.

Pryor, Felix. *Elizabeth I: Her Life in Letters*. Berkeley and Los Angeles: U of California P, 2003.

Queen Victoria in Her Letters and Journals: A Selection by Christopher Hibbert. New York: Viking, 1985.

Quirk, Lawrence J. *Claudette Colbert: An Illustrated Biography*. New York: Crown, 1985.

Redgrave, Vanessa. *Vanessa Redgrave: An Autobiography*. New York: Random House, 1994.

The Reign Continues: Making Elizabeth: The Golden Age. *Elizabeth: The Golden Age* DVD Special Feature. Universal, 2007.

Rev. of *Marie Antoinette*, dir. W. S. Van Dyke. *New York Times* 17 Aug. 1938. *The New York Times Film Reviews, 1913–1968*. 7 vols. New York: *New York Times*/Arno, 1970. 2:1523.

Rosenberg, Eleanor. *Leicester: Patron of Letters*. New York: Columbia UP, 1955.

Royster, Francesca T. *Becoming Cleopatra: The Shifting Image of an Icon*. New York: Palgrave, 2003.

Schwarzbaum, Lisa. Rev. of *Elizabeth: The Golden Age*, dir. Shekhar Kapur. *Entertainment Weekly* 10 Oct. 2007. ew.com.

Scott, A. O. "A Lonely Petit Four of a Queen." Rev. of *Marie Antoinette*, dir. Sofia Coppola. *New York Times* 13 Oct. 2006: B1.

Seger, Linda. *The Art of Adaptation: Turning Fact and Fiction into Film*. New York: Holt, 1992.

Shakespeare, William. *Antony and Cleopatra*. Ed. Barbara A. Mowat and Paul Werstine. New York: Washington Square/Pocket, 1999.

Sharpe, Howard. "The Star Creators of Hollywood." *The Talkies: Articles and Illustrations from a Great Fan Magazine, 1928–1940*. Ed. Richard Griffith. New York: Dover, 1971. 166–67, 333, 337.

Shaw, George Bernard. *Caesar and Cleopatra: A Page of History*. New York: Dodd, 1930.

Shirley, Lois. "The Girl Who Played Greta Garbo." *The Talkies: Articles and Illustrations from a Great Fan Magazine, 1928–1940*. Ed. Richard Griffith. New York: Dover, 1971. 133, 309.

Shulgasser, Barbara. "A Pair of Old Pros Rescue *Mrs. Brown*." Rev. of *Mrs. Brown*, dir. John Madden. *Examiner* 25 July 1997. http://www.sfgate.com/cgi-bin/article .cgi?f=/e/a/1997/07/25/WEEKEND1611.dtl&hw=queen&sn=097&sc=370.

Solomon, Jon. *The Ancient World in the Cinema*. New Haven, CT: Yale UP, 2001.

Somerset, Anne. *Elizabeth I*. New York: St. Martin's Griffin, 1991.

Stanley, Alessandra. "The Flinty Monarch with an Iron Fist." *New York Times* 21 Apr. 2006. nytmes.com.

Starkey, David. *Elizabeth: The Struggle for the Throne*. New York: Perennial, 2001.

Stein, Ruthe. Rev. of *Elizabeth: The Golden Age*, dir. Shekhar Kapur. *San Francisco Chronicle* 12 Oct. 2007: E9.

Sterritt, David. "Live Ullmann: Norway's Glittering Gift to World Film." *Liv Ullmann Interviews*. Ed. Robert Emmet Long. Jackson: UP of Mississippi, 2006. 78–81.

Stevers, Martin. "'Now I Help You,' Says Garbo to Gilbert." *The Talkies: Articles and Illustrations from a Great Fan Magazine, 1928–1940*. Ed. Richard Griffith. New York: Dover, 1971. 213.

Strachey, Lytton. *Elizabeth and Essex: A Tragic History*. 1928. New York: Harcourt, 1969.

———. *Queen Victoria*. 1921. New York: Barnes & Noble, 1998.

"Summary of Ancient Sources." Trans. Dwight Castro. New Wilmington, PA: Westminster College, 2003.

"Super Pan." *Time*. 14 May 1965. Available at http://www.time.com/time/ magazine/article/0,9171,898812,00.html.

Sylvia of Hollywood. "Beauty and Personality Are Inseparable." *The Talkies: Articles and Illustrations from a Great Fan Magazine, 1928–1940*. Ed. Richard Griffith. New York: Dover, 1971. 188–89, 344.

Taraborrelli, J. Randy. *Elizabeth*. New York: Warner, 2006.

Tillyard, E. M. W. *The Elizabethan World Picture*. 1943. New York: Vintage, [1964].

Towers, Courts and Cathedrals. *Elizabeth: The Golden Age* DVD Special Feature. Universal, 2007.

Uncovering the Real Elizabeth. *Elizabeth I* DVD Special Feature. HBO, 2006.

Vanderlan, Mike. "Mary of Scotland." *Magill's Survey of Cinema*. Ed. Frank N. Magill. Vol. 4. New Jersey: Salem Press, 1981. 1547–49.

Vickers, Hugo. *Vivien Leigh*. Boston: Little, Brown, 1988.

Victoria. *Leaves from the Journal of Our Life in the Highlands from 1848 to 1861*. Ed. Arthur Helps. 1868. Abridged ed. London: Folio Society, 1973.

Vieira, Mark A. *Greta Garbo: A Cinematic Legacy*. New York: Harry N. Abrams, 2005.

Waliszewski, Kazimierz. *The Romance of an Empress: Catherine II of Russia.* 2 vols. London: Heinemann, 1894.

Walker, Alexander. *Elizabeth: The Life of Elizabeth Taylor.* New York: Grove, 1990.

———. *Vivien: The Life of Vivien Leigh.* New York: Grove, 1997.

Wallace, Tim. "Biography of Jean Simmons." 2000. http://www.geocities.com /clannad47.

Wanger, Walter, and Joe Hyams. *My Life with Cleopatra.* New York: Bantam, 1963.

Weber, Caroline. *Queen of Fashion: What Marie Antoinette Wore to the Revolution.* New York: Holt, 2006.

Weintraub, Stanley. *Victoria: An Intimate Biography.* New York: Dutton, 1987.

Weir, Alison. *The Life of Elizabeth I.* New York: Ballantine, 1998.

Wharton, Edith. "The Fullness of Life." *Collected Stories, 1891–1910.* New York: Library of America, 2001. 12–22.

Williams, Neville. *The Life and Times of Elizabeth I.* New York: Shooting Star, 1995.

Williamson, David. *Kings and Queens of Britain.* New York: Dorset, 1992.

Wolff, Ruth. *The Abdication.* Woodstock, IL: Dramatic, 1971.

Woodcock, Sandra. *Catherine Zeta-Jones.* London: Hodder & Stoughton, 2002.

Woodham-Smith, Cecil. *Queen Victoria: From Her Birth to the Death of the Prince Consort.* New York: Knopf, 1972.

Wren, Melvin C. *The Course of Russian History.* Prospect Heights, IL: Waveland, 1979.

Zevin, Alexander. "Marie Antoinette and the Ghosts of the French Revolution." *Cineaste* 32, no. 2 (2007): 32–35.

Zweig, Stefan. *Marie Antoinette: The Portrait of an Average Woman.* 1933. Reprint, New York: Harmony, 1984.

———. "History and the Screen: Austrian Author Discusses Filming Events of Bygone Times." *New York Times* 8 Apr. 1934. *The New York Times Encyclopedia of Film.* Ed. Gene Brown. New York: *New York Times* Books, 1984. Unpaginated.

Films Discussed

The Abdication. Dir. Anthony Harvey. Perf. Liv Ullmann and Peter Finch. Warner Bros., 1974.

Antony and Cleopatra. Dir. Charlton Heston. Perf. Hildegarde Neil and Charlton Heston. Folio Films, 1972.

Antony and Cleopatra. Dir. Jon Scoffield. Perf. Janet Suzman and Richard Johnson. ABC, 1975.

Caesar and Cleopatra. Dir. Gabriel Pascal. Perf. Vivien Leigh and Claude Rains. United Artists, 1945.

Catherine the Great. Dir. Paul Czinner. Perf. Elisabeth Bergner and Douglas Fairbanks Jr. United Artists, 1934.

Catherine the Great. Dir. Marvin J. Chomsky. Perf. Catherine Zeta-Jones, Jeanne Moreau, and Omar Sharif. A&E, 1995.

Cleopatra. Dir. Cecil B. DeMille. Perf. Claudette Colbert and Warren William. Paramount Pictures, 1934.

Cleopatra. Dir. Joseph Mankiewicz. Perf. Elizabeth Taylor and Richard Burton. Twentieth Century–Fox, 1963.

Cleopatra. Dir. Franc Roddam. Perf. Leonor Varela and Timothy Dalton. ABC, 1999.

Elizabeth. Dir. Shekhar Kapur. Perf. Cate Blanchett, Geoffrey Rush, and Joseph Fiennes. Universal, 1998.

Elizabeth: The Golden Age. Dir. Shekhar Kapur. Perf. Cate Blanchett, Geoffrey Rush, and Clive Owen. Universal, 2007.

Elizabeth I. Dir. Tom Hooper. Perf. Helen Mirren, Jeremy Irons, and Hugh Dancy. HBO, 2006.

Elizabeth I: The Virgin Queen. Dir. Coky Giedroyc. Perf. Anne-Marie Duff and Tom Hardy. Masterpiece Theatre, 2005.

Elizabeth R. Dir. Claude Whatham, Herbert Wise, Richard Martin, Roderick Graham, and Donald McWhinnie. Perf. Glenda Jackson and Robert Hardy. BBC, 1971.

Marie Antoinette. Dir. W. S. Van Dyke. Perf. Norma Shearer and Tyrone Power. MGM, 1938.

Marie Antoinette. Dir. Sofia Coppola. Perf. Kirsten Dunst and Jason Schwartzman. Columbia Pictures, 2006.

Mary of Scotland. Dir. John Ford. Perf. Katherine Hepburn and Fredric March. RKO, 1936.

Mary, Queen of Scots. Dir. Charles Jarrott. Perf. Vanessa Redgrave and Glenda Jackson. Universal, 1971.

Mrs. Brown. Dir. John Madden. Perf. Judi Dench and Billy Connolly. Miramax, 1997.

The Private Lives of Elizabeth and Essex. Dir. Michael Curtiz. Perf. Bette Davis and Errol Flynn. Warner Bros., 1939.

The Queen. Dir. Stephen Frears. Perf. Helen Mirren and Michael Sheen. Miramax, 2006.

Queen Christina. Dir. Rouben Mamoulian. Perf. Greta Garbo and John Gilbert. MGM, 1933.

Queen Victoria: Evening at Osborne. Dir. Richard Stroud. With Prunella Scales. Thames Television, 1991.

Rome. Dir. Stephen Shill. Perf. Lyndsey Marshal and Ciaran Hinds. HBO, 2005–2007.

The Scarlet Empress. Dir. Josef von Sternberg. Perf. Marlene Dietrich and John Lodge. Paramount Pictures, 1934.

Victoria and Albert. Dir. John Erman. Perf. Victoria Hamilton and Jonathan Firth. A&E, 2001.

Victoria the Great. Dir. Herbert Wilcox. Perf. Anna Neagle and Anton Walbrook. RKO, 1937.

The Virgin Queen. Dir. Henry Koster. Perf. Bette Davis and Richard Todd. Twentieth Century–Fox Film Corp., 1955.

Young Bess. Dir. George Sydney. Perf. Jean Simmons, Stewart Granger, and Deborah Kerr. MGM, 1953.

Young Catherine. Dir. Michael Anderson. Perf. Julia Ormond and Vanessa Redgrave. Turner Pictures, 1991.

Index